CINEMATIC ENCOUNTERS 2

JONATHAN ROSENBAUM

CINEMATIC ENCOUNTERS 2
PORTRAITS AND POLEMICS

UNIVERSITY OF
ILLINOIS PRESS
Urbana, Chicago, and Springfield

© 2019 by Jonathan Rosenbaum
All rights reserved
Manufactured in the United States of America
1 2 3 4 5 C P 5 4 3 2 1
♾ This book is printed on acid-free paper.

The cataloging-in-publication data is available from
the Library of Congress

ISBN 978-0-252-04255-3 (hardcover)
ISBN 978-0-252-08438-6 (paperback)
ISBN 978-0-252-05139-5 (ebook)

To the memory of Peter Thompson

Contents

INTRODUCTION In Defense of Polemical Criticism 1
CHAPTER 1 Chantal Akerman 9
CHAPTER 2 James L. Brooks 20
CHAPTER 3 Luis Buñuel 29
CHAPTER 4 Pedro Costa 32
CHAPTER 5 André Delvaux 41
CHAPTER 6 Jacques Demy 49
CHAPTER 7 Carl Dreyer 58
CHAPTER 8 John Gianvito 67
CHAPTER 9 Jim Jarmusch 81
CHAPTER 10 Jia Zhangke 96
CHAPTER 11 Jerry Lewis 106
CHAPTER 12 Richard Linklater 122
CHAPTER 13 Guy Maddin 135
CHAPTER 14 Elaine May 152
CHAPTER 15 Manoel de Oliveira 157
CHAPTER 16 Ermanno Olmi 171

CHAPTER 17	Yasujiro Ozu	183
CHAPTER 18	Sally Potter	194
CHAPTER 19	Mark Rappaport	202
CHAPTER 20	Alain Resnais	211
CHAPTER 21	Jacques Rivette	220
CHAPTER 22	Béla Tarr	241
CHAPTER 23	Tsai Ming-liang	263
CHAPTER 24	Orson Welles	272
	Index	295

INTRODUCTION

In Defense of Polemical Criticism

THIS IS THE SECOND VOLUME of a two-volume collection devoted to my critical encounters with filmmakers. *Cinematic Encounters: Interviews and Dialogues,* the first volume, was published last year, and it has only been recently, during the preparation of this second volume, that I've become aware of a structural influence on my decision, here and earlier, to develop a matching pair of books in a dialectical relation to one another. The first foray of this kind came when I decided, in the early 1990s, to title the first retrospective collection of my film criticism *Placing Movies: The Practice of Film Criticism* (1995), in deliberate juxtaposition with my first published book as a writer, *Moving Places: A Life at the Movies* (1980), which was being reprinted at the same time by the same publisher. Inverting the title of my first book was a way of contrasting the first sixteen years of my life as an Alabama moviegoer who largely grew up in my family's movie theaters with my thirty-odd years in New York, Paris, London, San Diego, Hoboken, Santa Barbara, and Chicago as a film critic. I also took care to produce other rhyme effects and musical or poetic matches of various kinds—such as a division of each book into five sections, and matching accounts of rides with my father between his theaters when he was a movie exhibitor in Alabama and a ride with Manny Farber back to a San Diego suburb after seeing a couple of movies with him in Los Angeles, each account of which involved an undercurrent of sibling rivalry (we both grew up with—and as—competitive brothers), as well as very different accounts of *Gentlemen Prefer Blondes* in each book.

Shortly after I moved to Chicago in 1987 to start my twenty-year stint as film critic for the *Chicago Reader,* I had occasion to review four short films by a local filmmaker I'd never heard of:

> The four films to date of independent Chicago filmmaker Peter Thompson form two diptychs: not films to be shown simultaneously side-by-side, but successive works whose meanings partially arise out of their intricate inner rhymes and interactions. *Two Portraits* (1982), which has already had limited exposure in Chicago, describes the filmmaker's parents: *Anything Else,* devoted to Thompson's late father, combines stop-frame images of him, in an airport and outdoors, with a painful recording of his voice taken in a hospital and a multifaceted verbal portrait delivered by his son; *Shooting Scripts* juxtaposes the filmmaker's mother, Betty Thompson, reading from her own diaries with a minimalist view of her sleeping on a beach chair, alternating stop-frames with privileged moments of movement. Together these films create a rich tapestry, but the more recent hour-long pair, *Universal Hotel* and *Universal Citizen* (1987), receiving their premiere here, create a still more ambitious and dense interweaving of objective and subjective elements. As Thompson puts it, this diptych deals with three main themes: "the emotional thawing of men by women, the struggle to disengage remembrance from historical anonymity, and nonrecoverable loss." In the first film, Thompson describes his involved research about medical experiments in deep cold conducted on a Polish prisoner and a German prostitute by Dr. Sigmund Rascher at Dachau in 1942; photographs culled from seven archives in six countries, as well as a subjective dream set in the Universal Hotel, form the main materials. In the second film, the filmmaker's offscreen meetings with a Libyan Jew and former inmate of Dachau who works as a smuggler in Guatemala yield a complex personal travelogue that leads us not only to the Universal Hotel (a real place, as it turns out), but also to the public square in Siena that appears at the beginning of the first film. These are all films that have grown out of years of reflection, and Thompson's background as a still photographer serves him well in his haunting and original historical meditations; these works reverberate powerfully with a sense of the passage of time and the mysterious coalescence of disparate strands in a varied life.

Not too long after this, I saw an interview with Thompson on Chicago cable TV that led me to contact and befriend him as a kindred soul. How much his own diptychs may have exerted an unconscious influence on formulating my own is impossible for me to gauge from a distance of almost a quarter of a century, but the likelihood that they did is only belatedly becoming apparent to me. So the facts that my 2009 interview with Thompson is the last chapter in volume 1 of *Cinematic Encounters* and that my account of the impact of his own two diptychs on my students at film.factory in Sarajevo shortly after his death in 2013 appears in the twenty-second chapter here seem entirely appropriate.

Thompson may be the least well-known filmmaker treated in both volumes, but his overall influence has been decisive. What I've adapted from his work for my own purposes is a two-part structure that is both complementary and dialectical, allowing for rhyme effects and repetitions between the two parts (as well as within each part) and various forms of counterbalancing opposition, all in the interests of a richer set of affective options for the audience/reader—that is, a greater use value and more formal coherence. The impulse to reconcile disparate portions of our lives (such as living both in the United States and abroad, very different forms of closeness with our respective parents, and, in Thompson's case, deep involvements in classical music, poetry, and still photography as separate artistic disciplines that parallel some of my own involvements in jazz, prose, and film) is undoubtedly part of the motivation behind these two-part structures and what we wish to accomplish with them. No less important, though perhaps more unusual, is a desire to combine and reconcile various procedures of "nonfiction" (such as journalism, criticism, research, observation, reflection) with those of making art— something that was also a cherished notion of Farber, and perhaps his older friend James Agee as well. Concluding what I regard as Farber's last major critical text is the following: "I get a great laugh from artists who ridicule the critics as parasites or as artists *manqués*—such a horrible joke. I can't imagine a more perfect art form, a more perfect career than criticism. I can't imagine anything more valuable to do, and I've always felt that way."

Even though *Cinematic Encounters* was originally conceived as a single volume in two parts, until Daniel M. Nasset, my editor, suggested that I turn it into successive books, the two-part structure was there from the beginning, awaiting further elaboration. As it has turned out, the organization of *Interviews and Dialogues* is chronological and the arrangement of *Portraits and Polemics* is alphabetical. And running parallel to the first volume's overall focus on critical interactivity, this second volume's emphasis on polemics doesn't mean that each of the essays here is concerned with controversial debates—only the majority of them.

The list of filmmakers covered in both volumes doesn't qualify precisely as a list of favorites because many of the latter—such as James Benning, John Cassavetes, Charlie Chaplin, Alexander Dovzhenko, Howard Hawks, Alfred Hitchcock, Hou Hsiao-hsien, Abbas Kiarostami, Fritz Lang, Nicholas Ray, Erich von Stroheim, Jacques Tourneur, and Edward Yang—aren't included but have already been discussed in previous collections of mine, and some of those who *are* included (for example, John Carpenter, Paul Morrissey, Ermanno Olmi) aren't favorites. But I've tried to strike a balance between well-known and lesser-known figures in both books. Furthermore, because I've previously collected many other essays but few of my interviews (apart from those in *Film: The Front Line 1983,* a book that only recently went out of print), the majority of the pieces here are more contemporary: in fact, few of them predate the new millennium, although there are many more of them (forty-nine) than in the previous volume, despite almost the same number of chapters (twenty-four instead of twenty-five).

In both volumes, I implicitly adhere to the position that film critics are ideally mediators and facilitators in a public discourse that exists independently of them rather than solitary voices or "experts" who should have the first or last word. In *Interviews and Dialogues,* the emphasis is on sympathetic conversations with filmmakers and other members of the film community. Here the emphasis is more on disputation and argument—sometimes on behalf of the filmmakers and how they're understood, and sometimes in relation to issues posed by their work.

In both books, I'm interested in a certain amount of dialogue and debate *between* as well as within certain essays—so that one of the films by Richard Linklater considered here is about Orson Welles (while another is compared with the work of Wong Kar-wai—who might deserve but doesn't receive a section of his own—just as one of essays about Guy Maddin is also partly about Alfred Hitchcock, another deserving but omitted figure), and the essays here about Jarmusch, Rappaport, Resnais, Rivette, Tarr, and Welles can be cross-referenced with my interviews with those filmmakers in the previous volume. And more specifically, my argument in 2018 for privileging Luis Buñuel's notions about class over his notions about sex directly contradicts my 2008 criticism of Oliveira's *Belle toujours,* his sequel to Bunuel's *Belle de jour,* for doing precisely that.

As envisioned by this book, one form of cinematic encounter is argument, even when the argument in question happens to be with myself (as in pieces about Luis Buñuel, *Ne Change Rien, Day of Wrath, A Touch of Sin, Journey to the West,* and *Stray Dogs*). On other occasions, arguments are waged with the filmmakers, for example, Chantal Akerman, Richard Linklater, Manoel De Oliveira, Mark Rappaport, and Béla Tarr. Most often, however, either implicitly or explicitly, they're waged with other writers: with Wikipedia and Pauline Kael about Jacques Demy, with the *Hollywood Reporter* and *Variety* reviewers of Jarmusch's *The Limits of Control,* with David Thomson about James L. Brooks, and with a good many American and English film critics about Jerry Lewis, Guy Maddin, Yasujiro Ozu, Potter, and Welles. (I can't legitimately include as an example my swipe against James Wolcott for dumping on Resnais's *Providence* because he hasn't bothered to register any critical argument about the film, only a jeer and a gatekeeping reflex; Susan Sontag never published anything about the film either, but my own critical arguments for dissing the immoderate reverence for the first two *Godfather*s are spelled out in my previous collection, *Goodbye Cinema, Hello Cinephilia*.)

One reason for including four separate pieces about Alain Resnais in this book is that I feel that, along with Jerry Lewis (the focus of my longest essay), and both Abbas Kiarostami and Orson Welles (the focus of two of my other books, and someone else who gets four pieces), he's one of the filmmakers who has been most flagrantly and frequently misrepresented in the United States, and often for ideological reasons that are less than obvious. As I argue in "The Lewis Contradiction," the most important misrepresentation about Lewis isn't the simple factoid about "the French" loving him—indeed, Chris Fujiwara's excellent book about him fully demonstrates that we don't need French criticism in order to understand Lewis's art—but the steadfast denial about Americans loving him in the 1950s far more than the French ever did or have ever since. Perhaps the most important misjudgment about Resnais in the United States isn't so much misreading him as a cold intellectual as one that corresponds to some of the misunderstandings that have greeted Welles: the capacity to reinvent himself stylistically with every new film testifying to a refusal to allow his talent to become commodified, and a willingness to take radical risks unshared by his colleagues. (They paid dearly for this courage in the number of cherished projects that went unrealized—a staggering list in both cases.) Some of this willingness was shared by Kiarostami, although in his case he was protected far more by his modest production budgets and his ease at moving back and forth between arthouse venues and gallery spaces. I believe more significant misunderstandings relate to his skills as a master illusionist in articulating his narratives, coupled with a tendency to exercise them to fool audiences about his more experimental and/or self-critical interests.

There are certain recurring untruths in film criticism—such as the notion that Dreyer had a strict religious upbringing or that Stroheim based his script for *Greed* on a page-by-page adaptation of Frank Norris's *McTeague*—that are widely believed not because of any actual research but because of a formula designed to paper over a gap that then gets endlessly repeated. (The fact that both Kenneth Rexroth and Susan Sontag repeated the Stroheim myth naturally gives it more credence.) Part of my effort as a journalist has been to combat these expedient untruths—some of which are dubious interpretations rather than factual errors—whenever I can.

Given the number of recurring themes and chords in this book, it should quickly become apparent that as a journalist I find many opportunities to repeat myself, even when it comes to synopsizing the same obscure Kafka tale in my reviews of two separate Jarmusch features (both of which, uncoincidentally, make great use of repetition). The fact that I've had to read Maurice Drouzy about Dreyer and Shigehiko Hasumi about Ozu mostly in French has encouraged me to convey portions of what they've had to say in English on numerous occasions. My pet notions about rural avant-garde artists and the role of sex in films made under totalitarian regimes crop up more than once, as does my comparison of Elaine May with Stroheim, which is something I take very seriously. Both filmmakers are mainstream figures with the temperaments of transgressive artists; Orson Welles's description of Stroheim's style as "Jewish baroque" also fits May's quite well; and perhaps most significantly, both of these highly obsessional writer-director-performers create films populated almost exclusively by monsters, yet characters whom their creators clearly love. May might even be considered more radical than Stroheim because one can't cite a single villain in her four features—unlike, say, Schani the butcher (Matthew Betz) in Stroheim's *The Wedding March*. Furthermore, for me, the two greatest Stroheim films, *Foolish Wives* and *Greed*, are echoed in many respects by *The Heartbreak Kid* and *Mikey and Nicky*, the two best films of May.

Considering that only ten of the following chapters include single essays, and that fewer than half of these qualify as adequate career summaries (indeed, one of them, on Dreyer, essentially focuses on a single film), this is necessarily a somewhat untidy book that is governed more journalistically by what Raymond Durgnat once called "occasions arising" than by the diverse Procrustean beds of academic decorum and unifying formats and formulas.

And I haven't even troubled to omit most of the details of these occasions because they're part of the history and context that gave birth to these pieces. Factoring in the lack of any sustained hospitality I've received from most of the various academic institutions I've worked for, so that library passes would invariably expire on the same day that semesters or quarters ended—with the result that when I happily moved east from Santa Barbara to Chicago to start my twenty-year stint at the *Chicago Reader,* people who knew far less about film than I did assured me that even my position as an adjunct lecturer at the University of California branch where I'd been teaching for four years wouldn't be renewed, even after they put me in charge of their summer school, because I didn't have the proper degrees (only an M.A. in English and American literature). With this send-off in mind, I've often felt an impulse to say good riddance to such "experts" and follow my own standards for scholarship and professionalism rather than what I regard as their more dubious ones. In keeping with this bias, there are a fair number of pieces here in which my literary or musical interests might be said to bisect with my cinematic encounters, sharing the French notion that cinema can sometimes qualify as literature, music, painting, or dance by another means—or such is my polemical presumption.

J.R.
Chicago, January 2019

CHAPTER 1

Chantal Akerman

As with Sylvia Plath, Chantal Akerman's critical stock seemed to shoot up as a direct consequence of her suicide, giving far too much ill-considered value, in my opinion, to both her bipolarity and her final film, *No Home Movie* (2015). By neglecting her fiction films, this essay, commissioned by Icarus Films for their DVD box set *Chantal Akerman: Four Films* in 2016, can't pretend to encompass the full range of her work—her status as a Belgian surrealist, for example, which links her to another filmmaker considered in this book, André Delvaux, is overlooked—but I hope it can provide a useful starting point. An even longer and more comprehensive survey of Akerman's work, though it only goes up to 2004, can be found at https://www.jonathanrosenbaum.net/2012/02/chantal-akerman-the-integrity-of-exile-and-the-everyday-tk/.

Place and Displacement: Akerman and Documentary

> When you try to show reality in cinema, most of the time it's totally false. But when you show what's going on in people's minds, that's very cinematic.
> —Chantal Akerman

If I had to describe the art of Chantal Akerman (1950–2015) in a single word, I think I'd opt for "composition." This is a term that needs to be understood in its plastic as well as its musical meanings: a visual object that has to be framed in space, a musical object that has to be composed in time. And if we factor in the implied definitions offered above by Akerman regarding what's reality and what's cinematic, what's going on in people's minds and what's going on in front of a camera and microphone, then we have to acknowledge that what she chooses to compose represents a kind of uneasy truce between all four elements (or five elements, if we regard sound and image as separate). How much she and we privilege mind over matter and cinema over reality—or vice versa—has a lot of bearing on what's derived from the encounter.

The four Akerman documentaries included in this box set—*D'est* (*From the East*, 1993), *Sud* (*South*, 1999), *De l'autre côté* (*From the Other Side*, 2002), and *Là-bas* (*Down There*, 2006)—and the documentary about her included as an extra (Gustavo Beck and Leonardo Luiz Ferreira's 2010 *Chantal Akerman, From Here*) are all self-described in relation to place. Yet all five films are deeply involved with *dis*placement, thanks to the uneasy truces between their elements that I've just alluded to. *Chantal Akerman, From Here* is further displaced from the four Akerman films by virtue of the fact that it may appear superficially to resemble her own films in its handling of space and time, although I would argue that in fact it does something that's actually antithetical to her methodology: a fixed camera position that seems *un*composed, at least in relation to Akerman's own monumentally forceful and weighted framings, and a use of real time that seems similarly haphazard and unfocused in contrast to the more structured uses of real time that she periodically employs. As Akerman herself points out in the interview proper, which gives *Chantal Akerman, From Here* its undeniable value and relevancy, the household rituals of Jeanne Dielman in her most famous fiction film, even if they seem to unfold in "real time," are in fact "recomposed." And even more relevant are her remarks in this interview about the viewer's perception of time passing, as opposed to the more commercial norm of time "flying by"—a subjective experience that is far removed from the notion of "real time" adopted by Beck and Ferreira. ("If I have a reputation for being difficult," she once said, "it's because I love the everyday and want to present it. In general people go to the movies precisely to escape the everyday.") This helps to explain why, in the same interview, she notes that documentaries gave her more freedom as an editor than her narrative features by virtue of allowing her more choices in how to combine disparate materials. Freed from the tyranny imposed by the necessity of following stories and characters, her best documentaries can arguably call on a fuller range of both her aesthetic resources and the imaginations of her viewers, which is implied by the title she gave to her 1995 installation related to *From the East, Bordering on Fiction.*

A brilliant French television producer once showed me a paper he wrote arguing that Akerman's greatest films were her documentaries, and he asked me for comments. My main comment was to ask about the 201-minute *Jeanne Dielman, 23 Quai de Commerce, 1080 Bruxelles* (1975), only to discover that he'd never seen it. But despite this major caveat—his overlooking of one of Akerman's greatest films, with an indelible depiction of housework and other forms of female entrapment, a subject that becomes no less worthy of epic proportions than those of *From the East* and *From the Other Side*—I think his overall point has some merit. It's especially valid once one acknowledges that like many of the other greatest filmmakers, Akerman worked in a zone in which nonfiction and fiction frequently intermingle and sometimes even trade places. The final sequence of *From the Other Side* is arguably more novelistic in the depth of its feeling and in its creation of a fictional temporality than anything in her no less distinctive adaptation of Marcel Proust, *La captive* (2000), while the final sequence in her only other (and no less free) adaptation of a novel, Joseph Conrad's *Almayer's Folly* (2011), ends with a striking use of extended real time that becomes in effect a documentary about its lead actor, Stanislaus Merhar. Furthermore, it is easy to conclude that *Les années 80* (1983), her documentary about the making of her only musical, *Golden Eighties* (1986), is far more successful and expressive, even *as a musical,* than the finished work (largely because of Akerman's own contributions during the recording sessions)—a bittersweet tale of crossed romantic destinies that unfolds almost entirely inside a shopping mall.

Returning to Akerman's statement about what's cinematic, I think it's fair to say that *From the East, South, From the Other Side,* and *Down There* are only nominally and incidentally films about a journey from Berlin to Moscow, or the town of Jasper, Texas, or the border between the United States and Mexico, or a narrow patch in Tel Aviv mainly consisting of a room in Akerman's rented flat and its immediate environs. More basically, they're films about the states of Akerman's consciousness, her thoughts and feelings of displacement and alienation in relation to those places. Such displacements can be found throughout her work—perhaps most memorably in two films linking her sense of homelessness with the figure of her mother: *News From Home* (1976), occasioning what was perhaps her first major use of autobiographical and documentary materials (letters from her mother that are read by Chantal over shots of New York), and *No Home Movie* (2015), her final film (mostly conversations with her mother, shortly before her mother's death, during which she tries and fails to get her to open up about other family members—conversations that, as Janet Bergstrom has written, are "filled with the tension of Akerman's need to interrogate her mother about things that were taboo for her since childhood").

Akerman's personal investments—or lack of same—in the places that she films have a great deal of relevance to her thoughts and feelings about them. Born in Brussels as the daughter of Polish Jews who were Holocaust survivors—including a mother, Natalia, whose own parents and other relatives perished in Auschwitz—and with one younger sister who eventually emigrated to Mexico (and who appears, along with Natalia and Chantal herself, in *No Home Movie*), she maintained throughout her career a refusal to participate in identity politics regarding her sexuality or her feminism outside the realm of her filmmaking, although her identity as a Jew remained crucial. Apart from her Judaism, she refused to accept tribal definitions and categories, although she was by no means apolitical or unaffiliated in her positions. Thus her voyage from Germany to Russia shortly after the fall of the Berlin Wall in *From the East* is directly inflected by the fates of other Eastern Europeans at that historical moment; her lack of a personal connection to the American South in *South* (apart from her horrified response to the brutal murder of a black man by several white men in Jasper, Texas) obliged her to forego much of her customary lyricism in that film and to function mostly as a journalist (not generally her forte); her own perceived status as a homeless alien who moved between Brussels and Paris (and, less often, New York) for most of her career informed her treatment of borders in *From the Other Side,* as, more specifically, did her various visits to her sister in Mexico; and her difficulty in engaging with Israel in *Down There* has to be seen in relation to her father's' decision not to settle there after the war, choosing instead to move to Brussels, which she describes in some detail in her closing monologue.

In addition, our own personal responses to these films are necessarily and unfortunately affected by Chantal Akerman's suicide in Paris at the age of sixty-five, on October 5, 2015, after extended periods of hospitalization for her depression following her mother's death. As with the suicide of Sylvia Plath at the age of thirty in 1963, this is a suicide that retroactively informs our sense of the anguish and despair underlying much of her work, even to the extent of distorting it through overdetermination. Like the facile and mainly unhelpful slotting of her work into some brand of so-called lesbian or bisexual cinema, it oversimplifies far too much of the torment and anger as well as the exuberance and pleasure found in her work in diverse media.

■ ■ ■

The haunting masterpiece *From the East* documents without any commentary, dialogue, or subtitles Akerman's several-months-long trip from East Germany to Moscow, offering a formally rigorous inventory of what the former Soviet bloc looked and felt like at the time. Yet despite the overall narrative trajectory, Akerman's painterly penchant for finding Edward Hopper wherever she goes has never been more obvious. This travelogue seemingly offers vistas that any alert tourist could find, yet it delivers a series of images and sounds that are impossible to shake afterward, seeping into our consciousness as if by osmosis: the countless tracking shots of street life, the sense of people forever waiting, the rare occurrence of a plaintive offscreen cello over an otherwise densely (and sometimes deceptively) ambient soundtrack, an on-screen solo cello performance (by the previous cellist's teacher), static glimpses of roadside sites and domestic interiors, everyday activities inside other domestic interiors, the periphery of an outdoor rock concert, a heavy Moscow snowfall, and a crowded terminal where weary people and baggage are huddled together like so many dropped handkerchiefs. The only other film I know that imparts such a vivid sense of being somewhere is the Egyptian section of Straub-Huillet's 1982 *Too Early, Too Late*. Everyone goes to movies in search of events, but the extraordinary events in Akerman's sorrowful, intractable film are mainly the shots themselves.

Although it may not be precise in all of its particulars, the most telling account of what *From the East* does appears in the lengthy prospectus Akerman wrote before making the film, reprinted in the Walker Art Center catalogue for her multimedia installation two years later, *Bordering on*

Fiction: Chantal Akerman's D'est. To quote only the opening paragraphs, before she broaches her personal investments in the material (including her parents' Polish origins, her Belgian upbringing, and an earlier trip to the Soviet Union):

> While there's still time, I would like to make a grand journey across Eastern Europe.
>
> To Russia, Poland, Hungary, Czechoslovakia, the former East Germany, and back to Belgium.
>
> I'd like to film there, in my own style of documentary bordering on fiction. I'd like to shoot everything. Everything that moves me.
>
> Faces, streets, cars going by and buses, train stations and plains, rivers and oceans, streams and brooks, trees and forests. Field and factories and yet more faces. Food, interiors, doors, windows, meals being prepared. Women and men, young and old, people passing by or at rest, seated or standing, even lying down. Days and nights, wind and rain, snow and springtime.
>
> And everything I see along the way that is slowly changing—faces and landscapes. All these countries in the throes of great change. Countries that have shared a common history since the war and are still deeply marked by this history, even in the very contours of the earth. Countries now embarking on different paths.
>
> I would like to record the sounds of this land, to make you feel the passage from one language to another, the differences, the similarities.
>
> A sound track only partially in sync, if at all. A river of diverse voices borne along by images. Voices that will tell stories both great and small, often very simple ones that we won't always need to understand but can grasp anyway, like music from a foreign land, only more familiar.
>
> Why make this trip to Eastern Europe?
>
> There are the obvious historical, social, and political reasons, reasons that underlie so many documentaries and news reports—and that rarely indulge a calm and attentive gaze. But although these are significant, they are not the only reasons. I will not attempt to show the disintegration of a system, nor the difficulties of entering into another one, because she who seeks shall find, find all too well, and end up clouding her vision with her own preconceptions.
>
> This undoubtedly will happen anyway; it can't be helped. But it will happen indirectly.

We don't have access to Akerman's prospectus for *Sud*—whose title suggests that it was originally intended as a complementary offshoot of *From the East*—but reportedly her original intention was to create a more general portrait of the American South, inspired in part by her admiration for the work of William Faulkner. This plan was quickly overtaken by her response to a horrifying hate crime in Jasper, Texas that occurred a few days before her arrival in June 1998 and received international attention, in which a black man named James Byrd Jr. was beaten and tortured by three white supremacists, chained to the back of a truck, and dragged three miles to his death through a predominantly black neighborhood, severing both his head and his right arm in the process. This crime had many repercussions, including the arrests of the three men responsible (one of whom has since been executed) and the passage of hate crimes legislation, but Akerman's film, made shortly after the arrests, is clearly limited by having been made off the cuff, without much preparation.

The assumed audiences of both *From the East* and *South* are mainly if not exclusively Francophone, so that the "foreignness" of the settings won't register in the same way for Eastern Europeans or Russians who see the former, or for Americans (or more specifically, American southerners or East Texans) who see the latter. This is especially relevant in the case of *South,* which might be said to resemble Jean-Paul Sartre's 1946 play *La Putain respectueuse,* inspired by the Scottsboro case, in being consciously or unconsciously addressed to a non-American audience.

Speaking as a non-Texan southerner, I can identify two brief moments in *South* that evoke poetically (as opposed to literally) the small town in Alabama where I grew up: the sounds of insects heard at the beginning before any image appears, and a lovely, melancholy, slow-moving shot through Jasper's main street at dusk. But maybe this latter shot speaks to me directly because it's virtually the only shot in the film that shows white pedestrians. All the other neighborhoods seen in the film are peopled by blacks, and only three white people are shown and interviewed in interiors, all of them men, in contrast to the many black women and men encountered.

Given Akerman's feelings of solidarity and identification with Jasper's poor black population, this is understandable (as is her decision to omit her own questions and her presence throughout the film), but it makes her portrait of the community far from complete. Nineteen of the film's seventy minutes pass before we see a single white person, even though a white town official whom we see much later estimates that Jasper is two-thirds white (contrary to Wikipedia, which claims an almost even split between blacks and whites based on a 2010 census), and the only commentaries we encounter about this part of the community are a few personal anecdotes from black people, a brief description by a white man of the Aryan Nation and Christian Identity movements, and the aforementioned interview with a local official, who predictably tries to soft-pedal Jasper's racial strife by arguing that the town's problems are chiefly economic. The two longest sequences are a memorial for Byrd held in a black church (thirteen minutes) and the concluding shot, roughly half as long, filmed from the back of a car driving down the three miles of Huff Creek Road where Byrd's body was dragged. There's a disquieting clash between the beauty of the shot and the horror of what it signifies and asks us to imagine, but all Akerman can do with such a shot is bear mute witness to the crime.

In *From the Other Side,* we hear Akerman interviewing Mexicans in Spanish and Americans in English. This time it's far more evident that her interest in her subject goes well beyond sympathetic tourism. The final sequence here, shot from the front of a car traveling down a freeway at night, features her own beautiful and moving monologue, spoken in French, in which she speculates about the fate of an interviewee's mother, who disappeared after crossing the border into the United States. We never see this woman, and she isn't mentioned before this monologue, so we wind up imagining her as we would a character in a short story. Akerman traces some of her jobs and finds oblique references to her in the stray comments of other people, following the woman's elusive trajectory as if she were a ghost fading into the anonymity of the hypnotic superhighway. This character's fugitive and semifictional existence, which flits in and out of our consciousness before vanishing, provides a heartbreaking summation of all the hard facts about her and other Mexican migrants we've been absorbing over the previous ninety minutes. This is both sensitive portraiture and sharp investigative journalism, maintaining a respectful, inquisitive distance from its subjects that recalls some of Walker Evans's photographs of Alabama sharecroppers in his book with James Agee, *Let Us Now Praise Famous Men.* In a way, Akerman's powerful monologue serves as a kind of counterpart to Agee's impassioned and empathetic prose.

She begins the film by interviewing a twenty-one-year-old Mexican on the Mexican side of the border about his older brother; he tried to cross to the United States with a group, and all of them eventually perished in the desert. Next, she focuses on portions of the border itself—a wide, dusty road, a field where three kids play baseball, and another road flanked by a high wall. Then she interviews Delfina, a woman in her late 70s, about her family, including the son and grandson she lost when they tried to cross the border. Her husband less stoically bemoans their loss. Akerman then turns back to the various landscapes along the border. Only much later in the film does she finally get around to people and places on the American side—spending time in a restaurant, then talking to a rancher and his wife, who express fears about Mexicans "taking over and doing a lot of damage" by, for instance, carrying diseases. We hear Akerman ask them if September 11 has changed things. The wife says, "It makes us realize life is short." Her husband responds by saying he considers anyone who comes onto his property a trespasser, and the warning sign doesn't have to be in Spanish either. "This is America," he concludes.

The cumulative impact of the eventless shots of the border wall that appear periodically over the course of the film is striking. In themselves the shots are fairly nondescript and uninteresting, but the more we accept the wall as part of the everyday surroundings, the more disquieting and menacing it becomes. This is especially true after we see lights on it at night and helicopters with searchlights moving along it, giving the settings some of the ambience of a lunar landscape. And we can't shake that impression when we see illegal aliens being tracked from the vantage point of a plane in the daytime. The wall that appeared to be a neutral dividing line at the beginning of the film seems more and more like a scar once we see the kinds of pain and anguish it causes. And as Akerman's title suggests, which side of the border we're viewing it from can make all the difference.

Down There, the most recent of her films included in this set, is at once the most subjective *and* the most objective, as well as by far the most radical and challenging. It is closer to autobiography than the others by virtue of often suggesting a diary film, even more than *From the East,* yet Akerman's various ways of objectifying her own subjectivity ultimately makes this more of an essay film than the others as well. (One could easily imagine a multimedia installation derived from this film entitled *Down There, Bordering on Essay.*) Much as *La Captive* has often been viewed as a personal work partially inspired by Hitchcock's *Vertigo,* this film can be regarded as a personal meditation on many of the implications of *Rear Window*—albeit one in which we are pointedly made unsure about whether it is Akerman, her film, or simply we ourselves who are spying on her neighbors.

As pointed out by Akerman's friend and sometime cinematographer Babette Mangolte, *Là-bas* is "less a documentary on Tel Aviv, where the film was shot, than an essay film on an existential question: how do we live near others?" The fact that we are mostly watching some of her neighbors (or their absence, on other occasions) through bamboo blinds is only one of the elements that complicates, mediates, or even interferes with our voyeuristic responses; others include the offscreen sounds we hear inside Akerman's flat and Akerman's own presence whenever she fleetingly moves into the visual field, reminding us that what we're seeing and what she's seeing can't really be equated, and *how* we're seeing and hearing becomes as much of an issue as what we're seeing and hearing. For example, her offscreen monologues about her thoughts, memories, and daily activities, which clearly weren't recorded at the same times as the shots, add still another layer of complication.

The topics addressed in these monologues—suicides in both Tel Aviv and Brussels, the nearby violent deaths occurring from a terrorist bombing, her mother and other family members, Judaism, language, food, the state of her health—are all deeply personal, but more overtly so than in the preceding films. They call to mind a statement of hers cited by critic Ivone Margulies: "I haven't tried to find a compromise between myself and others. I have thought that the more particular I am the more I address the general."

Akerman's visit to Tel Aviv was for a teaching stint that she alludes to only in passing, but it's one of the many paradoxes of this film that in spite of her reluctance to leave her rented flat (and, by the same token, physically engage with Israel, apart from her job)—making her few excursions to the roof of her building or to a nearby beach (which occasions the only time in the film in which she allows the camera to linger on her own presence) almost heroic as well as climactic interludes—her focus is mainly on other people.

■ ■ ■

Throughout her career, Akerman moved freely between narrative and nonnarrative, relatively independent and relatively industrial forms of filmmaking. Broadly speaking, the documentaries considered here belong in the "relatively independent" category—in contrast to such features as

Les Rendez-vous d'Anna (1978), *Golden Eighties* (1986), *Night and Day* (1991), *A Couch in New York* (1996), *The Captive* (2000), *Tomorrow We Move* (2004), and *Almayer's Folly* (2004). But they are still closer to being narrative films than nonnarrative films in their overall trajectories, and the story she has to tell in all of them reaches to the core of her being—her story and ours.

Note

The author's thanks to Janet Bergstrom for her advice and support.

CHAPTER 2

James L. Brooks

The following essay was written for a collection edited by Adam Cook, *Making the Case: Contemporary Genre Cinema*, whose publisher belatedly changed his mind about publishing it, making this appearance the first one between book or magazine covers. But at least the assignment gave me a chance to further explore and articulate what for me makes James L. Brooks one of the most paradoxically neglected auteurs in mainstream American cinema—despite (or is it because of?) the fact that, apart from Jerry Lewis, he is the most mainstream director to have a chapter in this book.

In the January–February 2011 issue of *Film Comment*, I speculated as follows about Brooks's own evisceration of *I'll Do Anything*:

> It may have been the wrenching honesty of this insider's take on the brutality of studio politics more than the conventions of the musical numbers that preview audiences rejected—or, rather, rejected immediately after they saw the movie, before they had time to adjust to its strangeness. (Who knows what they might have thought or felt a couple of hours later, which the voodoo science of test-marketing routinely ignores?) There may have been other factors that contributed to the turn-offs—such as the creepy performance of Whittni Wright as Nolte's bratty, precocious little girl (part of whose icky solo number, alas, is the only song retained in the final version). But the best numbers were what got removed, and the raw, crippled feelings they embody are what one misses most.

James L. Brooks: High-Stakes Gambling, the Ethics of Over-Privilege, and the Comedy of Dysfunction

Out of his half-dozen comedy features to date as producer-writer-director—*Terms of Endearment* (1983), *Broadcast News* (1987), *I'll Do Anything* (1994), *As Good as It Gets* (1997), *Spanglish* (2004), and *How Do You Know* (2010)—James L. Brooks has had three big commercial successes (the first two and the fourth) and three absolute flops (the third, fifth, and sixth). And because all six of these movies are concerned equally with personal failure and personal success, functionality (emotional and professional) as well as dysfunctionality (emotional and professional), it somehow seems fitting that each one has represented a highly ambitious as well as a highly risky undertaking.

The above paragraph has the disadvantage of making Brooks seem so unexceptional as a commercial filmmaker that one might wonder, on the basis of this description, whether he's worth examining at all. Some might also question whether all six of his movies qualify as comedies, despite Brooks's own insistence that they do. (He's even suggested that the comedy of *Terms of Endearment* represents his "solution" to the problem of how to make an entertaining movie about someone dying of cancer.) But arguably the only other assertion that might be considered questionable in my paragraph is the claim that they're all "high-risk undertakings," at least insofar as they all have bankable stars in them. Yet the real sticking point, especially among cinephiles, is whether they're worthy of extended analysis. Because I consider them all profound, troubled, often contradictory, and endlessly fascinating autocritiques, I think they are.

A good illustration of how and why they usually aren't can be found in the five-paragraph Brooks entry in the sixth edition of David Thomson's *Biographical Dictionary of the Cinema* (New York: Alfred A. Knopf, 2014). Thomson's taste isn't invariably mainstream—consider his enthusiasm for Jacques Rivette and his dislike of John Ford—yet one could argue that his popularity as a cinephile-pundit often rests on his capacity to engage with mainstream taste without seriously challenging it, and from this standpoint, his treatment of Brooks is exemplary. His first two paragraphs are devoted to praising with justifiable extravagance Brooks's TV work: "Jim Brooks is living proof that American television, week after week, can deliver smart, well-written, beautifully played comedy series that are devoted to being decent and humane without seeming smug or idiotic. This is an extraordinary achievement, and one to be borne in mind whenever the mood takes us to think the worst of TV." But before returning to this TV work in his third paragraph, here's all he has to offer on Brooks's first three features:

> When he moved sideways, into feature films, he took Larry McMurtry's novel [*Terms of Endearment*] and made a smart hit for which he won the Oscars for script, direction, and best picture. A few years later, *Broadcast News* was only a little less successful while being a tender portrait of the confusion and hypocrisy in doing TV. *I'll Do Anything* is the least of his movies, but it was a musical once. When test screenings showed that it was failing with audiences, Brooks had the skills (and the freedom) to re-edit it. Nevertheless, it is his single large venture to result in disappointment.

Regarding the second three Brooks features, Thomson ignores *Spanglish* (which he omits from his Brooks filmography), skates past *How Do You Know* (which he adds a question mark to in the filmography), and regards *As Good as It Gets* as "another very effective social comedy for the big screen . . . which actually embodied TV ethics (be nicer to one another) and paired a movie star (Jack Nicholson) with a TV star (Helen Hunt). It was a picture like soap in your hands—but, afterwards, you felt cleaner and better."

But the most damning portion of Thomson's critical summary is his preceding paragraph:

> Brooks has spoken about trying to chart the urge toward decency, a mainstream subject one might suppose, yet one ignored by so much of Hollywood. There is a case to be made, I think, that Brooks remains unknown as a personality—he is a manager of good material, a producer who likes to make work. He lacks the edge of, say, a Lubitsch or a Buñuel. But, of course, you say—whoever thought that American TV was open to such people? True enough, but then we have to face the fact that mass media may always move in search of a kind of anonymous, benevolent proficiency more suited to politicians than to artists.

Leaving aside the question of whether Lubitsch and Buñuel belong in the same category (or whether Lubitsch is really inimical to contemporary American TV), one of my underlying premises in everything that follows is that James L. Brooks is every bit as personally embedded in his features as Lubitsch or Buñuel are in theirs. Moreover, the fact that his personal presence and investment remain invisible to Thomson and many other cinephiles doesn't mean that I'm the only one who thinks otherwise: in the ninety-seventh issue of the French quarterly *Trafic,* dated Spring 2016, Murielle Joudet's provocative and persuasive eighteen-page essay, "James L. Brooks, le secret magnifique," even goes so far as to identify "a Brooksian touch" in such features as Alan J. Pakula's 1979 *Breaking Away* (which Brooks wrote and produced), and Penny Marshall's 1988 *Big* and her 2001 *Riding in Cars with Boys* (both of which Brooks produced).

Furthermore, though I wouldn't necessarily dispute Thomson's claim that *I'll Do Anything,* as released, is the "least" of Brooks's movies to date, I would also argue that the original musical, which I've managed to see, is in many ways his most substantial and exciting achievement. (The slim likelihood that this will ever surface commercially is said to be a matter of costly song rights.) Therein lies the Brooksian paradox that I wish to explore here, tied in many ways to his success as cowriter and producer in TV comedy (for example, *The Mary Tyler Moore Show, Taxi, The Simpsons*), where test-marketing might be said to play an even greater role than it does in Hollywood features. And it's important to add that, in spite of what Thomson has to say about Brooks's "skills" and "freedom" in reediting that movie (which is largely and ironically concerned with Hollywood test-marketing, and in many respects can be regarded in part as a sort of West Coast "remake" of *Broadcast News*), the reedited version grossed only slightly more than a fourth of the film's total budget of $40 million (approximately double the budget of *Broadcast News*). This raises the question of whether the original musical version might have ultimately fared better. (We might also wonder what material we might have lost in other Brooks features; *Spanglish* reportedly went through thirteen previews.) For it's an axiom of movie test-marketing that it can test only immediate responses, not lingering impressions, and the undeniable strangeness of what Brooks was originally up to—which combined nine original songs by Prince and at least two others by Carole King and Sinéad O'Connor with twitchy choreography by Twyla Tharp—was the most obvious risk factor in that project.

■ ■ ■

For better and for worse, Brooks's features are marked by his TV training. The negative side of this was noted by Dave Kehr in reviewing *Terms of Endearment:* "Brooks was one of the architects of the [*Mary Tyler Moore*] sitcom style, and he has television in his soul; his people are incredibly tiny (most are defined by a single stroke of obsessive behavior), and he chokes out his narrative in ten-minute chunks, separated by aching lacunae." The positive side is the way that he orchestrates and juxtaposes his ten-minute chunks, single-trait portraiture, and stylistic overkill, yielding arresting, dialectical collisions that produce something far richer than can be found in his sitcoms. The potential casualties of this approach—such as the overwrought, strident gargoyles of Jack Nicholson in *As Good as It Gets* and *How Do You Know,* and Tea Leoni in *Spanglish*—can't be wished away, but neither can the fruitful collisions that they make possible.

Broaching what makes all of Brooks's features personal, it makes sense to start with *Broadcast News* and *I'll Do Anything* because they're the two whose subjects come closest to his own experience. (He began his career in television working for CBS News, and he has said, in reference to the years of research he usually spends in preparing his features, that *I'll Do Anything* was the only one that required none.) In both films, he's concerned with ethical issues involving talented people in media who fail (Albert Brooks in *News,* Nick Nolte in *Anything*) as well as succeed (William Hurt in *News,* Nolte's character's daughter Jeannie [Whittni Wright] in *Anything*), and equally concerned with talented successful people (Holly Hunter in *News,* Albert Brooks in *Anything*) with massive, neurotic personality disorders. Much of the plots in both films come from pitting these various types against one another dialectically, personally as well as professionally. Thus Albert Brooks's Aaron in *News,* who sweats too much to succeed as an anchorperson and is romantically smitten with his best friend, Hunter's Jane (who is attracted in turn to Hurt's more camera-ready Tom), feeds ideas to Jane by phone during Tom's news report on Libya, and Jane speaks into a concealed earpiece to Tom. (The complex means by which Aaron's expertise gets translated into Jane's editorial savvy, which is in turn translated into Tom's charismatic delivery, is excitingly conveyed—even though the rightness or wrongness of what's being conveyed is never addressed.) Nolte's Matt in *Anything* fails his screen-test with Burke (Albert Brooks) but is hired as his part-time chauffeur and sleeps with Burke's script-reader Cathy (Joely Richardson)—who has set up his screen-test, but winds up betraying him during its evaluation because of Burke's hectoring—meanwhile befriending Burke's mistress

Nan (Julie Kavner) while his bratty little girl Jeannie, whom he mentors, succeeds in acting in a sitcom that is then canceled.

The intricate webs of succeeding and failing professionally and/or personally in these worlds, set respectively in Washington, D.C., and Los Angeles, are far more elaborate, even in their dialectical crosscurrents, than these bald if breathless summaries can suggest, and the close relationship between these two worlds is even pinpointed in an early speech given by Nan in *Anything* that compares Washington to L.A.: "Both places have a lot in common: Overprivileged people crazed by their fear of losing their privileges. Alcoholism. Addiction. Betrayal. The near-total degradation of what once were grand motives. The same spiritual blood-letting." And in keeping with Brooks's ongoing ethical obsessions, these are basically the concerns of all his pictures. The fact that Burke and Jeannie figure as virtual doppelgängers, both illustrating portions of Nan's description, only begins to account for their status as Brooksian staples.

"I conceived the story [of *I'll Do Anything*] as a musical because musicals have a heightened sense of reality," he has said. "Through song you can get closer to the truth." In fairness to both Brooks and to test-marketing, I should concede that some of the musical numbers in the original *I'll Do Anything*—such as two that are sung by Albert Brooks, including the title tune—fail both as memorable songs and as "truthful" expansions of the dramatic material. But the fact that all the numbers comprise logistical as well as aesthetic gambles, and ones that pay off in some other cases, is clearly what gives them part of their dynamic value. And the two that are, for me, the most affecting and powerful are the ones where dialectical forces are most hyperbolically at play: a production number devoted to actors hysterically preparing their auditions (punctuated by the contradictory riffs and mantras, "You've got to make believe!" and "It's only a movie!") and an even more emotionally wrenching and complex number in a chic restaurant where Nan is breaking up with Burke because of his compulsion to glad-hand all the other customers—her declaration given in a mournful song on the upper level ("I can't love you anymore,/So I'm walking out the door") while his grotesquely cavorting behavior is seen below in comic choreography.

So it isn't surprising that *As Good as It Gets* periodically evokes the hyperreality of musicals: Greg Kinnear's gay Village painter calls to mind Gene Kelly in *An American in Paris*—a notion planted when he plays some of the Gershwin suite on his stereo—while Jack Nicholson's neurotic writer noodling on his piano next door becomes a clear stand-in for Oscar Levant; and when the writer gets ejected for his boorish behavior by Helen Hunt's waitress from a coffee shop and the other customers applaud, we still might be on an MGM soundstage, even if it looks like a real location.

Similarly, Nicholson's monstrousness here and in three other Brooks films makes him the natural partner of another monster (Shirley MacLaine) in *Terms of Endearment,* and the veritable soul brother of such Brooksian misfits as *Anything*'s Burke and *Spanglish*'s Deb (Tea Leoni), to cite the only two films where he doesn't appear. All these walking disasters periodically register as ferocious autocritiques of Brooks's own obsessiveness as a filmmaker, and the fact that we wind up cherishing the witty putdowns they receive from their mates and/or family members (such as Cloris Leachman as Leoni's mother in *Spanglish*) only intensifies the self-inflicted spiritual bloodletting. Even though Albert Brooks has confirmed that the ostensible model for Burke was Joel Silver, the man who wrote this character has also admitted that he was thinking partially of himself.

■ ■ ■

Even though only two of the Brooks features are about media, all of them are about performers who are conscious of performing and are continually critiquing and correcting their own and one another's performances to each other. This process of compulsive revision becomes literalized in *How Do You Know* when a character named Al whom we barely know hands the hapless executive hero (Paul Rudd) a video camera to record his impromptu marriage proposal to his girlfriend—the hero's former secretary and best friend, who has just given birth to their baby boy in a hospital. The hero's own "performance" in recording Al's speech fails because he forgets to hit the red button, so the proposal then has to be given a second time, with prompts from everyone else present, in a second "take," this time correctly recorded. "We're all just one small adjustment away from making our lives work," this hero says to the heroine at the film's climactic juncture, and it's probably the closest Brooks has ever come to formulating an epigraph (or epitaph) to his cinematic oeuvre, which is obsessively composed of nothing but small adjustments.

It's the credo of an optimistic gambler and a compulsive reviser, recklessly going for broke.

If the trade papers are to be believed (a dubious concept in itself), *Spanglish* had a production budget roughly double that of *I'll Do Anything*, and although it grossed more than five times as much, it still lost money. By contrast, *How Do You Know* cost ten times as much as *I'll Do Anything* and made slightly less than half of that budget back—which suggests that we may have to wait some time before a seventh Brooks feature comes along.

Without presuming to guess where and how all that money was spent, the subject and focus of both these features already earmark them as high-risk ventures: the experiences of a Mexican immigrant (Paz Vega) as a maid with the family of a wealthy chef (Adam Sandler) in Bel Air and Malibu, as recounted in flashback by her teenage daughter (Shelbie Bruce); a thirty-one-year-old professional softball player (Reese Witherspoon) who loses her professional status because of her age and then has to choose romantically between a cheerful, promiscuous, self-involved pitcher (Owen Wilson) and a hapless but honest executive (Paul Rudd) who has just lost his job at the company run by his father (Jack Nicholson) after being targeted by a federal criminal investigation for a crime committed by his blustery dad. *Spanglish* was probably further hampered commercially by having a lot of unsubtitled Spanish dialogue (a language Brooks didn't speak himself), and *How Do You Know* may have been further handicapped by appearing to deal with baseball while retaining only the barest minimum of sports footage. Both of these commercial liabilities point to Brooks's seriousness in addressing his chosen topics, which have much more to do with ethical performance, familial obligation, romance, and class than they do with translingual communication, sports, or corporate crime.

Both *News* and *Anything* stage crises around moments when performers produce tears on-camera. In *News*, these tears are faked by Tom while giving a report about date rape, and Jane, his producer, about to run off with him on a tryst, changes her mind after she learns from Aaron about his fakery. In *Anything*, Jeannie knows she'll be required to cry in the kids' TV show she's appearing in and is afraid she won't be able to. Matt advises her to either think of something that makes her sad or to forget that she's pretending; she opts for the former, enabling Matt to succeed finally in his otherwise futile efforts at parenting. In this case, producing tears is seen as unambiguously desirable (in contrast to Jeannie's previous crying jags that manipulate her father) whereas in *News* it's regarded as odious, but curiously, in neither case is the effect or quality of the TV show made an issue. This implies that Brooks is either rethinking his moral position or reasoning that authentic emotion matters in a news show but is irrelevant in a staged fiction (even if the kids watching it or the kid performing it may not grasp the difference). You might say he's stuck in the existential dilemma of show biz itself and all that it entails, and whether he wills this or not, we're stuck in the same conundrum. You might even say that vexing, ambiguous, and delicate ethical questions of this kind are what all his films are about. And in an era when reality TV and celebrity culture have yielded a Donald Trump, it's hard to think of a subject more contemporary or relevant.

CHAPTER 3

Luis Buñuel

Given the brevity of this account of Luis Buñuel, it qualifies more as a footnote to a career summary than as a summary in its own right. For more detailed accounts of the French, Mexican, and Spanish portions of his oeuvre, all three centered on individual films, readers should check out my earlier essays on *The Discreet Charm of the Bourgeoisie*, *The Young One*, and *Viridiana*, available both on my website (jonathanrosenbaum.net), which is where the following first appeared, and in three of my previous collections, *Movies as Politics*, *Essential Cinema*, and *Goodbye Cinema, Hello Cinephilia,* respectively. And for a hilarious, affectionate tweaking of both Buñuel and his legendary aura, check out Carlos Saura's *Buñuel and King Solomon's Table* (2001), at least if you can find (or don't need) an English subtitled copy; for reasons that escape me, this immensely entertaining fantasia is virtually unknown in the English-speaking world.

Luis Buñuel, Our Contemporary

I've been revisiting a good many of Buñuel's films lately, and a couple of traits of his work as a whole that I haven't been sufficiently aware of in the past have been the centrality of class issues and his uncanny ability to predict or anticipate the future—not only the rise of terrorism but an escalation in income inequality and even, to my surprise, some of the lessons of feminism. These are traits that come together most tellingly and provocatively in his final feature, *That Obscure Object of Desire* (1977).

I've previously regarded this film as a bit of a letdown after the formal radicalism and thematic freedom of its immediate predecessors, *The Discreet Charm of the Bourgeoisie* (1972) and *The Phantom of Liberty* (1974). But it's now more apparent to me that the play with multiple narratives really starts with *The Milky Way* in 1969 (or, much earlier, with *Un chien andalou* and *L'age d'or*), that the inability to complete a sex act in *That Obscure Object* complements and rhymes with the inability to finish a meal in *The Discreet Charm,* that the economic and sexual exploitation of *That Obscure Object* is already present in *Tristana* (1970), and that despite Buñuel's reputation for kinkiness and cruelty, sadomasochism has never been his particular forte. So unlike Josef von Sternberg's 1935 *The Devil is a Woman,* based on the same novel (Pierre Louÿs' 1898 *La femme et le pantin*), *That Obscure Object of Desire* isn't the film of a masochist—nor is it really the film of a sadist, either.

In a highly informative interview included on the StudioCanal Blu-Ray, Jean-Claude Carrière points out that when he and Buñuel collaborated on their half-dozen late scripts, he typically spoke for the male characters and the supposedly macho Buñuel spoke for the female characters—including the chambermaid in *Diary of a Chambermaid,* the title heroine of *Belle de jour,* and Conchita in *That Obscure Object of Desire*. Consequently, insofar as *That Obscure Object* needs to be seen beyond the complacencies of male privilege and class entitlements, it actually anticipates the recent "Me too" movement. Above all, it recognizes that male entitlements and class entitlements usually turn out to be densely interwoven.

Simply identifying with the sexual frustrations of Don Mateo, the narrator-hero played by Fernando Rey, as I did back in 1977, typically means dismissing or at least minimizing the economic frustrations and resentments of Conchita (played alternately by Carole Bouquet and Angela Molina). And as Raymond Durgnat once pointed out, the two Conchitas/actresses "[aren't] just two facets of one woman. They're different women. Differences of physique become differences of style, differences of style becomes class differences. The brunette is classically proletarian, the blonde is characteristically petit bourgeois." Even so, neither of these Conchitas is anywhere close to being an economic match for Don Mateo, whose glibly unexamined entitlements are similar to those of Don Lope (Fernando Rey again) in *Tristana.*

The first two films of Buñuel are those of a spoiled rich kid, consigned by his partner in entitlements, Salvador Dali. *Las hurdes* changed that profile, and the twenty or so Mexican films that followed confirmed his proletarian humanism, with only *The Exterminating Angel* anticipating most of the late French films in returning to Buñuel's own class. I've often pondered the reasons why Raúl Ruiz always preferred the Mexican Buñuel to the French Buñuel, and I'm now inclined to think that class had a lot to with it. (Even if Buñuel spoke for Conchita at the scripting stage, Carrière notes that he had two on-screen surrogates who represent his two male class positions, Francisco Rabal and Fernando Rey.)

To cite only one example of *That Obscure Object*'s uncanny relevance to the present, consider the very last glimpse that we have of Don Mateo and Conchita as a couple, just before the latest terrorist bomb explodes—a nearly exact replica of the gesture caught of Melania rejecting Donald's hand when they traveled abroad.

CHAPTER 4

Pedro Costa

People who customarily describe Portuguese filmmaker Pedro Costa as "neglected" often seem to mean only that he isn't a mainstream figure. Given the number of retrospectives around the world that have been devoted to him and the reverence his name typically and justifiably evokes, despite the difficulties commonly posed by his films as narratives, he might be said to illustrate the maxim that the quality of one's audience is far more important and consequential than the quantity. A cinephile with soul who has taught himself how to make films with minimal crews and relaxed timetables, he offers a bracing model to the world at large of how to film people.

    The first of the articles in this chapter was commissioned by the Dutch magazine *Filmkrant* for its special "Slow Criticism" issue in February 2010 (no. 318); the second was commissioned by *Artforum* for its May 2016 issue. It seems worth adding that, in spite of Costa's growing renown, *Ne Change Rien* was the first of his films to be shown at the New York Film Festival.

Finding Oneself in the Dark: Costa's *Ne Change Rien*

There's a personal reason why *Ne Change Rien* comes together for me in a way that few music documentaries do. Eight years ago, I was approached by Rick Schmidlin, the producer of the 1998 reedit of *Touch of Evil* (on which I'd served as consultant), about writing or directing—in any case, helping to conceptualize—a documentary about jazz pianist McCoy Tyner. This led to a lengthy conversation with Tyner in Chicago and then a three-page treatment that I prepared with cinematographer John Bailey via phone and email, which concluded: "Any film that's about listening, as this one will be, will also be about looking—predicated on the philosophy that the way one looks at musicians already helps to determine the way one listens to them."

For me one of the ruling ideas was that few jazz films, apart from a handful of the very best, focused enough on the spectacle of jazz musicians listening to one another. And I saw (and heard) the whole thing as a two-way process—the way one listens should dictate the way one looks, as well as vice versa. Perhaps the most remarkable examples of this happening on film are footage of Charlie Parker reacting delightedly to Coleman Hawkins playing a solo in Gjon Mili's never-completed 1950 film *Improvisation* and Billie Holiday responding to Lester Young's desolate yet intensely compacted eight bars on "Fine and Mellow" in the 1957 CBS special *The Sound of Jazz*—her way of looking, listening, tilting, and moving her head back and forth with what appears to be equal amounts of pleasure and grief, both ecstatic, the two folded together into some tragic form of boundless love. In fact, filming Holiday in *The Sound of Jazz* is one of the few models cited by Pedro Costa, along with Godard filming the Rolling Stones in *1 + 1* (1968).

None of this is meant to imply that *Ne Change Rien* can be reduced to such a simple formula of musicians responding to musicians, even if this principle does assume an important part of its texture. More generally, the film's "ideas" can't be limited to either those of Jeanne Balibar and her accompanists and accomplices or those of Costa and his own helpers because they nearly always comprise an interweaving of them all. And this being a Costa film, who starts what is a perpetual mystery—and not one in which our own responses necessarily correspond to those of either the performers or the filmmakers, although modulations and transmutations of various kinds between various players and spectators (including us) are clearly part of the game. It's the same radical process suggested by Tati's *Parade,* according to which one can't determine when anything starts and when anything stops. Perhaps the most significant difference is that Costa's play with darkness and the nonvisible adds our imaginative investments to all these fluctuations. (Interestingly enough, he settled on black and white only after accidentally discovering neck veins on Balibar that didn't register in color).

Something comparable happens in *Where Lies Your Hidden Smile?* (2001), Costa's most accessible film, which shows Jean-Marie Straub and Danièle Huillet editing *Sicilia!* in another dark studio space. Aptly described as a romantic comedy, it's the only Costa feature that isn't dark in spirit. And it's a telling sign of Costa's radicalism that he can approach the work of artists as dramatically dissimilar as Balibar and Straub-Huillet in comparable ways.

Blood (*O Sangue*, 1989) already announced the essence of his cinema by declaring every shot an event, regardless of whether or not we can understand it in relation to some master narrative, and *Casa de Lava* upped the ante, adding color and Cape Verde while composing some of the most thrilling landscape shots in contemporary cinema, meanwhile critiquing Costa's own role in composing them. (This prompted me to ask Costa—in Lisbon, November 2008—why he hadn't made any more landscape films. "It's too easy," he said—which might serve as a working motto for his entire oeuvre.) *Bones* (*Ossos*, 1997) discovered some friends and relatives of characters in *Casa de Lava* in Lisbon's Fontaínhas slum, and the next four films, not counting *Where Lies Your Hidden Smile?*, remained there, implacably and patiently—not so much waiting for things to happen as witnessing either the survival or the decimation of his friends, their various evolutions, and, eventually, their expulsion from their (and Costa's) elected turfs.

The fairy-tale poetics of disturbed innocence and threatened violence in *Blood* evoke Charles Laughton's *The Night of the Hunter* (1955)—milky whites, inky blacks, and delicate balances of light and shadow already forecasting the graded intensities of *Ne Change Rien* while recalling certain shades of Fritz Lang's *The Big Heat* (1953). *Casa de Lava* (1990) is plainly an eccentric remake of Jacques Tourneur's *I Walked with a Zombie* (1943), and Costa has also described his short *Tarafal* (2007, from *O Estado do Mondo*) as a remake of the same director's *Night of the Demon* (1957). Thom Andersen aptly calls *Colossal Youth* (*Juventude em Marcha*, 2006) a remake of Ford's theatrically lit *Sergeant Rutledge* (1960), with the traumatized Cape Verdean patriarch Ventura standing in for Woody Strode. Costa's frequently dazzling color palettes derive in part, he says, from having watched Ford's *She Wore a Yellow Ribbon* (1949) "very, very stoned," and he has even compared *Ne Change Rien* to a Nick Ray B-film about "three guys lost in a forest and [finding] some shack," where there's a fire, some coffee, and a guitar.

But I have to be frank. Not only does most of Balibar's music have little to say to me, unlike the music of Hawkins, Parker, Holiday, Young, and Tyner; on my second trip through *Ne Change Rien,* I found myself actively recoiling from it. (The major exception is a hypnotic stretch, mostly wordless, of a droning vamp that begins twenty-two minutes into the film and proceeds in a lovely Coltrane-like trance for fourteen minutes; if there's even a trace of this on *Paramour,* the arty, self-conscious CD that emerged from all this work, I managed to miss it). How much this disaffection comes from electric guitars or diva stances is probably secondary. My first trip through the film didn't pose much of this problem, because I thought and felt I was attending to Costa's ideas, only some of which might have been tributaries of ideas from Balibar, Rodolphe Burger, Arnaud Dieterlen, and a few others, that is, sound engineer, voice teacher, pianist.

In short, what comes together for me as a film often comes apart as music, and maybe this is as it should be. The film begins with Balibar in the darkest of speckled profiles, singing "You're torturing me" (uncredited lyrics by Kenneth Anger) at some unidentified club date, and I knew exactly what she meant and felt—or rather, what she was professing to feel, because I can rarely figure out in her songs what statements belong between or outside quotation marks. Or whether they even qualify as statements as opposed to questions, or as enactments as opposed to acts. All I knew was that they were torturing me.

Questions from Costa in the form of shots, no matter how challenging, are still easier for me to entertain than events performed by Balibar in the form of notes and gestures, rehearsed or remembered or both. In the film, where it's no simple matter to distinguish the dancer from the dance, or the dance from the filmmaker filming the dance, I'm no longer recoiling—just weaving in and out, along with the filmmaker and the musicians, in and out of abstraction, in and out of referentiality, and, even by design, in and out of music.

But insofar as filmmaking itself is a kind of music, I'm reminded of a 1928 statement by F. W. Murnau—which becomes all the more resonant when one acknowledges that fiction and documentary in both Murnau and Costa are merely two sides of the same coin:

> They say that I have a passion for "camera angles." . . . To me the camera represents the eye of a person, through whose mind one is watching

the events on the screen. It must follow characters at times into difficult places, as it crashed through the reeds and pools in *Sunrise* at the heels of the Boy, rushing to keep his tryst with the Woman of the City. It must whirl and peep and move from place to place as swiftly as thought itself, when it is necessary to exaggerate for the audience the idea or emotion that is uppermost in the mind of the character. I think the films of the future will use more and more of these "camera angles," or as I prefer to call them these "dramatic angles." They help to photograph thought.

The fact is, even while clarifying the movement of thought, Murnau has to obfuscate whether the thought belongs to himself, his character, or his audience, choosing to collapse all three within the same privileged zone of voluptuous transport. So when Costa combines the flickering flames of a furnace in a dark recording studio with disconnected phrases of Balibar and Burger noodling, how much this music is being rehearsed or performed or explored or questioned is secondary to the dance of the flames and notes and faces that accompanies this process, which we're asked to join even before we can think of observing it. Most of the time, it's the personal transactions and the fantasies we all spin around them more than the actual notes that hold the screen, so it's small wonder that when we see Balibar and her pals performing "Johnny Guitar" in a club just afterward, it's the romance of the idea and the atmosphere as much as the song itself that carries us along: shack, guitar, fire, and coffee finally giving way to Nick Ray mythology, complete with grandiloquent hand gestures. And dark, humanized space, which we recognize from the Fontaínhas films, more than the groping, stammering sounds inside it.

Lost Intervals, Doomed and Waiting Souls: Pedro Costa's *Horse Money*

> DOCTOR (OFF): Has this happened to you before?
> VENTURA: It will happen again, yes it will.

Trying to rationalize Pedro Costa's *Horse Money* in terms of a synopsis is ultimately a fool's game, but connecting it to recent Portuguese history is a necessity. The April 25, 1974 military coup known today as the Carnation Revolution, led by the left-wing MFA and ending the Estado Novo dictatorship that lasted almost half a century, took place when Costa was in his early teens. Ventura, Costa's slightly older principal protagonist in practically all of his other recent films—a Cape Verdean immigrant and construction worker, always playing himself and scripting his own dialogue—was around in Lisbon, too. But as Costa told Mark Peranson in an interview in *Cinema Scope,* Ventura's experience of the same events was radically different:

> I was very lucky to have been a young man in a revolution, really lucky. . . . And I was discovering a lot of things, music and politics and film and girls, everything at the same time, and I was happy and anarchist and shouting in the streets and occupying factories and things like that—I was 13 so I was a bit blind. It took me 30 years to discover that Ventura had been at the same place, at the same time, crying, very afraid, of what I was doing, and what the soldiers were trying to do. So this is an interesting thing. I was shouting the slogans, the common revolutionary words with the banners and the stuff, and he was hiding in the bushes with his comrades, the black immigrants, that had started coming in 1968 from all the Portuguese ex-colonies.

Even for a filmmaker as radically transgressive as Costa, *Horse Money* represents a sharp departure from the long takes of *In Vanda's Room* (2000) and *Colossal Youth* (2006) in its privileging of traumatic memory and consciousness and all the narrative fragmentation this entails over any sustained continuity of space or chronology. Speaking to a packed film festival audience in Hong Kong that I was part of last spring, Costa further noted that in all the photographic records that he's seen of the Carnation Revolution, the roughly 100,000 black immigrants who were in Portugal at the time are completely absent, and *Horse Money* is a willful construction of a fantasmatic world devoted to the survivors (and the non-survivors) of that exclusion.

In terms of surface impressions, this 105-minute feature offers mainly a series of institutional spaces, alternately decaying, dark, and prison-like and tidy but blank and anonymous interiors resembling a hospital through which an ailing and troubled Ventura moves or lingers, his hands often shaking, dressed in pajamas, underwear, or work clothes, as well as ruined work spaces suggesting his former employment in construction (where his godson also appears, saying he's been there for twenty years awaiting an overdue paycheck). Occasional exterior shots, which also include a forest at night, only extend the Caravaggio-like gloom, as in some of the films of Val Lewton and Jacques Tourneur, intensifying rather than alleviating the overall claustrophobia. A few key painful incidents in

Ventura's past, mostly relating to his own teens, including a knife fight in the forest and an arrest by the MFA, are often recounted or recalled, but almost always as if they were recurring in the present—culminating in a lengthy sequence in which he's stranded in an elevator with a motionless armed soldier covered in dull silver paint who appears to speak (but without his lips moving) along with many other unseen voices. This scene, the first one shot for the film, appears in a differently edited version as *Sweet Exorcism,* Costa's contribution to the 2012 portmanteau feature *Centro Histórico,* and as this alternate title implies, Ventura's wrestling with his own demons here is a kind of therapeutic exorcism, both confession and trial. "Some people say they make films to remember," Costa told Peranson. "I think we make films to forget."

It's imperative to note that what *Horse Money* "says"—or, more precisely, what it sobs or sings—is far less important than what it does. In the same interview with Peranson, Costa acknowledges the direct influence exerted by Jean-Marie Straub and Daniele Huillet's *Not Reconciled* (1965)—an adaptation of Heinrich Böll's novel *Billiards at Half-Past Nine,* covering several decades in a Cologne family during and after the Nazi era that Straub described at the time of its release as follows: "Far from being a puzzle film (like *Citizen Kane* or *Muriel*), *Not Reconciled* is better described as a 'lacunary film,' in the same sense that Littré defines a lacunary body: a whole composed of agglomerated crystals with intervals among them, like the interstitial spaces between the cells of an organism."

Stated differently, a seeming narrative discontinuity of time, space, and even identity is superseded by an underlying continuity of mood and feeling that belongs to a form of consciousness itself—what might be described somewhat inexactly as public and political consciousness in the case of *Not Reconciled* and private and personal consciousness in *Horse Money*. What keeps this description inexact is that it leaves out the more private, even solipsistic manifestations of this consciousness in *Not Reconciled,* as well as the elements of Ventura's own traumatized consciousness that can be described as shared—shared with a middle-aged woman named Vitalina Varela, another important character in *Horse Money,* who has returned to Lisbon for the funeral of her husband Joaquin, and shared with Costa himself in the collaborative process of composing/constructing *Horse Money* with Ventura, Vitalina, and a few others.

Vitalina, who has an even more commanding sculptural and vocal presence in the film than Ventura, is often seen and/or heard reciting or reading the contents of official documents relating to the birth and death of her husband, her own birth certificate, and their marriage certificate—most of this delivered in an intense, breathless whisper suggesting her furtive existence as an undocumented alien. Ventura periodically tells her that her husband is still alive and in the same hospital, but we don't believe him—or, rather, we can only believe him in the sense that, as Faulkner put it, the past is never past, that we live only in the present (where the past also continues to live), and when Ventura later gives her a letter that he says her husband wrote to her, we can only surmise that this must be the same letter that we have previously seen Ventura writing, with a pen taken from one of his doctors. When she exchanges her white smock (which makes Ventura wonder if she's a doctor herself) for black clothing, she gravitates into a ritual with beads accompanying her recitations that suggests voodoo, as if she were in a trance. Identity and ritual are in some ways as fluid and as unstable here as the time frames, and pain is ultimately the only constant. When Ventura, in one of his ruined former work spaces, drags a disconnected phone behind him by its severed cord, which makes a grating sound on the floor, this rhymes plaintively with the sound of Vitalina, newly arrived from Cape Verde, dragging her suitcase across a public square at night.

Since his earliest features, *O Sangue* (*Blood*, 1989) and *Casa de Lava* (1994), made before he arrived at the small-scale and more collaborative methods of his more recent work, Costa has presided over a series of uncanny shotgun marriages between fiction and nonfiction, narrative flow and nonnarrative stasis, the materialism of Straub-Huillet and the immaterial spirituality of haunted, doom-ridden fantasy suggested by Lewton and Tourneur. A hardcore cinephile whose filmmaking taste owes as much to the heroic, sculptural, and populist Soviet portraiture of Boris Barnet, Alexander, Dovzhenko, Sergei Eisenstein, and Dziga-Vertov as to the expressive and expressionist lighting and color schemes of such Hollywood artisans as John Ford, Howard Hawks, Nicholas Ray, and Tourneur, Costa has even described *Horse Money* in commercial, generic terms as a "horror action film," and the seeming paradox of marrying the blunt realities of a Ventura and a Vitalina with the studio-contrived artifice of a Lewton quickie is central to both his methods and the philosophical suppositions underlying them.

A romantic attempt to bridge the unbridgeable, Costa's form of alchemy can be contested for its effort to exalt abjection, yet to renounce that endeavor is to deny its tragic poetry and its visionary power. It's important to recognize that when he begins *Horse Money* with a display of mostly black-and-white photographs by Jacob Riis of New York immigrant tenement dwellers in the late nineteenth century—a disconnected and somewhat awkward overture and prologue matching the heroic portraiture of Cape Verdeans at the start of *Casa de Lava,* for better and for worse—the tattered condition of the mournful photographs themselves seems as relevant and even as essential to the expressiveness as the dilapidated people and places shown. And there's an undeniable pleasure as well as pain to be found in the process—most clearly, in a musical montage sequence devoted to lonely ghetto inhabitants that comes midway in the film, offered to us as a kind of gift, a reward to us for waiting. For in effect, the institutional, Kafkaesque nightmares depicted in the film all involve different forms of waiting, and it's entirely consistent with Costa's method of sharing that we're invited to wait endlessly along with his characters, even if this means waiting for some form of deliverance that is unlikely to arrive.

CHAPTER 5

André Delvaux

One of the least well-known filmmakers discussed in this book, Delvaux has been marginalized not only because of his Belgian nationality but also because of several other factors addressed in this essay, such as the divisions between the French and Flemish branches of his work (taken up thematically in one of his best but most neglected and hard-to-access films, *Un soir, un train*) and that, like Orson Welles, he tended to reinvent himself with each new project. Even some of those critics who have celebrated individual features of his (most often his first, *The Man Who Had His Hair Cut Short*) seem unfamiliar with most of the others.

    The following career piece was written in late 2012 and early 2013 for *Film Comment,* but this bimonthly magazine's editor at the time liked to improvise the contents of every issue at the last moment, and this article was edited, scheduled, and then pulled from two consecutive issues. For me, it had immediate relevance because of the release of a Delvaux DVD box set in Belgium on the excellent Cinematek label; from the editor's more land-locked Manhattan perspective, it could be published at any time without making any difference because, as the editor put it, Delvaux was dead anyway—unlike, say, someone else's latest thoughts about *The Searchers*, which were presumably more urgent matters for the magazine's readers. Rather than run the risk of this delay happening a third or even fourth time over the remainder of that year, and because I believed, rightly or wrongly, that jonathanrosenbaum.com (now jonathanrosenbaum.net) may have had a larger readership than *Film Comment* anyway, I made a last-minute editorial decision of my own and posted it there, originally in August 2013, thereby forfeiting the expected $1,000 fee for the piece. It's probably the biggest financial sacrifice I've ever made in the interest of journalistic currency.

André Delvaux's Buried Treasures

Part of the strength of André Delvaux (1926–2002) as a filmmaker is that, like the otherwise very different Samuel Fuller and Jacques Tati, he was already pushing forty when he directed his first feature. By then he had studied music, German philology, and the law, and also taught Germanic languages and literature before he became a pioneer in teaching film at Belgian state schools, where Chantal Akerman and *Hitler in Hollywood*'s Frédéric Sojcher were among his pupils, meanwhile playing piano to accompany silent films at the Brussels Cinémathèque.

In various ways, Delvaux's cultivated and detached, standoffish protagonists tend to reflect this multidisciplinary background—the pianist hero of *Rendez-vous à Bray*, for instance, is seen at one point accompanying a contemporary screening of *Fantômas*—although these portraits, never wholly sympathetic, sometimes register as critiques (or autocritiques) of these characters' passive-aggressive traits. (A friend of Cinémathèque director Jacques Ledoux, Delvaux wound up marrying the latter's secretary, Denise Debbaut, who went on to become both a major force in Belgian television and an invisible collaborator on her husband's work, reportedly as important to his filmography as Alma Reville was to Hitchcock's.)

One reason why Delvaux isn't better known outside his home turf, where he's widely regarded as the greatest *and* most Belgian of Belgian filmmakers, is our difficulty in navigating (as well as sometimes distinguishing between) Flemish as well as French strands in that country's culture—and part of Delvaux's distinction comes from his roots in both. Born in a Flemish-speaking part of Belgium, he entered a French-speaking school at age six when his family moved. And the day before he died, at an international conference in Valencia, he spoke ruefully and at length about the potent cultural mix that characterized his country before it became a federal state where subsidies supporting Belgian filmmaking had to come from either the French or the Flemish community but never from both—a move that effectively banished Flemish cinema from most people's awareness.

Delvaux's first and still best-known feature, *The Man Who Had His Hair Cut Short* (1965), is Flemish; his next three—*Un soir, un train* (1968), *Rendez-vous à Bray* (1971), and *Belle* (1973)—are French, but the first of these freely adapts a story by Johan Daisne, the Flemish writer whose novel Delvaux had adapted in his previous film, and the conflicts between Flemish/Dutch and French speakers (including the lead couple, played by Yves Montand and Anouk Aimée) are central to the plot; similarly, shifts between languages crop up frequently in the other shorts and features. Delvaux's next two films—*With Dieric Bouts* (an extraordinary short essay from 1975, juxtaposing painting with film and past with present, in which Delvaux's contrapuntal use of sound is particularly remarkable), and *Woman in a Twilight Garden*, a 1979 feature—were cowritten in Flemish with Ivo Michiels, and the second of these broached the then-taboo subject of Flemish (and Belgian-Catholic) collaboration with Germany during World War II. Delvaux next followed that feature's French lead actress, Marie-Christine Barrault, to the United States, to make a feature-length documentary in English about her next film, *Stardust Memories*, entitled *To Woody Allen, From Europe with Love* (1980)—the only Delvaux film mentioned above that I haven't yet seen—followed by a feature mostly in French with Fanny Ardant and Vittorio Gassman (*Benvenuta*, 1983), set mostly in Ghent as well as Milan, and a final feature in French partially set in Flanders (*L'oeuvre en noir* aka *The Abyss*, 1988).

As noted above, we usually confront Belgium's bilingual culture by ignoring the Flemish part—as I just did in the previous paragraph, by giving English titles to all the Flemish films—and sometimes confusing the country with France. But now that the excellent Belgian DVD label, Cinematek, has brought out most of Delvaux's major work with English subtitles, in slim, handsomely designed trilingual editions (go to cinematek.be/index.php?node=30&dvd_id=44&category=14)—six of his seven fiction features, and four of his major shorts (with other extras, including part of the speech he gave the day before he died) on a seventh disc—this situation should improve. The only missing fiction feature—my second favorite, *One Night, a Train*, which remains unavailable because of rights issues—was formerly available on the now-defunct http://thepiratebay.se, and its presence on YouTube tends to fluctuate. (Most recently, I could find only a brief excerpt there.)

...

It's both tempting and limiting to call Delvaux a Belgian surrealist—or, as many prefer, "magical realist." French surrealism is an actual movement, but the other two categories are, at most, tendencies. For me, one significant difference between French and Belgian surrealism is that the former is in rebellion against the bourgeoisie while the latter virtually equates the bourgeoisie with the cosmos—but this latter position can't really be identified in national terms, because Franz Kafka and Sadegh Hedayat, among others, seemed to share it.

Un soir, un train, the Delvaux film that comes closest to both Kafka and Hadayat, follows a Flemish linguist (Yves Montand) as he departs on a train to give a lecture in another town—first quarreling with his longtime French partner (Anouk Aimée), who walks away from him shortly before he leaves, but later unexpectedly joins him in his compartment, then mysteriously disappears from it while he dozes off. After the train stops in a desolate wasteland, things become progressively stranger as he gets off with an older and younger man and they eventually wander into a mysterious town. I've recently discovered that the "incomprehensible," untranslated language they hear in this town is in fact Farsi—which has made me wonder whether certain affinities of the story with the Iranian Hedayat's nightmarish novella *The Blind Owl* might have prompted this.

More generally, Delvaux's seamless transitions from waking life to dreams tend to follow an emotional progression that retroactively seems logical, even inevitable. In the same film, for instance, the hero's failure to have a child and his inability to find his father's gravesite together seem to have some relation to the younger and older men who turn up as the hero's companions in the story's increasingly terrifying second half. And the overall narrative development in *The Man Who Had His Hair Cut Short* from normality to insanity is comparably unnerving. The schizophrenia of the hero in Daisne's novel—a middle-aged family man and lawyer who teaches at a local high school and is quietly obsessed with a graduating female pupil—is established by presenting his story as a flashback from a mental asylum. But the film, far less guided by its first-person narration, introduces this schizophrenia so incrementally and ambiguously that we're held in a queasy kind of abeyance, and can't even be sure at the end whether or not he's murdered his former pupil, after running into her at a hotel years later. (Meanwhile, he's quit his job to become a court clerk and attended an autopsy, in both cases with obscure motivations.) That he barely looks at her during their climactic dialogue in her hotel room is only part of what's so weird about the scene. There are odd hints about his condition throughout the film, from his behavioral tics to Delvaux's unconventional edits, but the fact that we can't distinguish between his mental reality and our objective perceptions is a constant.

There's a similar tendency in other Delvaux films, *Belle* especially, to switch from apparent objectivity to subjectivity and back again without clarifying when or how the transitions occur—although one of the more remarkable facets of *Appointment in Bray* is that it contains no literal fantasy, even in the *Fantômas* clip, yet virtually all of it feels magical. To cite Delvaux himself about the two best-known Belgian surrealist painters (speaking to Dan Yakir in 1977), what he found striking in René Magritte was "the way he uses real elements in an illogical way," and in his namesake Paul Delvaux, "the use of mystery, or settings I know well, old places with much charm, where people live as if they weren't there." At least two famous Delvaux paintings, *Soledad* (1955) and *Trains du soir* (1957), seem to have inspired a female nude on a railway platform in *Belle*, first seen in a dream with the title heroine (who may not even be real), and then evoked with the hero's grown daughter in the "real" world, whose upcoming marriage and his anxiety about it are tied somehow to Belle's unexplained appearances.

But Delvaux's relation to music, informed by his virtually career-long collaboration with composer Frédéric Devreese, runs still deeper than his relation to painting. His art is largely composed of subtle structuring devices that work via emotions more than ideas (one of his many affinities with Alain Resnais), and sometimes their subversiveness is so subterranean that it seems to reach us via osmosis. Like Delvaux's first feature, *Belle* and *Benvenuta* are both films about the central character's sexual obsession, and that this is related to incestuous impulses—the hero's toward his daughter in *Belle*, Benvenuta's toward her father—is partly conveyed through visual rhymes in the first case, editing patterns in the second. (Moreover, Benvenuta's passion for an older man and father figure, played by Vittorio Gassman, who becomes her lover, is juxtaposed with the relation of an older woman [Françoise Fabian], a novelist, recounting Benvenuta's fictional story to a younger man [Mathieu

Carrière], a filmmaker, who wants to adapt it into a screenplay.) If we consider juxtapositions between repressed normality and kinky desires, a possible parallel between Belgium and Canada is suggested, at least if one considers the films of David Cronenberg, Atom Egoyan, and Guy Maddin. There also seems to be a common preoccupation with death and decay—ranging, in Delvaux's case, from the rotten fruit at the end of the opening sequence of his first feature to his last film, the eight-minute *1001 Films* (1989), included on Cinematek's shorts DVD—dedicated to the Belgian Cinémathèque and largely preoccupied with the deterioration of celluloid.

■ ■ ■

My first encounter with his work was *Appointment in Bray,* which I now regard as his masterpiece (it was Delvaux's favorite as well). It is his most subtle and delicate film, and is the hardest to describe. Based on a Julian Gracq novella, "Le Roi Cophétua" (an English translation of which is still in print), it has a dense Gothic atmosphere and even denser erotic texture that defy any synopsis—perhaps because, as Delvaux has pointed out, it is structured more in musical terms (specifically as a rondo) than as a narrative. It concerns a young pianist and musical journalist, Julien (German actor Mathieu Carrière), in 1917 Paris, receiving a telegram from his composer friend Jacques (Roger Van Hool)—who is in the air force—inviting him to his country house in Bray, only a short distance from the battlefront. On the train, Julien—a noncombatant from neutral Luxembourg whose German accent provokes some hostility from the French—begins to recall various prewar encounters with Jacques and a fellow musician, Odile (Bulle Ogier, in one of her most delightful and inventive comic performances); there are hints of a potential *ménage à trois* that evoke *Jules et Jim,* albeit with far more sensual (and homoerotic) imagery; Jacques and Odile are already involved, but Julien seems to shy away from her sexual interest, and it's suggested that he's a virgin. Arriving at Jacques's roomy mansion, Julien is greeted by a mysterious woman (Anna Karina, at her most luminous) who says that Jacques hasn't yet arrived, and serves him tea and then dinner. In fact, Jacques never turns up and the woman eventually takes Julien to her bed, but we never discover either her relation to Jacques or the reason for his absence, and in the morning Julien heads back to the train station, where he lets the train leave without him, then hesitates about his next move.

A perfect and exquisite work filled with question marks that somehow thrives on its multiple mysteries, *Appointment in Bray* leaves such a pungent aftertaste that, in spite of my reverence for Akerman, if I had to select a single Belgian film to take to a desert island, I'd pick this one in a flash. Undoubtedly part of what makes it so satisfying is the sheer musicality and dialectical charge of its eroticism—the way that the story in the present and its implied *ménage à trois* seem to resolve the sense of incompletion in the flashbacks without resolving much of anything in the storyline.

■ ■ ■

In the early '60s, Delvaux made four documentary miniseries for Belgian TV about Fellini, Jean Rouch, Polish cinema, and Demy's *The Young Girls of Rochefort,* and these experiences undoubtedly helped to shape his subsequent features. A wonderful forty-minute episode from the latter, *Behind the Screen,* is included in Cinematek's DVD of Delvaux shorts; in it we get to see Demy directing Gene Kelly and working with Michel Legrand on the score, plus a dance rehearsal and joint interview with Catherine Deneuve and Françoise Dorléac. Delvaux met the lead actress of his first feature, Beata Tyszkiewicz (Andrzej Wajda's wife), in Poland, and from *Rochefort* he recruited an executive producer (Mag Bodard), cinematographer (Ghislain Cloquet—a Belgian who'd also done major work for Bresson and Resnais), and sound technician (Antoine Bonfanti, who'd also worked extensively for Resnais and Godard) who would all work with Delvaux a number of times.

With the exception of *Belle*—an original script written before *Bray* but realized afterward—all of Delvaux's features are inspired by the fiction of contemporary authors with whom he corresponded, freely adapting their work with their approval. Reportedly at least half the plot of *One Night, a Train* is Delvaux's own invention, and in *Bray,* he converts Gracq's hero from a wounded French World War I vet into a Luxembourgian civilian who no longer narrates, and he adds lengthy flashbacks that include an invented character (Odile). Like Stroheim working from *McTeague* to produce *Greed,* you could call Delvaux an adaptor more faithful to the spirit than to the letter of his sources, using his chosen texts as starting points for his own inventions.

Reading most of the few accounts of Delvaux's work written in English—especially those by the late Tom Milne, probably his most sympathetic critic—one often gets the impression that all his features after his first were relative disappointments. This is the drift of Tony Rayns's recent appreciation of *The Man Who Had His Hair Cut Short,* and even Milne regarded the political turn in *Woman in a Twilight Garden,* a film about a Flemish Catholic youth leaving his French wife to collaborate with the Nazis, as a lapse (although arguably Delvaux was already critiquing Belgian society in *The Man Who Had His Hair Cut Short, One Night, a Train,* and *Belle,* and would also critique its Catholicism in *Benvenuta* and *The Abyss*). These aren't my biases, even though I'd concede that Delvaux's last three available features are weaker than his first four.

The Man Who Had His Hair Cut Short may indeed be Delvaux's most significant contribution to Belgian cinema, and it's clearly a major advance over his 1962 short *School Days,* beautifully filmed but relatively slight. But I can't say I love it the way I cherish *Appointment in Bray, One Night, a Train, Behind the Screen,* and *With Dieric Bouts.* (I haven't yet seen either his experimental 1985 feature *Babel Opéra ou la répétition de Don Juan* or his 1986 short that grew out of it, *La Fanfare a cent ans.*) The feature that has so far engaged me the least is Delvaux's final one, *The Abyss*—a grim tale about a Flemish doctor and alchemist in flight and in hiding during the Spanish Inquisition—but even this might well warrant a closer second look. No two Delvaux films are alike, and within my experience, they all prove to be far richer than they first appear.

CHAPTER 6

Jacques Demy

One way that I've attempted to compensate for the absence of a section of this book devoted to Agnès Varda is my discussion of her and Demy as fellow self-indexers at the beginning of this essay—which was commissioned for a Demy retrospective catalog, published by the San Sebastian International Film Festival, September 15–24, 2011, the same year that I headed the New Directors Jury there and the third time that I attended this wonderful festival. Otherwise, I've tried to polemicize my understanding of Demy's work here by focusing on various ways in which it's been misunderstood, especially in the United States, and by discussing some of his points in common with other filmmakers—not only Varda, but also Yasujiro Ozu, Frank Tashlin, and Jean-Luc Godard.

Two or Three Things I Know About Demy

> Braque, Picasso, Klee, Miro, Matisse. . . . C'est ça, la vie.
> —Maxence in *Les Demoiselles de Rochefort*

> Life is disappointing, isn't it?
> —Kyoko in *Tokyo Story*

1

I've never come across any critical discussion of common traits in the separate films of Jacques Demy and Agnès Varda, who lived together for three decades. Their oeuvres are in fact quite different and distinct from one another, but one striking characteristic they share as filmmakers is their preoccupation with indexing and cross-referencing their own works within their own films.

In chronicling and excerpting her own previous work, Varda's *Les Plages d'Agnès* (2008) brings this tendency to a climax, but her DVD containing *Les Glaneurs et la Glaneuse* (2000) and its sequel, *Deux Ans Après*, already formalizes and optimizes this tendency—which can be traced within and between some of her previous films—by allowing one to leap via one's remote control from a character in the former documentary to the same person being filmed two years later (or vice versa). In a comparable spirit, Demy transplants Cécile/Lola (Anouk Aimée), the title heroine of his first feature (1960), from Nantes to Los Angeles in his fifth feature, *Model Shop* (1968), after having had her killed offscreen in Rochefort in his fourth feature, *Les Demoiselles de Rochefort* (1966). In *Model Shop*, he also has Lola explain that Michel (Jacques Harden), her long-lost boyfriend who returned for her at the end of *Lola*, eventually abandoned her to run off with Jacqueline Demestre (Jeanne Moreau), the heroine of Demy's second feature, *La Baie des anges* (1962). Meanwhile, Roland Cassard (Marc Michel), the young man in Nantes who fell in love with Lola before leaving for Johannesburg, reemerged in Cherbourg in *Les Parapluies de Cherbourg* (1964), Demy's third feature, as a successful diamond merchant to marry the pregnant and abandoned Geneviève (Catherine Deneuve), the heroine of that film.

Bearing this common trait in mind, Varda's wonderful documentary *L'univers de Jacques Demy* (1993) manages to cross-index her late husband's work in many effective ways—cutting directly, for instance, from the father-daughter incest in Demy's final feature, *Trois places pour le 26* (1988) to the father-daughter incest in his earlier *Peau d'Âne* (1970), or cutting between a suspension bridge remembered in Demy's childhood to several bridges of this kind in his films (for example, the credits sequence of *Les Demoiselles de Rochefort*, the backdrop of some dance performances in *Trois places pour le 26*)—and also cross-references his work with her own (as well as with their separate and their interconnected lives) in many other ways.

Part of the point of stressing all these interconnections is that Demy (like Varda), in spite of all the frustrations and economic imperatives that frequently interfered with his plans—and indeed, perhaps in part because of them—has to be seen as the author of an oeuvre, not simply as the author of individual films (and one, moreover, who assumed sole screenwriting credit on most of them). The iris shots that end both his first feature, *Lola,* and his last, *Trois places pour le 26,* are echoed fairly precisely by the iris shot that opens his second feature, *La Baie des anges;* and the blazing colors of the wallpaper in his third feature, *Les Parapluies de Cherbourg,* are already anticipated in the blazing red wallpaper of the only set in his short film *Le Bel Indifférent* (1957), made three years before *Lola.*

We know, of course, from the superb documentation of Jean-Pierre Berthomé's *Jacques Demy ou les racines du rêve* (Nantes: L'Atalante, seconde édition, 1996), that Demy rarely (if ever) got the opportunity to make his films according to his original conceptions. In the case of *Le Bel Indifférent,* he would have preferred to have adapted Cocteau's *La Voix humaine; Lola* was conceived as a Michel Legrand musical, and he had to dispense with color and (for the most part) songs when his budgetary restrictions made this impossible; he wanted to cast Nino Castelnuovo, the male lead of *Cherbourg,* in *Rochefort,* until he had to rewrite the script and assign this part to Grover Dale; and comparable revisions of this kind can be found throughout his filmography. Yet at the same time, the autobiographical elements that got worked into his scripts and projects are equally constant, accounting for everything from the garage in *Cherbourg* (inspired by the one where his father worked in Nantes) to the aforementioned suspension bridges.

2

To broach the issue of how Jacques Demy is misunderstood and misperceived in English-speaking countries, one should go to the English-language version of Wikipedia, The Free Encyclopedia (at wikipedia.com), where the second sentence of the entry on Demy comes close to summarizing many of the major misunderstandings and historical confusions:

> Jacques Demy (5 June 1931—27 October 1990) was one of the most approachable filmmakers to appear in the wake of the French New Wave. Uninterested in the formal experimentation of Alain Resnais, or the political agitation of Jean-Luc Godard, Demy instead created a self-contained fantasy world closer to that of François Truffaut, drawing on musicals, fairytales and the golden age of Hollywood.

At the beginning of the respective careers of Demy, Godard, Resnais, and Truffaut, one might counter that certain signs of "political agitation" came from Resnais as well as Godard (in *Le Petit Soldat*)—a trait especially apparent in Resnais's first major short film, *Les Statues meurent aussi* (1953), an essay about African sculpture made in collaboration with writer Chris Marker and cinematographer Ghislain Cloquet, an essay film whose attacks on racism and colonialist appropriation in its final reel led to the film being banned for almost half a century. Moreover, all four of these directors, along with Jacques Rivette, clearly had some interest in formal experimentation, and in the case of Demy, this interest had a great deal to do with confronting "musicals, fairytales" and "the golden age of Hollywood" with the real world, including such real cities as Cherbourg, Los Angeles, Monte Carlo, Nantes, and Rochefort—a confrontation, moreover, that had (and still has) many political ramifications.

So one way of perpetuating the historical misunderstandings and confusions found in these two sentences would be to assume, as this Wikipedia entry does, that "formal experimentation" and "political agitation" are necessarily alternative paths to take in filmmaking rather than, at least in certain cases, as two manifestations of the same impulse, and that the creation of "a self-contained fantasy world" that is misleadingly attributed here to both Truffaut and Demy represents a third path. Yet the moment one starts to consider what could be meant by "self-contained fantasy world[s]" in the early features of Demy and Truffaut, one would presumably also have to include such themes as parental neglect (*Les 400 Coups*), World War I (*Jules et Jim* and *La Chambre Verte*), the plight of a single mother (*Lola*), the French war in Algeria (*Les Parapluies de Cherbourg*), the U.S. war in Vietnam (*Model Shop*), and a shipyard labor strike (*Une Chambre en ville*) as parts of the presumed "unreality" of these fantasies—along with the unorthodox and unstable genre mixes of, say, *Tirez sur la pianiste* and *Les Demoiselles de Rochefort*.

Most musicals shift back and forth between story (spoken dialogue) and song-and-dance numbers—sometimes creating queasy transitions just before or after these shifts, when we're uncertain where we are stylistically. But *Les Demoiselles de Rochefort* often daringly places story and musical numbers on the screen simultaneously, mixing them in various ways and in different proportions, which wittingly or unwittingly produces a certain malaise, or at least a certain amount of disquiet or discomfort, along with some exhilaration. (Two freakish American musicals of the 1930s, *Love Me Tonight* and *Hallelujah, I'm a Bum,* display a related metaphysical impulse to perceive the musical form as a continuous state of delirious being rather than a traditional story with musical eruptions, with comparably unstable results.) One of the stars may be simply walking down the street, for example, while many or each of the pedestrians around her are dancing, and she can be seen slipping momentarily in and out of their choreography. The feeling of uncertainty or instability arising from this mixture produces powerful and deeply felt yet conflicted emotions—exuberance combined with confusion or a sense of absurdity, a kind of transport underlined or at least threatened by an almost constant sense of loss, yearning, and even tragedy. All of which makes it explicable why both *Rochefort* and the '30s musicals just cited failed at the box office in the United States, and why *Trois places*—which contains similar moments of uneasy transition in relation to its choreography—has never received a commercial run there. (By way of contrast, the commercial success of *Cherbourg* in America can probably be explained in part by the continuous use of song and the absence of choreography, both of which result in an avoidance of the kind of instability I've been describing.)

3

I suspect that the problems being broached here are ultimately philosophical ones—specifically, the empiricism of Anglo American culture trying to make sense of some of the Cartesian underpinnings of French culture. For me, one way of expressing the philosophical paradoxes of Demy's films would be to say, " I think, therefore I am, and dreaming is a part of thought, therefore a part of life and existence; ergo, I dream, therefore I exist." Or, more simply, "I dream, therefore I live." Consequently, the impressions of both artificiality and of actuality in Demy's work can be highly deceptive: the use of "natural" locations that have been freshly repainted (as in *Cherbourg* and *Rochefort*), the supposed simplicities of fairy tales and "innocent" Hollywood genres complicated by such things as incest (in *Peau d'Âne* and *Trois Places pour le 26*) and an ax murder (in *Rochefort*). Serge Daney once aptly described *Une chambre en ville* as Bizet's *Carmen* revisited by Visconti, and it is important to bear in mind that operatic and melodramatic modes are as pertinent to Demy's art as cinematic ones. (Significantly, he often recalled that his formative filmgoing experience as a child was *Les Dames du Bois de Boulogne*.)

A somewhat different spin on this position can be found in a famous statement of the Irish poet William Butler Yeats: "In dreams begin responsibilities." And what responsibilities are these, in the case of Demy? Among others, formal and political ones. The formal responsibilities include his uses of "musicals, fairytales and the golden age of Hollywood," along with operas and melodramas, and the political responsibilities include his considerations of the "real," the world of the everyday as it brushes past or collides with these various modes of fiction and artifice.

For Pauline Kael, writing about *Model Shop* (in the *New Yorker*, February 22, 1969), Demy's first film in English, about Los Angeles, commits the fatal flaw of treating its setting and characters realistically after he excelled as a master of movie-based fantasy in *Lola, La Baie des Anges*, and *Les Parapluies de Cherbourg*, and, according to Kael, "misunderstood" the conventions of Hollywood musicals in *Les Demoiselles de Rochefort*. But I believe it's a serious error to assume that any of Demy's features can be classified quite so simply or unambiguously, which can only be done by overlooking the complex mixtures that inform his work at virtually every moment. Even the forays in his work that appear to come closest to "pure" actuality or artifice, such as the Los Angeles of *Model Shop* or the fairy-tale trappings of *Peau d'Âne*, are contradictory portraits, especially if one considers all the coincidental and chance elements of the former and the conscious anachronisms (such as the hash pipe and the helicopter) in the latter.

By comparing Demy with three other filmmakers—Yasujiro Ozu, Frank Tashlin, and Jean-Luc Godard, all of them quite dissimilar to one another—I would like to suggest that what we generally mean by such terms as "fantasy" and "reality" are invariably grounded in alternative sets of film conventions that need to be defined as such. One could argue that even the more "realistic" employments of French locations and social mores in Demy's first four features are informed and inflected by various film traditions (such as those deriving from Bresson, Cocteau, Ophüls, and various musicals from Hollywood and elsewhere), so that Hollywood and other forms of commercial filmmaking serve to shape as well as filter many of the "realistic" details.

A famous line uttered in Ozu's *Tokyo Story*—"Life is disappointing, isn't it?"—could serve as a virtual motto to *Lola* and *Les Parapluies de Cherbourg*, and it is worth adding that Demy is every bit as preoccupied as Ozu with the formulas, ceremonies, and rituals of everyday life—not only rituals such as getting married, going off to war, having children, and losing or finding work, but also such minor rituals as saying "Good morning" and "Thank you"—with the full span of generations and age groups informing the social interactions of particular neighborhoods and their hangouts (mainly cafés), as well as the dynamics of family life. One of Ozu's sublime late films, *Good Morning,* is very much concerned with that particular salutation—as is *Cherbourg,* which has more than its share of *bonjour*s, each one musically placed. It may say something about the difference between Japan and France—as well as the difference between Ozu and Demy as artists—that Ozu's films are full of father figures and Demy's are more often bereft of them (with a few exceptions in the latter portion of his career). But their views of the human condition are surprisingly similar.

By contrast, the similarity of Demy to Frank Tashlin is relatively limited—circumscribed by the fact that both directors entered film via animation and that both had a special taste for "loud" primary colors—and one should emphasize that their differences are just as relevant. Tashlin's satirical mode, to begin with, was almost entirely foreign to Demy. When the latter charts in *Cherbourg* with withering accuracy the steps that Geneviève's mother takes to snare the diamond merchant—a process that begins even before she discovers that Geneviève is pregnant—he doesn't view the process satirically or even judgmentally; he's simply observing in detail the way French people behave in such situations, with a kind of accuracy and fidelity that seems comparable to that of Ozu in chronicling the behavior in his own country.

The dialectical play between documentary and fantasy in Godard seems far more relevant, especially as it figures in a film such as *Alphaville*. Indeed, the two features of Demy that to my mind have been most critically underrated and neglected are arguably the ones in which the play between actuality and artifice is the most complex and unconventional, *Model Shop* and *Trois places pour le 26*. The nature of both the realities and the contrivances that figure in each film, I should add, is quite different, and these films need to be considered separately.

In *Model Shop,* one should consider first of all a portrait of everyday life Los Angeles in 1969, particularly in relation to the counterculture of that period, that seems remarkably accurate and authentic (especially if one compares the film to Antonioni's relatively expressionistic depiction of Los Angeles in *Zabriskie Point* a year later), placed inside a "drifting" narrative that unfolds over a few hours that is essentially framed by the hero (Gary Lockwood) driving around, attempting to borrow money to prevent his car from being repossessed, his chance encounter with and pursuit of a French model (Anouk Aimée), the discovery during a phone call to his parents that a draft notice has been sent to him in San Francisco, and his eventual breakup with his girlfriend (Alexandra Hay) back at their bungalow. This narrative material—which is paradoxically both action-packed and, in terms of most Hollywood conventions, devoid of incident, and in which the sprawling topography of Los Angeles figures as a constant documentary presence—plays against contrary elements that can be characterized as "auteurist": a very contrived and artificial back story bringing together diverse characters from Demy's first three features (which I've already described in the second paragraph of this essay) as well as an employment of the film's title location as a self-referential device that addresses Demy's own activity as a "photographer" and director. (One should also cite the use of film stills from both *Lola* and Godard's *A bout de souffle,* two low-budget nouvelle vague features sharing the same producer and cinematographer; in a similar spirit, *Lola* employs a still of Elina Labourdette from *Les Dames du Bois de Boulogne* to represent her character's past as a dancer.)

In *Trois places pour le 26,* one finds Yves Montand not only playing himself, but doing so in a musical revue in Marseille that is based on his own life, with allusions to his real-life romantic involvements with Edith Piaf, Simone Signoret, and Marilyn Monroe. The plot's main narrative thread, however, involves a wholly fictional affair of Montand with a Marseille prostitute (Françoise Fabian) more than two decades earlier, producing a daughter (Mathilda May) whose existence he never knew about, who winds up costarring in his musical revue *and* having sex with him.

In this case, where Montand's own life provides the documentary subject in almost the same way that Los Angeles figures in *Model Shop,* the "back story" is even more contrived, to the point of hyperbolic provocation: not only do father and daughter sleep together unknowingly, but the daughter, once she discovers the facts, contrives to bring her mother along with her on the show's tour, rejoining her with Montand in the final scene—a dénouement that seems conceivable only in France, and "acceptable" only because of its outrageous contrivance.

This dialectic between the real and the false matches the unending struggle in Demy's work between blind chance and overdetermined control (and between chaos and symmetry), reaching a kind of temporary climax in *Rochefort*. It's part of the film's overarching design that characters who are perfectly matched keep missing one other as they go about their daily routines, in most cases not even realizing that they're in the same city. And even though *The Young Girls of Rochefort* could be described as Demy's most optimistic film—the one in which every character eventually finds the person she or he is looking for—the missed connections preceding this resolution are relentless. Indeed, the split second by which Maxence (Jacques Perrin) misses Delphine (Catherine Deneuve) at the café before he leaves Rochefort might well be the most tragic single moment in all Demy's work, perhaps even surpassing the grisly suicide at the climax of *Une chambre en ville,* when Edmond (Michel Piccoli) slits his throat on-camera in the presence of his wife Edith (Dominique Sanda). By contrast, when this "ideal couple" does eventually meet—an event represented only obliquely and offscreen—this mainly registers as a sort of offhand diminuendo and postscript, a simple concession to musical-comedy convention. What reverberates more decisively is the earlier moment of dreams just missing their realization. The same might be said for the hyperbolic "happy" ending of *Trois places,* and, for that matter, the conclusions of all of Demy's other best films—*Lola, La Baie des Anges, Cherbourg, Model Shop, Une chambre en ville.* The vision of these works is ultimately closer to tragedy than it is to comedy.

CHAPTER 7

Carl Dreyer

The late films of Carl Dreyer have been an ongoing preoccupation of mine at least since I wrote about *Gertrud* (1964), his last film, in the mid-'80s for *Sight and Sound*—an essay subsequently included in my first collection, *Placing Movies* (1995). But I also previously reviewed Dreyer's *Vampyr* and *They Caught the Ferry* for the *Monthly Film Bulletin* in 1976 and David Bordwell's book about Dreyer for *Film Comment* in 1981. More recently, in 2008, the Australian DVD label Madman commissioned essays from me about *Day of Wrath* (1943) and *Ordet* (1955). The latter of these can be found in my 2010 collection *Goodbye Cinema, Hello Cinephilia,* and the former can be found below; both of these, along with all the other pieces cited here, are also available on my website.

Figuring Out *Day of Wrath*

I first encountered Carl Dreyer's work in my teens, but it wasn't until my forties that I became ready for it. I mainly had to rely on lousy 16mm prints, so ruinous to the sounds and images of *Day of Wrath* that I could look at that film only as a form of painterly academicism, a repressed view of repression. The film defeated me with its unalleviated Danish gloom and its dull pacing, which I associated with Dreyer's strict Lutheran upbringing.

Most of this perception was sheer nonsense, as I discovered once I had access to better prints, information, and reflexes. For one thing, contrary to many would-be reference works, Dreyer's upbringing was neither strict nor Lutheran, and he was born a Swede, even if he grew up in Denmark. He was born out of wedlock in 1889 to Josefine Bernhardine Nilsson, a Swedish servant living and working in a large country estate—a woman who died horribly a year and a half later trying to abort a second child in her seventh month of pregnancy by taking a box and a half of matches, cutting off their heads, and swallowing them, which led to a painful and hideous death from sulfur poisoning. After brief stints with foster parents, in an orphanage, and then with another family, the baby was adopted by the Dreyers in Copenhagen—a typographer named (as his adopted son would be) Carl Theodor Dreyer and his wife Inger Marie, who already had an illegitimate daughter, Valborg. Marie, who felt cheated that the infant Carl's real mother hadn't lived long enough to pay child support, reportedly made a habit of complaining to her adopted son about it, and often punished him by locking him in a closet, and he grew up despising her; when she died many years later, he refused even to attend her funeral. According to his biographer Maurice Drouzy, Dreyer worshiped his real mother and hated his adopted one with equal amounts of passion, and good as well as bad mother figures subsequently abound in his films. (Gertrud, the title heroine of his last feature, is perhaps the only female character in his work who combines these two figures, mythically speaking, even though she happens to be childless herself.)

Even though at the age of two he was christened in a Lutheran church, Dreyer the future filmmaker essentially had a nonreligious upbringing. (When he later went to Sunday school at a French Reformed church, this was mainly done to sharpen his French.) What I and many others had taken to be Dreyer's religious beliefs were actually calculated challenges to belief and nonbelief alike. And according to what Dreyer's friend Ib Monty once told me, he wasn't religious at all. (There *is* some evidence, however, that Dreyer believed in paranormal phenomena as a way of explaining certain things that might be interpreted as supernatural—including the miracle that occurs at the end of *Ordet*.)

Indeed, part of what's great about *Day of Wrath* is a passionate ambiguity that leaves all major questions frustratingly unresolved yet vibrantly open, quivering and radiant with life and meaning. The slow pacing is needed for both the intensity and the sensuality under the gloom to fully register. Adapted from a Norwegian play—Hans Wiers-Jenssen's *Anne Pedersdotter*—that Dreyer had first seen in 1909, *Day of Wrath* looks today more cinematically advanced than any other movie released in 1943. (The play, on the other hand, apparently hasn't been available in English since 1917, and used copies of the English translation that occasionally turn up on the internet are unusually pricey.)

The heroine of Wiers-Jenssen's play is a historical figure in Norway who was accused of being a witch and was burned alive at the stake in 1590. Dreyer's adaptation is quite free, and it appears that the main similarity between the play's Anne Pedersdotter and Dreyer's own heroine of that name, apart from their shared fate, is that both were married to clergymen named Absalon Pedersson. The historical Pedersdotter was first accused in 1575 of having murdered her husband's uncle, a bishop, through sorcery to make her husband a bishop; but she was cleared and managed to get a pardon from the king of Denmark. Fifteen years later she faced trial again—this time for killing half a dozen people, including children, through witchcraft—and this time she was found guilty. The main transgression of Dreyer's Pedersdotter, who had a mother burned as a witch (a fact kept hidden from the local community by Absalon), is developing a passion for Absalon's son by his first marriage, Martin, when he returns home from his theological studies—a transgression that ultimately leads to her wishing for her husband's death and then causing it with the direct expression of her hatred for him, which leads immediately to his collapse. One of the many changes Dreyer made to the play was to desexualize the figure of Absalon (Thorkild Roose)—a character who was more clearly drawn to Anne (Lisbeth Movin) for her beauty in the original—and thus give further motivation to her becoming sexually attracted to her stepson (Presben Lerdorff-Rye).

The film's handling of period is unparalleled, achieving a narrative richness that may initially seem confusing, and anticipating many of the positions held by historians today about the witch trials, understandings that were not yet widely held in 1943. Set in 1623–1633, years after the real Pedersdotter's execution, but during a time when people still believed without any question or doubt in witches—and shifting the setting from Norway to Denmark—the film views that world from a contemporary perspective without for a moment dispelling our sense of what it must have felt like from the inside. Dreyer pulls off this difficult task through his singular style, part of which involves a sensual form of camera movement that he invented: the camera gliding on unseen tracks in one direction while uncannily panning in another direction. It's difficult to imagine—a three-dimensional kind of transport that somehow combines coming and going in the same complex journey—but a hypnotic experience both to follow and to keep up with. The film's first real taste of it comes fairly early, when we follow Anne in her sinuous progress toward the interrogation of Hertlofs Marte (Anna Svierjier) by her husband. The camera tracking with Anne around a pillar prompts our involvement in both her curiosity and her stealth in satisfying it, while its simultaneous swiveling away from her establishes our detachment from both—at the same time that it suggests an anticipation of her future impulses and desire by literally racing past her.

Enhancing the strange sense of presence that results from this emotional complexity and ambiguity is Dreyer's rare employment of direct sound rather than studio post-synching—giving scenes an almost carnal impact that becomes lost in smudgy and static-heavy prints. And, in keeping with the subsequent practice of Robert Bresson to replace images with sounds whenever he can, Dreyer uses sound to force us to imagine many of the details of the pursuit, torture, and extermination of an old woman in the opening sequences of the film rather than show us any of these things in any extended detail.

There are many ways of interpreting the eerie story. We can believe that the characters, oppressed by sexual repression, conjure up fantasies about witches; or we can believe that witches really exist, and this story is showing us how one particular society, working through the church, produces them. Either way, Dreyer's hatred for intolerance and institutions, the clergy in particular, is evident throughout, though all the characters can be said to have their own reasons, and simple hypocrisy is never an issue. The bottom line is that everyone in this society believes in witches—including the women suspected and accused of being witches, who regard many of their own passions as a form of sorcery and power. Herlofs Marte, the old woman accused of witchery in the opening sequence, who asks for Anne's help in hiding her, never denies being a witch, and Anne never does either. And even though Dreyer's focus throughout is on his characters' psychology, there's really nothing in the film that supports the proposition that either of these women is being falsely accused or misunderstood.

Merete (Sigrid Neiiendam), Absalon's elderly and widowed mother, who resembles W. C. Fields at odd moments, may be the closest thing in the film to a villain—Drouzy suggests that the very fact that her name sounds a bit like Marie may have carried some emotional weight for Dreyer. But her perception and understanding of what's going on between her grandson and daughter-in-law as their quasi-incestuous affair develops is more acute than anyone else's, and she's clearly nobody's fool. Furthermore, we accept Absalon as a good man, or at least as a sincere and honest old fogey—struggling to be responsible about his own sense of virtue and justice—at the same time that we feel complicitous with his son and wife when they're betraying him, caught up in their blazing passion for one another. And however much we may regard Anne as a heroine for related reasons, we can't say that Dreyer idolizes her either; believing that her sexuality is tied in some way to sorcery, she's also as complicitous in the society that condemns her as everyone else is.

Some combination of all the above is operative at every moment, lending a multidimensional impact to each gesture, word, and emotion. We bear the frightening knowledge that genuine evil resides in this confined world, but without a capacity to locate it either in literal sorcery or in particular individuals, at least with any sense of finality, we might paranoiacally find it everywhere and nowhere—in a kind of collective virus infecting a whole community.

This film was made and had its premiere during the grimmest days of the Nazi occupation of Denmark, when Jews were being deported. The curfews in force instituted by the Germans had the effect on limiting all forms of public entertainment, including film exhibition, to the afternoons. In spite of this latter restriction, *Day of Wrath* ran in Copenhagen for six months, though according to Jean Drum and Dale M. Drum's *My Only Great Passion: The Life and films of Carl Th. Dreyer* (Lanham, Md. and London: Scarecrow Press, 2000), this was mainly because the cinema playing the film wanted to find an excuse not to show German films during this period; apparently attendance was minimal, and, again according to the Drums, "*Day of Wrath* was almost universally condemned by the Danish critics, mostly on the ground that the action was too slow." (The film wouldn't play outside Denmark until after the war, when it received mixed reviews and mainly poor business in the United States and elsewhere in England.) So it's a cruel irony that the leading Nazi-run newspaper at the time gave *Day of Wrath* a rave review, correctly implying in this case that the Danish didn't know how to appreciate their native talent, while less plausibly arguing that Germany could make better use of such a filmmaker as Dreyer. Indeed, it was the interest shown in Dreyer by Nazi officials based in Denmark, after the release of *Day of Wrath,* that led directly to him emigrating to Sweden with his wife for the war's duration.

How relevant is it that the film was made during the Nazi occupation? Like many other issues raised by this perpetually vexing film, this is a complex question with no simple answer, perhaps even with no final answer at all. It is especially so because Dreyer paradoxically combines a vivid present-tense quality with a distanced historical perspective, almost as if we were watching the action simultaneously from opposite ends of the same telescope, so that we're deeply implicated in the events yet also able to analyze them. Drouzy surmises that Dreyer may have cast a blonde actress as Anne to avoid charges that he was making a political allegory. On the other hand, the contemporary Danish film scholar Casper Tybjerg persuasively argues that any film made in occupied Denmark that had a trace of political allegory would likely have been recognized as such by most members of the Resistance as well as most Nazis, thereby endangering the filmmakers involved—and that any political allegory *we* might be tempted to find is ultimately confounded by the fact that Dreyer's portrait of a society in which everyone believes in the existence of witches finds no clear counterpart in the persecution and extermination of Jews. Tybjerg also offers the plausible hypothesis that Dreyer's refusal to show any signs of hope for liberation among his characters probably influenced as well as inflected the film's poor critical reception in Denmark.

For many years, I've regarded *Day of Wrath* as one of the great Resistance films, but now, after brooding at length over Tybjerg's arguments, I'm inclined to regard this description as a seductive but facile error: anti-totalitarian, yes; but pro-Resistance? Not really, because there's no Resistance of any kind to be found anywhere in the world of *Day of Wrath*—which is part of what's so maddening about it.

Like all of Dreyer's greatest films, this is a masterpiece that keeps changing and eluding us whenever we try to pin it down. According to the late Scottish critic Tom Milne, Dreyer "always insisted that any such political overtones to the film were strictly unintentional"—which means that *Day of Wrath* is the reverse of a conscious allegory like Arthur Miller's *The Crucible,* a play that opened on Broadway ten years later and clearly used the witch trials in Salem, Massachusetts in the late seventeenth century—a full century after the death of Anne Pedersdotter in Norway—to stand in for the contemporary reign of terror unleashed by Joseph McCarthy against actual and suspected Communists, including Miller himself. Yet it's also worth stressing that Miller's play was almost certainly influenced by Dreyer's movie—a fact that becomes particularly apparent in the 1996 film version of *The Crucible* with Daniel Day-Lewis and Winona Ryder, directed by Nicholas Hytner, which Miller adapted himself. It also seems pertinent that the American critic who wrote most memorably about both *Day of Wrath* and *The Crucible,* Robert Warshow, attacked the latter for what he called Miller's "steadfast . . . refusal of complexity" in perpetrating various allegorical mismatches between the past and present; but he failed to note any contemporary relevance at all in *Day of Wrath,* and perhaps he was correct in not doing so.

Nevertheless, Dreyer's persistent denial that he was saying anything about the German occupation of Denmark in *Day of Wrath*—apart from acknowledging in a 1950 interview that "one never knows, of course, what goes on in one's subconsciousness"—also suggests that some works of art ultimately know and say more than their makers do. Like one of the characters in his masterpiece, Dreyer was trapped in his own personal obsessions, yet he remained so faithful to his art that he may have wound up saying more about his own times than most direct commentators. For *Day of Wrath,* whatever it lacks in close or sustained correspondences between seventeenth-century witches and twentieth-century victims of totalitarianism, may still be the most profound depiction that we have on film of what it means and feels like to live inside a totalitarian society. That is to say, it has an emotional authenticity even when the historical analogies don't match up—a defense that some critics would make of *The Crucible* as well.

Let me hypothesize another possible reading of *Day of Wrath,* which could be regarded as another way of proposing a legitimate allegorical reading. If a direct political allegory would have entailed a distortion of the historical truth as well as a serious risk for the filmmakers, there's another conscious or unconscious route that might have been taken by Dreyer and the other creative participants on the film that is worth considering. In most of the more honest depictions of totalitarian societies that have been made, consciously or unconsciously, by people living inside them, one can find a fairly systematic displacement of the theme of political enslavement and persecution to the theme of sexual enslavement and persecution. Two of the clearest examples of this trend that come to mind are Henri-Georges Clouzot's *Le Corbeau* (*The Raven,* 1943)—made the same year as *Day of Wrath,* during the German occupation of France—and Juan Antonio Bardem's *Calle Mayor* (*Main Street,* 1956), made by a Communist filmmaker working under considerable difficulty in Franco Spain. Bardem, in fact, was even arrested in the middle of his shooting, until his lead actress, Betsy Blair—herself a Communist and a victim of the Hollywood Blacklist—refused to resume work with any other director, even after Bardem gave her permission to do so, and thereby exerted enough economic pressure to force the Franco government to release him.

The plot of *Calle Mayor,* concerning bored men in a provincial Spanish town who dream up an ugly practical joke of courting and proposing to a spinster (Blair) and then rudely dumping her—an exceptionally cruel story that anticipates that of Neil LaBute's 1997 film *In the Company of Men,* with its own anticapitalist agenda—implicitly becomes a pointed commentary of the ugliness of human behavior under totalitarianism. Much the same could be said about the plot and characters of *Le Corbeau,* and similar examples of political oppression being obliquely reflected in sexual terms can surely be found elsewhere, in everything from the treatment of homosexuality in the posthumously released second part of Sergei Eisenstein's *Ivan the Terrible* (1958) to the theme of feudal sexual enslavement in Zhang Yimou's *Ju Dou* (1990) and *Raise the Red Lantern* (1991). In the Clouzot and Bardem films, where the settings are contemporary, the absence of any political theme apart from male-female relations makes this displacement especially evident. In the two Zhang Yimou films, one could argue that sexual persecution isn't so much a displacement of the political theme as the principal aspect of it that's being addressed—the sexual aspect of feudalism in contemporary China.

Day of Wrath could also be considered more simply as a film that addresses the dynamics of sexual behavior in a totalitarian society. In this respect, it shares some traits with the nonallegorical treatments of an illegal abortion in Romania during the 1980s in Cristian Mungiu's *4 Months, 3 Weeks, and 2 Days* (2007) and some details of everyday totalitarian life in postrevolutionary Tehran in Marjane Satrapi and Vincent Paronnaud's animated *Persepolis* (2007)—with the key difference that Dreyer is viewing oppression in the remote past rather than the recent past. These latter examples don't involve any displacement of emphasis or any strategy for skirting censorship, but they nevertheless seem relevant in a more general way—by showing, respectively, how the anti-abortion laws of Romania in the '80s permitted an authoritarian and totalitarian exploitation of women by men, and how a practical joke of the heroine as a teenager—claiming to a police officer that an innocent boy looked at her salaciously, which led to his arrest—shows how easily and thoughtlessly anyone can drift into totalitarian behavior, especially when prudish sexual mores are involved.

In conclusion, I've had far too little to say about *Days of Wrath*'s remarkable visual style so far apart from its innovative camera movements. It's one that creates a universe with particular spatial and rhythmic laws of its own, relating to claustrophobic interiors and exteriors where the no-less-threatening forces of nature often seem to overtake the social constraints. There are the evocations of Rembrandt found in some of the interiors—which Dreyer himself claimed partially stemmed from the fact that the 1623 setting was contemporary with Rembrandt. One should also mention Dreyer's insistence that none of the actors wear make-up—an injunction Lisbeth Movin later admitted she surreptitiously defied, by applying just a dab of rouge when Dreyer wasn't looking—and his effective use of authentic period furniture. Above all, one should stress the uncanny, otherworldly way that Movin's Anne is often lit, with particular attention given to the passion burning in her eyes—which ultimately helps to make her final speech, addressed to the corpse of Absalon, carry the cumulative tragic weight and force of the entire drama, concluding, "I killed you with the Evil One's help, and with the Evil One's help I have lured your son into my power. Now you know, now you know. I see through my tears, but no one comes to wipe them away."

CHAPTER 8

John Gianvito

Like Travis Wilkerson (*An Injury to One, Did You Wonder Who Fired the Gun?*) and Jon Jost (*Last Chants for a Slow Dance, They Had it Coming*), John Gianvito is a radical American independent whose low profile in spite of his considerable talent and originality can partly be attributed to his absolute lack of compromise. Significantly, all three of these filmmakers contributed segments, along with Minda Martin and Soon-Mi Yoo, to the 2012 collective protest feature *Far from Afghanistan,* which Gianvito initiated, with its title inspired by the 1967 French feature *Far from Vietnam*. It's the recent Gianvito film that is most neglected in the two pieces below, written respectively for *Film Quarterly* (Winter 2008–2009) and *Film Comment*'s blog (February 2, 2016).

Historical Meditations in Two Films by John Gianvito

It's been gratifying to see the almost instant acclaim accorded to John Gianvito's beautiful, fifty-eight-minute *Profit Motive and the Whispering Wind* (2007), especially after the relative neglect of his only previous feature-length film, the 168-minute *The Mad Songs of Fernanda Hussein* (2001).

The more recent film—a meditative, lyrical, and haunting documentary about grave sites that won the *grand prix* at the Entervues Film Festival in Belfort in 2007 and both a Human Rights Award and a special mention at the Buenos Aires Festival of Independent Film in 2008—also received an award at the Athens International Film and Video Festival in Ohio and was named the year's best experimental film by the National Society of Film Critics. (Full disclosure: I nominated *Profit Motive* for the last of these awards, and headed the jury of the same Buenos Aires film festival in 2001, which gave *The Mad Songs* its top prize.)

The Mad Songs focuses on the irreparable effects of the First Gulf War in 1991 on three separate powerless people in New Mexico (which is where the film in its entirety was shot). *Profit Motive* focuses on the grave sites of several dozen heroes of progressive struggles throughout American history. These topics are of course quite different, yet the differences between the films aren't nearly as substantial as they might initially appear. Both are predicated on and filmed around subjects that are physically absent—the Persian Gulf in *The Mad Songs*, the dead heroes of *Profit Motive*—and ones that viewers are invited to imagine, think about, and mourn in some fashion. In fact, I think both films are enhanced and complicated immeasurably as soon as one sees them in relation to one another rather than as separate and isolated forays. Both films are dedicated to examining political struggles in the United States and how these struggles are emotionally, intellectually, and historically assimilated.

Never morbid, and too gentle to qualify as strictly didactic, *Profit Motive and the Whispering Wind* invites us to accompany Gianvito on a casual, fact-finding tour of American history that's as much concerned with what is lost as what is found. It was shot over the course of three summers whenever Gianvito wasn't teaching; the 16mm Bolex that he used prevented him from filming any image continuously for any longer than twenty-five seconds, although he managed to disguise the cuts he made on a few occasions when he needed to accord the viewer more reading time.

He includes in his pantheon such famous figures as Thomas Paine, John Brown, Henry David Thoreau, Chief Crazy Horse, Frederick Douglass, Susan B. Anthony, Harriet Tubman Davis, Eugene Debs, Mother Jones, Emma Goldman, Medgar Evers, Lorraine Hansbury, Malcolm X, John Dos Passos, Paul Goodman, Paul Robeson, and Dorothy Day as well as a virtually equivalent number of unknown or lesser-known names, deliberately goading our curiosity to learn more about them. (One critic has expressed skepticism to me about the absence of certain key figures, such as Martin Luther King, but it's important to note that Gianvito's selection remains highly personal without in any way aspiring to exhaustiveness.)

At first glance, Gianvito appears to have gone from boiling, impotent rage about a few marginalized victims and dissidents in *The Mad Songs of Fernanda Hussein* to a kind of hushed, mourning tranquility in *Profit Motive* as he ponders the lives and memory traces of a good many activists—all of whom appear to have had a far greater historical impact than the characters in *The Mad Songs* (even though their remains are in mainly unremarked locations). This may help to account for the much wider and warmer appreciation accorded to the latter film in both the United States and abroad, despite the fact that *The Mad Songs* has been available on DVD (issued by the small-label ELF, or Extreme Low Frequency) since 2005. But of course a radically different change in political climate since early 2001 has also surely had a lot to do with the respective receptions of both films—more, I would argue, than any particular change in Gianvito's politics or in his measured mastery of framing and editing. The distance traveled from the embrace of the American public of the First Gulf War in 1991 and the same public's eventual (if belated) recoil against the occupation of Iraq a decade and a half later is considerable, but this is a journey that is in some ways implicitly recorded in the juxtaposition between Gianvito's two features.

Both films are the poetic and pantheistic expressions of a committed leftist, a fiercely determined independent ready to brook all obstacles, and a passionate cinephile with an extensive curatorial and programming background, known particularly for his work at the Harvard Film Archive. (The second section of the three-part *Mad Songs* is titled, "Orphans of the Storm.") Both films can be said to have overall structures that seemingly move from isolated and lonely individuals to a massive and potent collective experience—though one should add that the single collective experience viewed at the end of *The Mad Songs* is regarded far more darkly and complexly than the celebratory montage of footage from various protest marches in Boston, New York, and Washington, D.C. concluding *Profit Motive,* which relate to the Iraq war, immigrant rights, and gay rights, among other issues—footage played against throbbing drumbeats that is clearly and effectively employed for agitprop and rallying purposes. Furthermore, both films employ a kind of stylistic bricolage that can shift abruptly from meditative lyricism to passionate agitprop and from conventional documentary to musical interludes, art and literary references, and personal experimental filmmaking verging on abstraction.

In *The Mad Songs,* Gianvito can also shuttle with some regularity between conventional documentary and conventional fiction when he isn't intricately mixing the two, or veer off into a brilliant and devastating montage sequence devoted to Desert Storm war toys and various things inscribed on them (for example, "not recommended for children under three years old"; "Eat lead, Cobra!"; "Let's party!"). In *Profit Motive,* he can suddenly make room for brief flashes of discontinuous and seemingly unrelated animation (his own) punctuating his live-action footage. Yet for all their eclecticism, both films are principally emotional rather than intellectual experiences.

Read superficially, both films are susceptible to the accusation of belonging to a leftist syndrome, "the ennobling of victimization," astutely analyzed by Thom Andersen in his essay "Red Hollywood": "The ennobling of victimization is dangerous, I think, because it requires the victims to keep in their places to maintain their moral claims. If they revolt they must be defeated if they are to keep our sympathy and indulgence. They must remain victims. When Castro's rebels in Cuba and the Sandinistas in Nicaragua won their revolutions, they immediately forfeited the considerable goodwill their seemingly hopeless struggles had earned them in the United States."[1] Citing Robin Blackburn ("Bourgeois sociology only begins to understand modern revolutions in so far as they fail"), Andersen goes on to critique from this vantage point the romanticizing and glorifying of "revolutionary defeats" in such revered political films as *Viva Zapata!* (1952), *The Battle of Algiers* (1967), and *Burn!* (1970).

In fact, *The Mad Songs,* by centering on three figures who are principally seen as victims, is theoretically more open to this charge than *Profit Motive,* which is more concerned with political struggle per se than with either success or failure. But one must also acknowledge that *The Mad Songs* is largely conceived as a kind of therapeutic gesture, an attempt at healing—comparable, *mutatis mutandis,* to something like *The Best Years of Our Lives.* As Gianvito said to Ray Privett in an interview, "I feel that to some extent the Gulf War is like this monster in the closet that we don't talk about, but about which somehow in our conscious or unconscious minds we carry a lot of shame and unresolved feelings. And I think people know that. The rapidity and intensity with which it unfolded and the rapidity with which it vanished left the country traumatized. And unless we face up to and examine those traumas, we will continue to behave in more and more wounded manners."[2]

I should confess that my gratitude for *The Mad Songs*—which is part of what led me to lobby successfully for it being awarded the jury prize in Buenos Aires—is closely tied to its therapeutic power. Gianvito himself says that he made that film in order "to keep [himself] from going crazy": "The whole thing emerged out of inarticulate rage I carried within me, not only during the Persian Gulf War but through the years that followed, as I progressively learned more and more about what had in fact transpired during the war and its unfolding consequences on the lives of so many people."[3] To make it, Gianvito had to travel repeatedly from his home in Massachusetts to New Mexico, which he selected as his location largely because of its physical resemblance to the Persian Gulf.

For me, the personal effect of this feature was almost like hearing a cry of shared pain and rage after a decade of deafening silence. The problem wasn't simply that so many friends and family members, virtually all of them liberals, supported the war without qualification (as some of them would also do of the Iraqi invasion, at least before its stated motives proved to be spurious); it was that so many of them were positively gleeful about it, even after admitting in their euphoria that it entailed killing a substantial number of innocent civilians. For me this offered early glimmers of a terrifying conviction that persists for many Americans today—that we can not only "liberate" countries we know next to nothing about, but also that we can confidently define our military goals while remaining indifferent to the wills and lives of the people we are supposedly devoted to liberating. (It's important to stress that the principal reason given by editors at the *New York Times* for rejecting an Op Ed piece by John McCain in summer 2008 was his refusal or inability to pinpoint what he meant by a military "victory" in Iraq. To all appearances, the operative phrase in his vocabulary on this topic is "with honor," which clearly alludes to the welfare of Americans, not Iraqis.) Given such bloodlust and such a glib desire to remain uninformed (as reflected in a TV clip in *The Mad Songs* where we see TV talk-show host Arsenio Hall quip in 1991 that "Iraqi intelligence" is an "oxymoron"—a "bright" observation that obviously required no illustration or backup to get rounds of laughter and applause), it's hardly surprising that so many were easily persuaded to invade Iraq on a flimsy pretext in the Second Gulf War.

The three fictional stories of *Mad Songs* intersect only twice—or possibly three times, an ambiguity the film prefers to leave open. The title heroine is a young Latina (Thia Gonzales, the only professional in the cast) in Los Lunas, separated from her Arab husband (who returned to Egypt when he couldn't find work), whose two children are killed because of their surname shortly after the outbreak of the war. A teenage boy in Santa Fe named Raphael (Dustin Scott) is so alienated by his parents' intolerance of his antiwar sentiments and activism that he leaves home and becomes a street person. (Gianvito has a cameo as one of Raphael's teachers, someone who shares his beliefs.) And Carlos, a Chicano and vet returning to his home in Pecos, is so troubled by his experiences in Saudi Arabia, including some atrocities he participated in, and by such consequences of his service as losing his former job and a rash that appears to derive from Agent Orange, that he finds it easier to relate to the two hookers he hires than to his loyal girlfriend.

The first two of these plots clearly intersect when one of Raphael's friends reads aloud a news story about Fernanda Hussein, describing some of the aftermath of her own story. (Having become mentally unstable, she's arrested for the murder of her own children and subsequently released, then disappears and reportedly has become homeless, either in Mexico or near the border.) Much later, she reappears at the home of an old friend, having by now regained her sanity. And toward the beginning of the film's final sequence, at a large fiesta held in Santa Fe in which an ancient ritual known as Zozobra takes place (featuring a gigantic burning effigy, and for me evoking some accounts of the Mexican Day of the Dead), the first two plots intersect a second time when Fernanda is one of the passing members of the crowd who signs Raphael's antiwar petition.

Less conclusive but highly suggestive is an earlier moment, in a canyon, that takes place before Fernanda's first reappearance, when Carlos, in a hysterical and frustrated rage after trying to describe his wartime experiences to his girlfriend, starts to rape her, and his attention is suddenly drawn away by an eerie and sustained cry of misery that he hears resounding through the open spaces and that he can't identify. Whether or not this is one of the mad songs of the title and belongs to Fernanda is left entirely up to our imaginations.

This is a fairly simple, even simplistic schema for a lengthy narrative feature, and some of the execution of it is rudimentary. But even though *The Mad Songs* can be described in some ways as an amateur production, it arguably has the kind of amateur credentials called to mind by filmmakers as diverse as Jean Cocteau, Emile De Antonio, Robert Kramer, and Jean Rouch. And even if it begins in rage, it concludes, in the powerful and cathartic Zozobra sequence, with intimations of sorrow, mystery, simple curiosity, and awe as Gianvito steadily contemplates, through the giant burning figure and its orgiastic effect on a large crowd, all the things he has been railing against for the past two and a half hours. In some respects, this sequence recalls his earlier screed against war toys (which intersperses a lavish fireworks display with a comparable rhythmic effect), but here the tone is much more detached and mellow, and the aforementioned emotions—awe, curiosity, mystery, sorrow—dominate. And these are more or less the same emotions with which *Profit Motive and the Whispering Wind* begins.

■ ■ ■

As previously noted, the main focus of *Profit Motive* is grave sites and markers scattered across the United States and their various inscriptions, all of them belonging to heroes and/or victims of progressive struggles from the sixteenth century up through the twenty-first. These sites and markers are all cited in the final credits like a cast list, and they seem fairly evenly divided between relatively known and relatively unknown figures. They progress from the colonial period and early slave revolts to the present day—all the way from Anne Hutchinson (1591–1649), banished from the Massachusetts Bay Colony in 1638 for maintaining that ordinary people could interpret the Bible on their own (though killed with her family in Long Island over a decade later, by Native Americans, simply for being in "the wrong place at the wrong time," as Gianvito put it in an interview with Benjamin Strong[4]), and Mary Dyer, a "witness for religious freedom" hanged on the Boston Common in 1660, to I. F. Stone (1907–1989), buried with his wife, and César Chávez (1927–1993).

The majority of the names and struggles are taken from Howard Zinn's *A People's History of the United States,* which Gianvito credits as his inspiration and dedicates the film to. The film's epigraph (by Claire Spark Loeb, a name unknown to me) is, "The long memory is the most radical idea in America"; this is immediately followed by the sound over black leader of an 1894 recording of a Native American chant, "Kiava Ghost Dance No. 12," transliterated and then translated in subtitles.

In the film's opening stretches, Gianvito is even more attentive to the inscriptions and markings of time and weather on gravestones than he is to the man-made inscriptions, the words and art, found on the same objects. That is to say, the lives celebrated here initially appear to be almost stumbled-upon incidental data in locations that are already being regarded as places of meditation, reflection, and worship. History, the film seems to be saying, is something to be teased out and approached somewhat circumspectly rather than something to be delivered to the viewer directly. The names and statements engraved on the stone are only part of the story.

The film's principal artistic inspiration seems to be the landscape films of Jean-Marie Straub and Danièle Huillet, in which natural settings, past political struggles, and the wind play similarly prominent roles. In fact, one might say that the wind gets far more play in this film than death does—or the profit motive, for that matter. Gianvito's various ways of approaching the graves, memorials, and shrines through the surrounding landscapes that nestle and sometimes hide these largely unremarked sites is every bit as important as their inscriptions. Like the Straub-Huillet landscape films (which include, among many others, *Fortini/Cani*, *Too Early, Too Late*, *The Death of Empedocles*, *Cézanne*, and *Workers, Peasants*), *Profit Motive* may sound minimalist but in fact is very far from being so, in part because the leisurely meditative mode both allows and invites the viewer to become far more attentive to details and nuances than one can be in most narrative films.

Where Gianvito deviates most crucially from Straub-Huillet's example is in his desire to explain on-screen whom these people and what these struggles were, almost always through allowing us to read the inscriptions; one might even say that the central role played in Straub-Huillet films by recited texts, usually on-screen, is performed here by these inscriptions, and Gianvito carefully provides us with all the time we need to read them. (By contrast, the repeated pan of Straub-Huillet's *Europa 2005—27 octobre*, a 2006 video without text or title of any kind, appears to presume that the date is all that's needed for viewers to identify the French location and what happened there—a position that I believe can be criticized as provincial rather than elitist.)

To make another comparison, the grave-site markers in *Profit Motive and the Whispering Wind* are filmed with the same contemplative attentiveness that James Benning shows toward the trains rushing through his *RR* (2007), and their cumulative impact has a comparable expansive effect. Yet the historical sensibility of Gianvito exercised on his settings registers quite differently from Benning's. Benning seems to regard the industrial waste associated with trains both nostalgically and apocalyptically, seesawing dialectically between these extremes as he invites us to perceive the trains both in relation and in opposition to the various landscapes they pass through. Gianvito's more lyrical sense of setting is much closer to the transcendentalism of a Thoreau or a Malick, imparting an almost preternatural sense of primeval (and at times even timeless) calm—a mystical communion with deserted landscapes that calls to mind the fact that Gianvito recently edited a collection of interviews with Andrei Tarkovsky.[5] Unlike *RR,* which suggests at times the kind of epic exhaustiveness being aimed for in John Dos Passos's *U.S.A., Profit Motive and the Whispering Wind* wants to widen our horizons without pretending to stretch them to the limits, repeatedly making us realize that there are many other unrecounted stories of struggle waiting to be told. Its sense of modesty is enhanced and replicated in most of the sites that it visits.

■ ■ ■

One of the more useful premises of Zinn's engaging, 729-page book, established in its first chapter, is "that we must not accept the memory of states as our own. . . . Nations are not communities and never have been. The history of any country, presented as the history of a family, conceals fierce conflicts of interest (sometimes exploding, most often repressed) between conquerors and conquered, masters and slaves, capitalists and workers, dominators and dominated in race and sex."[6]

Profit Motive can be said to benefit from the same overall vision, even if it's necessarily restricted in most cases to the particular understandings displayed in the site inscriptions (so that, for instance, we learn about why Anne Hutchinson was banished from Massachusetts, but not about why she and her family were slain by Native Americans). And I hasten to add that the film is also somewhat limited by the kind of slant that Zinn readily owns up to, a couple of pages earlier, when he insists that his "argument cannot be against selection, simplification, emphasis, which are inevitable for both cartographers and historians," but goes on to insist that the distortions of mapmakers are necessary for everyone who needs maps. Moreover, "The historian's distortion is more than technical, it is ideological; it is released into a world of contending interests, where any chosen emphasis supports (whether the historian means to or not) some kind of interest, whether economic or political or racial or national or sexual."[7]

A good example of what Zinn means by this can be seen in his brief treatment of Rosa Parks (1913–2005), the seamstress whom he rightly credits with launching the civil rights movement in late 1955 when she refused to relinquish her seat near the front of a bus in Montgomery, Alabama, was arrested for her defiance of the Jim Crow laws in doing so, and sparked the Montgomery bus boycott. Zinn typically follows the lead of Martin Luther King in giving Parks full credit as an activist but none as a strategist, overlooking the fact that earlier in 1955 she'd attended a workshop on nonviolent, pro-integration tactics at the Highlander Folk School in Monteagle, Tennessee, some of whose workshops King also attended. Eliding this part of Parks's contribution could be interpreted both as a shrewd tactical move (to make her rebellion appear more spontaneous than it actually was) and as a sexist omission that was all too characteristic of '60s male leftists, including King himself, who may have wanted to figure in the public eye as the only prominent tactician of the movement. Either way, Zinn's treatment of Parks perfectly illustrates his own point.

I should stress that Parks's grave site, in Detroit, is *not* one of those filmed by Gianvito, though it theoretically could have been. Its epitaph reads, apparently by her own choice, "Rosa L. Parks, wife." This further suggests that the implication of Gianvito's handling of history—that an important part of it can be (and is) written on headstones—is limited in much the same way as Zinn's is. Yet this is a limitation that comes naturally and inevitably with a desire to expand our historical parameters in the choice of people to be examined, as Zinn is also interested in doing.

In one of the rare instances in which he doesn't depend exclusively on a grave or memorial inscription for identification, Gianvito devotes a lengthy intertitle to explain who Uriah Smith Stephens (1821–1882) was—the cofounder and first leader of the first national labor union in the United States, the Knights of Labor. With the demeanor of a patient schoolteacher (echoing his cameo in *The Mad Songs of Fernanda Hussein*), he's interested in sharing discoveries with us, materially as well didactically, drawing upon whatever materials he needs, and he accompanies his fact-finding and soul-searching journeys with a sense of poetry and a kind of passion that are found in the finest instructors.

Notes

1. Thom Andersen, "Red Hollywood," in *"Un-American" Hollywood,* edited by Frank Krutnik, Steve Neale, Brian Neve, and Peter Stanfield (New Brunswick, N.J. and London: Rutgers University Press, 2007), 234.

2. www.sensesofcinema.com/contents/02/20/gulf_war.html.

3. From a Director's Statement dated February 2001 and included with the DVD of the film released by Extreme Low Frequency.

4. www.thefanzine.com/articles/film/242/interview_with_director_john_gianvito/3.

5. John Gianvito, ed., *Andrei Tarkovsky: Interviews* (Jackson: University Press of Mississippi, 2006).

6. Howard Zinn, *A People's History of the United States,* rev. ed. (New York: HarperCollins, 2003), 10.

7. Ibid., 8.

An Epic of Understanding: John Gianvito's *Wake (Subic)*

Consider the lengths of time between Jean Vigo's death and the first appearances of *Zéro de conduite* and *L'Atalante* in the United States (thirteen years), or between the first screening of Jacques Rivette's *Out 1* and its recent appearances on Blu-Ray (forty-five years), and it becomes obvious that the popular custom of listing the best films of any given year is unavoidably a mythological undertaking. By the same token, film history in the present should be divided between important filmmakers skilled and successful in hawking their own goods, from Alfred Hitchcock to Spike Lee to Lars von Trier, and those who, for one reason or another, aren't—a less definitive roll call that includes, among many others, Charles Burnett, Ebrahim Golestan, Luc Moullet, Peter Thompson, Orson Welles, and John Gianvito.

I haven't seen Gianvito's early shorts, one of which is called *What Nobody Saw* (1990), but its very title seems emblematic of his career—as does the epigraph from Cesare Pavese opening the first part of his first feature, *The Mad Songs of Fernanda Hussein* (2001), which introduced me to his work and remains my favorite: "Everywhere there is a pool of blood that we step into without knowing it." His second and best-known feature, *Profit Motive and the Whispering Wind* (2007), testifies to the same conviction, and his nine-hour documentary diptych, *For Example, The Philippines,* which he has been working on for the past decade, is an epic demonstration of the wisdom of Pavese's remark; *Vapor Trail (Clark)* (2010; 264 minutes) and now *Wake (Subic)* (277 minutes) concentrate on the human ravages left by the Clark Air Base and Subic Bay naval base—for almost a century, the two largest U.S. military compounds outside

North America—after the Philippine Senate voted to eject them in 1991. Departing without any environmental cleanups or any sense of responsibility about what remained, the United States left behind numerous toxic materials in the drinking water and elsewhere that tens of thousands of Filipino citizens knew nothing about, resulting in a massive health blight on successive generations that in many ways recalls the lead deposits in the drinking water of Flint, Michigan that have only recently been publicly acknowledged, with comparably catastrophic results.

The differences between Flint and two former military bases in the Philippines should be stressed—the diversity of toxic materials left behind in the latter (not to mention the alarming array of consequences, which include, to quote Gianvito, "premature births, deformed babies, miscarriages, skin allergies, heart problems, nervous system disorders, leukemia and cancers, problems that persist to this day") and the (very belated) attempts to rectify part of the damage in the former—but the institutional indifference compounded by capitalist greed and apparent racial entitlement in both cases is strikingly similar. In Gianvito's diptych, however, the buried scandal is viewed as only one part of a much larger picture, and *Wake*—which premiered at the Viennale last fall, and screens this week in Rotterdam—makes this broader canvas even more prominent than its predecessor.

Being a film poet and a historian (as well as a film historian, who worked for years at the Harvard Film Archive), not to mention an investigative reporter, Gianvito isn't content merely to expose an ongoing national disaster. He also meditates on the events as part of an even bigger issue, encompassing the no-less-neglected history of the Philippine-American War between 1899 and 1913, and, more implicitly, the environmental problems created by U.S. bases in Greenland, Iceland, Italy, Japan, Panama, Spain, and the U.K. (This scope accounts for the overarching title of Gianvito's project, *For Example, The Philippines*.) The ultimate focus of both *Vapor Trail (Clark)* and *Wake (Subic)*, like that of *The Mad Songs of Fernanda Hussein* and Gianvito's contributions to the omnibus feature *Far from Afghanistan,* is the legacy of U.S. military involvement and all that it entails.

Past and present are juxtaposed throughout *Wake,* with a musical precision in the editing and sound-mixing that makes intertitles (accounts of the Philippine-American War and bits of political speeches), still photographs and other archival materials (including silent newsreel footage and a 1908 recording of a William Howard Taft speech), Carolyn Forché's occasional voiceover narration, and actual music (some of which is furnished by Filipino filmmaker Lav Diaz) every bit as powerful, as pertinent, and as *present* as the contemporary footage. And the contemporary footage is not simply talking-head interviews and place-setting master shots but sustained encounters with particular people we get to know over the course of the film and lyrical interludes involving everyday life and landscapes. One of the most startling cuts, eighty-eight minutes into *Wake*, takes us from an archival black-and-white photograph of a city street in the 1920s or '30s to a moving color shot of what could be the same street today as the camera follows a car bearing a coffin. (Funerals and cemeteries in Gianvito's diptych are as important as they are in *Profit Motive and the Whispering Wind*.)

The facts presented about both past and present are devastating and often shocking, but Gianvito's scruples as a historian and commentator guarantee a vision that moves beyond simple didacticism. As I noted on this blog (on November 16, 2012) when *Vapor Trail* showed at the Viennale, it's characteristic of Gianvito "that whenever he encounters Filipino interview subjects who don't share his disgust with American negligence and indifference, even after losing many family members as a consequence, he doesn't hesitate to include their contrary responses in his film." Even the excruciating irony of his showing one of the deformed children—a contorted mute who has to use his feet to grasp objects—playing a war video-game with his toes isn't exploited as an isolated detail; it's shortly followed by a radical activist, Teofilo "Boojie" Juatco, expounding on how "colonial thinking" remains in the very "bones" of Filipinos today.

Indeed, Gianvito's handling of Juatco throughout creates an indelible portrait that is beautifully constructed, moving from his lengthy and moving account of his own life and career delivered directly to Gianvito's camera (complete with measured breaks and pauses) to his aforementioned thoughts about "colonial thinking" while driving a car, then to an extended sequence of him patiently and persistently coaxing a group of locals to organize themselves politically, next to a prolonged conversation with other people on the street about what's remembered (or, more often, forgotten) about the Philippine-American War, and finally to a moving performance of a song with his own guitar accompaniment behind the final credits.

More generally, Gianvito is as attentive to activists tirelessly working for the Alliance for Bases Clean-Up (his major collaborators) as he is to the families of stricken children and former base workers, many of whom contracted their health problems long before the bases were abandoned. An ethical purist who respects his audience as much as the people he films, Gianvito has this time outfitted his lengthy essay with a ten-minute intermission. As in his extended interview with Juatco, he privileges our capacity to think and meditate as well as feel.

CHAPTER 9

Jim Jarmusch

Few filmmakers of any national or aesthetic stripe can better illustrate the French critical attitude that cinema is literature by another means than Jim Jarmusch, who started out as a student and writer of poetry before he decided to become a filmmaker. This literary background is often overlooked by his reviewers, though it clearly comes to the fore in three of his best films, *Dead Man*, *Ghost Dog: The Way of the Samurai*, and *Paterson*, and it informs many of my observations in the first and last of the three items about him gathered here. (For more about *Dead Man*, see my BFI Modern Classic monograph; for more about *Ghost Dog*, see "International Sampler" in my *Essential Cinema* or on my website.)

The review of *Coffee and Cigarettes* appeared in the May 28, 2004 issue of the *Chicago Reader*; my defense of *The Limits of Control* was posted on my website on April 24, 2009; and my essay on *Paterson* was commissioned by the French quarterly *Trafic* and published in French translation in its 102nd issue (Summer 2017).

Short Cuts [*Coffee and Cigarettes*]

At first Jim Jarmusch's *Coffee and Cigarettes,* made over a span of seventeen years, looks like a departure for him. It consists of eleven entertaining, mainly comic short films in black and white that show people mainly sitting around in coffeehouses mainly drinking coffee, mainly smoking cigarettes, and mainly talking. But four of Jarmusch's seven previous fiction features were built out of similarly isolated episodes, and the remaining three—*Permanent Vacation* (1980), *Dead Man* (1995), and *Ghost Dog: The Way of the Samurai* (1999)—are all episodic. *Stranger Than Paradise* (1984) and *Down by Law* (1986)—also in black and white—each concentrated on three characters seen in three separate settings. *Mystery Train* (1989) had three separate sets of characters and three episodes set during the same day in Memphis. *Night on Earth* (1991)—focusing, like *Coffee and Cigarettes,* on what might be called downtime—had five separate episodes featuring cabdrivers and their passengers, occurring simultaneously across the globe.

The short form looks like a genuine alternative in Jarmusch's hands because of what he does with it. He's a master of minimalism, and his close attention to the form contrasts sharply with the isolated and detachable sequences that have become the calling card of film technique, the be-all and end-all of movie art. The fondness for fragments can be traced back largely to Sergei Eisenstein in the '20s, when famous set pieces began to define the "art of cinema" in many minds—the Odessa steps sequence in *Potemkin* (1925), the bridge-raising sequence in *October* (1927), and the cream-separator sequence in *The General Line* (1929), all eventually supplanted by the shower-murder sequence in Alfred Hitchcock's *Psycho* (1960). This tendency was further institutionalized by popular magazines such as *Premiere* and by countless "the making of" TV documentaries, which applauded the notion of separating sequences from their contexts.

The fragmentation of narrative form in current movies encourages the disassociation of the parts of a film. This may be fine when putting together a trailer, presenting a clip on a TV show, or making a point in a film class, but it undermines any sense of classical proportion or harmony. Few people would call Jarmusch a classicist, yet his fiction features show a concern for these qualities that isn't shared by many of his contemporaries.

A few critics have shrugged off *Coffee and Cigarettes* as slight and inconsequential, calling it an exercise in style, done in Jarmusch's usual "hip" idiom. But I think its form and content are much more notable and consequential than its style.

The film is less ambitious than *Dead Man* or *Ghost Dog,* though it's by no means less personal. The main themes are the ethics of celebrity, the tensions and irritations that can arise between close friends and family members, and two Jarmusch standbys, shyness and loneliness. These themes and the recurring formal elements—ranging from inserted overhead shots of coffee cups and checkerboard tablecloths or tabletops to abstract patterns in the dramaturgy—give *Coffee and Cigarettes* an overall artistic coherence that's far from common in current movies.

Having known Jarmusch for more than two decades, I think his celebrity status—he can't walk down the street in many cities around the world without being recognized—is something he both likes and dislikes. He loves the attention, but he's bothered by the inequities that arise from stardom. A lot of this movie is given over to some very funny observations and ethical reflections on that subject. In the segment titled "Cousins" we see Cate Blanchett playing in the same shots herself during a movie junket and her fictional punk cousin Shelly, who's seething with jealousy and resentment when Cate meets her in the lobby of her luxury hotel. It's a technical tour de force, flawlessly executed by Blanchett, Jarmusch, and his crew. I've heard that when Jarmusch posed for publicity photos during the shooting of this sequence, he chose to be photographed with Shelly rather than Cate, a telling indication of whom he feels more allied with.

Twenty-one of the twenty-seven actors play some version of themselves with the same name, and the majority of these actors are at least minor celebrities. (For the record, the six who don't play themselves are Joie Lee, Cinqué Lee in two separate parts, Blanchett when she's Shelly, Steve Buscemi, E. J. Rodriguez, and Mike Hogan.)

The project started when Jarmusch was invited to contribute a comedy sketch to *Saturday Night Live* in 1986, shortly after shooting *Down by Law,* and he cast one of that film's three stars, the then relatively unknown Roberto Benigni, along with stand-up comic Steven Wright. He shot the film's second sketch in Memphis (where he was shooting *Mystery Train*) three years later, and the third one four years after that. The remaining eight were all shot recently over a relatively brief period, meaning that Jarmusch had had plenty of time to plan these episodes individually and develop them as an ensemble, letting them echo and interact with one another and build a whole that's much greater than the sum of its parts. In this respect *Coffee and Cigarettes* resembles a cumulative, organically interrelated short story collection such as James Joyce's *Dubliners,* Sherwood Anderson's *Winesburg, Ohio,* Ernest Hemingway's *In Our Time,* or Ray Bradbury's *The Martian Chronicles,* rather than an assortment of loose pieces rattling around inside a common container, such as Bradbury's *The Illustrated Man,* Nelson Algren's *The Neon Wilderness,* Flannery

O'Connor's *Everything That Rises Must Converge,* or Thomas Pynchon's *Slow Learner.*

One of the more mysterious aspects of *Coffee and Cigarettes* is whether the form creates the content or the content suggests the form. A good example of what I mean can be found in one of the most provocative, though not best-known, stories of Franz Kafka, "Blumfeld, an Elderly Bachelor." The first part of the story recounts a comic fantasy: the grumpy title hero comes home to his sixth-floor walk-up, and "two small white celluloid balls with blue stripes" begin playfully following him around the room, coordinating their moves with his and with each other's. They bounce after him for the remainder of the evening, then resume their teasing play in the morning—until he lures them into his wardrobe and locks them inside. The second half of the story prosaically recounts his dull morning at the linen factory where he works, dominated by his irritation with the two assistants who share his tiny office. This story is remarkable not just for the fantasy that precedes the depiction of everyday normality, but for the playful form itself—the subtle and disquieting rhyming of the bouncing balls and the two assistants. One wonders whether Kafka's concept began with the bouncing balls, the assistants, or the echoes between the two.

There's a similar ambiguity in Jarmusch's playful two-part inventions. His second episode, "Twins," features Joie and Cinqué Lee, two of Spike Lee's siblings, playing twins (which they're not in real life); their petty bickering consists mainly of each contradicting and echoing the other. Their dialogue with a waiter (Buscemi) concerns the legendary twin of Elvis Presley, who died at birth, and the siblings' charge that Elvis ripped off the music of black musicians such as Otis Blackwell and Junior Parker (another form of duplication).

Five episodes later we get "Cousins" (one of my three favorite episodes), followed by "Jack Shows Meg His Tesla Coil," which features musicians Jack and Meg White, a former couple who pose as siblings. Then we get the hilarious "Cousins?" (one of my other favorites), in which Alfred Molina and British TV star Steve Coogan meet for tea in a Los Angeles restaurant, and Molina, hoping to establish some intimacy with Coogan, says he recently discovered that they're cousins. (In more ways than one, this is the most brilliant episode in the movie—an acute examination of showbiz and celebrity pecking order.) And in the episode after that, "Delirium," GZA and RZA, members of the Wu-Tang Clan, introduce themselves to Bill Murray as cousins.

Did Jarmusch think first of using twins, siblings, and cousins, or did he start off aiming for rhyme effects? I'm not sure it matters, but the pairings and doublings don't stop. Many lines of dialogue recur, and the movie opens and closes with separate versions of "Louie" (whose title is already a repetition). The sixth episode, "No Problem," begins and ends with Alex Descas taking a pair of dice from his pocket and rolling them three times; the results we see are all doubles. The ninth and tenth episodes both have two characters who order tea instead of coffee.

That Jarmusch's film registers as loose and offhanded despite so much formal control is one of the characteristic achievements of his minimalism. As in Eugen Herrigel's book *Zen in the Art of Archery,* he doesn't appear to care whether he hits the target, though he seldom misses. The only episode that strikes me as being undernourished is the fifth, "Renee," which lingers over a young woman (Renee French) smoking and drinking coffee while looking through ads in a gun catalog. She's interrupted by a waiter (Rodriguez) giving her an unasked-for coffee refill and later trying unsuccessfully to make conversation. Yet even this relatively meager segment manages to repeat some lines of dialogue and some formal elements from other sketches, and by focusing once on a character who prefers solitude to conversation, Jarmusch offers a meaningful contrast to the other episodes.

I assume one reason Jarmusch decided to home in on electricity pioneer and maverick Nikola Tesla (1856–1943) in another offbeat episode is that Tesla represents so many "alternatives"—not just alternating current and an alternative to Thomas Edison, but an alternative, utopian history that encompasses Tesla's ideas about free electricity, free transportation, and free communications. This also occasions what is probably the most poetic of the movie's recurring lines: "He perceived the earth as a conductor of acoustical resonance."

The many self-referential details increase the clubhouse atmosphere, and some of the reviewers who dismiss the film may be responding to this. For example, we get blackouts at the end of each section, as we did in *Stranger Than Paradise.* In the fourth section—which features Joe Rigano and Vinny Vella, who played aging Italian gangsters in *Ghost Dog*—there's a framed photo on the wall of Henry Silva, one of their colleagues in that film. And in the eighth segment, with Jack and Meg White, there's a framed picture of Lee Marvin; Jarmusch and some of his friends once founded a jokey, semisecret club they called the Sons of Lee Marvin.

Other gags can be traced to allusions of one kind or another. (Two that appear to have been studiously avoided: Jarmusch once played a coffee addict in Alex Cox's 1987 comic western *Straight to Hell,* and in Wayne Wang and Paul Auster's 1995 *Blue in the Face* he ruminated on what he claimed would be his last cigarette.) Jarmusch has noted in an interview that Tom Waits's speech to Iggy Pop in the third episode—about having just performed "roadside surgery" by delivering a baby and about combining "music and medicine" in his life—was improvised; when Jarmusch later discovered that RZA was into alternative medicine, he decided to duplicate parts of Waits's monologue in the episode that focuses on RZA and GZA. This mixture of improvisation and formal patterning justifies Jarmusch's description of *Coffee and Cigarettes* as a "series of short films disguised as a feature (or maybe vice versa)," as well as his formally pitched remark that the film is photographed "in black (coffee) and white (cigarettes)."

People who object to the in-jokes should consider that they might be just part of a dialectic with what could be termed the out-jokes—the more populist and obvious bits of humor. There's a close parallel in the dialectic between celebrities and nobodies that runs throughout the film, and there's the suggestion that inside every apparent improvisation is an element of determination, that juxtaposed with every conspiracy theory is an abyss of meaningless absurdity and chaos, and that next to the political incorrectness of the addictive coffee and cigarettes are politically correct demonstrations of social etiquette. Paradoxically, a certain kind of social chaos becomes most apparent whenever the characters are being most polite: when Isaach (Isaach de Bankolé) meets Alex for coffee at Alex's request, he can't believe he's been summoned just for the pleasure of his company, even though they're supposed to be best friends. This paranoid misunderstanding is played for comedy, but the fear of a gaping void remains.

The wistful and moving final episode, "Champagne" (my third favorite)—featuring Bill Rice and Taylor Mead in a dimly lit SoHo hangout called the Armory, drinking out of paper cups during their coffee break—seems at first to be at the farthest remove from Jarmusch's universe, yet it's a kind of tribute to his roots in the underground filmmaking scene of downtown Manhattan. Rice and Mead are closely associated with those roots through their roles in films by Scott and Beth B., Eric Mitchell, Amos Poe, and Andy Warhol, and they drink a toast at one point not only to

"Paris in the '20s" (Mead's suggestion) but also to "New York in the late '70s" (Rice's suggestion), which is when these films were being shot.

There's no better evocation of chaos in the film than the title of the beautiful Gustav Mahler song heard in this episode, "I Have Lost Track of the World." The overall abstractness of the location and the absurdist dialogue—including Mead's when he's periodically forgetful—call to mind Samuel Beckett's doleful tramps in their own sketchy settings. Curiously, Rice and Mead seem more settled and "placed" than any other characters in the film, perhaps because they seem older and wiser than everyone else—and perhaps because knowing who you are often entails knowing where you are.

Jarmusch Unlimited: *The Limits of Control*

Even if he didn't like Jim Jarmusch's latest film, which I found immensely pleasurable and mesmerizing, I'm glad that the *Hollywood Reporter*'s Michael Rechtshaffen at least picked up on the fact that Bill Murray, who turns up very late in the film, is "channeling" Dick Cheney when he does. This is by no means a gratuitous detail. Trust a minimalist to make absences as important as presences. None of the characters in this movie is named, all of them are assigned labels in the cast list, and the only label assigned to Murray is "American." Furthermore, unless I missed something, the European (specifically Spanish) landscape that Jarmusch and his cinematographer Chris Doyle capture so beautifully and variously, in diverse corners of Madrid and Seville, is otherwise utterly devoid of Americans of any kind—a significant statement in itself—until a foul-mouthed Murray makes his belated experience in a bunker, as ill-tempered as the American trade press is already being about this entrancing movie. Prior to that, we're told repeatedly, in Spanish, by a good many others in the film, that he who tries to be bigger than all the others should go to the cemetery to understand a little bit better what life is: a handful of dust.

It's no less pertinent that a Spanish boy on the street previously asks Isaach De Bankolé—who's channeling Lee Marvin in *Point Blank,* and is called "Lone Man" in the cast list—if he's an American gangster, and De Bankolé replies, "No." It seems like an act of prophecy that an American gangster like Cheney should meet his symbolic comeuppance in the same country that might now arrest him for war crimes if he should ever make an actual appearance there. It also seems relevant that the boy and his street pals are reluctant to believe what the Lone Man says. After all, American gangsterism is a style that seems designed for export. In *Point Blank*, directed by an Englishman, the terrain is supposedly Los Angeles, but Lee Marvin might as well be trekking across Mars; and in *Le samourai*, directed by a Frenchman—another obvious source for *The Limits of Control*—the terrain is supposedly Paris, but Alain Delon might as well be holing up somewhere in Tokyo.

I was originally going to wait until *The Limits of Control* opened in early May before posting anything about it, but I figure that if the trade press can sound off about it, so can I. Or at least offer a couple of first impressions of why I mainly prefer this movie to *Broken Flowers*.

For one thing, De Bankolé is a magnificent camera subject—a lot more fascinating to follow in his lonely rounds than Murray is in *Broken Flowers,* at least to me—and the urban and rural landscapes here do more for my imagination than the various American suburban stretches of Jarmusch's previous feature. Another thing: Tilda Swinton (identified as "Blonde," and lightly suggesting to me Bulle Ogier in Rivette's *Duelle*) observes to the Lone Man at one point that she likes films even when people are just sitting around in them and not saying anything—a declaration followed by a long pause.

"There are limits to artistic self-indulgence," begins Todd McCarthy's review in *Variety*. I disagree. And there are no limits to the pleasures that can be afforded from this kind of freedom.

I can't wait to see this movie again.

Jim Jarmusch's Lost America: The Pleasures of *Paterson*

1. Jarmusch as Dialectician

For some time now, Jim Jarmusch has been operating as an autocritical dialectician in his fictional features. Politically as well as commercially, *The Limits of Control* offers a sharp rebuke to his preceding film, *Broken Flowers,* by following Bill Murray as a protagonist—a bored and diffident Don Juan roaming across the United States to visit four of his former lovers, in order to discover which one he impregnated with a son—with Isaach de Bankolé as a protagonist, a hired assassin in Europe pursuing Bill Murray in the role of Dick Cheney as he hides out in a bunker until the assassin finally strangles him with a guitar string. But even more striking is the radical contrast between Jarmusch's most elitist feature (and in many ways my least favorite), *Only Lovers Left Alive,* about a romantic, middle-aged married couple played by Tilda Swinton and Tom Hiddleston—vampires named Adam and Eve who evoke junkies, rock stars, and pre-Raphaelite artists, living on separate continents in Tangier and Detroit—and Jarmusch's most populist feature (and one of my favorites), *Paterson,* about a younger romantic couple living together in Paterson, New Jersey, a bus driver named Paterson (Adam Driver) who writes poetry in his spare time and a housewife named Laura (Golshifteh Farahani) who cooks, specializes in creating black-and-white décor and clothing, and is learning to play the guitar.

The dialectical contrast between the last two films goes much further than the above description implies. Each of the romantic and mutually devoted married couples in these two films has a stronger and more dominant partner—the wife (Swinton) in *Only Lovers Left Alive,* the husband (Driver) in *Paterson*—who's focused on literature while her or his partner is more involved with music and plays the guitar. (Consequently, those American critics, myself included, who have complained that the wife in *Paterson* is treated somewhat condescendingly as an artist who fetishizes black and white have conveniently overlooked that a similar charge could be lodged against the narcissistic, childish, and even more self-absorbed husband in *Only Lovers Left Alive.*) The characters in the first film are split between stars and/or performing artists on the one hand (Adam, Eve, Christopher Marlowe, a Lebanese singer) and devoted groupies, fans, and assistants on the other; most of the stars are vampires and most of the others are defined (or at least described) as "zombies," whereas all the characters in the second film are perceived as social and cultural equals and all of them could be described as creative artists of one kind or another, whether they know it or not. (This includes even a hapless, lovelorn suitor named Everett who threatens to shoot himself with a toy gun, staging a violent crisis in a bar; and even the married couple's bulldog, Marvin, qualifies as a punk artist of sorts when he shreds the notebook of Adam containing all of his handwritten poetry.) The only "stars" evoked in *Paterson* are a few local celebrities, living (Iggy Pop) and dead (Lou Costello, Allen Ginsberg), whose photographs decorate the walls of a mainly black bar that Paterson frequents when he walks his dog.

2. Jarmusch as Minimalist

"I think the world has enough chaos to keep it going for the minute," Christopher Marlowe (John Hurt) declares to Eve in Tangier—a statement that recalls a repeated statement in *The Limits of Control*, "The universe has no center and no edges." Both of these somewhat terrified statements appear to motivate Jarmusch's carefully sustained and articulated minimalism as a calculated gesture against chaos, even though Marlowe himself, depicted here as the pseudonymous author of *Hamlet*, is hardly any sort of minimalist himself, any more than William Carlos Williams, the implied resident guru-poet of *Paterson*, is, especially in the sprawling and Whitmanesque book-length poem that gives the film its title.

Even the nameless minimalist hero-protagonist of *The Limits of Control*, played by Isaach de Bankolé—as centered and as edgy as Lee Marvin in *Point Blank*, one of Jarmusch's likely reference points, whose simple directness is offered as a salutary corrective to faceless multicorporate corruption—is a bit of a dilettante when it comes to appreciating art at Madrid's Museo Reina Sofia or flamenco dancing at a bar in Seville. The same applies to Forest Whitaker's Ghost Dog, an earlier version of a minimalist black hitman, with his taste for literature that highlights multiplicity and complexity—*The Wind in the Willows*, *The Souls of Black Folk*, *Rashomon*, *Frankenstein*—as well as his more minimalist guidebook, *Hagakure, or The Way of the Samurai*.

Yet it's part of the beauty and power of Jarmusch's minimalism as he's developed it in *Paterson* that it seems bountiful rather than deprived, an embarrassment of everyday miracles that yields an exquisitely uncluttered film about commonplace clutter—the kind that accumulates during a mainly ordinary week in the life of a New Jersey bus driver who also writes poetry, and one in which the ordinary flow of time is given an uncommon degree of orchestration: varying degrees of slow or fast motion—the hero's loping walk, the rushing second-hand of his wristwatch—superimposed over images of his poems as they're being slowly composed or recomposed, word by word on screen, and his lyrical reveries about cherished people and places, which periodically evoke the Vigo of *L'Atalante*.

3. Jarmusch as Fantasist

Like Leos Carax, Jarmusch is a filmmaker of romantic and poetic fantasy conceits in which a certain *nostalgie de la boue* always plays a part. But unlike Carax, Jarmusch's sense of fantasy is always grounded in at least a superficial sense of banal reality; even his century-old vampires occupy the recognizably mundane quarters of Detroit and Tangier. *Paterson* is of course less obvious as a fantasy than *Only Lovers Left Alive,* yet its utopian vision of small-town America as a friendly multiracial community in which every person appears to be some sort of artist is clearly sustainable only as a defiant poetic conceit that flies in the face of a Trump-led America, however gentle its multiple articulations might be. Furthermore, the preponderance of twins who keep turning up in Paterson, New Jersey is as fanciful as the abnormal and logically unjustifiable number of dog reaction shots in the film assigned to Marvin (anticipated by the dog reaction shots in *Ghost Dog: The Way of the Samurai).*

There's a particular moment about halfway through *Ghost Dog* when Jarmusch's strength and confidence as a fantasist intersect with his instincts as a poet. After Ghost Dog's rooftop home is destroyed by Italian gangsters, he sends them a message by carrier pigeon that's a quote from *Hagakure,* read aloud by Sonny Valerio (Cliff Gorman): " 'If a samurai's head were to suddenly be cut off, he'd still be able to perform one more action with certainty.' . . . What the fuck is that supposed to mean?" "It's poetry," explains Ray Vargo (Henry Silva). "The poetry of war." The sheer improbability and outlandishness of both the homing pigeon and this understanding of poetry from a New Jersey gangster is quintessential Jarmusch, as mannerist as a character in a Faulkner novel speaking the same way that Faulkner writes.

4. Jarmusch as Traditionalist

In many of his previous features, Jarmusch has offered his own eccentric versions of commercial film genres: western (*Dead Man*), hitman thriller (*Ghost Dog*), James Bondish spy thriller (*The Limits of Control*), and horror film (*Only Lovers Left Alive*). *Paterson* departs from this pattern by suggesting that ordinary American lives and traditions provide the only formal guidance needed. It's a form of artistic maturity that suggests that even though Jarmusch is technically a paying member of the Academy of Motion Picture Arts and Sciences, he is far too independent and far too "East Coast" as a filmmaker to qualify for an Oscar anytime soon.

5. Jarmusch as Formalist

One of the more mysterious aspects of *Paterson* is whether the form creates the content or the content suggests the form. A good example of this question can be Franz Kafka's "Blumfeld, an Elderly Bachelor." The first part of this story recounts a comic fantasy: the grumpy title hero comes home to his sixth-floor walk-up, and "two small white celluloid balls with blue stripes" begin playfully following him around the room, coordinating their moves with his and with each other's. They bounce after him for the remainder of the evening, and then resume their teasing play in the morning—until he lures them into his wardrobe and locks them inside. The second half of the story prosaically recounts his dull morning at the linen factory where he works, dominated by his irritation with the two assistants who share his tiny office. This story is remarkable not just for the fantasy that precedes the depiction of everyday normality, but for the playful form itself—the subtle and disquieting rhyming of the bouncing balls with the two assistants. One wonders whether Kafka's concept began with the bouncing balls, the assistants, or the echoes between the two.

There's a similar ambiguity in many of the playful two-part inventions of *Coffee and Cigarettes*. The second episode, "Twins," features Joie and Cinqué Lee, two of Spike Lee's siblings, playing twins (which they're not in real life); their petty bickering consists mainly of each contradicting and echoing the other. Their dialogue with a waiter concerns the legendary twin of Elvis Presley who died at birth and the siblings' charge that Elvis ripped off the music of black musicians such as Otis Blackwell and Junior Parker (another form of duplication). Then, five episodes later, we get "Cousins"—a playing out of the elitist versus egalitarian dialectic that later figures between *Only Lovers Left Alive* and *Paterson*—in which Cate Blanchett, within the same shots, plays both herself (a movie star) and her (fictional) punk cousin Shelly, seething with jealous resentment when Cate meets her in the lobby of her luxury hotel. This is followed first by a sketch featuring musicians Jack and Meg White, a former couple who pose as siblings, then by "Cousins?"—in which Alfred Molina and Steve Coogan, meeting for tea in Los Angeles, play in a variation on the Blanchett episode that hinges on whether these two actors might be cousins—and, finally, by "Delirium," in which two other musicians, GZA and RZA, both members of the Wu-Tang Clan (which provided the score for *Ghost Dog*), introduce themselves to Bill Murray as cousins.

The principal formal structure of *Paterson* is the seven days of the week and all the daily rituals contained in that structure (see #6, below). Whereas the more common way of viewing such rituals and repetitions is to view them as boring and tedious, both Paterson and *Paterson* find them pleasurable and comforting—that is to say, musical.

6. Jarmusch as Musician

As much a musician as a poet, Jarmusch is also partially responsible for *Paterson*'s score, as a member of the three-person rock band Sqürl consisting of himself, Carter Logan (Jarmusch's coproducer since *The Limits of Control*), and musical engineer and music producer Shane Stoneback. But more generally, his musical temperament can be felt in the numerous repetitions, thematic variations of verbal and visual motifs, and "rhyming" shots that abound in his films. In *The Limits of Control,* virtually everyone who meets Isaach de Bankolé's character begins by asking him, "You don't speak Spanish, right?"; this usually happens in Spanish cafés, where he habitually orders two espressos, and he also exchanges matchboxes with most of the people he meets. A repeated epigram in the same film: "Those who think they're bigger than the rest should go to the cemetery. There they will see what life really is: it's a handful of dirt."

There are also motifs that recur in separate Jarmusch features, such as guitars, twins (a preoccupation in his sketch feature, *Coffee and Cigarettes*), and matchboxes (the subject of one of Paterson's poems), and sometimes the same actors (Isaach de Bankolé, John Hurt, Tilda Swinton). *Paterson* is constructed around the repetitions and/or variations of motifs that occur over a single week, starting with the sleeping or waking positions of Paterson and Laura as each day begins, the time on Paterson's wristwatch that he observes just before he puts it on, the Cheerios he has for breakfast in the kitchen, and countless other daily rituals, including his walk to work, the habitual complaints of his Latino boss about his own troubles at home, Paterson's bus route, his checking the mailbox in front of his house when he returns home (sometimes correcting its bent position, which we eventually discover is by Marvin), his walking the dog, his tying of Marvin's leash around a pipe before entering the bar, and so forth. And I've already mentioned the strange proliferations of twins and dog reaction shots.

7. Jarmusch as Poet

Jarmusch studied poetry at Columbia University with New York School poets Kenneth Koch and David Shapiro, and reportedly has written some poetry as well, but only one of the poems heard and seen in *Paterson* was written by him—"Water Falls," attributed to a ten-year-old girl whom Paterson meets by chance while walking home and who reads it aloud to him. All the other poems in the film, apart from William Carlos Williams's "This is Just to Say" (read by Paterson to his wife) and some rapper poetry recited in a laundromat, were written by Ron Padgett (another New York School poet)—four preexisting poems and three others written for the film, all seven attributed to Paterson.

In many respects, *Paterson* is more concerned with the activity of writing poems than it is with the social functions of poems as cultural objects, and Jarmusch's preoccupation with his hero's creative processes is central to his focus on all the other people in Paterson whom he encounters or (as a bus driver) overhears among his passengers. All these people are viewed as artistically creative in one way or another, but without the egotism or ambition or desire for fame that we often associate with artists. This is especially true of Paterson himself; his wife chides him for not making copies of his poems, which exist only in his notebook, and there's no evidence that he has any desire to publish them. After Marvin shreds his notebook, Paterson, during a conversation with a Japanese poet whom he meets by chance, even denies being a poet himself, insisting that he's only a bus driver. But after the Japanese poet gives him an empty notebook as a parting gift, one feels that he has once again accepted "poet" as part of his identity.

In a 1996 interview with Jarmusch, we had the following exchange:

ROSENBAUM: In a recent essay about the dumbing down of American movies, Phillip Lopate writes, "Take Jim Jarmusch: a very gifted, intelligent filmmaker, who studied poetry at Columbia, yet he makes movie after movie about low-lifes who get smashed every night, make pilgrimages to Memphis where they are visited by Elvis's ghost, shoot off guns and in general comport themselves in a somnambulistic, inarticulate, unconscious manner."

JARMUSCH: I don't know, man. Once I was in a working-class restaurant in Rome with Roberto [Benigni] at lunchtime. They had long tables where you sit with other people. We sat down with these people in their blue work overalls, they were working in the street outside, and Roberto's talking to them, and they started talking about Dante and Ariosto and twentieth-century Italian poets. Now, you go out to fucking Wyoming and go in a bar and mention the word poetry, and you'll get a gun stuck up your ass. That's the way America is. Whereas even guys who work in the street collecting garbage in Paris love nineteenth-century painting.

Like many of the details in *Paterson,* this suggests that the evidence of almost nonstop artistic creativity that one witnesses in Paterson, New Jersey is neither plausible nor realistic but a poetic and utopian vision about what the town might be—or perhaps what it already is, hidden under the surface, or maybe also what it once was (given the film's implicit but omnipresent sense of nostalgia), before diverse middle-class and capitalist anti-art reflexes hid it from view.

To a large degree, this is what makes the film's poetic vision so precious: the sense that America as a community of friendly artists is not so much an impossibility as a transcendental potentiality, buried just beneath the surface of everyday activities—a "lost America" that conceivably could be found again, much as Paterson himself temporarily loses and then rediscovers it. In this respect, *Paterson* is the precise, dialectical opposite of my other favorite Jarmusch feature, *Dead Man,* where not even an accountant named William Blake (Johnny Depp) understands the significance of his name, which is understood and appreciated only by a Native American who is himself labeled by his fellow tribesmen as Nobody.

CHAPTER 10

Jia Zhangke

My favorite Jia Zhangke film to date probably remains *The World*, in spite of its confused and confusing ending, and I've reprinted one of my essays about that film in *Goodbye Cinema, Hello Cinephilia*. But as a freelance journalist who often depends on the assignments of others, I don't always wind up writing about my preferred films. All three of the articles in this section were commissioned, but neither *24 City* nor *A Touch of Sin* qualifies as a film I would have chosen to write about if I hadn't received the assignment. (In a pinch, I would have selected either *Platform* or *Still Life* instead.) Yet the challenge of confronting these films may have led me to discoveries I might not have made otherwise.

The first article here, slightly shortened to minimize repetitions (although I couldn't avoid them entirely), was written for a brochure to accompany a retrospective held by Northwestern University's Block Cinema in January 2008; the second was written for Cinema Guild's DVD of *24 City*, released in 2009; and the third was commissioned by Arrow Films for their dual format boxed set, *Jia Zhangke: Three Films*, released in the U.K. in early 2018.

Zhangke Jia, Poetic Prophet

What is it about Zhangke Jia that makes him the most exciting mainland Chinese filmmaker currently working? It might be oversimplifying matters to describe this writer-director, born in 1970, as a rustic avant-gardist. But the fact that he hails from the small town of Fenyang in northern China's Shanxi province clearly plays an important role in all his features to date. (I'm less certain about what role it plays in his two recent documentaries, *Dong* [2006] and *Useless* [2007].)

Jia attended the Beijing Film Academy, where he completed his first film, the one-hour *Xiao Shan* (*Going Home,* 1995). I haven't seen it, but according to critic Kevin Lee, it's about a country boy and unemployed cook in Beijing who wants to go home for the Chinese New Year and runs into numerous obstacles, and it utilizes literary intertitles (which also crop up in his last two features). Jia's identification with his rural hero is apparently underlined in a party sequence where he appears, speaking drunkenly in his semi-incoherent Shanxi dialect. (He can be found doing something similar in the opening sequence of *Unknown Pleasures*.)

Given that nearly all Chinese films are dubbed into Mandarin, this could be seen as a defiant move, comparable to the direct-sound recording of Taiwanese dialects in the work of Hou Hsiao-hsien, one of Jia's key influences. Fenyang is the main setting in *Xiao Wu* (*Pickpocket,* 1997)—another eccentric character study named after its leading character—and his second and most ambitious feature, *Platform* (2000), an epic following the teenage members of Fenyang's state-run Peasant Culture Group as they gradually mutate over a decade into the privatized All-Star Rock and Breakdance Electronic Band. In fact, *Platform* was scripted before *Xiao Wu* but made afterward because it was far more expensive to finance; like Jia's subsequent *Unknown Pleasures* (2002), it was an underground independent film—technically banned, though it circulated in China on pirated video.

Both *Unknown Pleasures* and *In Public* (2002)—a half-hour documentary shot on digital video that scouted locations for the feature—were shot in another small town in Shanxi about to be transformed by capitalism, Datung. And even though Jia returned to Beijing to shoot *The World* (2004), about alienated workers in a theme park, and went on to the equally spectacular Three Gorges Dam in central China for *Still Life* (2006), leading characters in both films hail from Shanxi province. So his roots remain, but he continues to grow. And now that he's officially recognized by the Chinese government, he shoots all his features on digital video.

Chinese Displacements in *24 City*

24 City is a documentary about the transformation of Factory 420 in Chengdu from the secret manufacture of military aircraft engines in 1958 to, after the Vietnam War, a downsized and remodeled facility producing consumer products, and then, more recently, into a privately owned real-estate development called "24 City." This sounds pretty straightforward, but because it's a Jia Zhangke film, it qualifies as an adequate description only in the most skeletal fashion. Factory 420 employed almost 30,000 workers, so a lot of life experience and displacement is involved in this multifaceted story—a good half-century of Chinese history. And Jia is so desperate to discover the truth of his subject that he's willing to employ anything and everything, including artifice, if this will bring him any closer to what urban renewal is in the process of quickly obliterating.

The theme of his film—of all his features to date, in fact—is the displacement coming from historical upheavals in China and the various kinds of havoc they produce: physical, emotional, intellectual, political, conceptual, cultural, economic, familial, societal. And sometimes the style involves a certain amount of displacement as well, such as when he cuts from a speech in late 2007 about recent changes in "24 City" before a full audience in an auditorium to a shot of an almost empty stairway that plays over the same speech, with one figure climbing the steps on two successive floors.

Jia addresses his ambitious theme by mixing documentary and fiction, a procedure he's been developing in various ways throughout his career. It's apparent here in the uses of music as well as in the mix of actors and nonactors, in both the *mise en scène* and the editing. But of course, blatant employments of theater and fiction, of prearrangement and construction, have informed documentary filmmaking since its earliest phases. It's never enough simply to assert that "capturing reality" is the aim; there are always other agendas, and teasing out those agendas is partly a matter of discerning various stylistic decisions. When the Lumière brothers filmed workers leaving their own factory in 1895, using a stationary camera setup explicitly recalled in *24 City*, the mode employed isn't simply "actuality" but also a form of surveillance. And by the time Robert Flaherty made *Nanook of the North* (1922), the mixture of modes had become still more complicated. In the film's first extended sequence, Nanook the Eskimo in his boat paddles to the shore and disembarks, performing the equivalent of a circus act in which many clowns emerge from a tiny car as he helps to bring out each member of his family from the boat's concealed interior: several children, his wife, the family dog. Documentary, in short, is a form of show business from the very outset, something constructed as well as found.

So when Kevin B. Lee, in his review in *Cineaste* (Fall 2009, 34, no. 4), rightly calls *24 City* "an oral history project transformed into performance art," we should acknowledge that Jia is being both innovative and experimental in one sense and highly traditional and commercial in another. Even if he's being more obvious about the arranged and/or fictional elements here than the Lumières or Flaherty were—by utilizing four professional actors and four actual factory workers for the eight interviews featured in this film, as well as a cowriter, Zhai Yongming, who comes from Chengdu—he is none the less adhering to certain conventions that are as old as the documentary form itself. It's important to realize, moreover, that Lu Liping, Chen Jianbin, Joan Chen, and Zhao Tao are all recognizable *as movie actors* to Chinese viewers. So the unconventional ways these actors are used has to be weighed against the various commercial benefits derived from their presence. In fact, although Jia started making features with state approval only after *Xiao Wu* (1997), *Platform* (2000), and *Unknown Pleasures* (2002), *24 City* (2008) has been his biggest commercial success in China to date, surpassing both *The World* (2004) and *Still Life* (2006).

Let's consider each of the roles played by these actors, as well as the overall historical development implied by the order in which they appear—a pattern that was carefully traced by James Naremore in *Film Quarterly* (Summer 2009, 62, no. 4) when he placed this film at the head of his annual ten-best list. Lu Luping, first seen carrying an IV drip bottle, plays Hao Dali, the oldest, who joined the factory the same year it opened, when she was twenty-one. Her heartbreaking story about losing her three-year-old son on a rest-stop during her journey by boat from Shanghai to Chengdu—whether this is a "real" story derived from an actual interview, a fiction, or something in between—followed by her watching an old propaganda film on TV, painfully dramatizes the degree to which nationalist and military obligations could supersede family in 1958. This is in striking contrast to the final interview with Su Na (Jia regular Zhao Tao), born in 1982 in Chengdu, who voices a very different kind of nationalist sentiment when she defends her capitalist career as a "personal shopper" who has purchased a new car to enhance her "credibility," and who tearfully says she wants to buy her factory-worker parents an apartment in the new 24 City development. (It's important to recognize that while westerners tend to view communism as "collectivist" and capitalism as "individualist," the Chinese state has tended to view each practice over half a century of social transformation as a particular form of civic duty.) And in between these polar extremes are the monologues delivered by Song Weldong (Chen Jianbin), born in 1966 in Chengdu—an assistant to the factory's general manager, seated at a counter, who recalls street-gang fights and having been spared from one beating by the recent death of Zhou Enlai—and by the somewhat younger Xiao Hua (Joan Chen), a factory worker named after the eponymous heroine of one of Chen's earliest films, who plays on audience recognition by discussing her close resemblance to Joan Chen. If the latter registers as a joke, it's a joke with some serious intent, because Jia evidently wants the Chinese viewers' emotions aroused by these monologues to echo those solicited by the same actors in fiction films, and he also wants the viewers to be aware of these echoes. And clearly the juxtapositions of nationalist consciousness with both street fights and business, as emphasized in these latter two monologues, are part of the ambiguities and ambivalences that Jia is intent on exploring, with pop culture and state policy both playing relevant roles.

It's important to add that the performative role played by nonactors is no less important to the film's feeling and design than the performances by the actors, and not simply or necessarily because they're always closer to "the truth." (Some of the formal poses of the portraits of workers are made to seem more artificial than some of the staged and written monologues, and the periodic fades to black, disrupting the flow of the interviews, discourages us from taking them as seamless documentary *or* fictional wholes.) Hou Lijun, born in 1953 and interviewed on a bus, may have more to say about displacements, family separations, and job loss than anyone else in the film, and her final statement, which Jia repeats as an intertitle—"If you have something to do, you age more slowly"—is clearly one of the key lines.

It's no less important to bear in mind that part of the financing of *24 City* came from the "24 City" development itself, much as the theme park that *The World* both explores and deconstructs also helped to finance that film. So there are multiple agendas at work here, some of them seemingly in conflict with one another, and the desire to experiment is tied to a kind of ideological juggling act that has made some Chinese viewers weep during portions of this film (reportedly, especially during the final sequence), but has also worried some critics, Chinese and Western alike, about some of the implicit compromises and cross-purposes involved in such an enterprise. But Jia has been an ambitious risk-taker throughout his career, and the topics as well as the emotions that he chooses to take on here are, perhaps by necessity, as ambiguous and as open-ended as China itself.

Many Touches of Sin

It's important to acknowledge that part of what makes Jia Zhangke the most exciting and important mainland Chinese filmmaker currently active also makes him one of the most disconcerting and sometimes even bewildering. This has a lot to do with his propensity for viewing fiction and nonfiction, and, even more radically, fantasy and reality, as reverse sides of the same coin, and, in keeping with this complex duality, a talent for bold stylistic shifts not only between successive films but between and within separate sequences. His ambitions are such that even his "failures" are worth more than the successes of many of his colleagues—and, for that matter, what we might describe as a Jia "failure" often means simply a film that we should see again and reconsider.

Confounding us still further in *A Touch of Sin* (2013), his seventh feature, Jia reverses his previous position of avoiding on-screen violence by delivering it this time by the bucketful. In his earlier features, treatments of violence tended to be reticent or elliptical, so that what may have been government executions in *Platform* (2000) registered as distant gunshots or drumbeats, and the tragic and fatal industrial accident of a construction worker in *The World* wasn't shown at all. By contrast, *A Touch of Sin* is already offering us graphic mayhem before all the credits appear, and even the appearance of the film's title is capped by an explosion.

Arguably, most or all of his shifts between reality and fantasy can be traced back to his cinephilia—or, more specifically, to his recognition that movie fantasies shape and alter various aspects of what we commonly regard as reality. This is the precise opposite of Quentin Tarantino's appropriations of, say, the German occupation of France and American slavery as mere tributaries of his cherished movie fantasies, so that, alarmingly but inevitably, some teenagers today wind up using *Inglourious Basterds*

(2009) and *Django Unchained* (2012) as historical primers. For Jia, the state of contemporary mainland China is his primary concern, and movie fantasies need to be referenced simply in order to examine part of what goes on inside people's heads. This is why, in his "documentary" *24 City* (2008), he can mix real factory workers with four movie actors (all recognizable as such to Chinese audiences) playing other factory workers.

Moreover, starting with *The World* (2004)—his fourth feature, and the first to be made with government approval—he begins to utilize highly original fantasy interludes. This is a logical step to take in a film about people working in a theme park outside Beijing devoted to fantasy replicas of such world-famous sites as the Eiffel Tower, Lower Manhattan (with the Twin Towers intact), London Bridge, St. Mark's Square, the Pyramids, the Taj Mahal, and the Leaning Tower of Pisa. These fantasy intervals are always sparked by moments when the film's alienated characters communicate with one another via text messages on their mobile phones, and they invariably take the form of animation—flights of fancy including the literal flight of one character sailing over the theme park. And quite apart from these cartoon stretches, *The World* also features a few song-and-dance stage performances that make the film as a whole resemble a backstage musical, with all the flights of imaginative fancy that this form implies—as well as a somewhat incoherently mystical and distinctly unsatisfying final sequence that creates another disturbance in the film's realistic narrative.

In Jia's next feature, *Still Life* (2006), the fantasies are live-action: a new state monument near the construction site of the Three Gorges Dam suddenly takes off into the sky like a rocket ship (as in an SF movie), and a tightrope artist walks across a high wire stretched between two new skyscrapers in the same vicinity (as in a circus movie). A maker of arthouse films by impulse and instinct, Jia also knows how to instill them with mainstream movie imagery, and indeed, it's largely his capacity to occupy both realms with equal assurance that makes his position within Chinese film culture so singular.

In *A Touch of Sin,* the fantasies at play are specifically tied to Chinese culture, Chinese movies in particular. They are also less original, but none the less startling for appearing in this unusual setting—a series of real-life stories gathered from the internet, most of them familiar to Chinese audiences, offering a survey of contemporary forms of moral and social corruption, and located specifically in all four corners of China and over the four seasons, proceeding backward in ages from a middle-aged protagonist to increasingly younger characters—all of which imply the sort of ambitions we might associate with an exposé, a manifesto of sorts, and an epic. (Furthermore, Jia periodically recalls some of the places and concerns of his previous features: the first episode is set in his native Shanxi province, the second returns us to the ferry crossing of *Still Life,* and the fourth is partially set in a sort of fantasy "theme park" brothel that reminds us of *The World,* and where Jia himself, to suggest his own implication in the fantasy, plays a cameo as the first wealthy customer that we see and hear in this segment.) The film's English title deliberately recalls King Hu's *A Touch of Zen* (1969) and the political implications of his martial arts action stories. (The Chinese title, *Tian Zhuding,* means "ill-fated," and a further gloss on the English title occurs in the final sequence—at a street performance of the classical opera *Yu Tang Chun* that formed the basis for King Hu's first feature.)

What makes these echoes so disconcerting is the way Jia stages shotgun marriages between realistic contemporary details and *wuxia* conventions, movie-fantasy poses, and the dynamic rhythms of pop-movie violence—all of which threatens to register at times as a reduction (or, for some viewers, elevation) of the characters to familiar icons. On my first viewing of the film—speaking now as a Jia partisan who was relatively unfamiliar with *wuxia*—it was an alarming reduction, especially in the case of the violence of Zhao Tao's character in the third episode, and given the rapturous critical response to this film from many of my colleagues, I was uncomfortably reminded of how Travis Bickle in *Taxi Driver* finally became a hero to everybody by turning into a righteous mass murderer: was Jia's depictions of righteous, generic bloodbaths delivered by clichéd killing machines winning him a comparable form of mass approval?

Not really, and certainly not exactly, at least in China. Despite many anticipations of commercial success, the film encountered some belated censorship owing to government worries about incitements to violence that delayed its release. In the meantime, the wide circulation of pirated copies brought Jia back to the status of cultish independence that he'd had on his first three features. And a more recent second viewing of *A Touch of Sin* immediately corrected my initial misimpression. In fact, the adoption by Zhao Tao of familiar *wuxia* poses after stabbing a sauna customer who's been slapping her with a wad of bills for not prostituting herself is clearly designed to function as a Brechtian "baring of the device" at the same time that it functions as an absurd fulfillment of the usual genre expectations. That is, it simultaneously invites our applause and makes us feel ashamed and/or embarrassed for applauding. As Jia said to interviewer Nicolas Rapold, "In *A Touch of Sin* the characters are ordinary people. They don't necessarily have kung fu skills. When they encounter these acts of violence and use their own violence to counteract what was inflicted upon them, they go through a transformation and become like the mystical warriors of the wuxia films. So I've treated every instance of violence in the film as a mystical event." It's worth adding that Jia's definition and understanding of violence extend to suicide, diverse kinds of mental cruelty and economic pressure, and, perhaps, above all, to repression and silence—in short, to the toleration of other forms of violence through passivity, fear, or defeated cynicism.

As Jia explained in another interview to Tony Rayns, all four of his main stories—and presumably some of the other stories and forms of corruption or social abuse alluded to only in passing—were found on Weibo, the Chinese equivalent of Twitter, although the first two occurred before Weibo was launched circa 2010, and Jia used the site in those cases for follow-up details:

1. "Black Gold Mountain": In a mining town in Shanxi, a middle-aged diabetic ex-miner named Dahai (Jiang Wu) attempts to lodge protests against an official who promised but then neglected to pay a percentage of the mine profits to the local populace after the state-run business became privatised, but his efforts are blocked at every turn, even by the local postal service. After being beaten so badly by the entrepreneur's henchmen that he becomes hospitalised, he loads a rifle and shoots several people in turn, including the corrupt official and a man he sees brutally beating an animal.
2. "Shapingba": In a village near Chongqing in the southwest Sichuan province, another lone wolf named Zhou San (Wang Baoqiang), a professional killer and thief—whom we have already seen on a motorbike slaughtering several hoods who attempt to rob him in Shanxi province in the precredits sequence—returns home to attend his mother's 70th birthday celebration and to briefly visit his family. We next see him disguising himself as a streetcleaner, stalking a wealthy couple making a large withdrawal at a bank and then killing them on the street, discarding his disguise, and fleeing.
3. "Nightcomer Sauna": Zheng Xiaoyu, played by Jia's wife (and habitual leading lady) Zhao Tao, tries to convince her married lover

to leave his wife before visiting her estranged mother and going to work as a sauna receptionist in Yichang (in Hubei province, in central China). After being beaten badly by her lover's wife and the latter's male friends or relatives, she gets harassed and abused by a sauna customer who insists on having sex with her, and she responds by killing him with a knife.
4. "Oasis of Prosperity": In Dongguan (in Guandong province, in southern China), a teenage boy named Xiao Hui, working a ten-hour shift on an assembly line at a clothing factory, causes an industrial accident by speaking to a coworker, thus becoming responsible for the coworker's salary while his wound heals. Further pressured economically by his mother's demands that he send her more of his wages, he goes to work as a waiter at an expensive brothel, where he falls in love with one of the prostitutes, who explains to him that her work rules out love and that she has a young daughter to support. Further harassed and bullied by some of his fellow tenants at the crowded workers' tenement where he stays, he leaps from an upper balcony there to his death.
5. In a final coda, Xiaoyu emerges from prison and moves to Shanxi, where she applies for a job assisting the widow of the corrupt entrepreneur murdered by Dahai. On the street, she watches the performance of a Chinese opera where she hears the recurring line, "Do you understand your sin?"

That Jia hails from the small town of Fenyang in Shanxi province clearly plays an important role in all his work. Like William Faulkner and Alexander Dovzhenko, he's a hick avant-gardist in the very best sense—someone whose outsider and minority status enhances and sustains both his humanity and his art. (In certain respects, his desire to shock and even shame his audience in *A Touch of Sin* calls to mind Faulkner's *Sanctuary*.) Working in long, choreographed takes, and mixing realistic accounts of working-class life with diverse forms of cultural shock and fantasy, he already qualifies as a poetic prophet of the twenty-first century, and not only for China.

CHAPTER 11

Jerry Lewis

The profound lack of curiosity in the United States about why Jerry Lewis was a huge American star for well over a decade is matched by an equivalent lack of curiosity about the reasons for the critical attention he received in France during roughly the same period. (As far as most American commentators are concerned, "the French" appears to represent an unvarying, permanent taste over the past seven decades.) This process of unthinking denial sometimes also extends to ignoring the critical reputations of Woody Allen in both countries somewhat later and their own motivations.

My own practically lifelong fascination with Lewis, which began when I saw *My Friend Irma* at the age of six, eventually led to this essay, written for the Viennale's catalogue accompanying its Lewis retrospective in October 2013, where it appeared in German translation.

The Lewis Contradiction

Why Did—and Do—the Americans Love Jerry Lewis So Much?

> . . . Jerry Lewis's face, where the height of artifice blends at times with the nobility of true documentary.
> —Jean-Luc Godard on *Hollywood or Bust*, July 1957[1]

The usual question—and by now a completely tiresome one—is, "Why do the French love Jerry Lewis so much?" People have been asking this question—mainly rhetorically rather than with any genuine curiosity about the answer—for more than half a century, yet if it was ever worth asking in the first place, this was only for roughly the first two decades of that period. As far as I can tell, this was a love that was first fully declared in detail (though it was far from being universally accepted even in France, then or later) in December 1957, when Robert Benayoun published an article in *Positif* entitled "Simple Simon ou l'anti-James Dean," although earlier appreciations, Godard's among them, had already appeared by then.

This was only about a month before Lewis, having ended his partnership with Dean Martin a year and a half earlier, and subsequently become his own producer on *Rock-a-Bye Baby,* purchased a mansion in Bel Air that had formerly been owned by the late Louis B. Mayer, containing more than thirty rooms, seventeen bathrooms, and three kitchens. And it seems fairly obvious that most of the money that paid for this lavish spread came from the love of Lewis's fellow Americans, not from any love of "the French."

Indeed, it becomes far too easy for us to forget that an estimated eighty million people saw *Sailor Beware* (1951), Martin and Lewis's fourth feature, and that their ninth, *Living It Up* (1953), another one of their best, made more money than *Singin' in the Rain, On the Waterfront,* or *The African Queen.* Indeed, the fact that the monster impact of Martin and Lewis on American society of the 1950s briefly preceded that of Elvis Presley suggests that, in their own manic fashion, Dean and Jerry helped to usher in the youth culture of the 1950s and its own liberating physical impulses (associated mainly with sex, drugs, and rock 'n' roll) in which Lewis's body spoke louder than his words (which often took the form of gibberish anyway) and seemed to have an erupting and convulsive will of its own, cutting through all the multiple restraints that characterized American society during this period. (See, in particular, the extraordinary and singular dances performed by Lewis in such films as *Sailor Beware, Living It Up, You're Never Too Young* [1954], *Cinderfella* [1959], *The Ladies Man* [1961], and *The Nutty Professor* [1962].) Despite the fact that Lewis was saddled with a producer at Paramount, Hal B. Wallis, determined to keep his and Martin's comedies as innocuous and as formulaic as possible—a service Wallis provided even more ruinously to Elvis Presley a little later by similarly and systematically deradicalizing and dry-cleaning his star's image and appeal in relation to sex, ethnicity, race, and politics—Lewis, unlike Presley, gradually acquired enough clout to exercise creative control as writer, producer, and director, even though he initially received no screen credit for this. Wallis fully succeeded, however, in depriving Lewis of any of the cultural prestige that he routinely assigned to his adaptations of Broadway dramas during the same period—many of these about frustrated middle-aged women (for example, *Come Back, Little Sheba, The Rose Tattoo, The Rainmaker, Summer and Smoke*)—and sometimes being rewarded for his good middlebrow taste with Oscars. For Wallis and his constituency, "art" usually meant the legitimate stage (especially Tennessee Williams), literature, and/or foreign actors such as Anna Magnani and Anthony Quinn—lessons that Woody Allen would benefit from (as would Arthur Penn, Francis Coppola, Martin Scorsese, among other culturally ambitious American directors) when he openly emulated European filmmakers and "serious" American playwrights, something Lewis has never done. (The only time when Wallis brought Lewis and his "higher" cultural aspirations together, it was the latter that clearly suffered, in a 1959 adaptation of Gore Vidal's *Visit to a Small Planet*.) Obviously, a large part of this cultural prestige had to do with targeting films for adults rather than children; to the extent that Lewis continued to regard his core audience as kids, lack of cultural stature was a given—as it was for the Elvis Presley films, pitched to a somewhat older but still non-adult public.

In fact, the alleged "French love" of Jerry Lewis has always really been a matter of highbrow prestige rather than one of either demographics or business. There are of course other occasions in film history when misunderstandings emerge from mainstream artists exhibiting some of the traits and temperaments of avant-garde artists: think of Chaplin, Stroheim, Val Lewton, Kubrick, Elaine May. But it's hard to think of anyone else apart from Lewis in which there's such a huge disparity between his or her mainstream and avant-garde profiles.

The distaste for Lewis expressed by many of his fellow Americans is largely a matter of rejecting what might be regarded as his excesses: lowbrow mugging, extreme physicality, infantile behavior, and recourses to sentimentality, in contrast to the dry and cerebral middlebrow and "grownup" comedy of Woody Allen. But considering the degree to which both tolerance and celebration of various kinds of excess define the American character, above all in cinema—so that mass slaughter is often regarded as a fit subject for family entertainment, and serial killers in such films as *The Silence of the Lambs* and *No Country for Old Men* are even perceived with a certain reverential awe as holy figures—it's worth asking why the excessive clowning and destructive consequences of an adult behaving like an out-of-control nine-year-old might be the cause for so much repulsion and recoil. Clearly other factors come into play.

There are striking class differences in the contrasting performance and directorial styles of Lewis and Allen as well: regardless of how many rooms his Bel-Air mansion had, Lewis's nouveau riche manner, like that of Elvis, kept his persona firmly within the realm of the working class (apart from a few strained exceptions, such as his early role in *That's My Boy*), and not at all ashamed or embarrassed to be there, whereas the class anxieties in Allen's comedies and dramas, as clarified especially in his recent *Blue Jasmine,* are entirely predicated on upscale privileges or their absence—often trumping and in effect replacing the various cultural and social anxieties that they appear to be about. (A rare and noble exception to this tendency is *Broadway Danny Rose.*) So even though it's worth bearing in mind that Woody Allen, a Lewis fan himself, asked Lewis to direct his first feature, *Take the Money and Run,* before deciding to direct it himself, the ideological differences between his comic persona and Lewis's remain profound.

So if a question that might have some pertinence for the mid-1950s through the mid-1970s, "Why do the French love Jerry Lewis," can be superseded by a question pertinent to the next four decades, "Why do the French *and* the Americans love Woody Allen?" the fact that the first question continues to get posed while the second question doesn't isn't because an answer to either question is self-evident. Perhaps even more to the point, why do the Americans love *and* hate Jerry Lewis? Clearly the degree to which he challenges, provokes, embarrasses, and sometimes even scares and troubles his public already sets him apart from Allen, Chaplin, Keaton, Lloyd, Langdon, and Tati, arguably placing his work closer to that of someone like Poe than to most other comics—though far removed from Poe's representational strategies or his sense of narrative continuity in its obsessive, nightmarish intensity. This intensity both reflects and solicits a sort of passionate ambivalence that could be traced back to Lewis's showbiz parents, who failed to show up for their only son's bar mitzvah and left most of their parenting chores to grandparents and an aunt. The begging and pleading for attention that soon became part of Lewis's performing style were clearly a response to a feeling of abandonment and to the panicky emotional hunger it fostered—an aesthetics of excess predicated on the assumption that even too much could never be enough.

If the Americans hadn't loved Jerry Lewis as much as they did between 1950 and the mid-1960s—so much that he wound up making two or three profitable features a year—it seems unlikely that the French would have "discovered" him. The ferocious Anglo American backlash that has ensued ever since is a far more interesting phenomenon than any presumed overestimation by "the French," already made somewhat dubious by Lewis's own avowal that he's been even more popular in other parts of the world. And it seems likely that the degree to which Lewis's persona has come to embody "America" for many people around the world helps to explain part of this backlash. In fact, French critics were the first to note the importance of Lewis's character in *Which Way to the Front?* (1970)—the richest man in the world, rejected by the draft and assembling his own army of misfits to win World War II—being named Byers, a pun for "buyers." (Byers's surreal and traumatized deformations of language brought about by references to him being "rejected," almost incantatory forms of unbridled babbling, are arguably even funnier than his physical deformations.) Exploring what attracted her to Lewis's movies in both prerevolutionary and postrevolutionary Iran, Mehrnaz Saeed-Vafa in her 2012 essay film *Jerry and Me* never explicitly links his films to political freedom, but she repeatedly associates him and his movies with America and all that it signified for her as a child, which includes the freedom to be nonsensical and irresponsible.

The Lewis Conundrum

> Lewis's films constantly put in question their own implied underlying meanings. Because the context he sets up is basically a show-business context—in which persons and their meanings are always constantly performed—the possibility always exists for a second- (or a third-, or a fourth-) degree reading of meanings as simulated or disavowed.
> —Chris Fujiwara, *Jerry Lewis*[2]

In certain respects, auteurist criticism has distorted and confused Lewis's achievements more than clarified them, by unduly privileging Frank Tashlin,[3] a major and misunderstood figure in his own right (though one tied much more to social and cultural satire than to Lewis's more metaphysically unstable form of self-scrutiny), by oversimplifying the intricate collaborative nature of Lewis's partnership with Tashlin in such films as *Rock-a-Bye Baby* (1958) and *Cinderfella,* and, above all, by privileging direction over performance and writing, which are always at the center of Lewis's art. (This is why I can't regard the 1970 *One More Time,* which Lewis neither wrote nor instigated as a project, as a "Jerry Lewis" film in the way that *A Woman of Paris* and *A Countess from Hong Kong* are Charlie Chaplin films.) The overall unity of Lewis's films as a performer regardless of who directed them—so that, for instance, some of the traits of Irma and Jane in the two *My Friend Irma* films (1949–1950) are echoed in the characters of Shirley MacLaine and Dorothy Malone in *Artists and Models* (1955)—begins to suggest some of the drawbacks in viewing Lewis simply as a director. Even in his work as solo director, privileging *mise en scéne* over *découpage* doesn't do justice to the full extent of his filmmaking. (One of Lewis's favorite stories, recounted in the chapter about editing in *The Total Film-Maker,*[4] describes the crucial difference made by cutting only two frames from a shot in *The Bellboy* in order to make a particular gag work—a gag he would restage twenty-one years later in *Hardly Working.*) Lewis's desire to resurrect the title hero of *The Nutty Professor* in both *The Family Jewels* (1965) and *The Big Mouth* (1967) clearly exceeds any narrative or stylistic function they might have in what is already an absurdist universe profoundly out of joint, both metaphysically and morally. To perform, existentially speaking, means in effect and at best to forge temporary meaning in a nihilist void, soon to be supplanted by other temporary meanings.

It could be argued that all comics deal with different forms of anxiety. Woody Allen's aforementioned class anxiety should be juxtaposed with the relative acceptance of Lewis's heroes being either working class or nouveau riche, where social maladjustment is only incidentally a matter of failing to meet the norms of middle-class conformity. This suggests in Lewis's case a form of pride and freedom harking back to his formation during the Depression, in contrast to Allen's formation nine years later, where "rising above" one's class origins—epitomized in his case by the move from Brooklyn to Manhattan—becomes the major aspiration. Lewis, by contrast, has proudly remained someone from New Jersey to the same degree that Frank Sinatra did throughout his own career. So it isn't surprising that in *The Caddy* (1953), the golfing careers of Martin and Lewis's working-class characters, recounted in flashback before they became a rich show-biz team exactly like themselves, derives most of their comic tension from their awkward entanglements with the country-club set, culminating in literal class warfare at a climactic tournament.

To revert to an ethnic stereotype, Lewis and Allen both project the personas of "pushy" (that is, aggressive) Jews, but in very different ways—modified in Lewis's case by a certain meekness that overtakes his own character once pathos becomes an important part of his image (which starts as early as *That's My Boy* in 1951). Prior to that, we find, in Lewis's first two film appearances—in *My Friend Irma* (1949) and *My Friend Irma Goes West* (1950), where he and Dean Martin both receive second billing—a persona noticeably different in some respects from the one that would develop later.

My Friend Irma, the movie spinoff of a popular radio show—one that I listened to with some regularity as a toddler before seeing the *My Friend Irma* films—focuses on two young women sharing an apartment in Manhattan and both usually working as secretaries, a level-headed brunette narrator named Jane (Diana Lynn) and her dizzy and dumb-blonde pal Irma (Marie Wilson), similar in some respects to the duo in *My Sister Eileen.* When Hal Wallis at Paramount successfully outbid his Hollywood studio rivals to sign a contract with Martin and Lewis—by then the hottest act in American show business (thanks to nightclub gigs, their own radio show, appearances on television variety shows, and even a single that they recorded at Capitol Records), after teaming up in 1946—he decided to cast Martin as Jane's boyfriend, Steve, which required only minor adjustments to the radio show by making Steve an aspiring singer. But when it came to casting Lewis as Marie's boyfriend—a sleazy con-artist named Al who resembled a Damon Runyon character and tended to live off Marie's income—the results of a screen test proved disastrous, and a hasty meeting with writer Cy Howard yielded a new character for Lewis named Seymour, Steve's partner in running an orange juice stand, and a decision to cast actor John Lund as Al.

One consequence of this rapid switchover is that some of Seymour's qualities (innocence, goofiness, a capacity to wreak chaos) seem like carryovers from Irma while certain others (abrasiveness, urban aggression, a tendency to whine and complain) suggest a few leftover traits from Al. And some of both can be related to Lewis's own personality. (From page 174 in *Jerry Lewis in Person,*[5] circa the early 1950s: "Many a night I'd get into my XKE Jaguar and speed down Sunset Boulevard, blasting the horn for no particular reason except to feel monumentally important.") And the standard practice of doubling characters in comedy seems to have led to Steve exploiting Seymour at work (it's Seymour who does all the physical orange-squeezing) to "rhyme" with Al exploiting Irma. As suggested above, it isn't until pathos and sentimentality become more integral to Lewis's persona that the sleazier aspects start to become minimized—even though Lewis has become sufficiently comfortable with Seymour in *My Friend Irma Goes West* (a considerable improvement over its predecessor) to create some of his freest inventions, such as a lengthy sequence featuring him with a chimpanzee on a cross-country train journey, which playwright George S. Kaufman reportedly acclaimed as the funniest thing he'd ever seen in a movie. But this isn't to say that major contradictions in Lewis's persona don't persist, all the way up to the present.

Chance and Spontaneity

> Show business constitutes, for Lewis, an alternate psychoanalysis, a therapeutic sphere in which he acts out his obsessions in public and transcends them (see the confession scene in the prom in *The Nutty Professor*). In several films, Lewis depicts show business as an alternate family.
> —Chris Fujiwara, *Jerry Lewis*[6]

One shouldn't assume that Jerry Lewis's first encounter with cinema in 1949 came out of nowhere. It came, specifically, out of live performance—first in nightclubs, and then on radio and television. It was live performances with Dean Martin (even when these were simulated and/or prerecorded on television while conveying the same improvisatory spirit that was part of the medium during that period) that made them stars before they went to Hollywood, and it's worth considering what special ingredients they brought to those appearances, which above all were a matter of spontaneity and the unexpected—a genuine sense of anarchy erupting during one of the most repressive periods in American history.

Indeed, one way of reading all their early features is to see them as mechanisms striving to approximate the same energies and freedom that brought them to Hollywood in the first place. Typically, a "straight" performance of a song by Martin gets repeatedly interrupted, disrupted, and deconstructed by Lewis's antics—a routine depending on the improvisational talent of Martin as well as Lewis—and variations of this routine turn up in virtually all these features, most often in nightclub or other live-performance settings. Paradoxically, such routines always required some preparation and even rehearsal, even when various improvisations provided additional sparks to the combustion of their chemistry, but the relative invisibility of these designs to the public kept the performances volatile, conveying the impression that "anything" could happen.

The fact that in many of his routines on the *Colgate Comedy Hour,* Lewis can be seen interrupting himself to laugh uncontrollably at his own jokes might seem the height of undisciplined show-biz behavior, but it also suggests both a complicity with the audience—he never laughs alone—and the impulse to deconstruct and even demolish the fictional "givens" of any particular sketch, including those that he might have dreamed up himself, a kind of perpetual auto-destruction that becomes an essential part of his filmmaking as he steadily gains more control over the writing and direction of his features.

One interesting parallel of Lewis with Charlie Chaplin is that they both had parents who were live performers, and both had their stage debuts performing a popular song at age five because of their family connection. In Chaplin's case, as recounted by his best biographer,[7] the song was "Jack Jones," and the five-year-old replaced his mother after her voice cracked and fell into a whisper. (In his *Autobiography,* Chaplin wrote, "That night was my first appearance on the stage and Mother's last.") When a "shower of money" was thrown at the boy during his singing, he stopped and "announced that [he] would pick up the money first and sing afterward," which "caused much laughter" that only increased when the stage manager helped him collect the money, and then increased again when he wound up imitating his mother's cracked voice during another song.

Lewis's stage debut occurred at a benefit for the Firemen's Association held at a hotel in the Catskills. Like many others during this period, his father had been performing the Depression standby "Brother, Can You Spare a Dime?" as part of his act, and at his son's urging, he allowed him to be brought onstage for an encore, after much rehearsing with his mother, who provided piano accompaniment. As Lewis remembered it later, while taking his bow, his foot slipped and caused one of the footlights to explode; "it scared me half to death," the audience laughed at his panic, and, as he put it in an interview on the Arts & Entertainment Network, "and I liked the laugh I got better than the applause I got."[8]

In both cases, one could say that the very first lesson learned, helping to set the terms for future performances, came from the audience. In

Lewis's case, this lesson becomes complicated initially by the presence of his partner (so that Dean Martin himself, who was nine years older, becomes both part of the audience and an audience surrogate as well as a co-conspirator—an "older brother" providing a sort of life raft to the seeming lack of control), and then, after the breakup of his partnership, with a kind of solipsistic self-scrutiny and self-interrogation once Lewis becomes a solo performer and the films become much stranger and, as a rule, less concerned with issues of narrative coherence. There's even less concern with verisimilitude in relation to period; *Which Way to the Front?*, opening in 1943 in Manhattan, alludes to "condominiums" in its first scene at least fifteen years before the first one existed. The same comic who would eventually build elaborate gag sequences in *Cracking Up* (1983) derived from his near-brush with a suicide attempt, the pain experienced from his surgery, and his attempts to stop smoking has in fact based most of his features on some of his most personal conflicts, issues, and wounds. Part of what's disconcerting about his preceding *Hardly Working*—his least Hollywoodish feature, made after more than a decade's absence from the screen—is its painful honesty about Lewis's aging and loss of stamina (which even becomes the point of certain gags, such as Bo Hooper's fantasy of being John Travolta in *Saturday Night Fever*) and the stark division of all the other characters into kids and adults who either love Bo and laugh at his every grimace or simply despise him; no one is allowed to be neutral.

As Fujiwara persuasively notes, show business serves for Lewis as both an alternate psychoanalysis and an alternate family—even though one should note that standard psychoanalysis isn't taken very seriously in either *Three on a Couch* or *Cracking Up*. But considering the degree to which Lewis's identity (which includes his life and family) are hard to separate from show business, a certain auto-critique that at times verges on self-loathing typically extends to show business itself and everything it entails, as in *The Errand Boy* and *The Patsy*. This self-hatred achieves its purest expression in *The Nutty Professor*'s Buddy Love, who is show business personified—and even to a lesser extent Lewis's title hero and Love's apparent opposite, Julius Kelp, who traces his own ineptitude directly back to his monstrous parents. (Part of the grimness of this film's "happy ending" is its suggestion that everyone ultimately prefers the brutal egotist to the meek professor; even the sweet-tempered heroine [Stella Stevens] packs two bottles of the secret formula on her way to the altar.) One reason why Lewis's performance in Martin Scorsese and Paul D. Zimmerman's

The King of Comedy (1982) resonates as strongly as it does is that it conforms to the impression that being a big-shot celebrity effectively means being a monster (and also sometimes having contempt for one's parents, as Robert De Niro's Rupert Pupkin does in his climactic comedy monologue), and perhaps even Lewis's telethons for muscular dystrophy can be viewed as a long-standing effort to compensate for this sort of troubling moral intuition.

Several years ago, when he was appearing onstage as the Devil in *Damn Yankees* during its Chicago run, Lewis graciously agreed to appear at an extended public discussion at nearby Columbia College—a session that lasted, if memory serves, for at least three hours. The sense of risk and danger in the auditorium that afternoon was palpable, and it came, I think, from the fact that Lewis stayed so close to the edge of his emotions, seemingly as a matter of both policy and temperament. The possibilities of being hurt, and of hurt being transformed into anger and rage, were never entirely absent, even though he managed to keep his cool on the few occasions when one of the questions betrayed some hostility—hostility that may have derived in part from some of the tension generated. (The absence of such tension and any feeling of danger in the work of Woody Allen is no less striking.)

The Lewis Contradiction

> There are two basic kinds of clown. In the classic circus, there's the clown who is white-faced, with a white cap, short trousers, and silk stockings. He has beautiful legs, and is very elegant. Every move he makes is perfect. The other clown, who works with him, is called an *auguste*, and he has baggy pants and big feet. What Chaplin did was to marry them, these two classic clowns, and create a new clown. That was his secret—that's my theory.
>
> —Orson Welles, *My Lunches with Orson: Conversations Between Henry Jaglom and Orson Welles*[9]

> "I love persons and people."
>
> "Persons and people. There's a difference?"
>
> "Oh, sure. There's a big difference. You see, persons . . . persons are people who have made it, who are rich and famous. So that, of course, makes them persons and they're not people anymore."
>
> —Fella (Lewis) to his Fairy Godfather (Ed Wynn) in *Cinderfella* (1959)

In *The Stooge* (1953), set in 1930, Lewis plays Ted Rogers, a hapless and clueless song-plugger (the one-time profession of Lewis's father) who gets hired by singer Bill Miller (Martin) at the insistence of his manager (Eddie Mayehoff) to beef up Miller's unsuccessful single act, using Rogers as a stooge who interrupts the singer's performance from a box seat. According to the plot, these interruptions are spontaneous and innocent, and Rogers doesn't even object when Miller refuses to give him any billing after the act is a smash success. Yet one night, when Miller is too drunk to go on and Rogers has to replace him as a single, he proceeds to imitate Maurice Chevalier singing "Louise."

Considering who the character is, this performance makes no sense at all; it's not even very credible that Rogers would know who Chevalier is, much less be able to perform a carefully rehearsed and meticulous pastiche of his singing style and mannerisms without any preparation. But one can fully understand Lewis calling *The Stooge* his best work with Martin, "because it transferred two nightclub performers to the screen properly. It came closest to capturing what Dean and I had as a team."[10] And it epitomizes the degree to which Lewis's character is founded on a contradiction as profound as the merging of two antithetical clowns in Chaplin's persona as described by Welles—or as Marilyn Monroe's Lorelei Lee in *Gentlemen Prefer Blondes* being simultaneously a very dumb blonde and a brilliantly conniving schemer.

It's a kind of contradiction that superstars are born to embody without the audience ever noticing it—unless one notices, for example, such details as Bo Hooper (Lewis), an out-of-work clown in *Hardly Working,* wearing the same expensive jewelry that Lewis habitually wears. For Lewis's persona is at once powerless and omnipotent, awkward and graceful, clueless and sophisticated, a snappy dresser (even as a misfit) as well as a slob, and these contradictions necessarily encompass other contradictions as well. The giddy megalomania of the man who spread his remarkably lavish boarding-house set over two of Paramount's soundstages in *The Ladies Man* (1961) and then filled them with nubile young actresses is difficult to reconcile with the fumbling idiot and the sexual panic of Lewis' own persona within that constructed space (who literally splits into four versions of himself when he sees all these women for the first time and flees from them), but ongoing disparities of this kind are fundamental to Lewis's art and the dream logic of his inventions. (It's worth adding that Lewis's major contribution as a technical pioneer—his invention of the video assist, introduced on *The Bellboy* [1960], his first feature—was motivated specifically by a desire to act and direct at the same time.) Even in *Visit to a Small Planet,* Lewis's hapless extraterrestrial character having telepathic and telekinetic powers doesn't seriously threaten the essential nature of his persona. The fact that, in some of his earliest recorded appearances with Martin, Lewis both cavorts like a spastic marionette and can be seen confidently conducting orchestras only begins to account for the duality he embodies and suggests, equally apparent in his pantomimes tied to music (the earliest form taken by his live comic performances). Yet the ideological safety net provided to virtually all his fictional characters is a perpetual yearning to conform to the status quo without challenging any of its basic principles. Typically, Fella in *Cinderfella* and Julius Kelp in *The Nutty Professor* are both apparently content to remain abject failures as "people" without ever questioning the successes of such "persons" as Fella's odious stepmother and stepbrothers or the equally obnoxious Buddy Love. Like Shakespeare's Cassius, these characters all seem to conclude, "The fault, dear Brutus, is not in our stars, / But in ourselves, that we are underlings."

In some films, the Lewis persona isn't simply contradictory but infinitely malleable, to the point of incoherence. On dance floors, even the withdrawn and graceless "Junior" Jackson in *That's My Boy* and Julius Kelp are compelled to break briefly into Lewis's gracefully jagged jitterbugging. In *You're Never Too Young,* Wilbur Hoolick runs the gamut from inept barber's assistant (when he first appears and in the film's closing gag) to two separate fake Frenchmen (one of them ancient) to an alternately bratty and sweet-tempered eleven-year-old to a conniving competitor for the affection of the heroine (Diana Lynn), plotting to get Bob Miles (Martin) shipped overseas in the army by perfectly imitating the voice of his boss's daughter (Nina Foch) over the phone; he also oscillates periodically between being fearless and terrified, and also offers a sustained Humphrey Bogart impersonation in one scene.

At least theoretically, one can subdivide not only Lewis but most of his pictures as writer-director-performer into two pairs of templates, best represented by his masterpieces *The Ladies Man* and *The Nutty Professor:* (a) nonlinear collections of gags versus linear narratives with beginnings, middles, and ends, and (b) free-form conceptual fantasies versus fictions grounded in some form of social commentary. But in practice, these features rarely opt for one or the other. Even the more nonlinear films (ranging from *The Bellboy* to the even more discontinuous *Cracking Up*), where narrative continuity is mostly perfunctory, are furnished with narrative setups and/or resolutions, and even some with more developed stories, such as *Three on a Couch,* have nonlinear interludes (for example, the remarkable and peculiar "slow dance" sequence with Janet Leigh) and brightly expressionist color schemes. (In the latter film, Lewis, for once, plays an "adjusted" adult, but the three men his character chooses to impersonate are even more maladjusted than Lewis's usual misfits, while the story's relatively "realistic" framework gets periodically jettisoned for fantasy gags that seem to belong to a different picture.) *The Ladies Man* is mainly a string of fantasies where anything can happen, but when a TV crew turns up at the boardinghouse to shoot a live show (a parody of Edward R. Murrow's *Person to Person*), the details become relatively realistic, as they do in many of the film-production details in *The Errand Boy*. Furthermore, the social commentaries often become abstracted into subjective fancies—one forbidden room in *The Ladies Man* becomes an all-white bedroom and then an open-air arena where Lewis dances with a predatory female in black to Harry James's orchestra; an offscreen pet that roars proves to be first a dachshund, then an actual lion—so that the usual distinctions between external and internal visions are systematically dissolved.

Lewis's first two features, *The Bellboy* and *The Ladies Man,* are set in very different kinds of hotels—the Fontainbleau in Miami, filmed on location, and an improbable boardinghouse for young women, constructed on Paramount soundstages—and are mainly nonlinear fantasies in which, speaking very broadly, each room provides a separate cell or sequence, and the third, *The Errand Boy,* expands this overall concept to a movie studio, where sets and locations seem interchangeable. At one point in *The Bellboy,* Lewis appears as himself entering the Fontainbleau, surrounded by a satirically huge entourage, and one sequence in *The Ladies Man,* also set in a common public space, is inspired by Lewis's knowledge of George Raft's early career as a dancer and features Raft playing himself (though it's predicated on Lewis's fictional character refusing to believe that Raft is Raft or that he had any background as a dancer).

In *The Errand Boy,* immediately after Lewis's character has a fantasy dialogue with a puppet named Magnolia that defends Hollywood's power to successfully sustain illusions (a scene in which Lewis's personal background as a moviegoer in New Jersey plays a part), he cuts to a very hokey dramatic death scene that is belatedly shown to be a movie scene being filmed (as if to undermine the preceding argument—a contradiction already propounded more systematically in the film's prologue, showing how various archetypal movie scenes are faked); and the film concludes with a variation of its opening gag juxtaposing Lewis himself with his hapless character Morty Tashman, who's clearly named after Frank Tashlin. By the same token, Chris Fujiwara has persuasively shown that for virtually every sentimental and conformist detail in Lewis's own films, one can find other details ridiculing or otherwise disavowing sentimentality and/or conformity: "Lewis's parodic impulse takes the form of a sententiousness that not only has no fear of parodying itself but doesn't even worry whether the parody is understood as parody: ambiguity is ever-present in Lewis, at least as a threat."[11]

Given Lewis's biography, it isn't surprising that most of his social commentaries relate directly or indirectly to show business and/or psychological self-scrutiny, and a good many of these partly consist of shattering whatever illusions the films and their stories and characters have been busy constructing. Combining the height of artifice with the nobility of documentary, as Godard put it, Lewis's face, like his cinema, is a calculated yet spontaneous contradiction of terms—suggesting the metaphor Godard once used to describe his own *Pierrot le fou* of a bathtub being filled by water and draining at the same time. So it's small wonder that contemporary mainstream criticism should find the more verbally based and rational comedies and dramas of Woody Allen more comfortable and digestible, especially in comparison to Lewis's brand of performative slapstick, where the universe itself remains profoundly and perpetually but also routinely devoid of purpose or meaning.

Notes

1. *Godard on Godard,* translated and edited by Tom Milne (New York: Da Capo, 1986), p. 59.

2. (Urbana and Chicago: University of Illinois Press, 2009), p. 48.

3. As Robert Benayoun points out in *Bonjour Monsieur Lewis* (Paris: Eric Losfeld, 1972, p. 240), *Living It Up* and *You're Never Too Young* (1955), both directed by Norman Taurog, can hold their own with Tashlin's *Artists and Models* (1955) and *Hollywood or Bust* (1956); indeed, all four of these films have their peaks and valleys.

4. (New York: Warner Paperback Library, 1971), pp. 128–29.

5. Jerry Lewis, with Herb Gluck, *Jerry Lewis in Person* (New York: Atheneum, 1982), p. 174.

6. Ibid., p. 57.

7. Stephen Weissman, M.D., in *Chaplin: A Life* (New York: Arcade Publishing, 2008), pp. 27–28.

8. *Jerry Lewis: The Last American Clown,* broadcast August 18, 1996.

9. Peter Biskind, ed. (New York: Metropolitan Books, 2013), p. 146.

10. James L. Neibaur and Ted Okuda, *The Jerry Lewis Films: An Analytical Filmography of the Innovative Comic* (Jefferson, N.C. and London: McFarland, 1995), p. 61.

11. Ibid., p. 45. See also pp. 33 and 46–49.

CHAPTER 12

Richard Linklater

Among the four films written and directed by Linklater since *Bernie*, three have struck me as disappointments in spite of their many virtues—*Before Midnight* (2013), *Boyhood* (2014), and *Last Flag Flying* (2017)—while *Everybody Wants Some!!* reverts gloriously to what I regard as Linklater's better impulses. Rightly or wrongly, I thought that *Before Midnight* would have been more interesting if it had followed Celine (Julie Delphy) when she storms out of the hotel room near the end of the movie rather than stayed with Jesse (Ethan Hawke), and I was happy to see *Boyhood* bringing Linklater wider media attention even if its interest as a long-range experiment may have exceeded its actual discoveries.

The first selection here appeared in the July 2, 2004 *Chicago Reader*; the second appeared in the online *Moving Image Source* (movingimagesource.us) on October 9, 2008; and the third appeared in a Spanish retrospective catalogue, *Richard Linklater: El tiempo en sus manos*, published in 2016.

Spur of the Moment (*Before Sunset*)

"The years shall run like rabbits,
   For in my arms I hold
The Flower of the Ages,
   And the first love of the world.

"But all the clocks in the city
   Began to whirr and chime:
O let not Time deceive you,
   You cannot conquer Time.

. . .

"O plunge your hands in water,
   Plunge them in up to the wrist;
Stare, stare in the basin
   And wonder what you've missed."
—from W. H. Auden's "As I Walked Out One Evening"

I wonder if the movies of the 1990s and the following decade might eventually be remembered as belonging in part to a couple of poets on opposite sides of the globe whose subject is time: Wong Kar-wai and Richard Linklater. From *Days of Being Wild* and *Slacker* to *Ashes of Time* and *The Newton Boys,* from *Happy Together* and *Dazed and Confused* to *In the Mood for Love* and *Before Sunrise,* these two lyrical and elegiac filmmakers are especially astute about telling us things about who as well as where we are, historically speaking. The romance and poetry of moments ticking by, the experience of living through and then remembering a particular slice of time, is a major part of what keeps their work so vibrant as well as haunting. Born only two years apart, 1958 (Wong) and 1960 (Linklater), they've become two of our key chroniclers—our stock-takers and casual historians.

Out of Linklater's ten features to date, more than half have narratives that take place over a span of a day or less. I can't remember if this applies to his unreleased first feature, the super-8 *It's Impossible to Learn to Plow by Reading Books* (1988), though I suspect it probably doesn't, and the temporal ambiguities of his animated *Waking Life* also leave me somewhat uncertain. There's no such compression of time in his two studio productions, *The Newton Boys* (1998) and *The School of Rock* (2003). But there's no question that it applies to the time frames of *Slacker* (1991), *Dazed and Confused* (1993), *Before Sunrise* (1995), *SubUrbia* (1997), *Tape* (2001), and now *Before Sunset,* an inspired sequel.

Only the last two of these features, however, take place in real time—over the same length of time it takes to watch them. And it might be argued that these two, both of which star Ethan Hawke, have a bit more ambiguity regarding the characters and their motivations than the other four. For this reason, I'm tempted to call them Linklater's most existential films—the ones that delve the most into characters' moment-to-moment decisions. It may also be worth mentioning that these are Linklater's two shortest features, with running times of eighty-six minutes (*Tape*) and eighty (*Before Sunset*)—and both are very much involved with anxiously hashing over a former romantic relationship. But in other respects they're polar opposites: *Tape* stays confined to one dinky motel room in Lansing while *Sunset*, if I've charted the geography correctly, skips across four arrondissements of Paris, moving from the Left to the Right Bank; the former charts suppressed hatred slowly rising to the surface, the latter something much closer to guarded love and affection.

It isn't necessary to have seen *Before Sunrise* in order to follow the sequel—especially because Linklater offers us a few quick, silent glimpses of Jesse (Hawke) and Celine (Julie Delphy) during their day together in Vienna in 1994 shortly after we're introduced to both characters in Paris in 2003. Both actors, one should note, are a decade younger than Linklater, placing them in their twenties in Vienna and in their thirties in Paris. Now he's doing a book signing at Shakespeare & Company at the end of a twelve-day, ten-city European tour promoting his novel, before returning to New York. He catches sight of Celine in the audience toward the end of his q and a, and even though he has only a little bit more than an hour before a driver will take him to the airport, he suggests they have a coffee. (Scholarly footnote: the Shakespeare & Company bookstore that we see isn't the famous one run by Sylvia Beach that published James Joyce's *Ulysses*—located several blocks east of there during the '20s and '30s—but a shop run by someone named George Whitman that's been around since the '50s and appropriated the name to attract gullible tourists. This doesn't mean that it isn't a respectable literary hangout in its own right, more Beat than Early Modernist in overall orientation.)

■ ■ ■

In *Before Sunrise*, Jesse (from Texas) and Celine (from Paris) meet by chance on a train in eastern Europe; he's on his way back home from a desultory European vacation after breaking up with his American girlfriend in Spain and she's returning from a visit with her grandmother in Budapest. They spontaneously decide to spend a day and then a night together in Vienna, sleeping in a park because he lacks the money for a hotel.

I'm sure it isn't coincidental that the day in question happens to be June 16, sometimes known as Bloomsday, during which the entire action of *Ulysses* is set. This isn't because *Before Sunrise* is an especially literary movie—even though Celine is reading Georges Bataille when they meet, Jesse quotes Auden (some earlier lines from the same poem quoted above) shortly before they part, and Joyce's English translation of Gerhard Hauptmann's first play, published posthumously in 1978, is entitled *Before Sunrise*. I suspect that Linklater uses the *Ulysses* reference because, like Joyce, he's interested in giving a lot of weight and gravity to the everyday, even though his acknowledged models in this case are Hollywood love stories such as Vincente Minnelli's *The Clock* (1944).

Ironically, when Jesse meets Celine, he's reading Klaus Kinski's relatively unliterary autobiography *All I Need is Love*. Yet nine years later it's he who's become a published novelist, while she's an activist working for an environmental group called the Green Cross. (This time, one should note, Linklater's cinematic models seem closer to the French New Wave—Eric Rohmer in particular—than to classic Hollywood.)

The novel that Jesse's promoting at Shakespeare & Company, a small best seller in the states, is in fact a fictionalized version of his earlier encounter with Celine, which ended with them promising to meet again in Vienna in six months—after deciding earlier that they wouldn't exchange last names or addresses, for fear of turning their relationship into something banal and routine. (In the novel, as in *Before Sunrise*, we have no way of knowing whether the couple will ever meet again.) A lot of viewers have speculated ever since whether in fact both or either of them would keep the date—and as critic Robin Wood has pointed out, in an essay in *Cineaction* no. 41 that rapturously celebrates the film as one of the greatest ever made, such speculation, far from being trivial, is inextricably tied to the ways that each viewer seriously relates to the film on a personal level. Wood should also be credited with coming very close to guessing correctly about both characters—though the fact that Linklater has long been aware of Wood's essay suggests that it may have actually exerted some influence on the eventual outcome.

■ ■ ■

Reseeing *Before Sunrise* between two viewings of *Before Sunset,* I find it impossible to say which film is better. Both seem to fulfill an ambition Jean-Luc Godard expressed in the '60s—to achieve "the definitive by chance." That is, each in its own way attains a kind of perfection while coming across as impromptu and offhand, which is surely a sign of the greatest mastery, and this accomplishment plainly owes to Hawke and Delphy as much as it does to Linklater and Kim Krizan (the director's credited script collaborator on both films).

But it would be wrong to view the second film as simply a "continuation" of the first in terms of style. The way in which it deliberately sets out to complement its predecessor is already apparent behind the opening credits. During the final stretches of *Before Sunrise,* we get a succession of shots of Vienna locations where Celine and Jesse spent time together, in their original order of appearance but this time without the presence of either of them—a kind of melancholy scrapbook. Reversing this process, *Before Sunset* begins with some of the Paris locations behind the credits where Celine and Jesse *will* spend time together, this time tracing their steps backward.

The switch seems appropriate, because this time the emphasis is much more on anticipation—theirs and ours—and on everything the passing of time does to exacerbate it. (Significantly, when Jesse is asked at Shakespeare & Company what his next novel might be about, he describes his aspiration of writing a story that could take place during the duration of a pop song.) As with the watch and clock that figure in the early meetings between Maggie Cheung and Tony Leung in *Days of Being Wild,* time itself becomes a tool of mutual seduction, the minute hand of a timepiece serving as a kind of Cupid's arrow. So it's hardly coincidental that Jesse's novel is entitled *This Time*—and that the cut on a CD that he chooses to play in Celine's flat, which she winds up doing an elaborate riff on, is a concert version of Nina Simone performing "Just in Time."

Even more of a two-hander than *Before Sunrise,* this film is talkier and offers us fewer distractions from the two leads. But it's also a film in which both characters have many more protective layers to peel away before they can arrive at their feelings, and this time the nature of those feelings is harder for us as well as them to recognize and define when they finally do arrive. Nine years ago, they contrived a couple of impromptu games to expose their emotions to one another—asking blunt questions on a streetcar and carrying on imaginary phone conversations with separate friends in a restaurant. Now that they're in their early thirties instead of their early twenties, there's far more dissimulation in both characters—and a kind of ambiguity to their already shifting cover stories that suggests they can't always be sure whether or not they're entirely true even when they're blurting them out.

Perhaps because Hawke and Delphy have had nine years to think about these people, there's an assurance as well as an excitement to their performances that I've never seen before in either actor. When Celine, in the back seat of a car with Jesse, starts to caress his head while he isn't looking and then suddenly pulls back, there's a sense of tragedy in the curtailment of that gesture that seems to come from the weight of years. Yet in constant competition with that tragic weight is the volatile and unstable lightness of the dangerous present—the onrush of minutes passing that keeps us and the characters equally suspended. Linklater's refusal to let go of that scary promise, even when the movie comes to an end, is a true master stroke—and one of the most perfect endings of any film that comes to mind.

This Way, Myth: *Me and Orson Welles*

"A writer's reputation," Lionel Trilling once wrote, "often reaches a point in its career where what he actually said is falsified even when he is correctly quoted. Such falsification—we might more charitably call it mythopoeia—is very likely the result of some single aspect of a man's work serving as a convenient symbol of what other people want to think. Thus it is a commonplace of misconception that Rousseau wanted us to act like virtuous savages or that Milton held naive, retrograde views of human nature."

Although Orson Welles is rightly regarded as someone whose creative work partially consisted of his own persona, he remains unusually susceptible to mythmaking of this sort. This is because he often figures as someone who both licenses and then becomes the scapegoat for vanity that isn't entirely—or even necessarily—his own. Quite simply, many of those (especially males) who obsess on the "meaning" of "Orson" are actually looking for ways to negotiate their own narcissism and fantasies of omnipotence.

It's part of the special insight of Richard Linklater's *Me and Orson Welles* to perceive and run with this aspect of the Welles myth, which is already implied in its title. This energetic and entertaining movie, which still lacks a U.S. distributor, was scripted by the couple Holly Gent Palmo and Vincent Palmo, closely adapting a 2003 novel by Robert Kaplow about a teenage boy in 1937 who joins Welles's legendary Mercury stage production of *Caesar* in the minor part of Lucius. This was a modern-dress, bare-stage presentation celebrated for the conceit of making Shakespeare's characters contemporary Italian fascists, and for employing "Nuremberg" lighting.

Even though the film—which is greatly assisted by much research into the original stage production and a very adroit impersonation of the young Welles by English actor Christian McKay—is limited both as history and as Welles portraiture, it remains wholly on target in suggesting some of the motives for Welles mythopoeia. Thus one of the key scenes depicts the liberated vanity of the Mercury Theatre players that immediately follows the triumph of the opening-night performance, as reflected in their idle chatter while they bask onstage in their victory. Indeed, the same euphoric self-regard can be found in virtually all of the film's young characters, including a writer (Zoe Kazan) befriended by the hero who isn't part of the Mercury troupe; in every case but hers, Welles is basically the magical force that unleashes and validates everyone's egotism.

Despite the fact that the movie celebrates collective effort, and benefits a great deal from its own version of it, self-regard is the main dish on display, and Welles is credited as both the chef and the narcissistic role model. In fact, the "me" that appears first in *Me and Orson Welles* also appears last in the story, long after the Welles character has evaporated into legend.

Kaplow's novel is also clearly attuned to this particular aspect of Welles fixation; on the book's second page, Richard Samuels, the teenage hero, is already gazing into a mirror and comparing himself to Gary Cooper, Cary Grant, and Fred Astaire (a conceit that the film's casting of teenage heartthrob Zac Efron in the part makes halfway plausible). But Kaplow complicates and muddles matters somewhat with some of his ethnic details—most notably, by making his Richard Jewish and then having Welles improbably call his Jewish set designer Samuel Leve a "credit-stealing, son-of-a-bitch Jew" after the latter complains about not getting credit for his work in *Caesar*'s program, which leads Richard to leap to Leve's defense.

The screenwriters, however, omit virtually all of the novel's Jewish details (including even the character of Marc Blitzstein, who composed

Caesar's incidental music), and given the particular story Linklater has in mind, this simplification actually clarifies the proceedings. The credit dispute remains in the story, but without the intervention of either anti-Semitism or Richard—whose own battle with Welles crops up later.

Welles mythopoeia may help to explain why the least researched of all Welles biographies, David Thomson's *Rosebud*—that is to say, the one most invented out of whole cloth—is commonly regarded by nonspecialists as the best, presumably meaning the most apt and insightful even while it imputes various failings to the man (including racism, classism, and declining productivity) that have no demonstrable basis in fact. Two characteristically unsupported sentences in *Rosebud:* "There is sometimes a perilous proximity of old-fashioned racial stereotype and yearning sympathy" (posited in Welles's affection for some black people and black music) and "Welles . . . always liked his revolutionaries to be sophisticated and well-heeled" (an assertion refuted by the Brazilian fishermen and communists he insisted on hanging out with in 1942, to the consternation of some "well-heeled" government officials and studio spies).

But because Thomson is clever enough to know what some people want to believe about Welles as well as what they prefer to ignore, the falsity of his portrait "rings true" according to the myth, and for many people it continues to hold water. To some extent, Kaplow seems to be banking on a similar trait in his own readers.

By his own account, Kaplow's hero Richard Samuels grew out of his efforts to imagine Arthur Anderson, the young lute player who appeared in a famous photograph of the Welles stage production—increasing his age by about three years so that his fictional counterpart could become Welles's romantic rival. Correspondingly, Kaplow's curiosity about what gave Welles's fascist *Caesar* its political resonance and impact in 1937 is minimal, so that one may be left wondering, in spite of his and Linklater's meticulous re-creations, why the production proved to be such a smash success. (John Houseman's memoir *Run-through,* clearly used as a major resource, conveys this period flavor much better.) And the film also sometimes reverts to standard-issue shorthand in establishing a late-Depression atmosphere—such as employing a pastiche of Benny Goodman's famous January 16, 1938 Carnegie Hall performance of "Sing, Sing, Sing," perhaps the most overused single emblem of swing music employed in American movies. (The second most overused emblem, Duke Ellington's "Solitaire," is also used.) More generally, it gives us the attributes of a young Welles that might inspire a teenager's envy and imagination while omitting many of the other traits that would complicate this scenario.

There's general agreement that Welles was self-absorbed. But one way of distinguishing mythopoeia from biography is whether or not his other distinguishing traits—such as his compulsive self-criticism (which could sometimes be even more severe than the charges of his detractors) and his desire to compensate for his self-absorption with certain forms of charm and generosity—are factored into the portrayal.

Me and Orson Welles (film and novel) is intermittently attentive to the latter but completely oblivious to the former, offering a Welles who insists on being called a genius and refuses any form of self-criticism. It also depicts him as a man who could nurse serious grudges over minor challenges to his authority—something my own research has failed to turn up. But insofar as Welles continues to be a shining beacon for the self-regard of others, the portrait hits a mythological bull's-eye.

The Paradoxes of *Bernie*

A prefatory caveat: My favorite Richard Linklater feature, *Bernie* (2011), is many different things at once, some of which are in potential conflict with one another. How we ultimately judge it depends on either reconciling or suspending our separate verdicts on how we judge it as fiction (and art) and/or how we judge it as fact (and justice). Because I've chosen to suspend my judgment on how we can judge the film as fact, for reasons that will be dealt with below, I can enjoy the luxury of celebrating the film as fiction and as art at the same time that I would maintain that it opens up factual questions about truth and justice that it can't pretend to resolve in any definitive manner.

Background

The film was inspired by a lengthy article, "Midnight in the Garden of East Texas" by Skip Hollandsworth, that appeared in the January 1998 issue of *Texas Monthly,* about the confessed murder of Marjorie Nugent, an eighty-one-year-old widow and the wealthiest woman in town, by thirty-nine-year-old Bernie Tiede, a former assistant funeral director in the same town (Carthage, with a population of 6,500) who had become her paid companion and the sole inheritor of her considerable fortune.

After having shot Marjorie Nugent four times in the back with a .22 rifle and stored her body at the bottom of a large freezer in her home for more than half a year, Tiede confessed to the police after the widow's son and his eldest daughter searched the house and discovered her body.

As Hollandsworth describes the local impact of the crime's discovery, Tiede was the most beloved member of the community, someone who had generously spent most of the money he had pilfered from Nugent (perhaps the most hated member of the community for her miserly traits, social snobbery, and ill temper) on others who needed it. And as suggested by the title of Hollandsworth's article—prompted by John Berendt's best-selling "nonfiction novel" *Midnight in the Garden of Good and Evil* (1994) and the 1997 Clint Eastwood film derived from it, about the killing of a male prostitute by a wealthy antiques dealer in Savannah, Georgia—Hollandsworth was more interested in the crime's local impact and what this said about the town itself than he was in the crime. The fact that east Texas is "southern" (close to the border of Louisiana), with a distinctly different culture from other portions of the state, is deftly and colorfully outlined in detail by one of the locals, Sonny Davis, early in the film, complete with animated maps behind him to illustrate his various points. That Linklater himself hails from east Texas, where one of his other most personal and inspired features is grounded (*The Newton Boys*, 1998, also based on a true story), obviously sparked his interest in the story and characters. Significantly, both *The Newton Boys* and *Bernie* are anarchistic and humanistic defenses of sympathetic criminals, although the crimes committed in the former are exclusively bank robberies. That *Bernie* mounts a comic defense for a thieving murderer makes it far more subversive and challenging, especially insofar as this defense is made to seem implicit and even secondary: as in *Midnight in the Garden of Good and Evil,* its principal aim is to celebrate the humor, eccentricity, and personalities of a small town, including the various moral paradoxes involved in its language and discourse.

A dozen years would pass between the appearance of Hollandsworth's article and the film's production, and not only did Linklater enlist Hollandsworth as his cowriter during this period; his script follows the particulars of the original article quite closely, meanwhile updating it to include the subsequent trial (which was held almost fifty miles away from Carthage, in San Augustine, owing to the partiality of Carthage residents toward Tiede), which both Linklater and Hollandsworth attended. There is one significant omission, however—the possibility (broached in Hollandsworth's article but missing from the film) that Tiede's confession of the murder may have been prompted by the fact that, after the discovery of Nugent's corpse, "deputies had confiscated nearly fifty videotapes from Bernie's house, some showing men involved in illicit acts." Although Tiede being a homosexual is not exactly overlooked in Linklater's film—we hear this euphemistically expressed as gossip that "Bernie was a little light in the loafers"—any hint of an active sex life in Carthage as a gay man is carefully avoided, perhaps because this would complicate the story and its various ramifications well beyond Linklater's own narrative agenda.

Further complications ensued after Tiede was sentenced to life imprisonment for first-degree (premeditated) murder, a sentence that is said to have been prompted largely by Tiede's handwritten confession. In May 2014, based on the argument that, after having been sexually assaulted as a child, Tiede committed the murder during a brief "dissociative episode" brought on by Nugent's abuse of him, Tiede was released on $10,000 bail in the custody of Linklater and allowed to live in his garage apartment in Austin. But almost two years later, in April 2016, Nugent's granddaughter, who had alleged that Linklater's film had unjustly led to Tiede's release, was able to get him retried, and Tiede was returned to prison for a life sentence, which he is currently serving.

Foreground

"WHAT YOU'RE FIXIN' TO SEE IS" and "A TRUE STORY" are the film's first two intertitles, both quaintly decorated in the style of silent movies, with praying hands and creeping vegetation. And the colloquial ring of the first intertitle both qualifies and focuses the didactic ring of the second. Both intertitles punctuate an academic lecture-demonstration by Bernie (Jack Black) on how to make a corpse presentable, a spectacle that is no less a blend of fact and folksy patter ("A little dab will do you"). This prepares us for the third intertitle, "WHO IS BERNIE?," which immediately follows, along with the movie's credits and Bernie robustly singly "Love Lifted Me" along with his car radio as he speeds down a leafy highway, entering and driving through portions of Carthage. This is intercut with shots of various Carthage residents in different locations praising him directly to the camera, before we arrive at Sam's Bar BQ, where inside the premises Sonny Davis delivers his aforementioned illustrated lecture about the separate partitions of Texas—yet another example of factual exposition delivered through flavorsome artifice. As in much of Linklater's other work, what identifies itself as and pretends to be a "story" is mainly a set of characters and a milieu, a celebration of a particular culture and a style of living.

Separating fiction from nonfiction in this volatile mixture is no easy matter. The film's final credits, after a few glimpses of the real-life Bernie and Marge (including a shot of the former in prison, conversing with Jack Black) identifies all the actors with miniature clips, starting with ten professionals (including Jack Black as Bernie, Shirley MacLaine as "Marge" Nugent, and Matthew McConaughey as local district attorney Danny Buck Davidson) before proceeding to thirty-one nonprofessional "townspeople," but it isn't always clear whether the latter are using their real names. (My favorite "townsperson," identified in the credits as "Kay Epperson," is addressed by Bernie/Jack Black as "Lenora" when we see her visiting him in prison.) And we already know from some of the earliest examples that we have of "documentary" and "fiction" cinema—the Lumières staging comical "real-life" events for their cameras, Méliès reenacting "current events" with actors, Flaherty casting his own Eskimo mistress to play Nanook's wife—that the protocols for making clear distinctions often amount to con games, or at the very least intricate mixtures of fact and fancy.

We don't see enough of Bernie Tiede's (first) trial to determine whether the harsh sentencing is the result of evidence for premeditated murder or cultural bias, but Linklater takes some pains to suggest that cultural bias plays a major role, especially when the cross-examination of Bernie/Black by Danny Buck/McConaughey focuses at length on a trip to New York taken by Bernie and Marge and their first-class air tickets, attending *Les Miserables* (grotesquely mispronounced by Danny Buck, correctly pronounced by Bernie), and knowing what wines should be drunk with fish, capped by Danny Buck's declaration, "That takes a lot of money to have culture so much, don't it? To enjoy the finer things in life that you know so much." Coupled with all the cultural activities in Texas that we've previously seen Bernie attending (often with Marge), participating in, and/or promoting or financing—classical music concerts, productions of musicals such as *Guys and Dolls* and *The Music Man* (with Bernie directing and playing leading roles), and a good many funerals, along with many other civic activities—this offers an adroit encapsulation of the American hatred for "art" as a form of social snobbery that Danny

Buck is counting on. Indeed, we're even left with the plausible presumption that it's Bernie's reverence for and support for the fine arts that helps to sentence him to life imprisonment.

Linklater's grasp of this attitude is complicated by a clear fondness for east Texan folkways that can also allow for affectionate satire and ridicule of hyperbole and other excesses. The same ambivalence toward his characters is fully evident in his most recent feature, *Everybody Wants Some!!*, set in 1980, as it is in his other "period" films set in Texas, for example, *Dazed and Confused* (1993, set in 1976) and *The Newton Boys* (1998, set mainly in the 1920s).

Apart from Alaska, Texas is the largest state in the United States, and one of the identifying traits of the country as a whole is a solipsistic conviction that it represents the entire cosmos, leading to the potentially dangerous and disastrous belief that this cosmos consists exclusively of Americans and "failed" Americans—the latter category composed of people who either want to be American or want to destroy America. Within this solipsistic mindset (which can arguably also be found to some degree in other large countries, such as Russia and mainland China), "Texas" is therefore another version of "America" reduced to its (perceived) essence. And "east Texas" is little more than a further refinement of the same concept—which is why both Hollandsworth's article and *Bernie* emphasize that Carthage "made it into the 1995 edition of *The Best 100 Small Towns in America*."

As a humanist with anarchistic impulses, Linklater honors all his characters in different ways, but apart from the magnificence of Jack Black in his multifaceted performance, it is the thirty-one townspeople and their choral role that dominate the proceedings. Indeed, defining Bernie apart from his community becomes an impossible task.

CHAPTER 13

Guy Maddin

The first two pieces in this section were published respectively in the July 3, 2003 issue of the *Chicago Reader* and in their May 14, 2004 issue almost a year later; the third appeared in the Spanish magazine *Found Footage* in March 2019. In terms of both academic and auteurist conventions, this is necessarily and unapologetically an untidy chapter, which seems appropriate for a filmmaker as untidy as Maddin. The first piece also deals with a film that isn't by Maddin and whose considerable interest can't be charted in auteurist terms, and the third piece is about a video with two codirectors that is cross-referenced with Hitchcock's *Vertigo*. Part of what's being addressed here is the fact that Maddin, for all his eccentricity and singularity as a filmmaker, has, like Chantal Akerman, been unusually adept in adjusting and adapting his art to other arts, other artists, and diverse circumstances, including installations.

   The second piece here occasioned one of the few thank-you notes I've received from a filmmaker for a review. I hope both Maddin and those reading this will forgive me for immodestly reproducing his email: "Dear Jonathan: I usually try to avoid setting precedents that violate what should be a no-fly zone between critics and filmmakers, but I must say that your review of *Saddest Music* left me feeling understood at last!!! What a feeling. Thank you for supplying this euphoria. You also win bonus points for the Laura Riding discovery—I always liked her characters' names. George Toles, who is terrified of reading reviews, will be thrilled to see his unsung name given its proper due.

Not only that, you disabled Anthony Lane's stinkbombs. A million thanks, Jonathan!! Warmest, Guy"

For more on Maddin, see my reviews of *Archangel* and *The Heart of the World* in *Essential Cinema: On the Necessity of Film Canons* (2004).

Brilliant Inaccuracies: *Down with Love* and *Dracula: Pages from a Virgin's Diary*

If a more interesting and entertaining Hollywood movie than *Down with Love* has come along this year, I've missed it. *Down with Love*—which has already closed in Chicago—is entertaining thanks to Eve Ahlert and Dennis Drake's clever script, Peyton Reed's mainly assured direction, inventive production and costume design, a musical number behind the final credits I'd happily swap all of *Chicago* for, and even a miscast Renee Zellweger pulling off a difficult climactic monologue. But I was knocked out less by these achievements, which are clearly deliberate, than by the film's authentic weirdness, which is apparently accidental.

One reason I took so long getting to see this movie was the number of friends who assured me it was nothing special. Most of them seemed to go along uncritically with the publicists' claim, echoed by reviewers, that it was a simple point-by-point pastiche of three late-'50s and early '60s comedies starring Rock Hudson, Doris Day, and Tony Randall: *Pillow Talk* (1959), *Lover Come Back* (1961), and *Send Me No Flowers* (1964). These films have never appealed to me in the slightest, though Mark Rappaport did an expert job of unpacking them in his 1992 *Rock Hudson's Home Movies,* just out on DVD.

But *Down with Love* is also an affectionate satire of late-'50s and early '60s studio glitz that often contradicts the pastiche. The filmmakers, who were too young to experience this era themselves, make plenty of errors, starting with a Fox CinemaScope logo (wrong studio and too late for that logo) and the snazzy rainbow credits (too hyperactive for the time). Then we get palatial Manhattan apartments (much more identified with *How to Marry a Millionaire* in 1953 and *The Tender Trap* in 1955) and bubble-gum-colored media blitzes (as in *Funny Face* and *Will Success Spoil Rock Hunter?,* both 1957), and culminating in the visual and verbal double entendres, anti-smoking gags, and overt references to feminism and homosexuality that are more identifiable with subsequent decades, all the way up to the present.

Furthermore, these subjective errors—coming from people too young to have encountered the period directly, characteristically collapsing and scrambling two decades into one, and therefore winding up with a hyperbolic dream of a dream—made the movie more fascinating and touching rather than less. By expressing a yearning for what's perceived (with debatable accuracy) as less cynical and more innocently romantic times, *Down with Love* has a lot to say about today. It also conveys an aching sense of absence that's too definitive to qualify as nostalgia. Nostalgia tends to shrink our image of the past into cozy pocket-size dimensions, something we already know, but this movie expands that image temporally as well as spatially—suggesting that in some ways the past is more sophisticated than the present, even if we can't say exactly how. It hovers ambiguously over a stupid and tacky trio of hypocritical comedies as if they contained awesome and precious secrets, and even though I can't quite swallow that premise as film criticism, I treasure its creative and poetic insights into the present.

Our embrace of technology and planned obsolescence—which remains vital to the further enrichment of the wealthy—condemns us to a myth of continuous progress. Yet we remain haunted by the feeling that we've left something substantial and untapped behind. Historian Eric Hobsbawm recently suggested that people in the nineteenth century had an edge on us in their capacity to distinguish war from peace. Hollywood filmmakers in the supposedly repressive 1950s found more ways to work social criticism into their movies than their counterparts today can manage, and some film directors in the 1920s knew things about their craft and art that the Scorseses, Spielbergs, and Lucases—with all their high-tech equipment—can't begin to fathom.

Winnipeg filmmaker Guy Maddin's work testifies to the notion that the past knows more than the present and that silent cinema is a richer, dreamier, sexier, and more resonant medium than what we're accustomed to seeing in the multiplexes. That may be why everyone I know who's seen his *Dracula: Pages From a Virgin's Diary* is crazy about it. There's been a gratifying expansion of Maddin's loyal band of followers ever since his seven-minute pastiche of silent Russian cinema, *The Heart of the World*, became a hit at the Toronto Film Festival two years ago, followed by its release along with his four previous features (*Tales From the Gimli Hospital, Archangel, Careful,* and *Twilight of the Ice Nymphs*) on two well-produced DVDs.

So Maddin, who will have another feature out later this year, is well on his way to becoming a household name like David Lynch. But if his *Dracula*, which opened last week at the Music Box, is reduced to its standard publicity labels—as *Down with Love* was—it could be shunned. A silent black-and-white film of a ballet based on Bram Stoker's novel and performed to portions of Mahler's first two symphonies—who could possibly want to see that? Warning signals are virtually programmed to go off in our heads when we hear terms like "silent," "black-and-white," and "ballet." In addition, horror buffs might blanch at the thought of ballet and Mahler, while ballet and Mahler fans could be put off by the prospect of a vampire film.

All of these elements are present in *Dracula*—to a point. Discreet sound effects make the movie not quite silent. The selective use of color—red blood, green dollar bills (American not Canadian), yellow intertitles, a blue cross, a rainbow-tinged mist—makes it not quite black-and-white. And even though this is a film of a ballet, it isn't in any usual way a ballet film. It would be more precise and telling to call *Dracula* simply a Guy Maddin movie, even though it's a commissioned work. Maddin has admitted that his lack of interest in both ballet and *Dracula* made him hesitate before accepting the assignment and that part of what finally persuaded him was his need for money, the dollar bills he makes so much of. That this is thoroughly a Maddin movie in spite of everything is its major triumph. Its secondary triumph is that it peels away the usual associations we have with black-and-white and silent cinema, ballet, Mahler, and *Dracula*, making inspired use of all of them.

Maddin has also indicated that even though he was bored by the Stoker novel, he was intrigued by the elements involving male problems with sexuality—including jealousy, rivalry, and paranoia, especially in relation to race, nationality, and ethnicity. This is apparent at the outset of the film, when graphic images of blood spilling across Europe are accompanied by such intertitles as "East Coast of England 1897," "Immigrants!" "Others!" "From Other Lands," "From the East!" and "From the Sea!" Maddin makes this theme even more nuanced by having Dracula played by a Chinese-Canadian, Zhang Wei-qiang, who periodically evokes the late French-Italian New Wave actor Pierre Clementi. This reading of the novel may, as critic Mark Peranson has suggested, be more faithful than any other we've had to date. (Most adaptations derive from Deane and

Balderston's play rather than the novel, and only Francis Coppola's splashy and underrated 1992 *Bram Stoker's Dracula* rivals Maddin's as a meditation on the historical period.) That Maddin films his dancers in none of the conventional ways—often moving in for close shots and sometimes using as many jump cuts as Godard did in *Breathless*—doesn't so much interfere with our appreciation of these dancers' moves as reconfigure it, assigning it a fresh kind of poetics.

Would it be correct, then, to call Maddin's works experimental? That's what the National Society of Film Critics did when it awarded prizes for the year's best experimental film to *Archangel* in 1991 and *The Heart of the World* in 2000. Maddin and NPR critic Pat Dowell have expressed some polite skepticism about the label. Having been part of the NSFC faction that lobbied for the prizes, I can say that we used that category because we knew it was the only way our organization could ever honor the films. Why? Because critics are just as hemmed in by packaging as publicists. It's frustrating that we all go to movies in search of something new, but when it comes to defining newness in the mainstream marketplace, the only acceptable ploy is to use old categories—thereby repudiating whatever is new and undefined. Simply put, the meager imaginations and resources of publicists and their mouthpieces, including critics, define the limits of what we're directed to see.

Bearing this in mind, Maddin's fans, like Maddin himself, might be seen as smugglers attempting to widen the possibilities of pleasure in movies whenever and however they can. Tapping the richness of 1920s filmmaking under the mask of irony (a principal tool of subterfuge in the present climate), *Dracula* offers a feast of rapid editing, fast lap dissolves, fade-outs, whiteouts, blackouts, tinting, superimpositions, irises, slurred motion, stop motion, and slow motion, along with the delectable textures of light, mist, snow, human flesh, vegetation, and Victorian upholstery. Yet it isn't so bound by the technical parameters of '20s pictorial film art that it can't make fruitful use of Super-8 footage and digital effects. That it's principally in black and white and mainly silent makes it more expressive and sensual rather than less—a premise that may seem hard to swallow because we've been trained to fetishize state-of-the-art technology involving color and sound.

In fact, Maddin makes better use of digital effects than most Hollywood-blockbuster wizards because he's an artisan, not a factory worker—the mark of his hand is everywhere. And this only makes it easier for viewers to enter and get lost in his fantasy. A good indication of the kind of art he's aiming for can be found in an appendix to Caelum Vatnsdal's helpful and engaging book *Kino Delirium: The Films of Guy Maddin* (2000), in a text Maddin wrote titled "A Letter in Severe Terms Suggesting a Four-Point Manifesto for Better Movies." Let me cite only the second point, devoted to actors:

> a) The studies of physiognomy and phrenology should be primary considerations in the casting of actors. Head bumps have long been ignored by the industry.
> b) Actors should have expressive fingers, real or artificial, for fingers represent up to ten more tongues, each capable of expressing a thought or a throb. The first finger—the tongue—should be used a lot less.
> c) Walking actors have forgotten how to walk. All actors should walk with latent or overt purpose, and cram a little poetry into their gaits while they're at it.
> d) Sitting or lying-down actors should sit or lie down with poetry. Modern directors have garbed such actors in prose for at least five decades. How they have done this is a mystery, for the sitting and lying-down actors suggest anything but prose—dreams knit within their heads; looms vigorously producing dreamy tapestries fling their stray threads into the air above these heads; the stray threads fall at random onto the floor in children's patterns of adult schemes, little primitive scraps of sordid wish fulfillment. The air and ground surrounding these actors should be strewn with mysteries, tangles, shreds, rent aromas, half-committed murders and doilies.
> e) Because of the above, the sleeping actor is the best actor—the poetically and psychologically truest representation of the human—and should be used as often as the sitting, lying-down, walking, running and flying actors.

The neosurrealist flavor of these directives lets us know that Maddin is no foe of the industrial film studio and what it can produce. More precisely, he belongs in the tradition of such obsessional, poetic tale spinners and studio craftsmen as Erich von Stroheim, F. W. Murnau, Josef von Sternberg, Jacques Tourneur, and Michael Powell, who bend public materials toward private ends, taking us along for a feverish theme-park ride.

Crying in Their Beer: *The Saddest Music in the World*

> To Guy Maddin, every contemporary story that feels true is at bottom an amnesia story.
> —screenwriter George Toles

> When all the archetypes burst out shamelessly, we plumb Homeric profundity. Two clichés make us laugh but a hundred clichés move us because we sense dimly that the clichés are talking among themselves, celebrating a reunion.
> —Umberto Eco, "Casablanca: Cult Movies and Intertextual Collage"

Guy Maddin has reached a new expressive plateau with *The Saddest Music in the World*. It reprises the key elements of his previous work—the look and feel of scratchy late silents and early talkies (mainly black and white, with a few lush interludes in two-strip Technicolor) and themes involving Canada, amnesia and other forms of repression, war and wartime loss, oedipal conflict, mutilation, and unabated romantic despair—all touched with deadpan comedy and melodramatic excess. New to the mix are two glamorous international stars (Isabella Rossellini and Maria de Medeiros), some of the accoutrements of a Hollywood musical, a more clearly conceived and executed narrative, more apparent emotion, and a hilariously apt satirical allegory about Canada, the United States, and the rest of the world.

As usual with Maddin, I can't even begin to furnish a synopsis without sounding hyperbolic and slightly breathless. The film is set in 1933, at the height of the Depression, in Winnipeg, Maddin's hometown. Beer baroness Lady Port-Huntly (Rossellini), whose name appears to have been suggested by Laura Riding's great '30s story "Reality as Port Huntlady," announces a contest to find the "saddest music in the world" as a way to promote her brew. Hoping the imminent end of prohibition in the United States will create a new demand for her beer and inspired by the *London Times*' selection of Winnipeg for three years in a row as the "world capital of sorrow," the self-styled Beer Queen of the Prairie invites musicians from around the world to compete for the $25,000 prize, appointing herself the sole judge. She even has a slogan: "If you're sad and like beer, I'm your lady."

Two countries compete at each preliminary session: alternating musical snatches are interrupted by Port-Huntly, operating a loud buzzer that suggests a tacky TV-game-show device, and the winner gets to slide down a chute into a huge vat of beer. Meanwhile radio announcers ad-lib about the proceedings as if they were sports commentators. When Siam competes with Mexico, one of them remarks, "Nobody can beat the Siamese when it comes to dignity, cats, or twins." Then Serbia goes up against Scotland, Canada against Africa, America against Spain. And it's not surprising given Maddin's flair for melodrama that when Serbia vies with America in the final playoff it's also brother against brother.

What's sad about Port-Huntly is that she's missing her legs, amputated years earlier by an alcoholic surgeon named Fyodor (David Fox) after an auto accident caused by her lover at the time, Fyodor's younger son, Chester Kent (*Kids in the Hall*'s Mark McKinney), who subsequently emigrated to the United States to become a flashy Broadway producer. (The character gets his name from the Broadway producer played by James Cagney in 1933's *Footlight Parade*.) But there are even sadder cases. Fyodor, who loved Port-Huntly when he was drunkenly sawing off her good leg and then her mangled one and loves her still, enters the contest under the Canadian banner, playing "The Red Maple Leaves" on an upended piano keyboard to commemorate Canadian casualties in World War I. Chester, down on his luck but indefatigably cheerful, is competing as an American, accompanied by his nymphomaniac and amnesiac girlfriend Narcissa (Medeiros). And Fyodor's older son, Roderick (Ross McMillan)—a Gloomy Gus cellist who emigrated to Serbia and has returned to compete as a Serbian, hidden behind an enormous black veil—is grieving inconsolably for his dead son (whose heart he keeps in a glass jar, floating in his own tears) and his missing wife, who went into an amnesiac funk when their son died; she of course turns out to be Narcissa.

"I'm not an American—I'm a nymphomaniac," Narcissa announces to Fyodor, now driving a streetcar, shortly after she and Chester arrive in town. In an equally goofy non sequitur Roderick eventually confronts her with their tragic Serbian past by asking, "Nine million dead, Narcissa—and you won't even remember one?" By contrast, when he recounts the source of one of his childhood grudges against Chester, his father reproaches him with, "Can't you ever forget anything?" Compounding the grotesquerie, Fyodor, still hoping to gain the affection of Port-Huntly, makes prosthetic legs for her out of glass, filled to the brim with her beer. But her heart still belongs to Chester.

Chester—refusing to admit to any sadness of his own, even when a Gypsy fortune-teller on the outskirts of Winnipeg forecasts doom for him—is determined to offer the sadness needed for the competition "with sass and pizzazz." He spells out his can-do philosophy early on: "Sadness is just happiness turned on its ass. It's all showbiz." This includes playing gigolo to Port-Huntly and buying up the disqualified musical acts and incorporating them into his own multicultural showstopper—a re-creation, in color, of the "Alaskan Kayak Tragedy of 1898": East Indian chorines in short-skirted blue Inuit outfits spear *papier-maché* fish while dancing to the rousing strains of "California, Here I Come," performed on banjo, panpipe, accordion, clarinet, violin, and sitar, with Chester conducting. Port-Huntly is so delighted with her new glass legs that she decides to make her first public appearance with them in the middle of this number; standing on a rotating glacier, cheerfully indifferent to conflict-of-interest issues, she sets the stage for an appropriately apocalyptic finale.

As more than one Canadian critic has noted, that Chester is Canadian and not American—despite his accent—only enhances the satirical implications of this setup. To be Canadian and consumed with self-hatred means to struggle with belonging to an American colony, existentially if not literally—the colonizing process that matters most is internal. It's worth adding that just as the success of Port-Huntly's musical Olympics will be determined by the American market—a fact underlined by the responses of an elderly American couple following it on the radio—the success of *The Saddest Music in the World* will depend largely on the response of American audiences.

More generally, to be Canadian means to be somewhat lost in terms of identity, which is why Maddin keeps returning to the theme of amnesia—though remembering everything can be just as much of a curse in his tormented universe as remembering nothing. (When Narcissa appears in Chester's first competitive music number, warbling "Swing Low, Sweet Chariot," the smell of her roses sends Roderick into a traumatic, red-tinted flashback, and he relives her telling him of their son's death.)

Not counting his 2002 ballet film *Dracula: Pages From a Virgin's Diary,* this is the first story idea Maddin didn't come up with himself. Instead, an unfilmed script by novelist Kazuo Ishiguro served as the starting point for

Maddin and his usual screenwriting partner (and former teacher) George Toles; an interview with Maddin and Toles in the fall 2003 *Cinema Scope* reveals that the original was set in London in the '90s and had nothing to do with Canada. Maddin notes that he eliminated the political allegory of the original, whose concerns "were almost entirely about the Third World [countries], comparing them almost to street beggars the way they desperately need charity from the 'have' nations." Toles, who hails from America but lives in Winnipeg, concedes that "there is something to the notion of competitive sadness, people trading away their tragic histories for image, and falsifying genuine tragedy." He adds, "Also, I'm a powerful Bush hater."

Yet in his essay about working with Maddin that concludes his 2001 collection *A House Made of Light: Essays on the Art of Film,* Toles speaks eloquently about the advantages of writing scripts intuitively: "It is frighteningly easy for an evolving narrative to perish under the weight of excessive premeditation or analytic control—the wrong kind of knowing. The imagination is like an oversensitive friend, who can regard any form of inquiry into its secrets as a terrible slight, and who can go into hiding without any warning when it feels betrayed." This suggests that the implicit commentary in *The Saddest Music in the World* about the American colonization of Canada is more felt than intellectualized, making it all the more persuasive.

Shot on a variety of film formats that were blended to create a luxuriant, dreamlike, and otherworldly expressionist atmosphere in 35mm, *The Saddest Music in the World* develops the ongoing Maddin project's affectionate form of ridicule, making it comparable to Jack Smith's *Flaming Creatures*. This is most apparent in the way it evokes, develops, and celebrates more than mocks some of the emotional extremes of commercial cinema—making the term "camp" inappropriate, despite the comedy. For instance, some of the musical numbers—Chester's showstopper, a commercial for Port-Huntly's beer with a '30s montage sequence—have parodic aspects, but others include ingenious variations on Jerome Kern's "The Song Is You" that give this plaintive anthem its full emotional resonance. Even the postmodernist and slightly anachronistic way Maddin sometimes mixes his visual effects—such as using a deep-focus '40s noir composition in the midst of a '30s setting with the mazelike *bric-à-brac* of a Josef von Sternberg interior—has an emotional logic that shows him to be anything but a dilettante. The grief expressed in the story is too keenly felt to be a target of derision; the facts may be cruel and monstrous, but the laughter provoked by them is almost always sympathetic and tender.

The mutilation of Port-Huntly seems inspired by some of the silent films of Lon Chaney, which Maddin wrote about in the winter 2003 issue of *Cinema Scope*. Chaney was a mainstream "A-list performer" with about forty starring film roles during the '20s, among them a dozen features that Maddin dubbed "disfigurement allegories," in which amputated limbs or other physical abnormalities reflect or stand in for "profoundly painful inner wounds." Maddin writes about Chaney in language that reeks of the mime of silent cinema and the extreme emotions it often trafficked in: "Riding the extreme parabolas of passion permitted by the wild genres in which he worked, he compelled his countenance to seethe, simmer, glower, yearn, lust, and quake in compound permutations of startling virtuosity, creating readable and emotionally complex sentences with the syntax of his features."

The New Yorker's Anthony Lane recently saw fit to scoff at Maddin for being a member of what he called the "derrière-garde"—a curious cause for complaint given that it's difficult to imagine Lane seeing an avant-garde film and almost impossible to imagine him reviewing one. The truth is, it's Maddin's great triumph that he's a traditionalist to the core, a trait that might seem odd only because the mainstream rarely sees film tradition going back further than three decades—for most of today's young cinephiles "the movies" started with *Jaws, The Godfather,* and *Star Wars*. But Maddin's style traces the art all the way back to the nineteenth century, so that, to paraphrase Marlene Dietrich in *Touch of Evil,* "It's so old it's new." In this respect, he's much closer to Roderick than Narcissa—condemned to remember in a universe ruled by amnesiacs.

The Green Fog and the Maddin Mist

As a critical commentary on cinematic depictions of San Francisco, Guy Maddin's *The Green Fog,* which he codirected with Evan Johnson and Galen Johnson, differs from Thom Andersen's *Los Angeles Plays Itself* not only in terms of its California city, employment of a voiceover (*The Green Fog* has none), and its running time (Maddin's 63 minutes versus Andersen's 170), but above all in its essential subject matter. Apart from the fact that Andersen habitually deals with found footage and Maddin usually doesn't work with found footage at all, Andersen's concern is basically with a film's factual and physical accuracy and its sociopolitical aspects, whereas Maddin, a perpetual student of romantic melodrama, is preoccupied with its audiovisual rhetoric. But both filmmakers are also highly knowledgeable and sophisticated film critics, so given the absence of any voiceover and the initial avoidance of any dialogue, there's an unmistakable irony in Maddin pointing directly to sound in his almost subliminal opening shot: a black-and-white close-up of a hand quickly twisting a recorder's dial backward from "talk" to "listen." But what we have to listen to usually turns out to be quite minimal, which is part of Maddin's point. Indeed, *The Green Fog* is so rich in its critical notations about what romantic melodramas and mystery stories do to us, and how they do this, that I've opted to examine only a little more than the first half of it. (For clip-spotting cinephiles, the video does the courtesy of identifying all its film sources, from *Greed* to *Star Trek IV* to *The Ten Commandments* to *The Lady from Shanghai* to *The Love Bug,* in the giddy closing credits.)

After the glancing reference to sound, we get diverse visual tropes, most of them in color, beginning with a brief zoom to a house front, then a reverse zoom away from a handcuffed male spectator (Rock Hudson) eating a sandwich (over which is superimposed a red filter and the title "Prologue"), accompanied by a melodramatic burst of music—apparently a clip from the 1970s TV series *McMillan & Wife,* with the music imported from elsewhere. (In fact, it's an original score by Jacob Garchik, performed by the Kronos Quartet.) While this aggressive music continues at full volume, this is followed by the opening of black-and-white theatrical curtains to a color screen image of a grotesque marionette that is being watched in a dark office by two male spectators while a third man, looking in the opposite direction, holds them at gunpoint (apparently footage from the same scene in *McMillan & Wife*), then more images of male spectators (including Rock Hudson again) and/or the words "San Francisco" appearing on a street sign (in black and white) and on a map (in color), comprising an implied series of angles and reverse angles culled from diverse sources. We next cut to an outdoor loudspeaker and a succession of diverse listeners of both sexes and various ages before finally settling on the title substance—a green fog hovering over the Earth, as viewed from a space satellite, dissolving into a Bay bridge smothered in the same green miasma, followed by many other San Francisco settings enveloped in what appears the same green murk thanks to a green filter, and sometimes shown in slow motion. In effect, Maddin seems to be doctoring a good many clips by others to transform all of them into a single, continuous Maddin set—at least until we see Karl Malden start and then fail to say something, over which is superimposed a red filter and the title "CHAPTER I/WEEKEND AT ERNIE'S." In short, it's quite a bewildering succession of disparate clips accompanied by the same aggressive music and, eventually, once the green fog appears, a few ambient or muffled sounds (such as footsteps).

And here's the rub: *The Green Fog* is Guy Maddin's cockeyed "remake" of Alfred Hitchcock's *Vertigo,* working almost entirely with clips from other films set in San Francisco. "Ernie's" is a fashionable, expensive local restaurant that appears several times in *Vertigo,* where John "Scotty" Ferguson, as if to prove his populist bonafides as a well-to-do retiree, seems to be practically the only male customer not wearing a tuxedo. The implied non sequitur of spending a weekend at such a place—derived from a deflating allusion to an awful gross-out comedy, 1989's *Weekend at Bernie's*—is only one of Maddin's many irreverent curveballs. Another is the complete absence of any shred of Bernard Herrmann's haunting and sumptuous *Vertigo* score, perhaps the principal means by which Hitchcock persuades viewers to overlook or otherwise bypass the film's emotional confusions and multiple plot improbables (such as the fact that Scotty doesn't ever see the body of Madeleine after her alleged suicide, even at an inquest or funeral). As Herrmann also demonstrated in his final film score, for *Taxi Driver,* the inordinate capacity of his music to override script flaws is an essential ingredient in his arsenal, and quite apart from Maddin's possible desire to avoid copyright infringement, removing any vestige of Herrmann's score allows us to see the romantic and melodramatic trappings of *Vertigo* far more nakedly, without window dressing.

And there isn't any green fog to be found anywhere in *Vertigo:* at most and at best, we hear a foghorn once or twice, and there's a very briefly glimpsed green mist that Kim Novak emerges from at one of the film's climactic moments—arguably *the* climactic moment—when she advances toward the camera and we discover that the transformation of Judy back into Madeleine via clothes and hairdo, as ordered and then as perceived by "Scotty" Ferguson, hoping to resurrect the supposedly dead Madeleine, with whom he's still hopelessly in love, is finally complete. This is precisely the point at which Scotty's mastery of his own *mise en scène* in "reproducing" Madeleine, which matches precisely the mastery and the *mise en scène* of Hitchcock, achieves its dreamlike apotheosis, in a moment that is far more dreamlike than Scotty's subsequent nightmare, illustrated with jazzy animated graphics (some of them green) and rear-projection. (Perhaps most dreamlike of all is the way the camera seems to turn 360 degrees around Scotty and Madeleine/Judy passionately kissing and embracing one another while the camera's angle on them remains frontal—a miraculous form of hocus pocus that Carl Dreyer once employed with a Jesus freak and a little girl in *Ordet,* and which many of the so-called Movie Brats such as Brian De Palma and Paul Schrader have also imitated after Hitchcock appropriated his own version of it, the latter most recently in *First Reformed.*)

Yet there isn't any actual fog anywhere in Hitchcock's picture, even if there *is* a great deal of signifying green: in costumes and décor, Madeleine's car, the water into which she and Scotty plunge in San Francisco Bay, the fireside cushions that Scotty brings for Madeleine to sit on in his flat, Scotty's sweater in the same scene, and much later, Judy's dress when Scotty first sees her on the street, and the neon light shining outside her hotel room's window. We even hear the word "green" several times in the dialogue, in locations outside San Francisco (the ancient sequoias and the Mission), in scenes where the word seems to signify both life and death.

Fog denotes emotional confusion and physical displacement—two Maddin specialties whenever he's dressing and otherwise contriving his own filmed romantic-melodramatic fictions, pursuing a game of smoke and mirrors and evoking fugue-like moods that are the exact opposites of Andersen's interest in clarity and placement. Hitchcock himself mainly enters this metaphysical realm only when he focuses on a cemetery or on sequoias, or when he briefly bathes Judy/Madeleine in that hallucinatory green mist. But for Maddin, mists or fogs of uncertainty and estrangement are always the main bill of fare.

"CHAPTER I" ushers us into the remake proper—mostly the opening action sequence of a rooftop chase, but reduced absurdly to the rhetoric of such a sequence more than to the action itself, crosscutting repeatedly between a man climbing up a building's exterior ladder and a bar or rail in the blue darkness waiting to be grasped, presumably by Scotty's hand, over frantic musical punctuations by strings. When this action continues on the rooftop with several different actors in the daytime and intermittently in black and white, it becomes even clearer that fictional consistency and continuity are being sacrificed to some abstract notion of action syntax.

Even Sidney Poitier and an overhead helicopter, from two other movies, are incongruously stitched into the linear progression. Once Vincent Price from Albert Zugsmith's delirious *Confessions of an Opium Eater* teeters on the roof's edge in slow motion, we've clearly entered the terrain of that B-movie's dream logic, so that when someone unidentifiable from another film clip falls to his death, it's a detail that could just as well have been cut from the same cloth.

The "dialogue" scene that follows, presumably standing in for Stewart's first scene with Barbara Bel Geddes—between Joseph Cotten cutting flowers on a high terrace and an actress I don't recognize—retains only the moments when the two are about to speak, intercut with various short black-and-white clips to illustrate Scotty's vertigo trauma, and his subsequent meeting with Gavin Elster is represented by still another actor being thrown into a plush office where he's promptly tape recorded by the Elster figure—although once again, the actual talk gets edited out. By the time we get to "Ernie's," we're witnessing a string of non sequiturs in the form of grimacing reaction shots from even more ludicrous replacements for Scotty, Madeleine, and Elster. Once again, and for most of *The Green Fog*, we're given all the physical accoutrements of dialogue without any words being uttered, a kind of verbal coitus interruptus that yields most of the style and flourish of dramatic conversation minus any of the content. (The first time "real" dialogue is heard in *The Green Fog*, more than sixteen minutes into the film, is in another part of the same *McMillan & Wife* scene, when a film projector breaks down and Hudson remarks, "It's the trouble with that old film"—a neat equation of "baring the device" with dismantling the device. And a few minutes later, we hear an offscreen prayer while we watch a teenage boy empty a beer can into a bouquet of flowers on a grave, from which a puff of green fog emerges—making an almost equivalent deconstructive point.) Like the mockery of conventional match cuts that approximates Scotty's tailing of Madeleine as various cars follow various other cars down assorted San Francisco streets, sometimes passing locations that are familiar from *Vertigo* or other movies, we're getting the bare bones of thriller and mystery mechanics without any of the thrills or mysteries, in contradistinction to all the musical signals. And when we see Karl Malden enter a florist shop, and converse (again wordlessly) with the florist, it seems appropriate that the piece of paper the florist shows to him shows us the green fog yet again, Maddin's signifier of the genre's rhetoric of mystification.

For some of the Hitchcock aficionados who helped to replace *Citizen Kane* with *Vertigo* in the last ten-best poll of *Sight and Sound,* the affectionate ridicule of *The Green Fog* may seem like an act of sacrilege, especially when we get a panoply of San Francisco cathedrals that are treated as interchangeably as all the cars and streets. But it might also be argued that Maddin's apparent scorn is in fact a kind of impious critical appreciation for all the tricks of romantic mystification that he and Hitchcock have in common. We have to bear in mind that seen in 2018, sixty years after its first release, *Vertigo* is already a kind of scrapbook—not only a scrapbook of famous and obscure locations in San Francisco and environs (which is part of what Chris Marker, the poet laureate of scrapbooks, is so fascinated with, paralleling some of Thom Andersen's investment in Los Angeles), but also a scrapbook of Hitchcock Moments, past and future. A policeman reaching out his hand for a dangling Scotty to grab in the opening action sequence anticipates Cary Grant reaching out his hand for a dangling Eva Marie Saint to grab on Mount Rushmore in *North by Northwest* a year later. James Stewart recovering afterward from his (unseen) accident, wearing a corset instead of his leg in a cast and complaining about being unable to scratch his itches, inevitably takes us back to Stewart in *Rear Window;* his gliding trip through a cemetery looks forward to Bruce Dern's visit to one in *Family Plot;* and Scotty's near-catatonia after Madeleine's apparent suicide offers many resemblances to Vera Miles's near-catatonia in *The Wrong Man*. Even more, one might say that a scrapbook entry becomes a textbook example when it comes to Hitchcock; the aforementioned 360-degree camera spin around Stewart and Novak that Hitchcock arguably cribbed and adapted from Dreyer has become a classic romantic cliché for De Palma, Schrader, and countless others. Which doesn't mean that the underlying emotions are necessarily inauthentic or unfelt, only that they're sufficiently shopworn to allow for a critical reading.

So even if we periodically lose track of which particular *Vertigo* scenes are being referenced, as I did, the overall intention to make its passions and conflicted emotions look, sound, and feel as absurd and as ridiculous as possible continues unabated. If we haven't seen *Vertigo* at all, I think we can still appreciate Maddin's unpacking of all its romantic mystifications and their various forms of punctuation—that is to say, their green fog.

Although Maddin appears to use a few glancing clips from *Vertigo* itself—such as the red flower petals that Madeleine drops into San

Francisco Bay—he makes sure to deflate them immediately, such as cutting next not to Madeleine dropping into the same Bay but to a black-and-white clip of a man falling with an oafish yelp into a swimming pool, and proceeding next to an underwater deep-sea-diver rescue, complete with snorkel gear, to replace Scotty's rescue of Madeleine. And when it comes to Madeleine's recovery in Scotty's flat, after having been implicitly stripped naked by him before she regains consciousness, Maddin replaces Novak with Gina Lollobrigida in a slip, already awake, and adds a whole subplot about their conversation being secretly recorded on reel-to-reel tape by operatives, even though characteristically none of their bedroom conversation is heard, apart from the male actor saying, "That makes two of us." This is because for Maddin, it's only their portentously adoring or puzzled looks at one another that really count—to which he adds another dollop of rising green fog.

The audio surveillance may remind us that Scotty and Madeleine's budding romance is in fact adulterous, a fact that Hitchcock either avoids or else makes even sexier by refusing to mention it (much as he refrains from showing Scotty removing Madeleine's clothing). A master throughout *Vertigo* of the Kuleshov experiment, Hitchcock knows that the best way to represent romantic longings is by omission, while Maddin makes eccentric omissions of his own to force us to consider what it is we might be missing—and might be helping to construct as a consequence.

After the tape gets rewound, and Maddin shows us the same bedroom non-conversation in rapid reverse, Rock Hudson, one of the operatives, expresses it best. John Shuck, another operative, asks, "What are we looking for, sir?" and Hudson, still the consummate film analyst, confidently replies, "I don't know. But at this point I'll take anything."

CHAPTER 14

Elaine May

The first of the articles written below was commissioned by the *Los Angeles Times* and ran in their June 14, 1987 Calendar section. For readers who might wonder how I could have ever gotten such an assignment, I should point out that in this period, the paper was running anti-*Ishtar* articles practically every day over several weeks, so I assume that my contrary position must have had some interest for them strictly as a novelty.

The second piece here was written for the DVD of *Mikey and Nicky* that was released by Home Vision Entertainment in 2004.

As May herself revealed to me when we subsequently met in Bologna on June 27, 2010, much of the biographical information that circulates about her (including my erroneous identification of her hometown) is false, mainly owing to her own idle inventions to the press over the years. She told me that she was actually born in Chicago, and further suggested that the story about her growing up in the Yiddish theater is not strictly accurate either.

Elaine and Erich

In all of Elaine May's films, one encounters a will to power, a witty genius for subversion and caricature, and a dark, corrosive vision that recalls the example of Erich von Stroheim. The legendary Austrian-born director who started out, like May, as an aggressive actor ("The Man You Love to Hate"), Stroheim the filmmaker was known throughout the '20s for his intransigence and extravagance—what one studio head termed his "footage fetish."

The thematic and stylistic parallels between May and Stroheim are equally striking. Broadly speaking, *A New Leaf* is her *Blind Husbands*—a bold first film about ferocious, cynical flirtation, with the writer-director in the lead part. The Miami of *The Heartbreak Kid* matches the Monte Carlo of Foolish Wives; the squalor and hysteria of *Mikey and Nicky* hark back to *Greed*. *Ishtar* is May's *The Merry Widow*—a piece of puff pastry enclosing a bitter almond. In all four films by each director, the personality of the film maker is markedly stronger than that of the producer involved.

If *Mikey and Nicky* and *Greed* are the ultimate testaments of a bleak vision of capitalism—just as the preceding *Heartbreak Kid* and *Foolish Wives* are more opulent celebrations of chicanery (on the part of director and hero alike)—*Ishtar* and *The Merry Widow* are closer to being pacts with the Devil. Made in each case by a compulsive perfectionist in love with retakes, and set in imaginary countries, they buckle into a blockbuster format at the outset, complete with familiar plot and superstars, and then proceed to subvert it from within.

Neither film is a masterpiece but there's no indication that either is trying to be one. The idea is merely to turn a war horse into something personal, perverse, and enjoyable.

■ ■ ■

None of this is supposed to matter. Insofar as the Reagan era reduces everything to business, Stroheim remains a villain in this town. We were reminded of this at the Oscars ceremony, when Richard Dreyfuss presenting an Irving G. Thalberg Memorial Award to Steven Spielberg, praised Thalberg's "courage" in firing Stroheim. He might have added that this exemplary act also entailed reducing *Greed* from twenty-two reels to ten—and burning the rest, according to Stroheim, for the forty-three cents worth of silver.

It isn't surprising that *Ishtar* is being weighed for its own potential silver. A publicist told me she caused some embarrassment simply by laughing at a press showing. A comedy costing $40 million-plus is no laughing matter.

■ ■ ■

Because my own investment in *Ishtar* consists of my respect for May's work and the price of a ticket, I can freely express my gratitude that

Warren Beatty, the producer and co-star, will never be the recipient of a Thalberg Award. Whatever else one could say about him, he doesn't play by the rules. In fact, he allowed the immensely gifted May to write and direct a film with a budget higher than one enjoyed by any other woman.

And May has rewarded him with a dopey comedy that manages to charm its audience while exposing the idiocy of America's role in the third world—from Irangate to Contragate and back again—without preaching or polemics. Not a sermon like *Salvador* or *Platoon,* which projects adolescent macho metaphysics about Good and Evil onto the same subject, not a genocidal romp like the Indiana Jones epics. Just a lighthearted farce about two aging misfits who combine show biz and politics with the same square and dimwitted charisma as our current president.

Like such equally obsessive filmmaking eccentrics as Jerry Lewis and John Cassavetes, May lavishes her attention on the unreclaimable rather than the conventionally heroic. But she always finds a surprising degree of heroism and humanity in these figures nevertheless, from her own Lewis-inspired performance as a klutzy horticulturist in *A New Leaf* to her inept innocents abroad in *Ishtar*. With Stroheim, she shares a knack for exploiting unexpected facets of actors, then pushing them to extremes. The former turned Zasu Pitts into a tragedian for *Greed;* May turned the usually sheepish Hoffman into both a stud and a maniacally jibbering auctioneer in *Ishtar*.

"Telling the truth can be a dangerous business," Beatty and Hoffman sing in *Ishtar*—a truism that May's career (like Stroheim's) amply illustrates. Stuck with a conventional Neil Simon script in *The Heartbreak Kid* and forbidden by contract to alter a word, she wickedly transformed the entire story by making the eponymous hero (Charles Grodin) and his newlywed wife (Jeannie Berlin) Jewish—thereby making the former's lunge after Cybill Shepherd during a Miami honeymoon a good deal more provocative. After exploring the cruelties of marriage in her first two movies, she has turned to male bonding in the second two, with equally paranoid overtones—a tragedy, then a comedy about mutually betrayed friendship.

The personal nature of May's work is more than just a matter of alluding to her hometown (Philadelphia) in one gag of *Ishtar* or reminding us of Mike Nichols's *The Graduate* (by way of Hoffman and Simon & Garfunkel) in another. Significantly, the stars of *Mikey and Nicky,* Cassavetes and Peter Falk, like those of *Ishtar,* are her contemporaries.

Her extraordinary capacity to identify with the loutishness of the former characters and the stupidity of the latter ones suggests an autocritique of deep and complex proportions. If *Ishtar* allows her to continue with this work—hopefully yielding her *Wedding March, Queen Kelly,* and *Walking Down Broadway* (Stroheim's last three films as director)—then this is money well spent.

Mikey and Nicky

Thanks to an appointment book, I can pinpoint that the first time I saw *Mikey and Nicky* was on January 7, 1977, at New York's Little Carnegie. The experience was a shock. In contrast to *A New Leaf* (1971) and *The Heartbreak Kid* (1972)—Elaine May's two previous features, both slick (if caustic) Hollywood comedies—this was a harsh gangster drama in drab urban locations, and, even stranger, a near-facsimile of John Cassavetes's raw independent features, costarring Cassavetes himself as Nicky and one of his regulars, Peter Falk, as Mikey. The editing was full of continuity errors, the garrulous performances free-wheeling and seemingly full of improvisations (as I then wrongly assumed Cassavetes's own features were). But the brutal force of an alternately nurtured and betrayed friendship between two small-time crooks over one long night in Philadelphia was so ferocious that it left me shaken as well as bewildered.

The second time I saw the film was in 1980, when I programmed it for "Buried Treasures" at the Toronto Film Festival; this inadvertently became the world premiere of the film's final version. The film looked even stronger, but most of the continuity errors had magically vanished. It was only later that I discovered that the original release version wasn't May's final cut but a cobbled-together version put out by Paramount. It was released after a dispute between the studio and the writer-director about the two years she'd already spent editing the 1.4 million feet of footage she'd shot, which culminated in her psychoanalyst helping her to remove some of the reels and hiding them somewhere in Connecticut. According to Janet Coleman—who reports these bizarre details in her history of improvisational comedy, *The Compass* (Alfred A. Knopf, 1990)—one can start to appreciate the sheer mass of the footage involved if one considers that 475,000 feet were shot for *Gone With the Wind*.

A friend who'd worked for May at the time told me she'd been editing the film in all sorts of different ways, and the way she'd been pursuing when the studio took the footage away from her was to splice together all the best line readings without paying any heed to continuity. And my misimpression that the film was partially improvised was also corrected; the script revealed that virtually all the dialogue had been written in advance.

In fact, *Mikey and Nicky* had started out as a play, and according to Coleman, May had already been working on a play with that title in Chicago back in 1954. There was also some reason to believe that the plot was inspired by an incident involving her older brother, Louis Berlin. And there are other likely personal references. As was noted by Stanley Kauffmann in 1977—who called *Mikey and Nicky* "the best film that I know by an American woman"—the film's title echoes the name of May's longtime associate Mike Nichols, with whom she'd formed a famous comic duo. (More recently Nichols has employed her as a writer when he directed *The Birdcage* and *Primary Colors*.) Even a detail in a speech by Mikey toward the end of the film—about his kid brother losing all his hair—may have been prompted by Nichols having lost his hair as a boy.

A certain amount of guesswork becomes necessary, because May has avoided interviews about her work almost as rigorously as J. D. Salinger and Thomas Pynchon. But I hasten to add that, well more than a quarter of a century later, *Mikey and Nicky* speaks pretty well for itself—and in fact always has, even in its original scattershot version. It even has clear links to May's other features. All four of her films to date include the same obsessive theme, the secret betrayal of one member of a couple by the other. The first two of these couples are newlyweds (in *A New Leaf* and *The Heartbreak Kid*) and the second two are heterosexual men and best friends (in *Mikey and Nicky* and the underrated *Ishtar*)—a Jew and a Gentile in both cases. But only in *Mikey and Nicky* is this theme pushed to its limits, beyond comedy.

It's a betrayal with many fluctuations, hesitations, reversals, and ambiguities, and May might be the least sentimental woman storyteller since Flannery O'Connor in her stark refusal to sweeten the pill. If her relentless realism evokes the epic sweep of Erich von Stroheim's *Greed,* her narrative still manages to cram a lifetime of troubled friendship, rivalry, money, and pain into the vicissitudes of a single night. And when women figure in the pivotal margins of this tragic tale, May is every bit as merciless as she is toward her two leads, whom she clearly loves as well as fears.

CHAPTER 15

Manoel de Oliveira

Since writing the following essay for the July–August 2008 *Film Comment,* I've paid two week-long visits to the Portuguese Cinémathèque in Lisbon, giving lecture series devoted to Welles and Stroheim, and during one of these I was finally able to see Oliveira's wonderful *Visit or Memories and Confessions* (1982), which according to Oliveira's own instructions could only be seen publicly after his death. Contrary to my speculation here, it isn't a political confession, but it does have a lot to say about his former house. Another update: Oliveira died in 2015 at the age of 106. And in keeping with the principles of delayed exposition that have characterized Oliveira's oeuvre from the outset, I ask for the reader's forbearance in allowing me to focus on some of Oliveira's lesser works before getting around to his supreme masterpieces.

The Classical Modernist [Manoel De Oliveira]

Films, films,
The best resemble
Great books
That are difficult to penetrate
Because of their richness and depth.

The cinema isn't easy
Because life is complicated
And art indefinable.
Making life indefinable
And art complicated.
—Manoel de Oliveira, "Cinematographic Poem" (1986)
(my translation)

Since this century has taught us, and continues to teach us, that human beings can continue to live under the most brutalized and theoretically intolerable conditions, it is not easy to grasp the extent of the, unfortunately accelerating, return to what our 19th century ancestors would have called the standards of barbarism.
—Eric Hobsbawm, *The Age of Extremes: A History of the World, 1914–1991* (1994)

I am large, I contain multitudes.
—Walt Whitman, "Song of Myself" (1855)

It's risky to insist that all great filmmakers contain multitudes, because it's possible to counter that all not-so-great filmmakers contain multitudes as well. Raúl Ruiz has observed that just as much labor can be expended on bad work as on good work, and this applies to the labor expended by viewers as well as by filmmakers. Life and art are both complicated, as Portuguese filmmaker Manoel de Oliveira points out, but that doesn't necessarily make them interesting.

So, from a practical standpoint, I'm afraid it won't do to argue to lingering skeptics about the greatness of Oliveira that they simply need to see more of his films—especially because following this advice usually leads to their seeing more of his bad stuff, resulting in a terminal allergy or permanent burnout whenever his name comes up.

Though familiarity with Oliveira's work as a whole does have its compensations—such as recognizing and enjoying his repertory company of actors, who seem every bit as loyal as John Ford's or Ingmar Bergman's, including such stalwarts as Luís Miguel Cintra (seventeen films), Leonor Silveira (sixteen films), and Oliveira's grandson Ricardo Trepa (thirteen films)—this doesn't necessarily redeem the less scintillating features. And you don't have to look far to find a film by Oliveira that's bad—or at the very least boring (such as *The Convent*) or pretentious (such as *The Divine Comedy*), or slight (such as *Christopher Columbus, The Enigma*), not to mention difficult (almost anything). And this problem is compounded by the fact that some of the lesser efforts of Oliveira are the easiest ones to access, probably because they often turn out to be the ones with stars.

These films also often turn out to be the talkiest, as well as the ones where Oliveira's own ideas—cinematic as well as thematic—seem too sketchy to sustain entire features, perhaps helping to explain why he sometimes alternates the gab with extended musical performances and/or establishing shots that linger. Two examples, among others: *The Letter* (1999) and *Belle Toujours* (2006). Both films, to be sure, have their charms and fascinations, but I'd hate to have to use either one to support any claims for Oliveira as a major figure.

The former transplants to the late twentieth century Madame de Lafayette's *The Princesse of Clèves* (1678), commonly described as the first great short novel in French—a tale about the self-abnegated love of the highly principled and married title heroine (Chiara Mastroianni) for the Duke of Nemours. (Reportedly the idea for both reading and adapting this novel came about two decades earlier, from Oliveira's principal French collaborator, translator, and exegete Jacques Parsi, who also proposed that Oliveira, given his fascination for frustrated love, read and adapt Paul Claudel's *The Satin Slipper*.)

Part of the promising and initially amusing two-pronged joke here appears to be the notion that aristocrats and their fussy distinctions hardly change at all from one century to the next—a conceit that works only if you don't think about it too much. The other part (or prong) is giving the role of the Duke to the real-life Portuguese rock star Pedro Abrunhosa, a dour, poker-faced dandy who hails from Oliveira's hometown (Porto) and never removes his sunglasses, playing himself the way that Dean Martin does in *Kiss Me, Stupid*.

Yet the campy humor of this double conceit over 105 minutes is so dry that it eventually becomes parched and arid. Oliveira neither runs nor plays with the two concepts; he simply and dully proceeds with them like a bulldozer, leading one to wonder if he eventually forgets that they're supposed to be funny and ironic. And if you go to YouTube to watch "Momento," the surprisingly conventional and humorless music video that Oliveira made with Abrunhosa three years later, you may start to wonder if he ever intended any sort of joke to begin with.

There's a similar mulishness present in *Belle Toujours,* recently released on DVD—an unlikely sequel/*hommage*/speculative footnote to Luis Buñuel's 1967 *Belle de jour,* which, unlike its model, has more to do with class than with sex, and whose only authentically Buñuelian touch involves the absurdist cameo appearance of a chicken at a climactic moment. In the original film, Séverine (Catherine Deneuve), a frigid bourgeois housewife who loves her husband Pierre (Jean Sorel), gets an afternoon job at a high-price brothel in order to satisfy her masochistic desires—a secret discovered by Pierre's friend Henri (Michel Piccoli), a rakish brothel customer. After Pierre is shot by one of Séverine's jealous clients, leaving him permanently mute and paralyzed, Henri announces that he'll tell Pierre everything, but we (and she) can't be sure whether or not he actually does this.

Oliveira, who couldn't persuade Deneuve to play Séverine again, got Bulle Ogier, the female lead in his 1986 *My Case,* to assume this role. Apart from the fact that she never comes across as the same character (a difference in conception that goes beyond casting), the story's focus shifts to Henri (Piccoli again) as he chases after a reluctant Séverine for most of the movie to invite her to a swank dinner, which she finally agrees to because she wants to discover whether he ever told Pierre the truth forty years earlier. As Henri pontificates to a young barman (Ricardo Trepa), he views Séverine as a masochist who became a sadist in order to work through her love for her husband. Yet it's his own unacknowledged sadism and glib narcissism that dominates the story—even though Oliveira, judging by interviews, appears to think that it's mainly about Séverine. One might even argue that some "civilized" form of misogyny is the main aristocratic attribute on display here, just as "civilized" xenophobia and/or misanthropy may be the key form of disdain in *A Talking Picture* (another star-laden production).

In sum, you might say that there's *some* sort of joke at play in both *The Letter* and *Belle Toujours,* but an extremely private one in both cases, and without a clearly demarcated punchline. Oliveira's seeming remoteness from both his characters (apart from his seeming complicity with Henri) and his audience creates a yawning distance that at times seems to define his method. There are plenty of attractive distractions along the way, such as the musical interludes in both films, for example, the performance of the second and third movements of Dvořák's Eighth Symphony at the Paris concert that opens *Belle Toujours*, where Henri first sights Séverine. But the fact that they often register as distractions rather than as essential narrative or nonnarrative forays is part of the problem.

It also won't do to try to cinch any briefs on Oliveira's behalf by pointing out that he'll be a century old this coming December. This is impressive in its own right, and it of course makes his ongoing productivity all the more remarkable—though he's pointed out himself that it's largely been his filmmaking that has been keeping him alive. Even so, this doesn't automatically validate the work being produced, at least beyond proposing that he may actually have more to tell us about the nineteenth century than James Ivory. Like Oliveira's celebrated early stints as a champion pole vaulter, diver, and car racer, you might say that his age adds more to his legend than to any better understanding of his filmography. (Some Oliveira fans seem to value *Christopher Columbus, The Enigma* most of all because Oliveira, as lead actor, can be seen driving a car in it. I suppose one could also relate Oliveira's principal assertion in this seventy-five-minute film—that Christopher Columbus was a Portuguese Jew—to John Malkovich's theory in *The Convent* that Shakespeare was a Spanish Jew, but I'm happy to leave the elaboration of this cross-reference to others.)

The son of a prominent industrialist—the first Portuguese manufacturer of electric lamps—Oliveira was an athlete, race-car driver, film actor (who appeared in the first Portuguese talkie), and college dropout who also helped run his father's factories and took over a farm inherited by his wife when he wasn't trying to make movies. But even though he finished his first film—the lovely, silent documentary short *Hard Labor on the Douro River* (1931)—when he was twenty-three, eleven years would pass before his first feature, then a whopping twenty-one more before his second.

Indeed, another off-putting aspect of his work is the highly asymmetrical shape of his career. He started out like Carl Dreyer with an overall average of one feature per decade for half a century, then continued with about one feature per year ever since. It's true that his initially sparse output can largely be attributed to the constraints of Salazar's right-wing dictatorship, which lasted from 1926 to 1974, and that the fairly steady flow of work afterward can largely be attributed to the resourcefulness of Paolo Branco, who produced all of Oliveira's films from *Francisca* in 1981 through *The Fifth Empire: Yesterday as Today* in 2004. That Oliveira's mastery as well as his modernism were firmly established in *Benilde* (1975) and *Doomed Love* (1978), before Branco came along—and that his average of one feature a year has continued since he left the same producer—only confirm that any simple cause-and-effect explanations of his unusual career are likely to be untrustworthy.

If he deserves to be regarded as a master—and I believe he does—this is at least partially in an eccentric category of his own invention, comparable to what could legitimately be called the mastery of Thelonious Monk as an idiosyncratic jazz pianist. And it's a mastery of sound and image that took shape fairly early—even though, as a director of actors, his foregrounding of artificial styles of performance doesn't always enhance the technical gifts of his players. A few of Oliveira's films are worth seeing principally for their actors: *Voyage to the Beginning of the World* (1997) offers Marcello Mastroianni's last screen performance (as an Oliveira surrogate); the all-star cast of *A Talking Picture* (2003) includes Catherine Deneuve, John Malkovich (in a hilarious portrait of a charming if self-absorbed American sea captain), Irene Papas, Stefania Sandrelli, and Leonor Silveira; Trepa's best turn probably comes in the decorous but static *The Fifth Empire,* where he plays clueless, despotic King Sebastian I (1544–1578); and Michel Piccoli is especially fine in representing the joys and sorrows of getting old in *I'm Going Home* (2001), perhaps the most accessible of Oliveira's fiction films. But none of these is exactly characteristic.

■ ■ ■

Making my strongest claims for *Doomed Love* and *Benilde* isn't likely to stir up many disputes. But this is partly because outside of scattered retrospective screenings, these features are almost impossible to see. Neither has ever been issued commercially on DVD or VHS anywhere in the world, and even if you want to try to track down *Inquietude,* which I consider nearly as good, you'll have to settle on French subtitles if, like me, you don't understand Portuguese.

The language barrier represents only one of many obstacles that stands between Oliveira and most of the rest of us. It's clearly a major strength of Randal Johnson's recent book on the filmmaker (University of Illinois Press, 2007), the first in English, that it can guide us through the features up through *Belle Toujours* and most of the twenty or so shorts and documentaries with all the contextual information that might be deemed essential, making it possible in many cases to follow the films in their basic thrust even when they aren't available with English subtitles (as in a Spanish DVD box set offering many films in Portuguese or French with Spanish subtitles). In this respect, apart from being more up to date, Johnson's book has been more useful to me than the five French books on Oliveira that I've acquired, three of them signed or cosigned by Parsi (as author or editor) and all published between 1988 and 2002; in comprehensiveness, it's topped only by the mammoth catalog produced at the Torino Film Festival in 2000.

But certain other cultural barriers persist. No less formidable are issues involving class (Oliveira's aristocratic background), political orientation (never directly stated in any of his films), the history of Portugal in the twentieth century (especially the aforementioned dictatorship), and history in general (specifically, how one situates Oliveira, a nineteenth-century modernist, in relation to *any* particular period, past or present).

Let's consider briefly the first three of these issues. (The fourth will be addressed a little later.) Despite some shared (and mutually avowed) cinematic influences, such as Bresson and Straub-Huillet, Oliveira and Pedro Costa might be said to occupy opposite ends of the spectrum of Portuguese culture in terms of the respective milieus of their films, ultra-rich and lumpen-proletarian. The working-class milieus of Oliveira's first two features, *Aniki-Bóbó* (1942) and *Rite of Spring* (1963), and his subsequent *The Box* (1994), can't of course be factored out. But these three features, which have practically nothing else in common with one another (and even less in common with any of Costa's films), are all so atypical of Oliveira's work as a whole that it becomes difficult to say much about them, apart from describing them respectively as a neorealist children's film, a documentary following a rural Passion play (à la Flaherty, with deliberate restagings and re-creations), and an adaptation of a play with a loose resemblance to Elmer Rice's *Street Scene*.

The elusiveness and ambiguity of Oliveira's politics may partially derive from survival tactics during a half-century of living under the repressive regime of Salazar's Estada Nova (New State)—including the first forty-three years of his filmmaking, which yielded only eleven shorts and four features. But one can't necessarily conclude from this that Oliveira was only or simply a victim of Estada Nova, even if, like many others, he was briefly jailed at one point (as he mentioned to me and a few others when he visited Chicago in 2005). Johnson reports that the occupation of the Oliveira dry-goods factory in Porto by leftists during the 1974 revolution led to its eventual bankruptcy and Oliveira losing "almost all of his personal assets, including the house where he had resided since 1940." The fact that both a conservative devout Catholic like Paul Claudel and an atheistic leftist scamp like Buñuel belong in his personal pantheon only begins to suggest that whatever his (undeclared) political positions might be, they aren't likely to be simple.

The same goes for Oliveira's mixed credentials as an avant-gardist. It's been a quarter of a century since I've seen his hour-long *Nice—À Propos de Jean Vigo* (1983), clearly meant as an *hommage* to Vigo's half-hour *À Propos de Nice* (1930), but I remember thinking later how strangely sedate and polite it all seemed as a tribute to a fire-breathing anarchist—certainly in contrast to, say, *Promenade*, Raúl Ruiz's genuinely wild contribution to the sketch feature *À Propos de Nice, la suite* a dozen years later (even if *that* was arguably much more of an *hommage* to *Vertigo* than to Vigo). My favorite Oliveira features (see below) are those that are the most transgressive, yet I also have to admit that part of what makes each of them qualify as avant-garde is the way its various transgressions rub shoulders with diverse forms of propriety and repression—the sort of traits that used to be called square. But then again, the ultimate avant-garde act may be to undermine what we mean by avant-garde.

■ ■ ■

At one time or another, I've seen twenty-six of Oliveira's twenty-nine features to date. One of the ones I haven't seen, the 1982 *Visit or Memories and Confessions,* according to Oliveira's own instructions, is not supposed to be screened publicly until after his death. (I wonder if it constitutes, among other things, a political confession; it's also said to be about a house he's lived in for years.) Another, which is the longest—the 400-minute *The Satin Slipper* (1985)—I've managed to see most of, but under uniquely frustrating circumstances: At an extended Oliveira event held at Brown University in 1998, repeated breakdowns in the projection of a 35mm print led to the entire audience being forced to leave well before the end in order to attend an already-scheduled panel discussion about the film—a perfect example of bureaucratic obtuseness at its most dysfunctional. (The other missing item for me is *The Past and the Present* [1971],

Oliveira's third feature—and this isn't counting his twenty-odd shorts and documentaries, only five of which I've seen.)

As hazardous and as tentative as such an undertaking might be, I'd like to rank all his other features in descending order of preference, to establish both where I'm coming from and, in terms of my own defense of his work, where I'm going. I've seen roughly half these films more than once, but my memories are much vaguer about many others, so the order assigned to the final ten is somewhat more arbitrary:

1. *Doomed Love* (1978)
2. *Benilde or the Virgin-Mother* (1975)
3. *Inquietude* aka *Disquiet* (1998)
4. *Porto of My Childhood* (2001)
5. *My Case* (1986)
6. *Francisca* (1981)
7. *I'm Going Home* (2001)
8. *Rite of Spring* (1963)
9. *No, or the Vain Glory of Command* (1990)
10. *Day of Despair* (1992)
11. *Aniki-Bóbó* (1942)
12. *Voyage to the Beginning of the World* (1997)
13. *Magic Mirror* (2005)
14. *The Letter* (1999)
15. *A Talking Picture* (2003)
16. *Belle Toujours* (2006)
17. *The Cannibals* (1988)
18. *The Uncertainty Principle* (2002)
19. *Valley of Abraham* (1993)
20. *The Box* (1994)
21. *The Convent* (1995)
22. *Word and Utopia* (2000)
23. *The Fifth Empire: Yesterday as Today* (2004)
24. *Party* (1996)
25. *Christopher Colombus, The Enigma* (2007)
26. *The Divine Comedy* (1991)

A few general points about these assessments:

(1) As far as I'm concerned, there is no "golden age" in Oliveira's career—even though what I take to be his supreme adaptations of prose fiction and theater, *Doomed Love* and *Benilde,* occur relatively early in

his career, and the superb and pivotal modernist musical scores of João Paes, which play substantial roles in Oliveira's films of the '70s and '80s, no longer figure in his work afterward. Nevertheless, masterpieces and less interesting or accomplished films turn up in all periods.

(2) Similarly, I can't entirely privilege the films in Portuguese over the films in French, or the adaptations (which comprise most of his features) over the original scripts (such as *Porto of My Childhood* and *No, or the Vain Glory of Command*), or the adaptations of stories or novels over the adaptations of plays. In fact, two of Oliveira's boldest and most original films, the Portuguese *Inquietude* and the French *My Case*, are derived from combining adaptations of theater with adaptations of fiction, while the no less adventurous *Porto of My Childhood* freely draws on the resources of both theater and fiction.

My Case chiefly consists of three successive onstage adaptations of a frenetic one-act Portuguese farce translated into French, José Régio's *O Meu Caso* (1957), but it also manages to work in portions of Samuel Beckett's *Pour finir encore et autres foirades* (a collection of stories known in the United States as *Fizzles*) and The Book of Job. *Inquietude* begins as another frenetic one-act Portuguese play (Helder Prista Monteiro's 1968 *The Immortals*); this turns out to be a play being performed in Porto in the 1930s, and attended by four of the characters in an adaptation of António Patrício's story "Suzy" (circa 1910); and one of these four characters recounts to another the film's third story, derived from Agustina Bessa-Luís's haunting and magical 1971 fairy tale, *The Mother of a River*.

(3) While some commentators have tended to privilege the eight Oliveira features derived from or cowritten by his novelist friend Bessa-Luís, I regard most of these as secondary, with the notable exceptions of *Francisca* and the third episode of *Inquietude*. Arguably no less important, and for me more interesting, is another writer friend of Oliveira's, José Régio (1901–1969), principally known as a poet, who wrote the plays Oliveira adapted in both *Benilde* and *My Case* as well as in *The Divine Comedy* (which also draws material from the Bible, Dostoevsky, and Nietzsche, but perversely ignores Dante) and *The Fifth Empire* (derived from Régio's play *El-Rei Sebastiã*, written only two years after *Benilde*). Although I've read nothing by either Bessa-Luís or Régio, I've mainly concluded, based Oliveira's adaptations, that Régio's troubled existentialism

and skepticism are far more fruitful and intriguing (at least from a dramatic standpoint) than Bessa-Luís's congealed and conservative Jamesian ironies. But I also must confess that when I saw *The Divine Comedy* seventeen years ago, I found it insufferably pretentious, hectoring, and dull; at their worst, Bessa-Luís's stories seem boring and snooty, but I wouldn't fault any of them for pretension or aggression. (Aggression, in fact, is what they sometimes appear to need the most. For me the most gratifying moment in *The Valley of Abraham* occurs in the third hour, during a character's interminable monologue about the decline of Western civilization, when another character suddenly lifts a purring cat from the heroine's lap and flings it straight at the camera, as if to wake us all up.)

As suggested by the somewhat bewildering mix of materials in *Inquietude* that are drawn from 1910, 1968, and 1971, in a film set in the 1930s, the settings of Oliveira's period films are sometimes difficult to date in relation to specific periods, apart from the specific periods of their major source materials (for example, the late sixteenth and/or early seventeenth century for *The Satan Slipper;* the seventeenth century for *Word and Utopia;* and the nineteenth century for *Doomed Love, Francisca,* and the unjustly overlooked and underrated *Day of Despair*—the trilogy relating to novelist Camilo Castelo Branco). Along with such contemporary tales as *I'm Going Home* and *Belle toujours, The Letter* provides a much clearer take on the twentieth century than the eight films related to Bessa-Luís, which for me often appear to exist in a kind of time warp related to both the insularity and preciosity associated with wealth and the freezing of history typically found in totalitarian regimes (such as Stalin's Russia, Franco's Spain, Mao's China, and Castro's Cuba).

(4) For a good many commentators, the 35mm, 167-minute *Francisca* has eclipsed or supplanted the 262-minute, 16mm *Doomed Love* as Oliveira's ultimate masterpiece about obsessive, unrequited love, maybe to some extent because its distribution, supported by Paolo Branco, has been much wider. My preference for the earlier and longer film (the first Oliveira work I encountered, explored in my collection *Placing Movies*), which has persisted over many repeated viewings of both, has a lot to do with the evident superiority of its source material (widely regarded as one of the greatest of all Portuguese novels) and its exceptional theoretical interest as a workshop of ideas regarding the cinematic adaptation of novels—rivaled to my mind only by *Greed*. It's a tribute to the epic staying

power of *Doomed Love* that it survived even a recent showing at the Brooklyn Academy of Music that denied it an intermission, omitting an important element in its dramatic structure. (At least this was preferable to the reverse error of granting it too long an intermission—something that happened at the Los Angeles County Museum's screening of the 450-minute *Sátántangó* the following weekend, where turning the second intermission into a dinner break fatally broke the spell for some viewers, who didn't return.)

(5) The strident, over-the-top acting featured in *My Case* and *The Immortals* is in striking contrast to the distanciated underplaying more typically found in most of Oliveira's other films, which sometimes come across more as "representations" than as performances (especially in *Doomed Love, Francisca,* and *The Satan Slipper*). And for me, the most impressively acted of the films occupying some middle ground between these extremes is *Benilde,* which also boasts the most astonishing opening shot to be found in any Oliveira film.

Like the original opening of *Touch of Evil,* this shot appears behind the credits—with Paes's bombastic, apocalyptic score, punctuated by manic screams and moans, accompanying a rapid, endless tracking shot that both snakes and pans around the labyrinthine backstage spaces of Lisbon's Tobis Studios until it finally arrives at and enters the décor, a room in the mansion where the play is set. Then, as in Michael Snow's *Wavelength,* the camera continues its journey all the way up to a framed photograph on a wall, in this case of a field, at which point the following title is superimposed: "The action of this film is supposed to take place in the 1930s."

The wickedly and subtly subversive "supposed to" introduces a note of existential doubt that's in fact central to *Benilde*—a film that for me indelibly captures the dread of living under totalitarian rule through following the same general approach adopted by Clouzot's *Le Corbeau* (1943) in Vichy France and by Bardem's *Calle Major* (1956) in Franco Spain, of reformulating political oppression in sexual terms. The eighteen-year-old title heroine, living sequestered with her widowed father and a maid, has become pregnant, and since she's an avowed virgin, she claims it's an Immaculate Conception. But she also sleepwalks, and some of the other characters think that a crazed village tramp is somehow to blame. And the remainder of the three-act play steadfastly refuses to confirm or refute either explanation. The remote setting, the spiritual ambiguity, the competing interpretations, the lighting and the *mise en scène*—all recall *Ordet* without the closing miracle. Instead of a miracle we get a shortened and slowed-down reversal of the opening shot at the end, making *Benilde* as much a theoretical statement about theatre and film as *Doomed Love* is a theoretical statement about literature and film. But this shouldn't imply that either masterpiece is any sort of formalist exercise; both are also claustrophobic hothouses of fierce meditation about ideological and spiritual as well as physical confinement. *Benilde* is a suffocating chamber piece throughout, while *Doomed Love,* which opens with an iron gate swinging shut, emphasizes the bars in convent and prison alike. (The latter, incidentally, was inspired in part by a viewing of *Chronicle of Anna Magdalena Bach*—as we learn from the book-length *Conversations avec Manoel de Oliveira,* by Antoine de Baecque and Jacques Parsi [Cahiers du Cinéma, 1996], the best of the French books devoted to his work.)

Superficially, *Benilde* might be said to bear some thematic relationship to *Magic Mirror* (2005), made thirty years later, about a wealthy woman (Leonor Silveira) determined to see an apparition of the Virgin Mary. But in fact I'm more apt to view it in terms of contrast, offering another illustration of the arguable superiority of Régio's existential skepticism over Bessa-Luís's more conservative wit and irony. (More mannerist than *Doomed Love, Francisca* for me periodically founders on its surfeit of hollow and posturing banter, its silly aphorisms such as "Death is only a moral accident" and "If fatality was a woman, I would marry her.")

■ ■ ■

The grandest claims to have been made for Oliveira, and in some respects the most persuasive, are those suggested more than a decade ago by Raymond Bellour, in a 1997 cycle of letters that I inaugurated that eventually grew into a book co-edited with Adrian Martin (*Movie Mutations: The Changing Face of World Cinema,* London: BFI Publishing, 2003). Bellour associates Oliveira's name with the word "civilization" ("a word far greater than cinema, its life or death"), and adds that "he could be greatest" of all working filmmakers today, "if this word had meaning," Bellour continues, "Oliveira's preoccupation is, to put it banally, the fate of the world, how to live and die, survive in harmony with the logic of an ancient and prestigious country, which was fortunate to discover the world when it was worth discovering, and the strange destiny of having in part escaped the worst conflicts of this century thanks to a cruel and miserable dictatorship. He is, I believe, the only filmmaker who knew how to tell, in a unique film, the history of his country, from its founding through a melancholy myth up to the end of its empire (*No, or The Vain Glory of Command*)."

This accounts for the difficulty of Oliveira's cinema as well as its importance and necessity—especially during a period when the fate of the world has been widely perceived to be a less pressing matter than the accumulation of wealth by a few individuals whose lack of interest in art is as conspicuous as their obsession with empire. As we return to what Eric Hobsbawm in my opening quote has described as barbarism from a nineteenth-century perspective, the civilized serenity of a broader view is bound to seem somewhat remote.

Note

The author's thanks to Scott Foundas and Richard Peña.

CHAPTER 16

Ermanno Olmi

Prior to writing this essay, Ermanno Olmi remained mostly a blank spot in my film education apart from *The Job* (1961) and *The Tree of Wooden Clogs* (1978), both of which I hadn't seen since their original releases. So being assigned to write about his work for a retrospective catalog published in Portugal in May 2012—*A Man Called Ermanno: Olmi's Cinema and Works*, published by Edições Il Sorpasso (in Lisbon)—provided me with an opportunity to dig deeper, to reacquaint myself with those films and to begin to explore some of his other works. I still have a long way to go before catching up with his oeuvre as a whole, which has been difficult to access, especially in North America, but I hope this essay suggests that such an investigation is well worth undertaking. . . . Sadly, Olmi died on May 5, 2018, as this book was nearing completion.

Problems of Classification: A Few Traits in Four Films by Ermanno Olmi

> For me, the cinema is a state of mind and a process of analysis from a series of detailed observations.
> —Ermanno Olmi, from a 1988 interview[1]

Ermanno Olmi first became well-known as a filmmaker during the period in the early 1960s when the nouvelle vague and, more specifically, François Truffaut's formulation of *la politique des auteurs*, were near the height of their international influence. Yet it seems that one factor that has limited Olmi's reputation as an auteur over the half-century that has passed since then is his apparent reluctance and/or inability to remain typecast in either his choice of film projects or in his execution of them. Indeed, the fact that he repeatedly eludes and/or confounds whatever auteurist profile that criticism elects to construct for him in its effort to classify his artistry results in a periodic neglect of him, followed by periodic "rediscoveries." And these rediscoveries are confused in turn by the fact that each rediscovery of Olmi's work seems to redefine his profile rather than build on the preceding one.

At least this has been the gist of my own experience. Although I'm clearly restricted by having seen only four Olmi features to date, the spotty and limited international distribution that his work has received has largely been responsible for this impasse. And the incomplete grasp that I have of Olmi as an auteur is not only a consequence of this problem but, more symptomatically, part of the problem itself insofar as it has inhibited me from making further explorations. In other words, he has largely fallen outside most international canons precisely because his work has resisted easy classification.

Olmi's style is frequently described as simple, but once any attempt is made to elaborate on this observation, this alleged simplicity often turns out to be far from simple—perhaps because Olmi's responses to his material usually turn out to be less pure than we initially assume them to be, and more intuitively open to chance, circumstance, and/or expressive variations than criticism often cares to admit. Consider, for instance, the brief sequence in *Il posto* (1961) that follows Domenico (Sandro Panseri) on his way home from Milan following a day devoted to his job application, during which he meets Magali (Loredana Detto), another applicant for a job at the same company. If we compare this sequence to Domenico's walk to the train station from his home the previous morning, the differences are striking.

We see him leave his family's third-story apartment with his brother Franco while their mother calls out questions to him about whether he has enough money. As we view them walking on the road in extended long shots (during which Franco gets called back to collect more money from his mother to give to Domenico), what we hear, such as the voices of Domenico and his mother and the passing traffic, appears to be recorded in direct sound. But that evening, after Domenico sees Magali depart on a bus, there's a cut to him walking through an apparently empty train, singing to himself, as seen from outside the train and through its windows, and the fact that we can clearly hear him singing despite the camera's position outside the train essentially proves that the sound in this sequence couldn't be direct. Moreover, after Domenico sits down in the train, the film cuts to various shots of the train as seen from the platform that seem to reflect Domenico's viewpoint even though the camera's placement is anything but subjective. And meanwhile, the sound of Domenico's singing becomes much louder and more assertive as we cut to him walking home from the train station; when we see him outside the door of his family's apartment, the fact that this isn't direct sound becomes confirmed by the imprecise lip sync. (We do know, however, from Olmi's own testimony that Sandro Panseri dubbed his own character, and that he systematically got his nonprofessional actors to dub their own roles.)

We might conclude from the contrasts in both image and sound between Domenico's walk from the train station in the morning and his walk back from the train station in the evening that the difference in approach from a relative objectivity to a relative subjectivity helps to illustrate a certain psychological observation—namely, the boost in Domenico's confidence which comes from having completed his job application and, perhaps even more, from having met Magali, which is only intensified once he returns to his home turf and shows that he can sing more openly there without any embarrassment. But in fact, neither the objectivity in the first sequence nor the subjectivity in the second sequence qualifies as pure; both are highly selective in what Olmi wants us to see and hear. And the differences may also be a matter of technical expedience. When Olmi spoke to the late American film critic Charles Thomas Samuels in Rome in spring 1971, he described his overall methodology and rationale as follows:

> I'm not so doctrinaire as Bresson. Since the visual element is the most important thing in a film, dubbing isn't too harmful. Furthermore, one touches up the visuals; why shouldn't one also touch up the sound track? However, I do try to take sound directly whenever that is possible. But when I shoot in 35mm, I can only take the sound directly when I am not using a hand-held camera, because obviously I couldn't find a machine small enough that would also record sound. When I need to be free of trolleys and so on, I dub.[2]

That Olmi most often shoots as well as edits his own films clearly gives them an artisanal quality that arguably becomes part of his films' content. "The talkies have become the walkies," Dwight Macdonald once wittily observed, while favorably reviewing *Il posto* in the August 1963 issue of *Esquire,* calling to mind the extent to which long walks often define as well as shape much of the Italian art cinema of this period—not only *Il posto* and *I fidanzati* (1963), but also, for instance, all of the films of Antonioni that were contemporary with them (*L'avventura, La notte, L'eclisse,* and *Il deserto rosso*). The nature of Olmi's observations, reflected in both his shooting style and in his principles of sound-mixing (including his uses of music), tends to be psychologically as well as socially oriented.

In the interview with Olmi included on Criterion's 2003 DVD release of *Il posto,* he gives an interesting rationale for his periodic inclusion of the sound of church bells during Domenico's walks through Milan. While most viewers would take them to be both realistic and nonconsequential, his description implies that they carry a certain commentary on the action that becomes part of the film's overall social statement, while his comparison of these bells to the sound of a mother's voice provocatively suggests a certain psychological dimension as well: "Why did I put in the bells? They come from a more rural, agricultural world where they marked the significant times of the day—a way of communicating with the rest of the community. . . . [They represent] an old world that will soon be gone."

It's worth adding that the periodic sound of church bells in *L'albero degli zoccoli* (*The Tree of Wooden Clogs,* 1978), which is probably Olmi's major representation of that "old world," while apparently more realistic and directly pertinent, appears at times to be used almost as intuitively and as expressively as it is in *Il posto.* Indeed, it has a similar kind of subliminal, psychological effect in creating the film's world—Lombardy at the end of the nineteenth century—as the recurring frontal camera angle in front of the huge farmhouse where most of the action is set, which often suggests the theatrical tableau framing of some of the earliest films, which were being shot at approximately the same time, and conveys cumulatively a certain rhyme effect that links particular scenes thematically and emotionally. (The recurrence of the same camera angles in the same settings, in this case many years apart, also informs much of the dramatic construction of Mizoguchi's 1939 masterpiece *The Story of the Last Chrysanthemums,* invariably leading us to recall earlier scenes and sequences while creating a certain overall sense of permanence that plays in counterpoint to seasonal and other temporal changes.)

The opening sequence of *I fidanzati* also uses sound at least partially in a manner that seems to be psychologically motivated. After Olmi slowly and methodically presents us with the routine, almost ritualistic opening in the evening of a dance hall that establishes the milieu and his leading characters, he presents a series of brief flashbacks in alternation within this setting that is quite unorthodox in terms of both their chronology and their succession (we even get one flashback within another flashback). All of this is clearly marked as the hero's subjective memories that are being propelled by the music, which is kept at the same volume level in the dance hall and in the other settings of the diverse flashbacks. When Samuels interviewed Olmi, there is a meaningful and interesting exchange on this topic. Samuels: "Why are you so fond of sound bridges from one scene to another?" Olmi: "To show that the psychological state remains even though outward reality changes."[3]

Another example of Olmi's expressive use of sound volume comes a little later in *I fidanzati*. Shortly after the hero, Giovanni (Carlo Cabrini), has flown to Sicily to embark on his new job and has found temporary lodging, he wanders into a drab, nearly deserted, but brightly lit café where a radio is loudly blasting incongruously cheerful music. The sharp disconnect here between sound and image perfectly captures the alienation and displacement being experienced by Giovanni.

Perhaps one could find no better illustration of Olmi's capacity to lend psychological *and* social significance to his sounds than the loud and relentless sound of a copying machine that accompanies both the final shots and then the closing credits of *Il posto,* which is again held at the same volume level. As in the earlier sequence that cuts away from Domenico at work to see depressing glimpses of his older colleagues at home, the present is metaphorically expanded to represent both the future and the shape of entire lives, thus making each character, in effect, a "copy" of the others that has been pressed out by the drudgery and monotony of work.

■ ■ ■

We tend to associate the nouvelle vague with both youth and various stylistic departures such as those that I've just been describing. In fact, the term itself was originally coined by the weekly magazine *L'Express,* in its October 3, 1957 issue, in reference to youth rather than to film per se, and it's worth recalling that Olmi's worldwide reputation only came with his second feature, *Il posto,* when he was already pushing thirty. (Regrettably, I haven't seen his first feature, *Il tempo si è fermato* [1959], so I can't discuss it here in any detail.) And his status as a stylistic innovator, which relates chiefly to his early features, seems determined and inflected most of all by his concern with content rather than any apparent desire to shake up film aesthetics; it was apparently arrived at more by default than by design. This content, moreover, might be described as a particular kind of speculative autobiography—that is, stories and situations based to some extent (and by his own testimony) on Olmi's own experiences, which are seemingly combined with some speculation about how his life might have developed if he hadn't become a filmmaker. Similarly, *L'albero degli zoccoli* might be described as a speculative account of his grandparents' life around the turn of the century. In the case of *The Legend of the Holy Drinker* (1988), the only other Olmi feature that I've seen, it could describe this literary adaptation as a form of speculative spiritual autobiography—precipitated in this case by his contraction of a rare and crippling neurological disease that interrupted Olmi's career between 1984 and 1987, and, by his own account, obliged him to anticipate and contemplate the prospect of his own death.

"I discovered my first subjects in myself," Olmi said to Samuels. "For example, the boy in [*Il posto*] is me; the worker who goes to Sicily in [*I fidanzati*] is also me. The young boy in my first film, [*Il tempo si è fermato*], is certainly me. Each film, except, obviously, [*E venne un uomo*], was about me—until [*Un certo giorno*]."[4] This autobiographical content covers the period when Olmi was working as a clerk for the Edisonvolta electric plant in Milan—a period during which Olmi first became involved with filmmaking, by shooting various industrial documentaries for the company, one of which surreptitiously grew into *Il tempo si è fermato*—although presumably the filmmaking itself is a subject that Olmi's early features fail to deal with.

■ ■ ■

Critical typecasting inevitably stems from a desire for simplification, but more often than not this is a sort of practice that can lead to various distortions. Several years ago, when I was still working as a regular film reviewer for the *Chicago Reader,* I received an email one day from a reader wishing to know how I could have possibly described *The Tree of Wooden*

Clogs as Marxist when it was so clearly a religious film. In fact, it had been Dave Kehr, my predecessor, who had written the *Chicago Reader*'s capsule review of Ermanno Olmi's feature back in 1985, two years before I'd started work on that newspaper, and the way he had employed the term "Marxist" is not something I would have agreed with myself: "The characters and situations are oppressively familiar; Olmi's wide-eyed, wondering point of view helps to freshen them, but not enough to overcome completely the Marxist sentimentalism inherent in the concept."

Nevertheless, under these circumstances, going into my disagreement with Kehr might have only led to more confusion, so adopting the usual reflexes of a journalist wishing to simplify issues rather than complicate them, I hastily emailed my correspondent that any Italian would tell you that Marxism could easily be seen as a form of religion. Afterward, I realized that this response was unnecessarily flippant and in its own way misleading—a prime instance of one form of simplification being used to "correct" another one. On further reflection, I concluded that it would have been better to say that Catholicism and Marxism have had a long and complex coexistence in Italy, and it was unrealistic to expect that they would be mutually exclusive as systems of belief; the complex and multifaceted career of Pier Paolo Pasolini stands as proof of how intimately the two can be intertwined, regardless of—or perhaps even because of—the various contradictions involved. This led me to think about how the similar characterizations of European Marxism in the United States tend to foster such confusion; indeed, it is even possible to argue that the term "Marxism" doesn't even mean the same thing in the United States and Europe. Shortly after this, I happened to read André Bazin's description of *The Bicycle Thief* as one of the great Communist films—an aspect of the film that I strongly suspect couldn't have been apparent to American audiences when it won the Academy Award for best foreign film in 1949. And still more recently, after reseeing *The Tree of Wooden Clogs* and Olmi's much earlier *Il posto* and *I fidanzati*, I realized that calling Olmi a Marxist in the same sense that Pasolini was one was already an oversimplification that can perhaps only be justified from a distant and American cold war perspective (and one that unhappily persists today), according to which almost any leftist-humanist European position can be—and often is—perceived as Marxist.

■ ■ ■

Typically, film directors become familiar to the public through various forms of critical packaging, and the difficulty in situating Olmi comfortably within the traditions of either Italian neorealism or the nouvelle vague have led to a blurry and uncertain critical profile that has only become more confused over time. His film career began in the shadow of what might be described as post–Italian neorealism—especially in his reliance on shooting in natural locations, but also in going further in neorealism's move away from the conventions of studio filmmaking by adopting the same procedure employed in *Banditi a Orgosolo* and *Accatone* (the first features of Vittorio De Seta and Pier Paolo Pasolini, both released in 1961, the same year as *Il posto*), to use only nonprofessional actors. And the use of both natural locations and nonprofessional actors in his subsequent and comparably well-known *I fidanzati* (1963) and *L'albero degli zoccoli* (1978) would appear to confirm that these characteristics were essential parts of his auteurist profile, to which one should add the aforementioned autobiographical elements.

Furthermore, the location shooting and some of the editing procedures of *Il posto* and *I fidanzati,* in addition to some of the autobiographical, psychological, and sociological elements and the uses of direct sound, parallel those associated with some of the French filmmakers of the nouvelle vague—in particular, Truffaut and Jean-Luc Godard regarding the autobiographical elements, Godard regarding the sociological elements, Resnais regarding the psychological elements, and Godard and Rivette in the employments of direct sound. (Unless one counts *Vivre sa vie* in 1962, Godard's uses of direct sound and his sociological interests as exemplified in *La femme mariée* and *Masculin féminin* suggests that *I fidanzati* might conceivably have influenced Godard, but it appears less likely that Godard influenced Olmi.)

Yet how, then, can one account for Olmi's 1988 *The Legend of the Holy Drinker*—one of his most famous and celebrated subsequent films, and apparently another personal project, winner of the Golden Lion at the Venice Film Festival? This latter film not only employs many professional actors and is largely studio-shot; it's also a close literary adaptation of a novel in German whose spoken dialogue is chiefly in English and secondarily in French, and it appears to have no direct autobiographical elements in relation to Olmi (although it does seem to have a few in relation to Joseph Roth, who wrote the story of the same title serving as the literary source). And even though the frequent use of sets appears to preclude the sort of direct sound employed in *Il posto, I fidanzati,* and *L'albero degli zoccoli,* one can nonetheless observe aspects of Olmi's expressive sound mixing, such as the way certain sounds precede their corresponding images (for example those of the Seine, which come before the film's opening shot), that seem consistent with those in the earlier features. (Equally consistent, alas, is the relatively conventional selection of musical pieces chosen as accompaniments, such as the Bach used in *L'albero degli zoccoli* and the Stravinsky used in *The Legend of the Holy Drinker*—not to mention the pop music used in *Il posto* and *I fidanzati.*)

Olmi, who has usually avoided literary adaptations, agreed to make this movie of the Roth story only after his friend and frequent writing collaborator Tullio Kezich (1928–2009) presented him with a copy of this story at a dinner party. According to Michael Hofmann, the English translator of the story, it was written "quite deliberately" as well as slowly, as Joseph Roth's final work of fiction while he was in the process of drinking himself to death in Paris at age forty-four.[5] Like Ulrike Ottinger's *Bildnis Einer Trinkerin* (aka *Aller Jamais Retour/ Ticket of No Return,* 1979), which deals with a similar theme, Roth's story is paradoxically a work of ironic celebration more than one of complaint or defeat, although the irony is far less apparent in the fate of Andreas Kartak (Rutger Hauer) in Olmi's version. As the British film critic Tom Milne pointed out in his review of the film, it is a very close and superficially very faithful adaptation, ending with the same epitaph on the death of Andreas—"May God grant us all, all of us drinkers, such a good and easy death"—yet "the explicit irony of Roth's personal voice, interjecting as narrator to cast cold water over [the] Biblical resonances, has been suppressed."[6] And indeed, as Olmi admitted to Don Ranvaud in an interview,[7] he deliberately avoided reading anything else by Roth or anything about his life before making the film: "He [Roth] became a perfect and discreet accomplice, perhaps not dissimilar from the stranger/ benefactor in the story."

One could hypothesize that, apart from Olmi's near-brush with death, the element in Roth's strange story that struck a personal chord with Olmi may well have been the almost obsessive recurrence of the word "miracle." For it would appear that the notion of miracles as responses to prayers has a very special meaning for this filmmaker, which can be seen not only in the seemingly miraculous recovery of the sick cow in *L'albero degli zoccoli,* but also in Olmi's own remarkable account of the arrival of the rainstorm in the final scene of *I fidanzati:*

> You must remember that in Sicily it never rains during August and September. You shouldn't tell anyone this story, because he will laugh at me! It exemplifies the mentality of a Catholic and a peasant. Here I was, needing a storm when there couldn't be any, so I started up an internal dialogue with my grandmother, who was no longer alive then. I kept praying for her to help me, and I went slowly on the retakes in the hope that she would. One day that oppressive Sicilian heat was so dreadful that no one could sleep, so we worked through the night. When I finally got to sleep, I had this crazy dream: I was shooting my last scene in a downpour so terrific that it was actually painful; even the trees were bending under it. I went on filming, while my grandmother looked on, happy and satisfied. Imagine how I felt when I awoke from that vivid dream to see an utterly clear sky. Nevertheless, I told everyone to get ready for work because it would rain that day. They looked at me as if I were crazy.... But by afternoon a storm came. Suddenly I found myself exactly as I had been in the dream, shooting in a downpour, with trees swaying all around me.[8]

■ ■ ■

Clearly we have to revise some of our presuppositions about what defines Olmi from an auteurist perspective if we wish to consider *The Legend of the Holy Drinker* as a meaningful part of his oeuvre. But in the process of this revision, we may also need to reconsider, once again, what we mean by both Italian neorealism and the nouvelle vague. For insofar as both these movements were very much collective phenomena—the result of friends having coffee and conversing and working together over protracted periods—Olmi needs to be considered separately insofar as he remains a relatively independent loner, creating and following his own laws. (One should note, however, that at least two of his children have also entered the world of cinema—Fabio as a cinematographer and Elisabetta as a producer.) In this respect, he may be more comparable to notable outsiders in the French cinema, such as Bresson and Jacques Tati, than he is to filmmakers associated with either post–Italian neorealism or the nouvelle vague. Like Bresson, he projects a spiritual sense of gravity over his plots, especially when he expands his expressive palette to suggest cosmic dimensions, yet like Tati he is also a master of "small" social observations. (Domenico and Magali each examining the bottoms of their coffee cups in an attempt to behave "typically" in a Milan café is a classic Tatiesque moment.)

Logically speaking, one can't postulate a tradition of eccentricity in any field of endeavor without perpetrating an oxymoron. But in attempting to describe as well as account for the eccentric styles, methods, and techniques of *Il posto* and *I fidanzati,* we can at least speak about a few tendencies that can be found in several other idiosyncratic "outsider" artists apart from Bresson and Tati.

One of these tendencies would be the reinvention of many of the basic practices and poetic principles of their specific art forms that is found in artists with rustic and/or small-town backgrounds, such as French painter Henri Rousseau (1844–1910), Ukrainian filmmaker Alexander Dovzhenko (1894–1956), American novelist William Faulkner (1897–1962), American filmmaker Jonas Mekas (born 1922), American filmmaker David Lynch (born 1946), and Chinese filmmaker Jia Zhangke (born 1970), among others—some of whom, like Olmi, might be said to invent their own forms of syntax.

Another tendency, much less common, would be for the artist to remain in his or her hometown or at least outside the main centers of culture and communication (that is, in Faulkner's case, outside New York; in Olmi's case, outside Rome), which typically results in both a delay in public recognition and remaining relatively unfashionable. In Olmi's case, it's worth pointing out that after *Il posto* opened in Paris somewhat belatedly, it tied with Nico Papatakis's *Les Abysses* for twenty-fifth place in *Cahiers du Cinéma*'s list of the best films of 1963, and *I fidanzati* did only slightly better the following year, winding up in seventeenth place—just behind Raoul Walsh's *A Distant Trumpet* and just ahead of Mark Donskoi's *Thomas Gordeyev*. (Uncharacteristically, however, and quite surprisingly, *I fidanzati* also occupied first place in Jean-Luc Godard's personal list of favorite films for that same year, 1964—just ahead of *Gertrud, Marnie, Man's Favorite Sport,* and *Il deserto rosso,* in descending order—which is partially why I have hypothesized the possibility of this film exerting an influence on Godard.)

One final tendency to note that's relevant to Olmi would be the relatively late start of some artists in discovering and/or practicing their particular art forms; restricting ourselves now only to filmmakers, we might think of D. W. Griffith, 1875–1948, who began making films in 1907; Robert Bresson, 1901–1999, who made his first short film in 1934 and his first feature in 1943; Jacques Tati, 1907–1982, who made his first feature in 1947; Nicholas Ray, 1911–1979, who made his first feature in 1947, and Samuel Fuller, 1912–1997, who made his first feature in 1949. Olmi, to be sure, made his first documentary shorts in his early twenties, but it also seems relevant that he only turned to fiction and feature filmmaking in his late twenties. As with Griffith, Bresson, Tati, Ray, and Fuller—a very prestigious and varied honor roll—it would be fair to say that Olmi's early features clearly reflect, and to their own advantage, the life experience of someone who has lived for many years outside the world of cinema. This remains an essential part of their mystery and their uncommon power.

Notes

1. Don Ranvaud, "A Discreet Accomplice: Ermanno Olmi," *Monthly Film Bulletin* 55, no. 657 (October 1988): 316 (back cover).

2. Samuels, Charles Thomas, *Encountering Directors,* 2nd ed. (New York: Da Capo, 1987), 101.

3. Ibid., 112.

4. Ibid., 100.

5. Translator's note, *Right and Left / The Legend of the Holy Drinker* (Woodstock, N.Y.: Overlook Press, 1992), 289–91.

6. *Monthly Film Bulletin* 56, no. 668 (September 1989): 277–78.

7. Ranvaud, "A Discreet Accomplice."

8. Charles Thomas Samuels in Ranvaud, "A Discreet Accomplice," 109–10.

CHAPTER 17

Yasujiro Ozu

Both of the following essays were commissioned by major DVD labels, the British Film Institute (in early 2011) and Criterion (in late 2017), but they presented me with quite different challenges. *A Hen in the Wind* is commonly (though to my mind unjustly) regarded as Ozu's worst film. *I Was Born, But . . .*, on the other hand, is my favorite among all of Ozu's films, although it was being treated as an extra on Criterion's release of *Good Morning*—mainly, I suspect, because it's a silent picture—so I was instructed that I had to devote less space to it than to *Good Morning* (which I also revere, though not as much). Like Criterion's critically debatable but commercially sound decision to title its edition of Orson Welles's *Mr. Arkadin* "The Complete Mr. Arkadin" (see "Orson Welles: The Consumerist Version," below), this is another salient illustration of the principle that criticism and promotion aren't always or necessarily compatible with one another. (In the early 1990s, when Voyager commissioned an essay from me about Welles's *Confidential Report*—an alternate version of *Mr. Arkadin*—for its laserdisc of that film, and I wrote that this was the second-best version of *Arkadin*, my remark was promptly censored.)

Building from Ground Zero: *A Hen in the Wind*

It would hardly be an exaggeration to call *A Hen in the Wind* (1948) one of the more neglected films of Yasujiro Ozu, especially within the English-speaking world. Made immediately before one of his key masterpieces,

Late Spring (1949), it has understandably been treated as a lesser work, but its strengths and points of interest deserve a lot more attention than they've received. It isn't discussed in Noël Burch's *To the Distant Observer: Form and Meaning in the Japanese Cinema* (1979) or even mentioned in Kyoko Hirano's *Mr. Smith Goes to Tokyo: Japanese Cinema under the American Occupation, 1945–1952* (1992), the English-language study where it would appear to be most relevant. Although it isn't skimped in David Bordwell's *Ozu and the Poetics of Cinema* (1988), its treatment in Donald Richie's earlier *Ozu* (1974) is relatively brief and dismissive. It seems pertinent that even the film's title, which I assume derives from some Japanese expression, has apparently never been explicated in English.

It may be an atypical feature for Ozu, but it is stylistically recognizable as his work from beginning to end, especially when it comes to its poetic handling of setting (a dismal industrial slum in the eastern part of Tokyo, where the heroine rents a cramped upstairs room in a house) and its use of ellipsis in relation to its plot. Ozu himself was more than a little disparaging about it; Richie reports that a decade after its production and release, he wrote, "Well, everyone has his failures. There are all kinds of failures, however, and some of my failures I like. This film is a bad failure."

Perhaps because the film testifies so powerfully to the fact and circumstances of Japan's shattering defeat during the American Occupation, Ozu may not have been disposed to recognize its truths years later, during a sunnier period. By then, one should note, the film had been widely written off by others as a failure, and chided for its lack of verisimilitude in certain details (such as the cleanliness and tidiness of a room in a brothel), as well as its violations of certain norms associated with other Ozu pictures, especially his usual avoidance of violence. One hardly expects to witness a rape or brutal spousal abuse in an Ozu picture, and this film shows us both.

Tokiko (Kinuyo Tanaka)—a young wife and dressmaker with a sick child, in financial straits while her husband Suichi (Shuji Sano) is away in the army—is forced into a night of prostitution by her son's hospital expenses, and the plot charts the couple's slow reconciliation after the husband returns and discovers what has happened. If we momentarily ignore the unusual constraints of the American censors during this period—which, according to Hirano's book, required a line of dialogue in *Late Spring* to be changed from a statement that the daughter's health had deteriorated "due to her work after being conscripted by the Navy during the war" to "due to the forced work during the war"—it's tempting to hypothesize what other Japanese masters of this period might have done with the same basic story. If Akira Kurosawa had treated this subject, one would expect him to focus more on the husband's war experience; Kenji Mizoguchi would likely have devoted more attention to the wife and her brief episode as a prostitute. Ozu, accepting the viewpoints of both wife and husband in turn, maintains a certain balance between them by showing us nothing of either the husband at war *or* the wife as a prostitute. Both of these essential elements are left up to our imaginations and the imaginations of the characters: we "see" the husband at war through his wife's sorrows at home, just as we "see" the wife's prostitution only through the husband's visit to the bordello much later. Both unseen experiences are ultimately viewed as devastations that have to be accepted, digested, and ultimately worked through—although significantly, it is the single night of prostitution, not the much longer period of the husband at war, that the film addresses and focuses on.

Tokiko had to sell her own last kimono shortly before her little boy Hiroshi became ill, and had previously resisted the advice of Orie (Reiko Mizukami), the woman who purchased it, that she turn to prostitution. But once she finds it necessary to take Hiroshi to a hospital, she discovers he has an acute catarrh of the colon, and even though one of the nurses kindly offers her a handout, which she accepts, Tokiko concludes that she has to follow Orie's suggestion in order to pay for the medical expenses, even without discussing the matter with her best friend, Chieko (Akiko Ida). She does this only once, with a single customer—an event kept offscreen, although we hear the customer complaining afterward in the brothel that she wasn't very good. And significantly, Ozu also keeps her confession of this act to her husband offscreen, and we learn about it only when she tells Cheiko about it afterward.

Suichi becomes increasingly despondent about Tokiko's revelation at his job, and back at home becomes obsessed with learning more, pumping his wife for more information, including the location of the brothel, and then, after raping her (an event shown elliptically), going to the brothel himself, pretending at first to be a customer and quizzing Fusako (Chiyoko Ayatani), the twenty-one-year-old sent to his room, about why she has succumbed to this profession. After leaving the brothel, he runs into Fusako again by chance and promises to find her another job. He tells a colleague, Kazuichiro (Chishu Ryu), also back from the war, who agrees to hire Fusako and urges him to forgive his wife just as he has forgiven Fusako; Suichi accepts his advice on principle, but in fact is still in such a rage that when he eventually comes home he winds up shoving Tokiko down the stairs when she begs him not to leave again. But once he finally agrees to forgive and forget her transgression toward the end, it is her gesture of accepting him—her hands clasping one another behind his back—that seals their reconciliation, before Ozu ends the film with everyday exterior shots of the neighborhood.

Despite the film's checkered reputation, it has been persuasively defended by the two most influential and distinguished contemporary Japanese film critics, Tadao Sato and Shigehiko Hasumi, albeit in very different ways. Sato, who also observed that the brutal wife-beating in both *A Hen in the Wind* and *The Munekata Sisters* two years later were striking exceptions in Ozu's work, has also suggested, according to Bordwell's summary of his argument, that "Tokiko's becoming a prostitute symbolizes a loss of national purity" that was central to Japan's sense of itself and its own spirit during the war: "Suichi's violence toward her becomes emblematic of the ingrained brutality of the war years, demonstrating that he has lost the noble purpose that had been used to justify the war. The film's lesson, Sato concludes, cuts deeper than those contemporary films that sloughed blame off onto villainous militarists and weak-willed collaborators." Supporting this theory is the fact that in the films of so many other countries under occupation or totalitarian rule, political issues, when they crop up at all, are commonly and covertly transposed into sexual issues. (Three examples of this tendency would be Henri-Georges Clouzot's *The Raven* in France and Carl Dreyer's *Day of Wrath* in Denmark, both in 1943, and Juan Antonio Bardem's *Calle Mayor/Main Street* in Spain in 1956.)

In further support of Sato's analysis is Ozu's pungent and highly suggestive use of his sordid settings—not merely the claustrophobic rented room, in a blocked corner of which the husband will rape his wife, but the stairs leading up to it from the ground floor, and, in a wasteland where the husband goes to brood, a large, gaping, exposed pipe, all of which contribute a great deal to the film's emotional dynamics. And it is in this general arena—architecture, settings, the cutting between interiors and exteriors—that Hasumi's own analysis of the film is especially illuminating.

Hasumi's highly original 1983 book about Ozu, which lamentably isn't yet available in English (I've read it in its French translation), addresses and responds to Sato's defense of the film in some detail, agreeing that the film is "an important work," even though he concedes that "it is impossible to believe in Kinuyo Tanaka's character," but focusing more on particular aspects of its unusual physicality. The film's climactic moment of violence—conceivably the most shocking single moment in Ozu's work—shows Suichi shoving Tokiko down the flight of stairs and painfully shows us this moment frontally, from the foot of these stairs. Hasumi stresses the disturbing fact that Ozu focuses so often and repeatedly on this staircase long before this event happens, always from the same angle.

Part of the shock comes from Tokiko's acceptance of her husband's abuse, even to the point of masochism. (Her denial about what happened afterward to her landlady, with the face-saving alibi that she had an accidental fall, is probably easier for most of us to understand, perhaps because we find this latter gesture more familiar.) But no less shocking is the fact that, as Hasumi points out, it is extremely rare for Ozu to show any stairs at all in any of his films; even when he implies their presence in various households, he almost invariably keeps them offscreen. Here he's not only showing us a particular staircase countless times; he even prepares us for the climactic moment of violence in another way, by showing us an earlier scene in which Suichi angrily kicks a tin can down those same steps and makes sure we hear the thuds as it hits every step.

Part of what makes Hasumi's book so provocative is its way of countering and at times even contradicting most of the other critical studies of Ozu that we have. In response to the frequent claim that Ozu was the "most Japanese" of Japanese filmmakers, Hasumi maintains that he may actually have been the *least* Japanese because of his (well-documented) obsession with Hollywood films, already evident in the movie posters seen in his features (including *A Hen in the Wind,* which has three of these in a single room). And when it comes to the climactic moment of violence in *A Hen in the Wind,* Hasumi conjectures that this may have been inspired by the fall of Scarlett O'Hara's down a staircase in *Gone with the Wind* (an accident that causes her miscarriage)—a film that Ozu saw in Singapore during the war, when he was viewing Hollywood films on virtually a daily basis.

It may seem paradoxical that Ozu's strategies for conveying Japan's sense of humiliation from the American occupation might have been drawn from the American cinema, but this possibility is supported by other things that we know about his taste. According to Richie, *Citizen*

Kane was his favorite film; and he once famously remarked, "Watching *Fantasia* made me suspect that we were going to lose the war. These guys look like trouble, I thought."

The film, in any case, is suffused with a sense of defeat, but it ends with some rays of hope, however characteristically elliptical Ozu makes their expression. Once Suichi finally agrees to forgive and forget Tokiko's transgression, it is significantly her gesture of accepting him—her hands clasping one another behind his back—that seals their reconciliation, before Ozu ends the film with everyday exterior shots of the neighborhood.

Structures and Strictures in Suburbia

From its very opening, *Good Morning* (1959) is deeply and delightfully musical, both in the orchestration of static visual elements in its first two shots (the juxtaposition of adjacent houses with fences and clotheslines, and all these horizontals with the verticality of electrical towers) and in its varying rhythmic patterns of human movement, which are no less orchestrated, as various figures cross the pathways between houses, between houses and hill, and on top of the hill itself—always, mysteriously, moving from right to left. And what could be more musical than the opening gag, occurring on the same sunny hilltop, of little boys farting for their own amusement, still another form of theme and variations?

All of which prompts me to disagree respectfully with the late Yasujiro Ozu specialist Donald Richie when he maintained, "*Good Morning*, in some ways Ozu's most schematic film, certainly one of his least complicated formally, is an example of a film constructed around motifs." Certainly the motifs are there, and these are vital; the two examined by Richie as sterling examples are the farting and the greeting embodied in the film's title, and numerous variations are run on both. But as soon as one focuses on the relations *between* these two motifs—including the realization that the farting game is the boys' way of saying "Good morning" to one another, and the fact that a housewife hears her husband's farts in another room as if he were summoning her—the possibilities of comic and formal play deriving from this, at once satirical and musical, become endless; and they are far from simple.

In a broader sense, the standardization of suburban life that can lead a drunken neighbor to come home one night to the wrong house and also lead the neighborhood as a whole to ostracize a bohemian couple is a central motif in *Good Morning,* and this too has formal and social implications—especially if one acknowledges that in Ozu, as in Jacques Tati, expressions of social forms and expressions of cinematic forms are simply two sides of the same coin. Because the society that Ozu depicts is essentially bound up in formality, it naturally follows that his sense of its boundaries and limitations is intimately related to its ritual social gestures. He is gently critiquing these gestures—greetings and farts alike—while also enjoying their absurdity and playing with their forms. Part of the unexpected brilliance of *Good Morning* (or *Ohayo,* as it's called in Japanese), for example, is how much formal ingenuity Ozu can exercise with visual rhymes in the riotous colors and identical square shapes (on quilts, other furnishings, clothes) of his scenic design, as if to refute or at least complicate the seeming monotony and replications of suburban neighborhoods.

Similarly, it's remarkable how much complexity and universal wisdom he can find in the crosscutting patterns of a Japanese sitcom. Minoru and Isamu, age thirteen and seven, are chastised by their mother, Tamiko, for watching television (mainly sumo wrestling, a Japanese craze at the time) at the nearby house of the bohemian couple instead of attending their English lessons; their English teacher, currently jobless, is given translation work by their aunt, while their equally jobless neighbor Tomizawa complains to the boys' father (Ozu standby Chishu Ryu) about the difficulty of being retired by his company. Meanwhile, there's consternation about the disappearance of the local women's club dues, and the fact that Mrs. Haraguchi (Haruko Sugimura, another Ozu regular), the treasurer, has recently bought a washing machine is the cause of some jealous suspicion, until Mrs. Haraguchi discovers that her mother has absentmindedly put the dues aside. This busy neighborhood interactivity, as conveyed through crosscutting that either contrasts or dovetails the separate intrigues, runs the gamut from trivial to profound and back again in such a way as to suggest how often serious and unserious matters can come to seem interchangeable—thanks to Ozu's acute sense of form.

Ozu's philosophical and formal equanimity, gauging both the significance and the inconsequentiality of everyday activities, is exemplified in the scene where Keitaro comes home to find his sons fretting because of Tamiko's refusal to buy a television. He says they talk too much and grows angrier when Minoru insists that grown-ups do the same, citing phrases like "Good morning" and "Fine day." They retaliate by taking a vow of silence—a serious gesture, yet one that leads to various absurd consequences when it comes to dealing with neighbors and teachers.

Devoted to both the profound necessity and the sublime silliness of gratuitous social interchange, *Good Morning* is therefore much subtler and grander than it might initially appear. Commonly identified as a remake of Ozu's silent 1932 masterpiece *I Was Born, But . . .*, also included in this edition, it is even more interesting for its differences than for its similarities—above all, the difference between what a father's authority meant in prewar and postwar Japan. The focus of the earlier film is a family adapting to a new suburban neighborhood by undergoing brutal social initiations: the father humiliates himself before his boss to get ahead, while the sons are accepted by their peers only after humiliating a local bully. Shocked by the behavior of their father, who insists that he must demean himself in order to feed them, the sons retaliate by going on a hunger strike. In the much lighter and far from tragic climate of *Good Morning*, twenty-seven years later, the setting is again middle-class Tokyo suburbia, but the family is now firmly settled, and serious problems—old age, unemployment, ostracism—are principally reserved for their neighbors and friends. The sons' complaint and rebellion are considerably milder. Significantly, it is the humiliations in the first film that provide much of the comedy, a subject assuming gravity only when it causes a rift between father and sons. But the more pervasive humor of *Good Morning* extends to the rebellion itself and all it engenders, as well as the local intrigues surrounding it; one no longer feels that the father's authority is a monument that can be toppled.

In his *Critical Handbook of Japanese Film Directors,* Alexander Jacoby notes that, despite his obvious importance, "Ozu has nevertheless been represented in partial and misleading terms in many Western accounts." Among the misunderstandings cited are the beliefs that Ozu "used an invariably static camera," that his devout Zen Buddhism somehow accounts for everything in his films, and that he was "the most Japanese of Japanese directors." But Ozu made almost twice as many silent pictures as talkies, and his early features abound in camera movements. Ozu ridiculed the assumption of some Westerners that his works could be explained by Zen, and as one of his sharpest and most insightful critics, Shigehiko Hasumi, has argued, he may have actually been the *least*

Japanese of major Japanese directors. His worship of Hollywood movies, which persisted throughout his life, even extended to setting most of his movies in the kind of clear and sunny weather you're more likely to find in southern California than in the drizzly and overcast climate of his own country. Indeed, it can be argued that Ozu's grasp of both reality and formality was much more tied to his sense of Hollywood studio filmmaking than to some idea of Japanese "otherness."

Lamentably, Hasumi's book on Ozu remains unavailable in English, apart from its closing chapter, pointedly titled "Sunny Skies." But I think the best summary of what Hasumi has to offer to our Western misunderstandings of Ozu can be found in the following sentence: "Ozu's talent lies in choosing an image that can function poetically at a particular moment by being assimilated into the film, not by affixing to the film the image of an object that is considered poetic in a domain outside the film." In *Good Morning,* the poetic charge he can somehow muster out of an unopened carton containing a new TV set in a hallway is a perfect illustration of this principle—another example of making something mundane and familiar into something luminous and special through strategic placement in an edited sequence.

In the interest of full disclosure, I should note that my first visit to Japan, in late 1998, came at Hasumi's invitation, during his stint as president of Tokyo University, to participate in a panel called "Yasujiro Ozu in the World" along with Hasumi himself, Taiwanese director Hou Hsiao-hsien, his screenwriter Tien-wen Chu, and French critics Jean Douchet and Thierry Jousse. This was part of a retrospective and exhibition devoted to Ozu, and for me the most memorable feature of the latter was a display of notebooks kept by the filmmaker on each of his features. Emblematically of how meticulous he was as a control freak, he neatly and precisely recorded how long he anticipated each shot would last and then how long each shot actually did last. (Undoubtedly the most luminous moment of the panel was being approached in the lobby just afterward by an elderly gentleman who spoke in Japanese to Hou and myself, shook our hands, and then walked away—a puzzling encounter that was immediately, and appropriately, explicated to me via mime, when Hou nimbly imitated the signature comic gesture of Tomio "Tokkankozo" Aoki, the younger son in *I Was Born, But . . .*—thus identifying the child actor discovered by Ozu and the performer behind the title antihero of *The Straightforward Boy,* also included in this release, who went on to enjoy a screen career that would last seventy-five years, encompassing even Seijun Suzuki's 2001 *Pistol Opera*.)

One of the funniest gags in *I Was Born, But . . .* is possibly the most blatantly self-reflexive moment in Ozu's oeuvre. Comparing the regimentation in the little boys' school with the regimentation in their father's office, Ozu shows the boys marching briskly past the camera in their schoolyard while the camera begins to track rapidly in the reverse direction. Then there is a cut to another rapid track in the father's office, moving at the same speed past workers at a row of desks, some seated and some standing. Each worker yawns, as if on cue, just as the camera passes him, except for one, until the camera moves back, stops, and waits for him to yawn as well; as soon as he does, the camera resumes the same rapid movement past other workers, all of whom yawn on cue. This is a rather exceptional self-referential moment in Ozu's work because it equates his own position of power as a director with the power of the state—specifically, with the power of the school and the office, the two principal zones of authority in the film apart from the more indeterminate zones of the field (ruled by the boys) and the house (ruled by the father).

Good Morning, of course, has its own ways of ironically comparing children and grown-ups, such as juxtaposing timid small talk between a youthful couple waiting for a train with the schoolboys' farting game. (There is also an implicit comparison in the depiction of the adults' childish envy when one household purchases a TV set and another one buys a new washing machine.) With a similar sense of scrupulous economy, there is the alternation of simply stated (if interlocking) mini-plots with complex camera setups, less bound by narrative advancement, depicting the physical layout of the neighborhood itself: the perpendicular passageways between houses and the overhead road on the embankment behind all cogently suggesting certain structures as well as strictures in a society of interdependent yet insulated busybodies. In a context where sliding doors and shot changes become integral facets of the same "architecture"—an interrelating complex of adjacent, autonomous units—the fascination is in the way even throwaway details become part of the design. For instance, movie posters for Stanley Kramer's *The Defiant Ones* and Louis Malle's *The Lovers,* combined with various glimpses of the sumo wrestlers on TV, allude not only to the recalcitrant sons but also to a sense of antagonistic parties chained together by circumstance that often seems to function just below the surface of the everyday pleasantries. A grandmother muttering gripes between her prayers, the drunken Tomizawa coming home to the wrong house, the young scat-singing couple being quietly hounded out of the community, a thoughtful Keitaro wondering if television will "produce 100 million idiots": all these moments are characteristically uninflected, and each goes straight to the heart of the film.

CHAPTER 18

Sally Potter

Apart from the two films considered here—in an essay written for the British Film Institute's Region 2 DVD release of *The Gold Diggers* in 2009, and in a review of *Yes* written for the July 8, 2005 *Chicago Reader*—I'm not sure whether I qualify as a Sally Potter fan. That is, while I've seen most (if not all) of her thirteen other shorts and features to date, and appreciated some of them to greater or lesser extents, the two discussed here are the only ones so far that I find I can return to repeatedly with pleasure and a renewed sense of discovery and edification. That they've both been widely and unfairly disparaged by other critics may have helped to intensify my support, but they certainly haven't caused it. And regarding most of the other Potter films I've seen, she should be praised for her refusal to commodify her special talents, which, like those of Peter Thompson, combine the fruits of her musical training with an acute if unfashionable sense of what can be expressed only in film—a sense, that is, of her own instincts that remain firm and unassailable quite apart from the inconvenience of their stirring up controversies.

The Gold Diggers Reconsidered

A quarter of a century after its initial unfriendly reception, it's worth puzzling over why a film as beautiful, as witty, as imaginative, and as brilliant as Sally Potter's first feature could have given so much offense to certain spectators in 1983. The recoil was so unforgiving in some quarters that

Potter, after touring extensively with the film, came to seriously question it herself—or at least the wisdom of having made it, insofar as it was already threatening to end her ambitious career in filmmaking almost before it had properly started, thereby eventually persuading her to withdraw the film from circulation. (By contrast, the exceptional success of her thirty-four-minute *Thriller* in 1979, an unpacking of Puccini's *La Bohème,* made with many of the same collaborators—most notably Colette Laffont, Lindsay Cooper, and Rose English—had clearly heightened her expectations.) Now that it's belatedly becoming available again on DVD, it's more than entitled to a fresh look—including a consideration of what originally perturbed some people about it.

Even after one totes up all of the most obvious of the possible objections that could be raised against *The Gold Diggers*—boredom, antifeminist backlash, envy of other independent filmmakers for Potter's lavish funding from the National Film Board, pretentiousness, allegorical and metaphorical density, sheer difficulty (as Ruby Rich, a sympathetic analyst, put it in her 1998 book *Chick Flicks,* "Its commitment to narrative [is] minor")—the inability or refusal of many viewers to grasp or even notice *The Gold Diggers*' no less obvious and unassailable strengths continues to confound me. Just for starters, there are the gorgeous images by one of the world's greatest cinematographers, Babette Mangolte—clearly her best work in black and white, as Mangolte has often maintained herself, and perhaps her most impressive work altogether. From the awesome opening pan across an epic Icelandic landscape, which suggests an etching or a woodcut almost as much as photography, the brilliance of Mangolte's high-contrast palette and its surrealist impact (which nowadays one would be more apt to call "Lynchian," and compare to Lynch's own first feature, *Eraserhead,* as well as its Victorian and equally neotheatrical follow-up, *The Elephant Man*), defying the chestnut about black and white being more "realistic" than color, already makes this movie an extraordinary achievement. As in Orson Welles's *The Trial,* the film creates an imaginary geography, multinational and labyrinthine, in which interiors and exteriors, locations and sets, and onstage and offstage spaces are often difficult to disentangle.

And even if one chooses to discount or ignore the historical (albeit extratextual) precedent of Potter hiring an all-woman crew, what about the grace and beauty of Julie Christie? The indelibly haunting and throbbing bassoon-heavy score by Lindsay Cooper, one of the film's three screenwriters? The bold, imaginative, and sometimes disturbing oversized sets by art director and costume designer Rose English, another one of the screenwriters? And what about the witty and pungent cross-referencing of film history by Potter herself (the third screenwriter)—making *The Gold Diggers* perhaps the only English feature that truly qualifies as Godardian, working out of a critical canon that's no less eclectic and wide-ranging?

Of course the opening offscreen monologue ("I'm born in the light and move continuously, yet I'm still") is also about cinema, and this ontological rumination ultimately informs everything else that the film chooses to consider—the "movement" of gold and money and blood, the exchange value of women, and the delight of breaking free from the usual habits and practices.

Like Elaine May's mainstream disaster *Ishtar* a few years later, I think that some of the outrage ignited by *The Gold Diggers,* unacknowledged and no doubt often unconscious, must have been ideological—a kind of transgression in Potter's case that had a certain relation to genre as well as gender. While May was castigated mainly (and improbably) for spending too much money, surely some of the bile provoked by *Ishtar,* despite this writer-director's clear affection for her dumbbell heroes, was her spot-on exposure of American idiocy in the Middle East, long before the First Gulf War was even a gleam in the eye of George Bush Sr. And I'm sure that at least part of the rage elicited by *The Gold Diggers* had to do with Potter's promiscuous cross-breeding of avant-garde and mainstream, gaily mixing together musical, anticapitalist satire, SF fantasy, western, quirky lesbian agitprop, silent melodrama, *Screen* magazine film theory about the male gaze and various kinds of capitalist discourse, period costume adventure, glum allegory, and deadpan farce—along with diverse forms of both modern dance (including tap dance) and landscape art, not to mention a glamorous commercial icon like Christie. And still another (and likely even more furious) part must have come from Potter having deliberately used her stereotypical male characters so marginally and incidentally that they mainly wound up registering as weak, silly, and interchangeable.

"Perhaps [the] determination to laugh in the face of power was what upset those critics more than anything that the film says explicitly," aptly writes Sophie Mayer in her recent *The Cinema of Sally Potter: A Politics of Love,* cinching the parallel with *Ishtar* a bit more precisely. So it seems entirely appropriate that the mocking laughter of Ruby (Christie) toward her former male captors would apparently elude Janet Maslin when she scornfully reviewed the film in the *New York Times* in 1988, expediently consigning the film's few overseas defenders to a different planet and implicitly declaring its *mise en scène,* cinematography, music, and art direction not even worthy of note, much less approval:

> There are critics in Britain who have praised Sally Potter's *Gold Diggers* as "witty," "visually entrancing," and "an absorbing pleasure," and there may also be like-minded individuals on the planet Jupiter. But by any reasonable earthly standard, this thing—a 1983 oddity, sort of a feminist, deconstructionist, riddle-filled anti-musical, much of it set on the Icelandic tundra—is pure torture. Its only noteworthy attribute is the presence of Julie Christie, who embodies some sardonic notion of the archetypal, unenlightened movie heroine through the ages. Like it or not, Miss Christie is infinitely better off playing such creatures straight than she is satirizing them here.

Launching a career bent on both lavish experiment and pleasing an audience, *The Gold Diggers* failed to perform the way that Potter's subsequent *Orlando* did, but this isn't to say that its own alchemical pleasures aren't fully available today—as they are in many of her subsequent features (such as my own current second-favorite of Potter's, *Yes.*) It's not enough to say that this first Potter feature, which wears its avant-garde credentials (that is to say, Potter's own background, in music, dance, *and* film) unabashedly, skirts pretension. More precisely, it glories in pretentiousness, which in this case basically means a free and highly creative assertiveness about ideas as well as appearances, ranging from its *Ubu Roi* sense of ritual to its diverse Klondike and gold-rush iconography. It's a film, in short, that proudly benefits as well as suffers from a surfeit of both significations and giddy percussive patterns, wallowing in excess only because it's bent on representing and unpacking a few of the excesses already rampant in the world, including cinema. Potter's savvy as both a film critic and a film historian can readily be gleaned from the films she programmed along with her own at the National Film Theatre in 1983, including among the over two dozen "fellow travelers" of *The Gold Diggers* such varied yet visibly relevant works as *Way Down East, The Smiling Madame Beudet, The Gold Rush, Gold Diggers of 1933, Alexander Nevsky, Dance, Girl, Dance, Hellzapoppin', Queen Christina, The Red Shoes, The Trial, Persona, Doctor

Zhivago, *Lives of Performers*, *The State of Things*, and *The Power of Emotions*. For me, perhaps the most conspicuous omissions here are *Dura Lex/By the Law* and *The 5,000 Fingers of Dr. T*. But then of course you can't always have everything, even if you take the kind of pleasure that *The Gold Digger* does—and the kind of immoderate pleasure it offers—in trying.

Love in the Time of Terror [*Yes*]

> **Yes**. A film that irrefutably deserves its title. A film of affirmation. Which is not the same as a story with a happy ending. . . . If the places in this story become characters, what is the scene? The area of world politics today, nothing less, is the scene—and, above it, the sky to which everyone, at one moment or another, prays.
> —John Berger

> Apparently sales of poetry go up in times of war.
> —Sally Potter

Many people feel a sense of helplessness about the ongoing war in the Middle East, feelings they're often unable to articulate, much less address. Sally Potter's *Yes* shows one way these feelings can be processed, and in doing so overturns some of the usual assumptions about what movies can and should do. It won't please everyone, and the sensitive topics it touches on may make some viewers mad enough to spit.

Yes is a post-9/11 love story, set chiefly in London, about a passionate adulterous affair between an Irish American scientist (Joan Allen), who's unhappily married to an English politician, and a somewhat younger Lebanese cook (Simon Abkarian), who's unmarried and used to work as a surgeon in Beirut. All the dialogue, which Potter wrote, is in rhyming iambic pentameter, ten syllables to a line, apart from a few direct declarations with eight syllables. Far from a gimmick, this is the ideal way to convey Potter's poetic intelligence and her feelings about the contemporary world. Moreover, the dialogue is delivered with such skill by the actors that it remains expressive without ever seeming mannered or show-offy.

Yes firmly, if offhandedly, undermines several received notions: that movies are a visual medium, so images matter more than sounds in general and words in particular. That rhyming dialogue, unless it's from Shakespeare or Dr. Seuss (as a reviewer in *Boxoffice* put it), is a fool's mission—though according to the *Reader's Encyclopedia,* "Insofar as one can generalize, [iambic pentameter] is the prevailing meter of natural English speech." That movies shouldn't try to address the state of the contemporary world. That using individual characters to represent nations, cultures, genders leads to facile generalizations (Potter's two main characters are named He and She, the heroine's maid serves as a Greek chorus, and the heroine's nameless dying aunt in Belfast stands for communism). That communism is dead and Cuba (where She flees after her aunt dies) isn't worth thinking about except to scoff at.

Potter's brazen movie seems to invite ridicule, though it's more lighthearted in its provocations than heavy-handed or bleak. *Variety,* the *Hollywood Reporter,* and the *New York Times* have run hyperbolically hostile reviews, yet Potter noted during a recent trip to Chicago (her blog is at sallypotter.com), "It is such a vindication for me and for all of those who worked on the film with such dedication that the very things that so many financiers found scary and to be avoided at all costs—the verse and the politics—are precisely the aspects of the film that people seem to find the most exciting. Audiences, it would seem, are ahead of the game, eager and bold."

Potter never discusses the war in the Middle East directly, though she started working on the film the day after 9/11. "What was evident was that there were going to be increasing levels of demonization of people from the Middle East and reverse levels of hatred of Americans," she said during an audience discussion. "So I asked myself, what can I contribute as a filmmaker? I thought a good starting point was a love story between a man from the Middle East and a Western woman, in which love and attraction initially transcend difference. But when world events, history, and national identity can no longer be kept out of the relationship, they have to slug it out."

This is the first Potter feature I've fully enjoyed since her first, *The Gold Diggers,* a black-and-white feminist SF musical received so poorly in 1983 that she's rarely allowed it to be screened since. Broadly speaking, the closest thing to a precedent for *Yes* is Alain Resnais and Marguerite Duras's 1959 *Hiroshima, mon amour.* Fourteen years after the first atomic bomb was dropped, Resnais and Duras found a way to deal with the emotional and ethical shock of that event through a series of spatial and temporal removes and through a love story that, like *Yes,* played out across a great cultural divide. That story, about a nameless French actress and a Japanese architect having a brief adulterous affair in the rebuilt Hiroshima, focused on the Frenchwoman recounting her traumatic persecution in France in 1945 for having had an affair with a German soldier. Without implying any sort of equivalence between her suffering and that of the bomb's victims in Hiroshima, the film nevertheless created an emotional gateway between those experiences, and the music of Duras's language and Resnais's exquisitely timed cuts and camera movements gave a healing and clarifying form of expression to the unbridgeable and the unimaginable. So it seems relevant that, trained as a musician, Potter still thinks like one.

She isn't dealing with a trauma buried in the past but one that's ongoing, though she too uses spatial and cultural removes. The hero isn't Afghan or Iraqi but Lebanese (and, reversing standard procedure, he's more sexually objectified and glamorized than the heroine), she's an American born in Ireland and living in England, and the film's set in London, Beirut, and Havana, not Kabul or Baghdad. Potter, who's a trained musician, is using her own poetic language, cuts, camera movements, canted angles, periodically slurred action, and other visual strategies to create emotional gateways into intellectual concerns. Differences in class parallel and overlap differences in culture, but her rhyming lines are clarifying, not vilifying. Consider these lines from three different parts of the film:

> SHE (TO HE): You cannot look me in the face
> And say I am your fall from grace.
>
> HE (WEARILY): From Elvis to Eminem, Warhol's art,
> I know your stories, know your songs by heart.
> But do you know mine? No, every time,
> I make the effort, and I learn to rhyme
> In your English. And do you know a word
> Of my language, even one? Have you heard
> That "al-gebra" was an Arabic man?
> You've read the Bible. Have you read the Koran?
>
> AUNT: A great big dream that's fallen pretty flat
> In all the other countries where they tried
> It. They'll regret it. Communism died,
> But what came in its place? A load of greed.
> A life spent longing for things you don't need.

The strengths and limitations of these characters are essentially those of Potter's poetic conceits, so they're somewhat generic—which is why they lack names, unlike the sympathetically portrayed estranged husband (Sam Neill), who's an English politician, as well as the cook's three coworkers, and a few others in the cast who project more prosaic and naturalistic social realities. Speaking most directly and intimately to us is the nameless maid (Shirley Henderson), who frames the film's action as she periodically looks up from her work to address the camera. She's the film's philosophical conscience, which is evident mainly in her discussions of dirt and its meaning. She's its Molly Bloom, providing the Joycean affirmation of the film's title, the last word in *Ulysses,* though unlike Molly, she has an intellectual lucidity that goes well beyond libido. Her obvious lesson is that no one can address today's problems without addressing our assumptions about a lot of things.

CHAPTER 19

Mark Rappaport

Mark Rappaport has been a good friend ever since I was assigned as a freelancer to write about the shooting of his fifth feature, *Impostors*, for the October 1979 *American Film,* shortly after I moved back to New York from San Diego, a piece available on my website (Look for "Man on a Shoestring.") A few years later, I devoted a chapter of my *Film: The Front Line 1983* to him, and subsequently reviewed at some length his *Rock Hudson's Home Movies* (1992) and *From the Journals of Jean Seberg* (1995)—his first two forays into fictional biography—for the *Chicago Reader*. My interview with him about the latter film for *Cineaste* is included in the first volume of *Cinematic Encounters*. He moved from New York to Paris in 2003.

The following essay was written for the ninety-ninth issue of *Trafic* (Fall 2016)—a revision and slight expansion of two previous essays written for *Fandor Keyframe* (January 2016) and *Found Footage* no. 2 (April 2016).

Fictional Biography as Film Criticism: Two Videos by Mark Rappaport

The rapidly and constantly expanding proliferation of films and videos about cinema is altering some of our notions about film history in at least two significant ways. For one thing, now that it has become impossible for any individual to keep abreast of all this work, our methodologies for assessing it as a whole have to be expanded and further developed. And second, insofar as one way of defining work in cinematic form and style that is truly groundbreaking is to single out work that defines new areas of content, the search for such work is one of the methodologies that might be most useful. In my case, this is a search that has led to considerations of two recent videos by Mark Rappaport: *I, Dalio—or The Rules of the Game* (2014, thirty-three minutes), and *Debra Paget, For Example* (2016, thirty-three minutes). Both are highly personal works that also define relatively new areas of on-film film analysis, forms of classification that can be described here as indexing.

Rappaport was born in New York and he lived and (mostly) worked there until he moved to Paris in 2003, although his work with found footage started more than a decade earlier with *Rock Hudson's Home Movies* (1992), followed by *Exterior Night* (made in Germany for German television in 1993), *From the Journals of Jean Seberg* (1995), *The Silver Screen: Color Me Lavender* (1997), and his 2002 short *John Garfield*. Since his move to Paris, he has published a collection of his (fictional and nonfictional) essays in French (*Le Spectateur qui en savait trop*, translated by Jean-Luc Mengus, Paris: P.O.L, 2008) and three online collections in English available in Kindle editions on Amazon: *The Moviegoer Who Knew Too Much* (2013), *(F)au(x)tobiographies* (2013), and *The Secret Life of Moving Shadows* (available in two parts, 2014). He has also exhibited photomontages in New York, Paris, and elsewhere over the past several years—and it should be added that his interests in the Victorian novel (which he studied at Brooklyn College), melodrama, and art history have informed much of his work, from his nine features made in New York to his more recent short videos (*Becoming Anita Ekberg*, 2014, *The Vanity Tables of Douglas Sirk*, 2015, *Our Stars*, 2015, *The Circle Closes*, 2015, and the aforementioned *I, Dalio* and *Debra Paget, For Example*, 2015, all made over the past three years).

Some of these videos, including *I, Dalio,* adopt the form of fictional autobiography that Rappaport used in *Rock Hudson's Home Movies* and *From the Journals of Jean Seberg*—employing actors who play the eponymous subjects recounting their careers (exclusively offscreen, by Tito de Pinho, in *I, Dalio,* speaking in English with a French accent) and commenting on clips from their films. The comments, all written by Rappaport, allow the actor's stand-in to serve as a kibbitzer (a Yiddish term for a commentator whose remarks are most often uninvited and irreverent) on the clips while pretending to be Hudson, Seberg, Ekberg, Dalio, or

Paget, and they frequently match the novelistic methodologies of his fictional essays by using fiction to broaden as well as dramatize Rappaport's analysis, sometimes creating in effect conversations between Rappaport and the films he discusses. And indexing certain roles and performances by these actors to make certain points is the most common procedure. Thus Hudson's closeted homosexuality and Seberg's ambiguous "blank" expressions, seen cumulatively over several roles and films, become the basis for social critiques and, in the case of Seberg, a certain amount of film theory tied to the famous "Kuleshov experiment." In the case of Marcel Dalio—born with the name Israel Moshe Blauschild in Paris's main Jewish neighborhood in 1899 (according to Wikipedia) or 1900 (according to Rappaport)—this becomes the basis of indexing Dalio's mainly unsympathetic roles in prewar French cinema, which are plausibly shown to be cumulatively and implicitly (if not always individually) anti-Semitic: "In the French films of the '30s, I play every kind of scoundrel, and I'm called every name imaginable—except one." Significantly, the two exceptions discussed are Jean Renoir's *La Grande Illusion* (1937) and *La règle du jeu* (1939), where he plays sympathetic aristocratic Jews, explicitly identified as Jewish. But then, after the Nazi occupation of France forces Dalio to emigrate to the United States, we discover that his Hollywood roles are subject to a different kind of typecasting in which his Judaism becomes both irrelevant and ignored and he becomes stereotyped simply as "French," most often in comic and whimsical parts.

After we see Dalio playing a hotelier named Frenchy in *To Have and Have Not* (Howard Hawks, 1944), we hear his stand-in say, "I was no longer the 'Jew' with quotes around it. No one cared about that anymore. Now I was simply The Frenchman. The rules of the game suddenly changed. It was that easy. It just depended on where you were and who was defining you." But this provocative conclusion is by no means all of *I, Dalio;* Rappaport also traces briefly the screen careers of Dalio's three wives (two in France, one in the United States) and his returns to Europe after the war (occasioning some reversions to being cast as more unsavory types), the less apparent Jewish identities of some of French colleagues and costars (such as Jean-Pierre Aumont and Simone Signoret, who didn't, like him, wind up on Nazi posters representing "typical" Jews—although Rappaport gets to imagine what such posters would have looked like), and other diverse tangents and asides that emerge from rummaging through

Dalio's filmography. Yet the unifying thread is Dalio's separate personas in French cinema and Hollywood, and many mitigating factors are brought into the discussion. "Paradoxically, the French respected me more, and I almost always got a full film credit (illustrated by several clips,) even for a small role," while a scene in the 1960 Hollywood musical *Can-Can* shows Dalio, "a Jew who fled Hitler," with two other stereotypical French actors, Louis Jourdan, "[who] fought in the Resistance," and Maurice Chevalier, "who did not resist very strenuously." The fictional Dalio then remarks, "You might well wonder what we talked about between takes," and the real Dalio (still in *Can-Can*) replies, "I'm not allowed to tell, sir."

This is shortly followed by the observation, amply illustrated, that "A Frenchman in America can play a priest, a Jew in France cannot." And finally, with the onset of old age, "I was no longer a type. I was neither Frenchy nor a devious Jew. I was just an old man." And then back in France, in 1973, ten years before his death, he plays Rabbi Jacob in a hit comedy.

This, in short, outlines the new areas of "content" created as well as discovered by Rappaport while indexing the found footage of Dalio's filmography, which also includes the effacement of his name from the credits and/or the effacement of his actual presence (as a Jew) in two 1938 French features when these were rereleased in Nazi-occupied France. And the obvious virtue of using film rather than prose to handle this material is that it proves Rappaport's points through concrete demonstration. (For the same reason, Rappaport's fictional and nonfictional essays often make integral uses of illustrations.) As Godard once said to Pauline Kael in a public discussion,

> the image is like evidence in a courtroom. For me, making a movie is like bringing in evidence. . . . That's why I'm not working in criticism anymore these days—practically—because *there* words always come first. . . . To me, a good review, good criticism (whether it is in *Cahiers du Cinéma* or *Film Comment*) would be trying not to say "I don't feel" "I don't see it the way you saw it," but, rather, "Let's see it, let's bring in the evidence" (Godard & Kael, 1982: 175–76).

Rappaport's own biography makes him ideally suited to index Dalio's work in this manner—not only because his own move from the United States to France predisposes him to observe differences in their two mainstream cinemas, but also because living in Paris clearly gave him access to a good many European films that he wouldn't have had otherwise.

■ ■ ■

Mark Rappaport and I have been friends for well over three decades. He's a year older than me, and even though our class and regional backgrounds differ, we're both film freaks and film historians who grew up with the same Hollywood iconographies, for better and for worse. How these experiences might qualify as better or worse have been the source of countless friendly arguments, all the more so when they converge on the same objects of fascination—as the title of his latest video puts it, *Debra Paget, For Example*.

Thirty-six minutes and thirty-six seconds long, this juicy video about the fifteen-year screen career of Debra Paget (1948–1963, ages fourteen to twenty-nine, including a busy eight-year stretch as contract player at Fox, 1950–1957) seems at times to cover almost as much material and as much cultural ground as Rappaport's two star-centered film features, *Rock Hudson's Home Movies* and *From the Journals of Jean Seberg* (1995). It might even be called a compendium of Rappaport's rhetorical strategies, such as using an actor to play the star in question—as in those two features, although here only offscreen (as was also done in *I, Dalio, or The Rules of the Game*), with Paget voiced by Caroline Simonds—and using Rappaport's own voice, as in another recent video, *The Circle Closes*. One might say that the reason why he employs two voices is what academic critics would call discursive: he has more to say, and this "more" can't be contained within a single voice; it also wanders every which way, as many of the best essays do. And to complicate matters, these two voices aren't so much in dialogue with one another as they are coming at us from different angles—fictional in the case of Simonds speaking as (or for) Paget, nonfictional in the case of Rappaport speaking for himself—even though the two of them share the same basic assumptions.

The voices aren't exactly in conflict, but they nonetheless point toward a divergence of positions that seem to make the two voices necessary. Let's call it a divided consciousness, marking a breach that I fully share with Rappaport. This divergence can be described in many different ways—for example, as art versus kitsch, as history versus memory, as reality versus fantasy, and maybe even as theory versus practice. Here is how Rappaport himself expresses the problem, roughly halfway through the video, starting with a parenthetical digression about Maria Montez in the 1940s and ending with the Golden Calf sequence in *The Ten Commandments:*

> She [Maria Montez] was called the Queen of Technicolor, but that was a euphemism. What they meant was the Queen of Kitsch.... But we're less likely to scoff at present-day kitsch, or even recognize it. In fact, we often embrace it.
>
> If Maria Montez was the Queen of Kitsch, surely Debra Paget is the Princess of Kitsch. But let's be careful here. One guy's kitsch is another guy's nostalgia.
>
> If you saw these movies at the right age, at a Saturday matinee or on TV when you were a kid, it would have made all the difference. And it's virtually impossible to explain it to other people who aren't there. You can't argue with someone's childhood memories. And who's to say that kitsch—or memories—or nostalgia, and the seemingly guilty pleasures they offer—are any less valuable in film history than, say, Ingmar Bergman or Antonioni? The jury's still out, and won't be in for awhile. For example—

Over the three labeled sections of *Debra Paget, For Example*—"1. Beginning," "2. The Middle Years & CinemaScope," and "3. Fritz Lang's Indian Film/Paget's Apotheosis"—the topics and positions toward them are indeed disparate. In the first part alone, among other things, we get Paget's skill in walking across a room ("not as easy to do as you might think"); then we get the queasy implications of fourteen-year-old Paget kissing a thirty-eight-year-old Richard Conte playing a gangster, in her first screen appearance in the 1948 *Cry of the City* (expressed by Rappaport and then seconded by Simonds, asking, "Why is my mother allowing this?"); we hear about Paget's mastery of "the sorrowful Madonna look" being both "a blessing and a curse"; Paget being cast in diverse ethnic parts (Italian, Native American, Polynesian); her skills as singer and dancer and her Vegas nightclub act; her playing second-fiddle to Jean Peters in *Anne of the Indies* (1951) and her desire for bigger parts and full stardom. Then, in part two, we hear about some of the mixed blessings of CinemaScope (such as the absence of close-ups, illustrated by a subdivision of the anamorphic frame into six medium shots of Debra), Elvis Presley's marriage proposal (nixed by Paget's mother) after they appeared together in *Love Me Tender,* diverse notations about *Demetrius and the Gladiators* and *Princess of the Nile* (both 1954), the latter of which gave her star billing for the first time, and much, much more.

I should add that my own, equally divided psychosexual investments in Debra Paget were explored in the first chapter of my first book, an experimental autobiography called *Moving Places: A Life at the Movies* (1980, published in 2003 by P.O.L in Jean-Luc Mengus's French translation as *Mouvements: Une vie au cinéma*), centering on my encounter at age eight with one of Rappaport's own privileged sites, *Bird of Paradise* (1952). Oddly enough, both our encounters are tied to Judaism: In my case, Paget's upsetting fate as a Polynesian maiden ordered to dive into a live volcano as a sacrifice for her interracial involvement with Louis Jourdan was tied in a subsequent nightmare to familial sacrifices occasioned by my older brother's bar mitzvah. Rappaport is mostly concerned with the Jewish identities of two other actors in the movie—Maurice Schultz (as the Kahuna who orders Paget's sacrifice), a major figure in Yiddish theater and Yiddish cinema, and Jeff Chandler (as Jourdan's American pal), born Ira Grossel in Brooklyn, Rappaport's hometown.

The reason for bringing all of this up is to point out that, to paraphrase Rappaport, one guy's kitsch is another guy's Judaism, and vice versa, and similarly, one guy's bad girl is another guy's good girl. In part two, Rappaport claims that Paget wanted more bad-girl parts like Marilyn Monroe in *Niagara* (1953), adding that this was what made her a star, whereas I would suggest that it was also the impossible mixture of Monroe's bad-girl smarts and her good-girl-innocence in *Gentlemen Prefer Blondes* the same year—which Rappaport also quotes from, but in a different context—that did the trick. And I would further argue that Debra's best parts all combine certain elements of saucy bad-girl irreverence with good-girl Madonna-like sorrow—even in *Bird of Paradise,* where she breaks the tribal taboo. But I don't mind him bringing up *Niagara* because it occasions a great line to accompany a shot of the heroine's demise ("Marilyn—frozen in a trapezoid of death"), even if this has nothing to do with Debra.

In short, we're talking here about a terrain where friendly quibbles are inevitable, and also ultimately irrelevant. I wasn't fully convinced that European actress Yvonne Furneaux was a dead ringer for Paget who could have played her twin, as Rappaport claims, until I happened to resee *Lisbon* (1956) while working on this review, which for me proves his point better than his own examples—but maybe that's because we view both actresses differently. I can't buy Rappaport's claim that Paget refused to give interviews after she ended her acting career after coming across two such interviews on YouTube (both concerned in part with her faith as a Christian), but of course one gal's acting career can turn out to be the same gal's religion (or vice versa) years later.

Furthermore, although I'm quite happy to call Lang's two-part Indian feature in 1959 "Paget's Apotheosis"—even when it ushers in another long digression about Billy Daniel's choreography (which allows for still another digression about Daniel's boyfriend Mitchell Leisen, another Rappaport favorite)—I would personally nominate another Paget dance with a different sort of voluptuous bump-and-grind as her erotic apotheosis: namely, her burlesque, bad-girl performance of "Father's Got 'em" in John Phillip Sousa's parlor in the 1952 *Stars and Stripes Forever* (accessible at www.youtube.com/watch?v=hwSK9u_4j6k), which allows her to sing as well as dance, with an equivalent number of shocked reaction shots. But this doesn't make me regret Rappaport's alternate choice, which permits him to add a riff about Paget's revenge on a snake erection in *The River's Edge* (1957), which further demonstrates that one guy's snake is another guy's erection (and vice versa). And even if he omits Fritz Lang's most erotic picture (*Spione,* 1928) while surveying his silent films, I can readily forgive him, because he also includes ravishing bits of two other versions of *The Tiger of Bengal* and *The Indian Tomb* that preceded Lang's own, neither of which I'd seen before.

■ ■ ■

A final remark about what makes Rappaport's work cinematic and not merely an alternate form of film criticism: Let me begin with two statements made by Rappaport himself about his earlier narrative features. The first paragraph is part of a statement written by him to introduce a screening of *The Scenic Route* (1978); the last four come from an interview with Tony Rayns in the February 1979 *Monthly Film Bulletin:*

> Love, jealousy and revenge. All standard components of melodrama—but a very "dry" melodrama. Expectations are thwarted and rechanneled. Instead of explanations and motivations, visual counterparts are offered. The film slides back and forth between passion and an irony which redirects it but doesn't dilute it. A film about myths and myth-making, about the Madame Bovary in each of us, about delusions and romance in a fragile world where violence erupts randomly and unexpectedly.
>
> The various elements only really fall into place when the narrations are there. The use of narration in low-budget films in general brings us back to finance; it's cheaper and more accessible than sync-sound

dialogue. But I *like* narration: I like the fact that you can create a discrepancy between what characters say and what you see of them. It's something that we've learned from Melville, via Bresson. I think it's an incredibly rich technique; it allows you to concentrate on essentials. Plus my mind is always full of ironic double-think . . . always re-assessing, always re-evaluating.

Movies like *Out of the Past* and *Sunset Boulevard* used narration for exposition, as a device for opening the closed door, always from a single character's point-of-view. I try to use it more centrally: what happens if you use narrations from *five* points-of-view?

I once described the entire script of *The Scenic Route* to someone (not the truncated version that I put on the screen), and he thought it was very dry, very dehydrated. But there's enough material there for *five* of the melodramas that Warner Brothers used to do! Only with all the melodramatic juices pumped out. The elements of melodrama (and of theatre) that I like have more to do with painting: it's the gesture, the *mise en scène,* the lighting, the arrangement, the pregnant moment right before something happens or right after it has.

The emotional tenor is not parody. If I'm parodying anything, it's the fact that we can only respond to emotional situations in prescribed ways. They're the only ways we have to respond to the trite elements of our lives. I guess it's more a matter of irony than of parody. I rely on associations to previous things as a kind of shorthand. It's not that audiences have to know which films I love, and I'm not interested in *hommages*. But it's all retreads—human relationships have been explored, re-explored, de-explored, and yet we still respond to the grain of truth that we recognize at the heart of these situations when they're represented on a screen. One wants the falseness to be true.

The above can read as Rappaport's own understanding of how he treats melodrama cinematically. And I think it could be argued that he treats his form of film criticism cinematically in the same way, at least if one replaces "narrations" and "points of view" with "critical positions" and "critical voices"—discursive avenues learned from literature and then translated into cinema. Wanting the falseness to be true is, after all, a central postulate of the cinematic experience.

… CHAPTER 20

Alain Resnais

As I've implied in my introduction, the most neglected and overlooked strength of Alain Resnais as a filmmaker was his courage in radically reinventing himself every time he embarked on a new film. I suspect that one of the reasons why this has been overlooked is that, unlike a more obvious and outspoken rebel such as Jean-Luc Godard, Resnais was a shy and withdrawn person who exuded an old-fashioned form of politesse; even if his films were invariably provocations, his style of addressing the public always seemed designed to make himself appear as conventional and as unthreatening as possible. This tended to confound his American reviewers, who interpreted his shyness as coldness and ignored his passion for such popular forms as comic strips and musical comedies when it mistakenly labeled him as an aloof intellectual.

The opening overview in this chapter was written to introduce a dossier in Farsi that was prepared by my friend Ehsan Khoshbakht in March 2012. The essay on *Statues Also Die*, perhaps Resnais' (and Chris Marker's) most neglected masterpiece, was posted online at *Moving Image Source* on November 6, 2009. My remarks on *Providence* come from my "Global Discoveries on DVD" column for the Canadian quarterly *Cinema Scope* (issue 39, Summer 2014), which I have been writing now for fifteen years, and my reflections on "Resnais' Secrets" is my thirty-first "En movimiento" column for *Caíman Cuadernos de Cine* (which I have been contributing for eleven years), written in March 2013.

On Alain Resnais

Alain Resnais is clearly one of our greatest living filmmakers. But he's also one of the most elusive, for a number of reasons. He started out as the most international of all the French New Wave artists, at least in his early features (especially *Hiroshima mon amour, Last Year at Marienbad, La Guerre est finie, Je t'aime, je t'aime,* and *Providence*), but then went on to become the most French of French directors (not only in obvious cases such as *Mon oncle d'Amérique, Stavisky . . ., Mélo, Same Old Song, Not on the Lips,* and *Wild Grass,* but even in films derived from English or partially American sources, such as *I Want To Go Home, Smoking, No Smoking, Private Fears in Public Places,* and *Life of Riley*). Even before he got around to making features, he made the greatest films in the history of cinema about racism and colonialism (*Statues Also Die*), the Holocaust (*Night and Fog*), plastic (*La Chant du Styrène*), and libraries (*Toute la mémoire du monde*). Among the most personal of modern filmmakers, he never signs his own scripts, always preferring, as Claire Denis once pointed out to me, to hide behind his screenwriters. He's also one of the greatest of all film critics and film historians, even without any printed criticism, if one considers how much he has taught us about Feuillade and Hitchcock in *Marienbad,* about Lubitsch in *Stavisky . . .,* and about MGM musicals in *Not on the Lips,* among many other examples. A poet of memory and emotion, he often gets mistaken for an intellectual (perhaps because he's French) and overlooked as a surrealist. Indeed, part of the richness of his films can be found in the fact that many of their treasures are hidden, apart from their beauty and feelings.

The Unknown Statue

It's fascinating to consider the possibility that the essential film oeuvres of both Alain Resnais and Chris Marker commence with the same remarkable, rarely seen essay film from 1953—a film whose direction is cosigned in the credits by Resnais (also credited for editing), Marker (script and conception), and Ghislain Cloquet (cinematography). (Cloquet [1924–1981], who went on to shoot most of Resnais' other major films until his own camera assistant, Sacha Vierny, basically replaced him, also subsequently shot major films by Jacques Becker, Robert Bresson, André Delvaux, Jacques Demy, Marguerite Duras, Louis Malle, and Roman Polanski.) And it's no less fascinating (and significant) to ponder the implications of the fact that the only Oscar-winning film of Resnais' career came five years before this neglected early peak. The film in question was the 1948 documentary *Van Gogh,* and in keeping with the Academy's procedures, the Oscar went not to Resnais, again the director and editor, but to the producer, Pierre Braunberger. Largely because I prefer to look at paintings from static vantage points and with my own itineraries, I've never felt entirely comfortable with Resnais' exploratory camera movements here and in *Paul Gauguin* and *Guernica* (both 1950). Unlike his tracking shots past or around various sculptures in *Statues Also Die,* former concentration camps in *Night and Fog* (1955), and various portions of the Bibliothèque Nationale in *All the Memory of the World* (1956) and a plastics factory in *The Song of Styrene* (1958), Resnais' other major early shorts, there's a tinge of academicism here, making it all the more unfortunate that these three films have influenced so many other documentaries about painters and paintings, including many otherwise good ones (for example, Jean-Pierre Gorin's 1986 *Routine Pleasures*) that track or pan across canvases in a similar fashion. From this standpoint, Jean-Marie Straub and Danièle Huillet's *Cézanne* (1989) and *A Visit to the Louvre* (2004) are exemplary (and relatively purist) examples of how to show paintings respectfully on film without superimposing particular trajectories across and around their surfaces.

The American reception of Resnais' work seems to have been a protracted series of misunderstandings and foreshortenings, beginning with *Statues Also Die* fifty-six years ago, when one might say that he made a decisive transition from films about art to films that can be described as literature (or, later, theater) by another means. More generally, one could maintain that the great undiscovered continent in Resnais' work consists of at least five of these aforementioned eight short documentaries that he made over the span of a decade, from 1948 to 1958, only one of which, *Night and Fog,* is very well known today. That film, I should add, remains for me and many others the greatest of all documentaries to date about the Nazi extermination camps, not only surpassing Claude Lanzmann's 1985 *Shoah* but also establishing the existential as well as formal terms—the use of the present both to evoke the past and to respect the degree to which that past is irretrievable—that made *Shoah* both possible and thinkable. If *Shoah* can be described as a kind of shotgun marriage between existentialism (associated with the present) and Judaism (associated with the past), *Night and Fog* can be seen as already providing an embryonic version of that forced encounter. Discounting another art documentary that followed *Van Gogh, Paul Gauguin,* and *Guernica, Le mystère de l'atelier quinze* (1957), codirected by André Heinrich and also written by Marker—which I've never been able to see, and which is seldom cited, much less discussed, in the criticism about Resnais that I'm familiar with—I think Resnais' stature as one of the greatest artists in the history of cinema is already firmly established in the remaining three shorts, each of which to my mind is as great in its own way as *Night and Fog*. And from the documentation we have about the production of these films, it appears that most or all of them required at least as much preparatory work as Resnais' subsequent features did. *All the Memory of the World* is a kind of creepy and morbid sequel to *Night and Fog* in which sequestered books in the Bibliothèque Nationale are perceived as if they were prisoners, squirreled away in a Borgesian labyrinth. *The Song of Styrene,* in color and CinemaScope (apparently Resnais' first encounter with each), is a quasi-abstract celebration of what appears to be sprouting buds of plastic, accompanied by a brilliant poetic narration by Raymond Queneau so rich in puns and literary references that English subtitles can offer only pale approximations. (Even though this may come closer to formalism than Resnais' other shorts, the vibrancy of the colors actually calls to mind some of the gusto of a Frank Tashlin.) Both of these treasures are bonuses in Criterion's *Last Year at Marienbad* box set, and *Night and Fog* is available from Criterion as a separate release. But many decades of neglect have so far kept *Statues Also Die* from receiving any equivalent treatment. Indeed, its screenings with English subtitles have been so rare that if you come across it in any venue that's showing a Resnais retrospective, you should drop everything to go and see it.

So regardless of whether or not one happens to revere such Resnais features as *Hiroshima mon amour* (1959), *Marienbad* (1961), *Muriel* (1963), *Providence* (1976), *Mon Oncle d'Amérique* (1980), *Mélo* (1986), *Not on the Lips* (2003), and *Wild Grass* (2009)—to cite only my own current favorites—his qualifications as a consummate film master can't rest simply or solely on these and other feature-length contenders. In many ways those short films are every bit as provocative, especially in their uncanny capacity to fuse literature and cinema. Marker begins his two-volume collection of offscreen commentaries, *Commentaires* (Paris: Editions du Seuil,

1961 and 1967)—filmed as well as unfilmed, and long out of print—with his dense, haunting, and blistering text for *Statues Also Die,* recited in the film by Jean Négroni. Here is how it begins, the words spoken over darkness: "When men die, they enter history. When statues die, they enter art. This botany of death is what we call culture." And then, as if to prove his point, the film's image lights up to show us the ruins of a few outdoor sculptures, speckled with sunlight and wizened by age and corrosion—strange botanical specimens.

What follows, over a striking montage of indoor specimens and some of their strolling museum spectators (first white ones, then a single black woman), is a kind of existential poetics of both art and history: "An object dies when the living glance trained upon it disappears. And when we disappear, our objects will be confined to the place where we send black things: to the museum." Resnais' Eisensteinian editing meanwhile peaks as an accelerating succession of graphic images and reaches a gorgeous crescendo and epiphany in a cut to the head of an African swimmer rising from underwater to the surface of a river. (Resnais' best work abounds in ecstatic or abrasive cuts of this kind, nearly always tied to sudden, unexpected human gestures and movements.) This gradually turns into a remarkable duet between Marker's literary fervor and a detailed as well as despairing political vision—a combination of speculative art history, precise journalism, and a grim meditation on the various places and functions Africa and its separate cultures have assumed within white civilization—and Resnais' musically and rhythmically orchestrated illustration of and counterpoint to this extraordinary text. Both of these strains can be said to embody, empower, and enhance as well as accompany the other, but it would be pointless to try to synopsize either Marker's multifaceted argument or Resnais' elaborately composed and articulated assembly of images, much less attempt to describe how effectively they complement one another. It appears that this film took years to put together, but it moves with a fluency and directness that is never labored. It was the final third of this half-hour film that eventually led to the film's suppression by the French government. Marker's passionate and angry polemic builds an indictment not merely of white colonialism but of the suppression, degradation, and in some cases irreversible extermination of black culture, taking on such ancillary topics as black athletes (including boxers as well as basketball players) and black musicians in the United States.

"Resnais might have been thinking of Howard Roark [the uncompromising architect hero of Ayn Rand's *The Fountainhead*] when he blocked for eight years the release of *Statues Also Die* in a form that was mutilated by the [French] censors," Luc Moullet recently remarked in his book-length study of King Vidor's 1949 film adaptation of that novel (*Le Rebelle de King Vidor,* Crisnée, France: Éditions Yellow Now, 2009). "Many of us haven't had the courage or even the occasion to confront [such a] problem." This was a principled stand that cost Resnais a good deal, because even after the film finally became sporadically available at a few venues, it was still apparently the truncated version, missing the final reel, that most people saw. But it's this reel that includes one of the most powerful and sustained antiracist statements that exists in cinema, even though its eloquence and moral force remain scarcely known, even in France. I can still recall coming across a story by Jean-Michel Frodon in the August 6, 1995, issue of *Le Monde* about the film's belated release once it was finally passed by the French censor, and *pace* Luc Moullet, this was not eight years after it was made but forty-two years, practically half a century. I also recall how disheartened I was to discover afterward that even though this event was deemed newsworthy in *Le Monde,* it was ignored completely in *Cahiers du cinéma.* In effect, the film's lengthy suppression had ultimately turned it into a key missing object in the careers of both Resnais and Marker. In fact, it's a monument that can't be said to have ever died because a diabolical combination of avoidance, ignorance, and indifference has never given it a proper chance to live.

On *Providence*

I shelled out $56.19 in U.S. dollars (including postage) to acquire the definitive and restored, director-approved DVD of *Providence* (1977) from French Amazon, and I hasten to add that this was money well spent. Notwithstanding the passion and brilliance of Alain Resnais' first two features, *Providence* is in many ways my favorite of his longer works, quite apart from the fact that it's the only one in English. And I can't ascribe this preference simply to the contribution of David Mercer (1928–1980). I recently rewatched the only other Mercer-scripted film I'm familiar with, Karel Reisz's *Morgan!,* and aside from the wit of its own sarcastic dialogue, I mainly found it just as flat and tiresome as I did in 1966, for reasons that are well expounded in Dwight Macdonald's contemporary review (reprinted in his collection *On Movies*).

Clearly part of what gives *Providence* more resonance now, writing less than a month after Resnais' death, is the theme it shares with his penultimate feature, *You Ain't Seen Nothin' Yet* (2013): an old writer facing his own death, and trying to create some form of art in relation to it. John Gielgud's performance as the old writer is for me one of the greatest bits of film acting that we have, and Dirk Bogarde's superb rendition of the writer's emotionally repressed older son may be as much of a self-portrait on Resnais' part. [2018 postscript: Resnais' final feature, *Life of Riley,* is also centered on a dying character, in this case one who remains offscreen.]

The DVD has some fascinating extras: François Thomas's very informative twenty-nine-minute audio interview with Resnais about the film (which Resnais conceived from the outset as a "documentary about imagination") and a fifty-one-minute documentary including detailed interviews with art director Jacques Saulnier, cinematographer Ricardo Aronovich, and actor Pierre Arditi (who doesn't appear in *Providence,* but whose work with Resnais in countless other films still gives him plenty to talk about), both thoughtfully provided with optional English subtitles. The single-disc set also includes both the original English and the French post-dubbed versions of the film (the latter of which Resnais supervised, and which includes many of the most famous actors in French cinema, even though the lip-sync isn't always up to the line readings).

On the box is a quote from Norman Mailer, of all people: "Le meilleur film jamais réalisé sur le processus de création," which translates as "The greatest film ever made on the creative process," and it's surely telling that I had to go to a French source to come upon such an apt and just description of this vibrant masterpiece. On the other hand, go to James Wolcott, one of Mailer's protégés, and you'll find him actually bragging about helping to create a ruckus with another of his mentors, Pauline Kael, at a New York press screening for having "dared take Alain Resnais' *Providence* (a meditation on death and creativity endorsed by Susan Sontag, swinging her incense ball) less than solemnly." I guess those fearless pranksters and indefatigable truth-tellers just didn't dig how much of *Providence* is a comedy. Too bad I was off in Europe during most of the mid-'70s; otherwise I might have been around to hoot and jeer at Kael and Wolcott swinging their own solemn incense balls to greet the far less witty and neo-Stalinist pomposity of *The Godfather Part II* (1974).

Resnais' Secrets

After recently having caught up with Alain Resnais' magisterial *Vous n'avez encore rien vu,* I belatedly discovered from diverse sources on the internet that "Axel Reval," the credited cowriter on both this film and *Les herbes folles,* is in fact a Resnais pseudonym, making it a typically sly acknowledgment of the personal nature of his filmmaking, which has been an essential part of his work since the 1950s. Remember the glimpse of the *Mandrake the Magician* comic strip found in the Bibliothèque Nationale in *Toute la mémoire du monde*? One could even argue that the fact that personal moments of this kind tend to be veiled or masked in Resnais only makes them more intense, as they sometimes are in the films of Sternberg. (Claude Ollier's alternate title for *The Saga of Anatahan* is *My Heart Laid Bare.*)

Indeed, it might make an interesting exercise to run through Resnais' oeuvre picking out such intense but half-hidden and fleeting details spelling out his personal investments in the films. An obvious example, in *L'année dernière à Marienbad,* is the life-size blowup of a photograph of Alfred Hitchcock, eavesdropping on hotel guests beside an elevator, shortly before X makes his first on-screen appearance. Less obvious, because much harder to locate, is the comparable Hitchcock cameo in *Muriel:* this time he's glimpsed on the street, in front of a restaurant, wearing a chef's hat. And if we add to this the crane shot around the exterior of a luxury hotel in Biarritz in *Stavisky . . .,* past the various windows of the opulent suite of Arlette (Anny Duperet) when Baron Raoul (Charles Boyer) is paying her a visit—Resnais' quintessential Lubitsch reference—we're talking mainly about the personal nature of Resnais' cinephilia, which, at least in this latter example, also proves that he's something of a film critic, working with sound and image rather than prose, much as Godard does in portions of *Alphaville* and *Made in USA.*

Yet in fact, what's most personal in this ravishing sequence isn't the Lubitsch reference but what Resnais subsequently does with it—a sudden shock cut from the Baron knocking on Arlette's bedroom to a close-up of her quickly turning her head with a startled expression—for me, one of the most beautiful and frightening cuts in the history of cinema, and one subtly encapsulating the entire film by turning Stavisky's dream of glamor into something like a nightmare. Or think about the apparently gratuitous crane shot over the hero's house in *Les herbes folles,* up one side and then across the roof and down the other side, providing a kind of stylistic explosion that's no less breathtaking but, for me at least, much harder to analyze in thematic terms. But as one character puts it in *Providence*—clearly speaking for Resnais, even if he's hiding in this case behind David Mercer's dialogue—the charge that style overrules any feeling rules out the salient possibility that style *is* feeling.

One of the most personal moments in *Vous n'avez encore rien vu*—perhaps the most personal of all, occurring after a veritable string of *coups de théâtre* combined with diverse contradictory and paradoxical reflections about death—is the Frank Sinatra song heard over the final credits, "It Was a Very Good Year," beginning with the line, "When I was 17 . . ." Even though Resnais was in fact nineteen when Anouihl's *Eurydice* opened in Paris, during the second year of the German Occupation—a play that, at least in Resnais' version of it, exudes the darkness, the cellar-like dinginess, and the paranoid taste of betrayals that one associates with that time and place, even more than Cocteau's *Orphée* would remember it a few years later—the bitter irony of those lyrics encapsulates the sweet (and yes, personal) anguish of everything preceding them.

CHAPTER 21

Jacques Rivette

Ever since I was a college freshman in the early 1960s, discovering *Paris Belongs to Us* with my friend and classmate Marc Haefele at Amos Vogel's Cinema 16 after reading about it in the first issue of *Sight and Sound* that I ever bought, Jacques Rivette has been a special interest of mine. This interest was rekindled in my early years in Paris when I attended a midnight screening of the over four-hour *L'amour fou* (for me, Rivette's second masterpiece), and later after I was befriended by his principal screenwriter Eduardo de Gregorio, which enabled me to attend several private screenings of *Céline et Julie vont en bateau* when it was still a work print. After I moved to London to work for the British Film Institute in 1976, I was able to help arrange for the world premiere of *Noroît* at the National Film Theatre, and one of my last sustained projects before leaving London for San Diego in early 1977 was editing *Rivette: Texts and Interviews,* a BFI publication.

The first essay here was written for Toronto's Cinematheque Ontario program guide (February 2007), which I've abridged and revised slightly. My Rivette obituary was written for the May 2016 *Artforum*; "*Out 1* and its Double" was written for the Carlotta dual format box-set release of that film in 2016. The latter draws on material from two previous essays ("Work and Play in the House of Fiction," *Sight and Sound,* Autumn 1974, and "Tih-Minh, Out 1: On the Nonreception of Two French Serials," *The Velvet Light Trap*, Spring 1996) and a few other previous texts, most of them available at jonathanrosenbaum.net.

Jacques Rivette: Babel and the Void

For better and for worse, and principally the latter, Jacques Rivette has been singled out as the former *Cahiers du Cinéma* film critic who makes the least-commercial films, as well as the longest ones. But for the record, the films of the always neglected Luc Moullet are generally less commercial than those of Rivette. And even what we mean when we say "longest films" is open to some debate. (After all, the more than twelve-hour *Out 1* was conceived as a TV serial, and Jean-Luc Godard's own first TV series, made a few years later, was just as long.)

The problem with such caricatures is they generally function as excuses for why some spectators won't deal with Rivette's films rather than as viable descriptions of what they offer. Yes, his features tend to be long and they work with duration. Furthermore, when two versions have been made of some of them—unauthorized in the case of *L'amour fou*, authorized in the cases of *Out 1*, *L'amour par terre*, and *La belle noiseuse/Divertimento*—the longer version is almost always superior.

Let me propose a few other traits that make Rivette stand out among his former critical colleagues. According to François Truffaut, he was the one who was most determined to become a filmmaker. He's also the one most interested in actors—even if this only started to become apparent with his second feature, when he could afford to hire professionals. I'd also argue that, along with Godard, he is the only one who has continued to be a critic as well as something of a theorist while functioning as a filmmaker—someone whose memory of other films and filmmakers often shapes his meanings, so that, for instance, *Give a Girl a Break* served as a kind of working model for *Haut/bas/fragile*, just as *The Seventh Victim* was a starting point for *Duelle*. (Regarding Rivette's appreciation of Hollywood, the 1974 *Céline et Julie vont en bateau* offers especially exuberant testimony.)

This latter tendency is already apparent in his first feature, *Paris nous appartient* (1960), when a group of friends are screening a print of *Metropolis*. Not only does Fritz Lang's Tower of Babel sequence comment on the complex paranoid plot of Rivette's film; once the film breaks and we're briefly confronted with a blank screen, this detail is equally pertinent. And in a way the dialectic present here between multiple languages and gaping void—too much significance and too little—is basic to Rivette's cinema as a whole.

* * *

His second feature, *La réligieuse* (1966), provoked a scandal when it was banned by the Gaullist government for its adaptation of Denis Diderot's anticlerical novel. Yet apart from its modernist soundtrack, it seems like a throwback to classical narrative in relation to the radical experimentation that precedes and immediately follows it (which for me figures as the most potent and exciting stretch in Rivette's work—roughly 1968–1981). But insofar as this film highlights Rivette's interest in what might be called "classical" *mise en scène,* which has dominated his work over the past quarter of a century, it no longer looks like a detour; among its most obvious successors are *Jeanne la pucelle* (1994) and *Sécret defense* (1998), both vehicles for Sandrine Bonnaire.

But it's only with Rivette's three-part TV documentary *Jean Renoir, le patron* (1966) that his formal agenda shifts and the creative contributions of actors become central, yielding the bold experiment of *L'amour fou* (1969). By Rivette's own account, it was partially the experience of editing Renoir clips that prompted this change, though his work with Andre S. Labarthe, coproducer of the Renoir series, who shot the 16mm footage of *L'amour fou,* also clearly played a role. Alternating between Labarthe's 16mm *cinéma-vérité* footage of theater rehearsals of *Andromaque* directed by Jean-Pierre Kalfon and Rivette's 35mm footage of the same rehearsals, meanwhile inviting Kalfon and Bulle Ogier to play a tormented fictional couple and generate much of their own characters and dialogue (which was also shot in 35mm), Rivette deliberately made his own position as spectator relatively passive, postponing his role as final arbiter to the editing stage. One might therefore postulate that Renoir and his own love of actors stands for the Babel side of the Rivettean dialectic, dominant during shooting, where too many meanings fight for supremacy, and the more misanthropic Lang stands for the void, articulated during editing, when most of the meanings get pared away.

Eventually, this shift would mean that Rivette's films would become defined mainly by their actors—and, in particular, their actresses. Arguably, *Le belle noiseuse* (1991) becomes even more a film about Emmanuelle Béart than a Balzac adaptation or a film about painting. *L'amour pare terre* (1984) is basically a meditation on Jane Birkin and Geraldine Chaplin, *La bande des quatre* (1988) is above all a film about Bulle Ogier, Laurence Côte, and Nathalie Richard, among others, and *Va savoir* (2001) ultimately has more to do with Jeanne Balibar than with Luigi Pirandello.

By the time of *Out 1,* actors had taken over Rivette's cinema during the shooting stage—a freedom underwritten by the radical premise that anything and everything an actor does is potentially interesting, and mixing seemingly incompatible acting styles becomes part of the interest. (This also has some effect on Rivette's framing, discussed with Serge Daney in Claire Denis's excellent 1990 documentary *Jacques Rivette, le veilleur.*) Enlisting actors as cowriters—as he would do again in *Céline et Julie,* his most popular film of this period, as well as in the much later *Haut/bas/fragile* (1995)—was then succeeded by obliging actors to stick to a fixed text in most of his subsequent features while seeking to solicit their creativity in other ways. In *Duelle* and *Noroît* (both 1976), where live improvising musicians share screen space with the actors, the creative expressiveness becomes gestural.

Conceived as the second and third parts of a projected four-feature series entitled *Scènes de la vie parallèle,* which were meant to be shot in swift succession, each film belonging to a separate genre, *Duelle* and *Noroît* both employ the same invented mythology involving goddesses of the sun and moon who struggle competitively for the means to remain on Earth past an allotted forty-day period.

Suffering a nervous collapse shortly after he began shooting the projected first part, entitled *Marie et Julien,* with Leslie Caron and Albert Finney, Rivette was forced to abandon the series, although his subsequent *Merry-Go-Round* (1993) and *Histoire de Marie et Julien* (2003) represent separate attempts to bring this unrealized project to some sort of closure. The latter in particular—in which Béart figures as the designated goddess/ghost, and the hero (Jerzy Radziwilowicz), Rivette's surrogate, is a solitary figure who repairs clocks—offers a suggestive combo that seems to bring certain aspects of Rivette's cinema full circle.

Jacques Rivette (1928–2016)

Although Jacques Rivette was the first of the *Cahiers du Cinéma* critics to embark on filmmaking, he differed from his colleagues—Claude Chabrol, Jean-Luc Godard, Eric Rohmer, François Truffaut—in remaining a cult figure rather than an arthouse staple. His career was hampered by various false starts, delays, and interruptions, and then it abruptly ended in 2009 with the onset of Alzheimer's disease, six years before his death. But his legacy is immense.

His career can easily be divided into two parts, although it's not so easy to pinpoint a precise dividing line between them. And for those who knew him well or even casually, as I did, it's hard to prefer the first portion to the second without feeling somewhat guilty.

Common to both parts is a preoccupation with *mise en scène* and the mysterious aspects of collective work, offset by the more solitary and dictatorial tasks of plotting and editing. Rivette's own collective work was frequently enhanced by improvisation—with actors, with onscreen or offscreen musicians, or with dialogue written just prior to shooting (either by actors or screenwriters)—while the more solitary work of plotting and editing emulated the Godardian paradigm of converting chance into destiny. Each of Rivette's films proposed a somewhat different method for arriving at this dialectical combination of elements, reinventing the director's role in the process, but it's hardly coincidental that the twin themes of togetherness and solitude are what invariably emerged from the alchemy.

The first part of Rivette's career encompasses both his activity over two decades as a film critic and his boldest experiments as a director. He began contributing to *Gazette du Cinéma* in 1950 and soon after to *Cahiers du Cinéma*, which he also edited from 1963 to 1965. Among his most significant critical engagements were those with Howard Hawks, Roberto Rossellini, Fritz Lang, and Jean Renoir—the latter especially in the three-part TV documentary *Jean Renoir, le patron* (1967). By Rivette's own account, the editing of Renoir clips helped to inspire his subsequent audacious experiments: *L'amour fou* (1969), *Out 1: Noli me tangere* (1971), *Out 1: Spectre* (1972), *Céline et Julie vont en bateau* (Céline and Julie Go Boating, 1974), *Duelle* (1976), *Noroît* (1976), and *Le Pont du Nord* (1981). This stretch also includes his heroically ambitious and haunting if relatively amateurish first feature, *Paris Belongs to Us* (1961), as well as the less characteristic *La religieuse* (The Nun, 1966) and the abortive *Merry-Go-Round* (1981).

It is of this first portion of Rivette's career that his fellow critic and director André Téchiné was speaking when he told *Le Monde,* shortly after the filmmaker's death this past January, that "For [Rivette], cinema was the equivalent of a lack of restraint, a leap into the void. His films defied rules, limits, the very notions of *mise en scène,* mastery, and duration. With *L'amour fou, Out 1,* or *Le Pont du Nord,* he invented the experiences of radical cinema, insanely exciting. I don't know any filmmaker who protected himself less than he did." His most important producer during this period was Stéphane Tchalgadjieff, who enabled him to make *Out 1, Duelle,* and *Noroît*—the latter constituting two parts of a projected four-feature cycle that capsized when Rivette suffered a nervous collapse a few days into the shooting of a third, the never-completed *Marie et Julien.* His most important personal relationship was with Marilù Parolini, an Italian photographer and screenwriter he briefly married, and with whom he can be seen (while she was working as a secretary at *Cahiers du Cinéma*) in Jean Rouch and Edgar Morin's 1961 *Chronique d'un été.*

The second part of his career, a dozen more features, was safer and saner, reflecting decisions made on behalf of life over art—not a betrayal of the concerns of his earlier work, but a more "reasonable" application of them: *L'amour par terre* (Love on the Ground, 1984), *Hurlevent* (Wuthering Heights, 1985), *La bande des quatre* (Gang of Four, 1989), *La belle noiseuse* (1991), *Jeanne la Pucelle* (Joan the Maid; in two parts, both 1994), *Haut/bas/fragile* (Up, Down, Fragile, 1995), *Secret défense* (1998), *Va savoir* (2001), *Histoire de Marie et Julien* (The Story of Marie and Julien, 2003—a belated retooling of *Marie et Julien* with a different cast and crew), *Ne touchez pas la hache* (The Duchess of Langeais, 2007), and, finally, *Around a Small Mountain 36 vues du Pic Saint-Loup* (2009). Rivette's only producer during this period was Martine Marignac, and his most important relationship was with Véronique Manniez, author of a 1998 book about *Secret défense*, who married him shortly after he was diagnosed with Alzheimer's and cared for him for the remainder of his life.

My own acquaintance with Rivette, in the mid-'70s to the early '80s, derived from my friendship with the late Argentinian screenwriter Eduardo de Gregorio, who worked on *Céline and Julie, Duelle, Noroît, Merry-Go-Round,* and the unrealized *Phénix.* Thanks to this connection, I attended several private screenings of *Céline and Julie* in its final work-print form, interviewed Rivette in my Paris flat, and observed parts of the shooting of both *Duelle* (in Paris) and *Noroît* (in Brittany), and even accompanied Rivette on a walking tour of London's West End prior to the latter film's world premiere. I can't claim to have known him well, but no one else I knew during this period did either. He was famously hermitic. With his shy, nervous giggles, he had the manner of a cheerfully enlightened monk. Though he was a familiar presence at the Cinémathèque Française (always occupying the same seat) and was always friendly, he was also a committed *solitaire* before and after the screenings.

A longtime defender of Rivette, over the years I've had occasion to revise some of my positions. I used to maintain that he was one of *the* major French film critics (together with Godard and the nonwriter Resnais)—which led me to publish a short collection of his criticism in English translation in 1977 (a project undertaken without his official consent, but with his tacit approval)—and that he remained a critic whenever he filmed. This explains why he used other films as critical models—*Artists and Models* (1955) for *Céline and Julie, The Seventh Victim* (1943) for *Duelle, Moonfleet* (1955) for *Noroît, Lady in the Lake* (1947) for the abandoned *Marie et Julien*. Yet once it became clear that he was the only member of the *Cahiers* team to refuse to allow his criticism to be reprinted—mainly, he said, because he no longer agreed with much of it—I began to realize that he had little sense of criticism as a vocation. (2018: As this book goes to press, Rivette's *Textes critiques* is about to be published posthumously in France by Post-Editions.) The lively late interviews he gave to the Parisian weekly *Les inrockuptibles,* for all their interest, weren't the musings of a major critic so much as cranky fan-boy arguments. Yet if his movies are themselves a form of film criticism, they are also, as Adrian Martin recently noted in a valuable essay on the director in the online journal *Lola,* "profoundly psychoanalytic" and quite open to auteurist investigation—but the principal auteur to be illuminated is Rivette himself.

I used to speculate that Rivette's decision to remove a hair-raising sequence from the thirteen-hour *Out 1* before the film was shown on European cable TV—the nervous breakdown of Colin (Jean-Pierre Léaud), alone in his room, in the final episode—was motivated by the director's concern for the emotional problems of Léaud. I'm now more inclined to believe it stemmed from Rivette's own identification with the character and his condition. Like the terrifying scene in *L'amour fou* in which Sébastien (Jean-Pierre Kalfon) lacerates his clothes and himself with a razor in the midst of a marital crisis, Colin's collapse was a dovetailing of an actor's improvisation into something resembling madness. And this contrasts sharply with the way Rivette would handle similar crises in the second part of his career. In *La Belle Noiseuse,* he calmly explores what the painting of a nude portrait does to the relationships among two couples (painter and wife, model and boyfriend). And later still, the troubled tensions between mortals and goddesses, living and dead characters, that once inflamed such fantasies as *Céline and Julie, Duelle,* and

Noroît are resolved in *The Story of Marie and Julien*'s unexpected happy ending, in which the couple are reunited.

In both parts of Rivette's career, the dissolution of a solitary self into a couple or a crew remains a constant. In one of his late interviews in *Les inrockuptibles,* he said, "I detest the formulation 'a film by.' A film is always [by] at least fifteen people.... *Mise en scène* is a rapport with the actors, and the communal work is set with the first shot. What's important for me in a film is that it be alive, that it be imbued with presence, which is basically the same thing. And that this presence, inscribed within the film, possesses a form of magic.... It's a collective work, but one wherein there's a secret, too."

Out 1 and Its Double

> [Ornette Coleman's *Free Jazz*] causes earache the first time through, especially for those new to Coleman's music. The second time, its cacophony lessens and its complex balances and counter-balances begin to take effect. The third time, layer upon layer of pleasing configurations—rhythmic, melodic, contrapuntal, tonal—becomes visible. The fourth or fifth listening, one swims readily along, about ten feet down, breathing the music like air.
> —Whitney Balliett, "Abstract," in *Dinosaurs in the Morning*

> If there is something comforting—religious, if you want—about paranoia, there is still also anti-paranoia, where nothing is connected to anything, a condition not many of us can bear for long.
> —Thomas Pynchon, *Gravity's Rainbow*

In the spring of 1970, Jacques Rivette shot about thirty hours of improvisation with more than three dozen actors in 16mm. Out of this massive and extremely open-ended material emerged two films, both of which contrive to subvert the traditional moviegoing experience at its roots. *Out 1,* lasting twelve hours and forty minutes, structured as an eight-part serial, originally subtitled N*oli me tangere,* that was designed for but refused by French television, was screened publicly only once (at Le Havre, September 9–10, 1971), still in workprint form. Twenty-seven and a half years later, at the Rotterdam Film Festival in February 1989, a somewhat reedited but nearly finished print was screened over several days for a much smaller audience, including myself, and then in the early '90s, a version that had apparently been reedited somewhat further by Rivette (including the deletion of a lengthy sequence featuring Jean-Pierre Léaud in the final episode) was shown at a few film festivals and on French and German television, and this version, to the best of my knowledge, is the one being presented here.

As I recall, no more than about five viewers in Rotterdam cared to watch the serial in its entirety in 1989, and very few others turned up even to sample it. But such are the conundrums of shifting fashion that when the Museum of the Moving Image in New York's borough of Queens screened the serial over a weekend in late 2006, tickets were sold out well in advance, and the entire event was rescheduled the following March to accommodate the others who wanted to see it. (In this case, an appreciative article in the Sunday *New York Times* by Dennis Lim clearly helped.)

Out 1: Spectre, which Rivette spent the better part of a year editing out of the first film—running 255 minutes, or roughly a third as long, and structured to include an intermission halfway through (as was Rivette's previous feature, the 252-minute *L'amour fou* in 1968)—was released in Paris in early 1974, and to the best of my knowledge, is the same version that is included in this release.

■ ■ ■

The organizing principle adopted by Rivette in shooting the raw material of both films was the notion of a *complot* (plot, conspiracy) derived from Balzac's *Histoire des treize,* where thirteen individuals occupying different sectors of French society form a secret alliance to consolidate their power. Consciously setting out to make a critique of the conspiratorial zeitgeist of his first feature, *Paris Nous Appartient,* Rivette also used this principle to arrange meetings and confrontations between his actors, each of whom was invited to invent and improvise his or her own character in relation to the overall intrigue. The only writing done as preparation came from Rivette's codirector Suzanne Schiffmann, who helped to prepare and plot the separate encounters, and from Rivette himself when he wrote three separate coded messages intercepted by one of the characters that allude to the *complot* and the "13."

Paradoxically, if one can get past the relative tedium of the theatrical exercises, *Out 1* might be the most accessible and entertaining of all of Rivette's works, with the possible exception of *Céline at Julie vont en bateau*—quite unlike *Spectre,* which probably qualifies as his most difficult film. (Arguably, these three films feature Rivette's most inventive and pleasurable uses of color.) But because of its initial rejection by French state television and its subsequent lack of availability, its reputation has assumed legendary proportions, inflating notions of its alleged difficulty owing to the length of its combined episodes (which few viewers would ever think of applying to other TV serials and miniseries, especially those in English). Soon after a pirated version of the serial as it was shown on Italian TV turned up on the internet, furnished with English subtitles provided by amateur fans, English critic Brad Stevens was moved to write the following in *Video Watchdog:* "It is surely evidence of how widely cinema is still considered a second-rate art that one of its supreme masterpieces has been denied to British and American audiences; if a similar situation existed where literature was concerned, we would only be able to read English translations of Proust's *À la recherche du temps perdu* in the form of clandestinely circulated photocopies. Yet one can hardly resist a wry smile upon discovering that *Out 1,* a work obsessively focused on conspiracies, has finally achieved widespread distribution thanks to what might be described as an Internet 'conspiracy.'"

It should be noted that repeated viewings of *Out 1* and *Spectre* help to clarify not their "plots" but their separate formal organizations. The analogy suggested above between Rivette and Coleman is far more relevant, however, to the notion of *performance*. Much like Coleman's thirty-eight-minute venture into group improvisation with seven other musicians, *Out 1*'s surface is dictated by accommodations, combinations, and clashes brought about by contrasting styles of "playing." The textures run the gamut from the purely cinematic skills of Jean-Pierre Léaud (Colin) and Juliet Berto (Frédérique) to the stage-bound techniques of Françoise Fabian (Lucie); from the relative nervousness of Michel Lonsdale (Thomas) and Michèle Moretti (Lili) to the relative placidity of Jacques Doniol-Valcroze (Etienne) and Jean Boise (Warok); from the reticence of Bulle Ogier (Pauline/Emilie) to the garrulity of Bernadette Lafont (Sarah). Most radical of all is the supposition that "everything" an actor does is interesting, effectively abolishing the premise one can discriminate in a conventional manner between "good" and "bad" performances, which is always predicated on some fixed notion of the real.

For Coleman as for Rivette, the thematic material is kept to a minimum and mainly used as an expedient—a launching pad to propel each solo player into a "statement" of his own that elicits responses from the others. Apart from the brief ensemble passages written by Coleman, there is no composer behind *Free Jazz,* hence no composition; the primary role of Coleman as leader is to assemble players and establish a point of departure for their improvising.

Rivette's role in both versions of *Out 1* is similar, with the crucial difference that he edited and rearranged the material afterward, assembling shots as well as players. And the assembly is one that works *against* the notion of continuity: sustained meaning, the province of an auteur, is deliberately withheld—from the audience as well as the actors. Consequently, it is hardly surprising that the "13" in both versions of *Out 1* never reveals itself as anything more than a chimera. It eventually becomes evident that the *complot* is a pipe dream that never got off the ground, an idea once discussed among thirteen individuals that apparently went no further. Aside from the efforts of certain characters (mainly Thomas and Lucie) to keep its real or hypothetical existence hidden, and the attempts or threats of others (Colin, Frédérique, Pauline/Emilie) to "expose" it, the "13" never once assumes a recognizable shape—in the dialogue or on the screen.

Both films begin by pretending to tell us four separate stories at once—although the beginning of the first and longer version could perhaps also be described, with greater accuracy, as presenting us with four separate and alternating blocks of documentary material with no narrative connection between them. We watch two theater groups rehearsing plays attributed to Aeschylus—*Seven Against Thebes* (directed by Lili) and *Prometheus Bound* (directed by Thomas), and also observe Colin and Frédérique—two rather crazed and curious loners, each of whom contrives to extract money from strangers in cafés. (Colin hands out cards declaring that he's a deaf-mute, and plays aggressively and atonally on his harmonica whenever someone hesitates to give him money; Frédérique, when she isn't hanging out with her gay friend Michel [played by her real-life gay husband at the time, Michel Berto], usually starts by flirting and/or inventing stories about her identity and background.) For the first three dozen or so shots of *Spectre*—ten of them black-and-white stills accompanied by an electronic hum—Rivette cuts between these four autonomous units, establishing no plot connections. The only links set up are occasional formal repetitions: a scene echoed by a subsequent still, two pans in separate shots of Colin and Frédérique in their rooms. Even within each unit, many shots are either "too long" or "too short" to be conventionally taken as narrative. Rivette often cuts in the middle of a sentence or a movement, and the missing pieces are not always recuperated. Conversely, a shot in which Colin's concierge reminds him to leave his key ends irrelevantly with her walking away from the camera and sitting down at a table to write. Like some of the cryptic stills punctuating later portions of the film, such a diversion proposes—without ever substantiating—yet another supplementary fiction.

Then almost miraculously, thirteen minutes and thirty-five seconds into *Spectre*—and thirty-five minutes and twenty-eight seconds into the second episode of the serial (or more than two hours into the overall proceedings)—two of the four "plots" are brought together: Colin is suddenly handed a slip of paper by Marie (Hermine Karagheuz), a member of Lili's theater group. On it is typed a seemingly coded message which he sets out to decipher, along with two subsequent messages he receives, following clues provided by references to Lewis Carroll's "The Hunting of the Snark" and Balzac (the latter gracefully explicated by Eric Rohmer in a cameo role). And when Colin's deductions eventually lead him to a hippy boutique called "l'Angle du hasard," the "plot" appreciably thickens: the boutique is run by Pauline, whom we later discover is a friend of both Thomas and Lili, another member of the collective; and all three are members of the alleged "13."

Meanwhile, Frédérique, the fourth narrative strand, has been making some unwitting connections of her own. After stealing letters from the flat of Etienne (another one of the "13," along with his wife, Lucie) for the purpose of possible blackmail, she dons a wig and arranges a meeting with Lucie: an incongruous match suggesting Mickey Rooney in an encounter with Rohmer's Maud. Then, when she fails to collect money, she turns up at the boutique to try the same ploy with Pauline.

This second encounter marks the fusion of all four "plots," and occurs just before the intermission of *Spectre*, although it doesn't occur in the serial until much later, during the fifth episode. It is the only time Frédérique and Colin ever cross paths (they are the only important characters who never meet), and the spectator may well feel at this point that she or he is finally being led out of chaos. But the remainder of the story in both versions, after drawing the four strands together more tightly, proceeds to unravel them again; and the final hour of *Spectre* and the remaining episodes of the serial leave us as much in the dark as we were at the beginning.

By this time, many of the characters have wound up revealing various secrets—Colin, for instance, starts talking a blue streak in one of the intermediate episodes, losing his deaf-mute pose for several hours—and the conspiracies paradoxically seem to grow thicker at the same time that both groups start to dissolve. Even though certain scenes toward the end defy explanation or decoding—in a dialogue between Colin and Sarah at the end of the seventh episode, some of her lines and one of his are literally played backward on the soundtrack, and Frédérique in the eighth episode is killed in an obscure intrigue with her recently acquired lover on a rooftop involving dueling pistols and a black mask (in effect, another romantic nineteenth-century fantasy that seems to rhyme with Colin's obsession with Balzac)—the overall design and meaning of *Out 1* become increasingly lucid as the serial unfolds. By the end, the paranoid fiction that the actors have generated has almost completely subsumed the documentary, even though the implied conspiracy continues to elude their grasp as well as ours. The successive building and shattering of utopian dreams—the idealistic legacy of May 1968—are thus reproduced in the rising and declining fortunes of all the characters, outlining both the preoccupations and the shape of the work as a whole.

Much as *folie à deux* figures centrally in *L'amour fou* and *Céline et Julie vont en bateau,* failed *folie à deux* gradually becomes the very essence of both *Out* and *Spectre*. The inability to "connect" reveals itself as part and parcel of the incapacity to sustain fictions, a failure registering most poignantly in the relationship of Ogier and Léaud, which begins with mutual attraction and ends in estrangement. Of all the "two-part inventions," theirs is the richest in shifting tensions, and the growing rift is brilliantly underlined by the staging of their scenes in the boutique—particularly when they're stationed in adjoining rooms on opposite sides of the screen, each vying in a different way for our attention. This spatial tension reaches its climax in their last scene together, on the street, when Ogier forcibly breaks away and Léaud mimes the invisible barrier between them by pushing at it in agonized desperation, finally wandering in a diagonal trajectory out of the frame while blowing a dissonant wail on his harmonica.

■ ■ ■

The ideal form of viewing the film would be for it to be distributed like a book on records, as, for example, with a fat novel of a thousand pages. Even if one's a very rapid reader—which, as it happens, isn't my case—one never reads the book in one sitting, one puts it down, stops for lunch, etc. The ideal thing was to see it in two days, which allowed one to get into it enough to follow it, with the possibility of stopping four or five times.

—Rivette describing the serial to Gilbert Adair, "Phantom Interviewers Over Rivette," *Film Comment*, September–October 1974

At least part of the impressionism you see in Duras and Straub (who, by the way, was totally hypnotized by a screening of the thirteen-hour *Out*) comes from their low-budget techniques. I aim at something a little different in my recent films; you might almost say that I am trying to bring back the old MGM Technicolor! I even think that the colors of *Out* would please a Natalie Kalmus [Hollywood color consultant 1934–1949].

—Rivette to John Hughes, "The Director as Psychoanalyst" (Spring 1975), http://www.rouge.com.au/4/hughes.html

Complot becomes the motivation behind a series of transparent gestures: specters of action playing over a void. We watch actors playing at identity and meaning the way that children do, with many of the games leading to dead-ends or stalemates, some exhausting themselves before they arrive anywhere, and still others creating solid roles and actions that dance briefly in the theater of the mind before dissolving into something else. Nothing remains fixed, and everything becomes ominous. Relentlessly investigated by Colin and blindly exploited by Frédérique, the specter of the "13" reactivates the paranoia of its would-be members, mainly increasing the distances between them. Other crises intervene (a stranger runs off with the money of an actor in Lili's theater group; Pauline threatens to publish the intercepted letters); fear begets fear; both theater groups disperse; Emilie and Lili are last seen driving off to meet the perpetually missing Igor; and Frédérique and Colin are each returned to their isolation. Repeated "empty" shots of Porte d'Italie in the final reel of *Spectre*—chilling mixtures of Ozu-like emptiness with Langian terror—embody this growing sense of void, which ultimately widens to swallow up everything else in the film.

The delivery of the first message to Colin is totally gratuitous, an act that is never explained or even hinted at, and most of the other "connections" are brought about by equally expedient contrivances. In a country house occupied at various times by Sarah, Thomas, Emilie (aka Pauline), and Lili, Rivette parodies the very notion of "hidden meaning" in a subtler way, by making sure that a single nondescript bust with no acknowledged relation to the "plot" is visible in every room. It even crops up in the locked room possibly inhabited by Igor, Emilie's missing husband, a room she enters only near the end of the film. Obviously the bust is a joke; but why is it there? To suggest a *complot*. And according to the tactics of *Out 1*, suggesting a *complot* is at once an absurdity and a necessity: it leads us nowhere except forward—a compulsive movement that often leads to comedy in the serial but mainly produces a feeling of anguish in *Spectre*.

For much of the preceding, I've been treating the plots of *Out 1* and its shortened and fractured "double" as if they were identical, but in fact the experiences and meanings of the serial and of *Spectre* are in many ways radically different, as they were meant to be. The opening shot of *Spectre*, for instance, occurs almost three hours into the serial, and the final episode of the serial largely consists of material missing from *Spectre*. One of the more striking differences in the long version is that Thomas (Lonsdale) emerges as virtually the central character (which he clearly isn't in *Spectre*)—not only because of his role in guiding his group's improvisations and psychic self-explorations, but also because his ambiguous role as a rather infantile patriarch, climaxing in his falling apart in his last extended sequence on the beach, becomes pivotal to the overall movement of the plot.

Beginning as a documentary that is progressively overtaken by fiction, the serial has no prologue, merely a rudimentary itinerary set down in five successive intertitles—"Stéphane Tchalgadjieff présente / OUT 1 / Premier Episode / de Lili à Thomas / Le 13 avril 1970"—followed by an opening shot of five actors in a bare rehearsal space performing elaborate calisthenics together to the sound of percussion. Minus the date, the same pattern of intertitles launches every other episode, each of which is labeled as a further relay between two characters, beginning in each case with the second character named in the previous segment. (In the sixth chapter, the relay is between two guises of the same character, Pauline/Emilie.)

All seven of the remaining episodes have prologues, each of which is structured similarly: fifteen to twenty-eight black-and-white production stills shot by Pierre Zucca that recap portions of the preceding episode, accompanied by the same percussion heard in the first shot of the first episode, followed by the one or two concluding shots of the preceding episode in black and white that carry their original direct sound. Thus the notion of precise links in a chain—between one episode and the next, between one character and the next—is maintained throughout as a strictly practical principle as well as a formal one. Each black-and-white prologue provides both a ghostly abstraction of the preceding segment as an *aide de mémoire* and a version of "the thirteen" (roughly, 2 x 13 = 26) as a compulsive rearrangement of existing data that might provide certain clues about what is to come. Similarly, each relay-title posits a beginning and an end to the trajectory of characters within each episode while establishing that each new beginning was formerly an end and each new end will form a new beginning—another form of abstraction-as-synopsis that retraces the action as if it were a kind of puzzle that might yield hidden meanings. (In *Spectre,* these titles vanish, but the black-and-white stills are reformulated at various junctures to provide cryptic extensions to as well as recollective summaries of the action, accompanied by a droning hum rather than percussion. As Rivette described this sound and function in a 1974 interview, "What we have is just a meaningless frequency, as if produced by a machine, which interrupts the fiction—sometimes sending messages to it, sometimes in relation to what we've already seen or are going to see, and sometimes with no relation at all. Because there are stills from scenes, especially toward the end [of *Spectre*], which don't appear in the body of the film and are frankly quite incomprehensible.")

In contrast to the serial, *Spectre* might be said to begin as a fictional narrative that is progressively overtaken by documentary—the precise opposite of its predecessor. Despite the fact that both theater groups are putatively preparing to perform plays ascribed to Aeschylus, there are no deaths at all in the serial apart from that of Frédérique, and apparently none whatsoever in *Spectre*. (One can't be entirely sure about the messenger played by the film's producer, Stéphane Tchalgadjieff—brained by Pauline with a blunt instrument in the back of the hippie boutique where she works, for no apparent reason, and never seen again.) Moreover, the meaning and impact of many individual shots and sequences are markedly different. Colin's efforts to get an Eiffel Tower trinket to swing back and forth thirteen times—a minor gag in the serial that parodies his manic efforts to impose meaning where there is none, to convert chance into destiny—becomes the final shot of *Spectre*. There it figures as an ironic metaphor for the viewer's frustration in trying to make sense out of the latter film. After repeated efforts, Colin finally concludes, "It didn't work," speaking now for Rivette as well as the spectator: the physical act becomes metaphysical.

■ ■ ■

ROSENBAUM: Why did you choose the title *Out*?
RIVETTE: Because we didn't succeed in finding a title. It's without meaning. It's only a label.
—"Phantom Interviewers Over Rivette," *Film Comment*, September–October 1974

Seen as a single work, or at least as two versions of the same work, *Out 1* strikes me as the greatest film we have about the counterculture of the 1960s. I hasten to add that unlike all the American or English examples one could cite, there is nothing in *Out 1* about hallucinogenic drugs (despite some riotously bright, psychedelic colors), and as a period statement that is related directly to the disillusionment that followed the failed revolution of May 1968, it projects a specifically French zeitgeist. (One could perhaps speculate that the Cartesian basis of French thought provided French culture with a sort of shortcut to the mindset provided by hallucinogenic drugs in North America, thereby delaying and otherwise limiting their cultural impact.)

But seen more broadly as an epic reflection on the utopian dreams of the counterculture as they manifested themselves on both sides of the Atlantic, *Out 1* remains an invaluable touchstone, above all in its perceptions of the options posed between collectivity and isolation, the major theme of Rivette's early features. Virtually all of *Out 1* can be read as a meditation on the dialectic between various collective endeavors (theater rehearsals, conspiracies, diverse countercultural activities, manifestos) and activities and situations growing out of solitude and alienation (puzzle solving, scheming, plot spinning, ultimately madness)—the options, to some extent, of the French left during the late 1960s.

Formally, the serial could be called Bazinian and Renoiresque in its preference for the long take and for *mise en scène* in deep focus over montage as a purveyor of meaning, and in this respect, the aggressively edited, splintered, and Langian *Spectre* forms a striking dialectic with it. In the serial, this ultimately leads to a kind of parodic summation of Bazin's notions about realism—a Rouch-like pseudo-documentary mired in fantasy—that might be said to undermine Bazinian theories more than simply illustrate them.

A major difference between Rivette's serial and the crime serials of Feuillade—accounting for their vast difference in popular appeal, at least to the audiences of their respective periods—rests in the notion of a stable base beneath or behind all the machinations. In *Les Vampires* (1915–1916) and *Tih-Minh* (1919), a supreme confidence in the fixed generic identities of heroes and villains and in the fixed social identities of masters and servants makes all the "revisions" of these characters and the improvised spirit of their enactments a form of play that never threatens their root functions and identities as narrative figures. In *Out 1*, the absence of this social and artistic confidence—a veritable agnosticism about society and fiction alike that seems to spring from both the skepticism of the late 1960s and the burden placed on all the actors to improvise—gives the narrative a very different status, entailing a frequent slippage from character to actor and from fiction to nonfiction. Because none of the masks seems entirely secure, the fiction-making process itself—its pleasures, its dangers, even its traps, dead-ends, and lapses—becomes part of the overall subject and interest. (The issue at stake isn't so much the skill of Rivette's actors—which varies enormously—as the perfunctory nature of many of the fictions that they embody.) Here there is no fixed text beneath the various proliferating fictions that might guarantee their social and generic functions; what one finds instead is a series of references and allusions—Balzac and Renoir, Aeschylus and Lang, Dumas and Rouch, Hugo and Feuillade—that can provide only theoretical pretexts or momentary, unsustainable models, as well as an overall spirit of drift and play.

Three Afterthoughts

> He who leaps into the void owes no explanation to those who watch.
> —Jean-Luc Godard, reviewing *Montparnasse 19* (1958)

1. Perhaps the most detailed comparison between the two separate theater groups in *Out 1* has been offered by Cristina Álvarez López and Adrian

Martin in two separate videos and an accompanying text commissioned by the Melbourne International Film Festival in late 2014 as part of an ongoing series of audiovisual essays and written texts about *Out 1*. (Kevin B. Lee and I provided the second video in this series, Álvarez López/Martin made the first and fourth, and David Heslin and Chris Luscri provided the third.) The following two passages are drawn from an essay posted in mubi.com/notebook on August 7, 2014 to accompany the first of these videos, "Paratheatre: Plays Without Stages (from I to IV)":

> The fact is that *Out 1* is an extraordinary, synthesizing document of many experimental movements in theater, dating from the immediate post-war period and surviving through to our day, in performance workshops grand and small across the globe. Although some of the commentaries indicate, in passing, that Rivette drew upon (through his actors) a mélange of influences including the Polish theatre guru Jerzy Grotowski and The Living Theatre from USA, it is dizzying to realize just how many traditions and tendencies are referenced in the physical work of the performers that Rivette records with such care, and at such length. The film is like an immense corridor through which the history of contemporary, experimental theatre passes.
>
> One group uses gestural and vocal work to explore and express, in highly stylized ways, Aeschylus's *Seven Against Thebes;* the other uses a radical form of improvisation, nominally based on the pretext of Aeschylus's *Prometheus Bound,* that is not quite psychodrama (its aim is not in the least bit therapeutic), but certainly reaches down to the roots of Artaud's Theatre of Cruelty—in the latter case, the written text slips further and further away. Both groups base their work on the types of rigorous exercises (Grotowski's exercises, psychophysical exercises, and ancient games such as mirroring) that are crucial, for instance, to Richard Schechner's The Performance Group (which later became The Wooster Group), whose production of *Dionysus in '69* was documented (in split-screen) by Brian De Palma in 1970.
>
> Both troupes talk, analyze and review their work a lot—but whereas the *Thebes* tend to re-work things practically (according to various kinds of 'scores' for voice and movement), the *Prometheus* group is more into research and self-critique, once they emerge from each 'trance.' Note, too, the dual orientation of both groups: while, in one way or another, they are fully avant-garde, they are also trying to plug back into mythic, sacred sources—the revival of theatrical spectacle as *ritual* which both attracted and disturbed Pasolini by the end of the 1960s.

Based on my own limited theatergoing experience in this period, I would add to this account that some of the "trances" in the *Prometheus* group closely resemble certain interludes in The Living Theatre's production of *Paradise Now* (which I attended at Brooklyn's Academy of Music in the fall of 1968, after the same group and production toured Europe).

2. The eventual knitting together of four seemingly autonomous and unrelated narrative strands—more cursory in *Spectre,* but central to the serial—might be seen as the belated fulfillment of an innovative aspect of Erich von Stroheim's original *Greed,* running at a length of some forty-odd reels, that is completely absent from the release version. As I've noted in my monograph about *Greed* (BFI Classics, 1993), an enormous amount of narrative material was added by Stroheim to the plot of Frank Norris's novel *McTeague:*

> Nearly a fifth of the plot (a quarter of the [latest version that we have] of the script—69 out of 277 manuscript pages) transpires before one arrives at McTeague eating his Sunday dinner at the car conductors' coffee joint, the subject of the novel's opening sentence. Mac's life prior to his arrival in San Francisco, which takes up about a quarter of this prologue—over twenty-four pages in the published script—comprises an elaboration of only two shortish paragraphs in the novel.
>
> A brilliantly designed and extended sequence that comes four pages later in the published script, and encompasses about thirty pages more, introduces all the other major characters in the film [including three that are entirely missing from the release version] on a "typical" Saturday, the day that precedes the novel's opening, without establishing any connections between them apart from the fact they live in the same building. It seems entirely plausible that Harry Carr—who described watching a forty-five-reel version of *Greed* between 10:30 am and 8:30 pm—had this sequence at least partially in mind when he wrote in *Motion Picture Magazine* (April 1924), "Episodes come along that you think have no bearing on the story, then twelve or fourteen reels later, it hits you with a crash."

3. Undoubtedly the most significant change brought about in Rivette's reediting of the serial between 1989 and the early '90s was his deletion of Léaud's powerful climactic scene, which is no longer part of the film. (The only other changes I'm aware of involve the order of certain sequences.) This lengthy *plan-séquence* occurred originally just after a comparably

lengthy scene between Bulle Ogier and Bernadette Lafont. (In fact, the final episode in its original, ninety-minute form showed three of the major characters—Ogier, Léaud, and Lonsdale—in a separate extended sequence; no trace of any of these sequences is to be found in *Spectre*. Lonsdale's scene is placed last, and his reduction from director-patriarch to a mass of blubbering jelly on a beach seems to bring the serial full circle from the wordless hysteria of his group's first exercise.)

I suspect that this hair-raising sequence, which showed Colin alone in his room in a state of hysteria oscillating between despair and (more briefly) exuberance, carried too many suggestions of Léaud's subsequent real-life emotional difficulties for Rivette to feel comfortable about retaining it. When Léaud appeared at the Viennale in 2013 to speak about the film, along with its heroic producer Stéphane Tchalgadjieff (whose other adventurous credits include *India Song* [1975], Rivette's *Duelle*, *Noroît* [both 1976], and *Merry-Go-Round* [1981], Straub-Huillet's *Fortini/Cani* [1976], and Bresson's *The Devil, Probably* [1977]; *Out 1,* moreover, was the first film he produced) and myself, he didn't allude to this deletion. But it also became clear that he's never seen the serial in its entirety; he spoke mainly about his earlier friendship with Rivette and the influence played by North African music on his harmonica wails.

Based on my notes taken at the 1989 Rotterdam screening, the missing sequence, punctuated by a few patches of black leader, showed Colin crying, screaming, howling like an animal, banging his head against the wall, busting a closet door, writhing on the floor, then calming down and picking up his harmonica. After throwing away all three of the secret messages he has been trying for most of the serial to decode, he starts playing his harmonica ecstatically, throws his clothes and other belongings out into the hall, dances about manically, and then plays the harmonica some more. Dramatically and structurally, this raw piece of psychodrama inevitably suggested certain parallels with the sequence relentlessly recording Jean-Pierre Kalfon's self-lacerations with a razor in Rivette's *L'amour fou*—a disturbing piece of self-exposure in which the fictional postulates of the character seem to crumble into genuine pain and distress, representing in both films a dangerous crossing of certain boundaries into what can only be perceived as madness.

CHAPTER 22

Béla Tarr

Hungarian filmmaker Béla Tarr is considered in this section in two separate capacities—as the director of *Sátántangó* and *The Turin Horse* and as the creator of and principal teacher at film.factory, a truly remarkable international filmmaking workshop that he established in Sarajevo in 2013 after he announced the end of his career as a filmmaker, and where I was privileged to teach for four separate two-week sessions during its three years of operation. I've remained in touch with Tarr, two members of his staff, and many of the film.factory students ever since. The school lamentably had to close because of a withdrawal of its financial support, although there are still hopes that it might reopen elsewhere.

The first two pieces here appeared respectively in *Music & Literature*, issue two: *László Krasznahorkai, Béla Tarr, Max Neumann*, 2013 (reprinted with corrections) and in *Film Comment*, September–October 2011. The third was posted on *Sight and Sound*'s website on July 18, 2013, and then expanded (by about 50 percent) for its French translation in *Trafic* #88, published in December 2013.

Sátántangó (Film and Novel) as Faulknerian Reverie

Part of the greatness of Béla Tarr's radical film adaptation of László Krasznahorkai's first novel, *Sátántangó*, is a curious combination of faithfulness and what might be described as the theoretical limits of any possible faithfulness in the "translation" of prose into sounds and images. There's something undeniably startling as well as radical about converting a novel that's only 274 pages long (in its graceful English translation by George Szirtes) into a film that lasts 450 minutes, but the relation between the long sentences of the former and the long takes of the latter is central to that conversion. The experience of following a sentence may not necessarily be identical to the experience of following one or more characters, whether this is on a page *or* on a screen, but the existential aspect of implicating us in the shape and duration of an event while we attend to it, with all the moral and political ramifications this "collaboration" implies, is common to both experiences.

In certain respects, one might argue that the political and social differences between novel and film are far less important than the separate cultural reflexes of Americans and Hungarians following the narrative in either of its phenomenological forms. A Cuban-born friend of mine who fought in Castro's army before fleeing to the United States has told me that the film *Sátántangó* captures the tragicomedy of Stalinist bureaucracy and surveillance better than anything else he has encountered, in film *or* in narrative prose, whereas Krasznahorkai and Tarr have both suggested in several interviews, no less plausibly, that nothing could have been further from their minds while composing this narrative in its separate forms. For them, it appears, the essential truth of the story is more metaphysical than sociopolitical, and a post-Christian and/or post-biblical context is what dominates. (This context is apparent even in the titles of the first two collaborations between Krasznahorkai and Tarr, *Damnation* and *Sátántangó,* and both men have acknowledged in interviews that their last film together, the apocalyptic *The Turin Horse,* is structured around the six days of creation found in Genesis.) But surely the playing out of its metaphysical meanings is contingent on the reader/viewer's sense of his or her own identity in relation to the story's blighted, godforsaken, and self-centered characters. Whichever side of the cold war one happens to be on, or whether one chooses to accept a cold war context at all, these arguably become the elected meanings more than the projected ones, although it's important to add that *Sátántangó* was written and originally published in the mid-1980s, when Hungary was still under Soviet Communist rule, and therefore a period when Communism couldn't be addressed directly, even if its bureaucratic manifestations are omnipresent and central to the narrative. It would perhaps be unduly facile to insist that the blatant (albeit twisted and perverted) religious context has replaced the suppressed political context in fixing the moral implications of the story, but it seems hard to deny that this relationship exists on some level.

By the same token, William Faulkner's *Light in August,* my favorite novel in any language, has almost never been described as a Communist novel. Yet if one reads it as a proletarian American novel of its period (1932), one could argue that it bears many of the characteristic attributes, formal and otherwise, that one might associate with that category as well as that era—for instance, the restless, almost twitching movement of the narrative from one location to the next (which one could also associate with, say, Charlie Chaplin's *Modern Times* and John Dos Passos's *The Big Money,* both from 1936), reflecting the economic instability of most of the characters.

As someone who grew up in northwestern Alabama and spent the first sixteen years of my life there (1943–1959), I have treasured *Light in August,* which I first read shortly after I left for a New England boarding school, as the novel that best captures the quasi-totalitarian climate of that culture, especially in relation to race. Even though this is clearly not addressed as directly as Faulkner addresses racism in *Light in August,* it seems no less clear that Tarr and Krasznahorkai recognize and understand this climate with comparable depth, not to mention sorrow and outrage, and regard it no less metaphysically as a blight on humanity. So, whether it's willed or not, *Sátántangó* deserves to be regarded in both its forms as one of the great narratives about Stalinism and its effects on alienating people from themselves as well as each other—including, one should stress, the lingering effects of that Stalinism on a capitalist society.

For many years, Béla Tarr and I have had a running debate about the relation of the film (and, by implication, the novel) *Sátántangó* to *Light in August,* which also focuses largely on the simultaneous events of a single day in a depressed, flat rural area as seen through the consciousness of several alienated characters—alienated from themselves as well as from one another—including a fallen patriarch who observes all the others named Reverend Hightower (a name and figure that already anticipates some of the structure and vision of Tarr and Krasznahorkai's film *The Man from London*), and who might have served as his community's conscience if they all hadn't deteriorated into an apocalyptic, post-ethical (and specifically post-Christian) stupor. Both novels are largely centered around shocking central episodes devoted to atrocious acts that, even more shockingly, are described with a certain amount of lyricism—in *Light in August,* the pursuit, castration, and murder of the racially ambiguous Joe Christmas by a racist named Percy Grimm who regards him as black; in *Sátántangó,* the torture and fatal poisoning of a cat by a feeble-minded young girl named Esti who then kills herself with some of the same rat poison.

Other rough parallels of *Sátántangó* with Faulkner, if not with *Light in August* per se, include a narrative that shifts between the separate viewpoints of diverse characters (see *As I Lay Dying*), an important section framed around the consciousness of a feeble-minded and innocent character—Benjy in *The Sound and the Fury,* Esti in *Sátántangó*—and a form of black comedy that forms around the meanness, pettiness, and spite of many of the central characters (the members of the failed farm collective in *Sátántangó,* the Snopes family in Faulkner's late trilogy—*The Hamlet, The Town,* and *The Mansion*—devoted to their ascendancy).

Béla Tarr doesn't see any connection between *Sátántangó* and *Light in August,* or, more generally, between Krasznahorkai and Faulkner; he has told me more than once that he finds the Hungarian translations of Faulkner so inadequate that he doesn't feel he knows this American author at all, and it's worth adding that one could also trace many of Faulkner's methods back to Joseph Conrad, for example, the events of one day perceived from the perspective of separate characters, as in *Nostromo.* (I can also readily acknowledge that the sarcastic wit of Krasznahorkai's story, for example, which arguably goes even beyond Faulkner's Snopes trilogy in its sense of absurdist and nihilist farce, seems quintessentially eastern European, making the apocalyptic pessimism of this novel distinct from both Faulkner and Conrad, even after one factors in the latter's Polish origins.)

But even so, there are certain similarities between long sentences by Faulkner and Krasznahorkai that are worth dwelling upon. Both convey a certain compulsive movement that can be described as a lyrical and rhetorical delirium around scenes and narrative situations that are virtually static, furious maelstroms that swirl around a void: not just the solitary and flabby inertia and impotence of Hightower and Krasznahorkai's doctor stewing in their own juices (which occasions a certain hilarious Beckett-like comedy in Krasznahorkai's novel and Tarr's film when they linger over the seemingly intense labor and straining effort required for an alcoholic to drink himself into oblivion, but only a kind of pitying despair or self-loathing identification in Faulkner's), but also the slow-motion progress of a wagon mounting a hill as perceived by Lena Grove in the present-tense opening of Faulkner's novel, and the relentless way Tarr's camera follows various characters walking down dusty roads throughout much of *Sátántangó*.

Nevertheless, the philosophical differences between Faulkner and Krasznahorkai are profound. The two major characters of *Light in August,* who never meet—Lena Grove (a pregnant and single young white woman on the road from Alabama, searching in Mississippi for the father of her child-to-be) and Joe Christmas (a doomed, bitter orphan of thirty-three with alleged biracial origins who can't ever discover whether he's white or black)—are presented generally in terms of the respective styles of *The Odyssey* and the Old Testament, at least as they're described by Erich Auerbach in "Odysseus' Scar," the brilliant first chapter of his *Mimesis:* seamless and untroubled in Homer, like figures on Keats's Grecian urn, and turbulent and full of gaps, like expressionist bolts of lightning, in the story of Abraham. As Claire Denis once suggested to me, *Light in August* may be the best novel ever written about racism, and it's also a profoundly troubled moral inquiry about the failure of southern Christianity to cope with racism. It boldly alternates pastoral comedy (Grove) with urban tragedy (Christmas), a cinematic form of stillness, presence, and unchanging persistence (Grove, who opens the novel in the present tense) with a very literary form of tortured narrative progression (Christmas).

Here is the way Auerbach summarizes the two styles:

> On the one hand [meaning Homer], externalized, uniformly illuminated phenomena, at a definite time and in a definite place, connected together without lacunae in a perpetual foreground; thoughts and feelings completely expressed; events taking place in a leisurely fashion and with very little suspense. On the other hand [in the Old Testament], the externalization of only so much of the phenomena as is necessary for the purpose of the narrative, all else left in obscurity; the decisive points of the narrative alone are emphasized, what lies between is nonexistent; time and place are undefined and call for interpretation; thoughts and feelings remain unexpressed, are only suggested by the silence and the fragmentary speeches; the whole, permeated with the most unrelieved suspense and directed toward a single goal (and to that extent far more of a unity), remains mysterious and "fraught with background."[1]

Krasznahorkai and Tarr clearly can't be identified with either of these styles—unless, perhaps, one tries to combine them into some sort of shotgun marriage between, say, Homeric uniformity and suspense, or between allegory and unbroken continuity. As I've already suggested, it can't be said to address Stalinism directly in the way that *Light in August* addresses Christianity, even though Stalinist bureaucracy and its bureaucratic surveillance, seemingly motored exclusively by mean-spirited self-interest and giving rise to a form of universal misanthropy, is one of its major sources of black comedy. But in spite of all this, *Light in August* and *Sátántangó* both qualify as moral indictments of hypocritical communities, a major source of their common power.

In any case, it's important to recall that the narrative of *Sátántangó* originated with Krasznahorkai, not with Tarr; and a 2012 interview with the former by Paul Morton concludes with a different spin on the issue of a possible Faulknerian influence:

> Question: "Finally, American readers will surely make comparisons between *Sátántangó* and Faulkner's novels. There are the long, rhythmic sentences. There is the small dying town cursed by a past and the constant jarring shifts in time. Did Faulkner's novels, either in English or Hungarian translation, or any of our other writers inform your work?"

Without clarifying whether he read Faulkner in English or in Hungarian translation—and before going on to praise Dostoevsky, Pound, Thoreau's *Walden,* West's *Miss Lonelyhearts,* and Thomas Pynchon—Krasznahorkai replied, "Yes, they had an extraordinary effect on me and I am glad to have the opportunity of admitting this to you now. The influence of Faulkner—particularly of *As I Lay Dying* and *The Sound and the Fury*—struck an incredibly deep echo in me: his passion, his pathos, his whole character, significance, the rhythmical structure of his novels, all carried me away. I must have been 16–18, I suppose, at one's most impressionable years."[2]

∎ ∎ ∎

Although the film *Sátántangó* is rigorously faithful to the novel's narrative and its narrative structure in most respects, one key difference is the exposition of the enlistment/induction—or, more precisely, reenlistment and reinduction—of Irimiás as a government spy (along with his sidekick, Petrina), which occurs in the second chapter of the novel, shortly after the release of Irimiás and Petrina from prison, but which we learn about in the film only retroactively and quite late in the proceedings, in the penultimate chapter. Both novel and film feature a dialogue with a captain/chief about their summons and their obligation to do government work, but in the film, the nature of this work is far more opaque and nonspecific; in the novel, there is a direct admission that their "job is to supply information."[3] Existentially, this puts us in a very different position regarding the failed farm collective who stand at the story's center, whose trust in Irimiás we're encouraged or at least permitted to share in the film, whereas in the novel we can only regard them throughout as gullible suckers and deluded victims of this false messiah's charisma.

This suggests that, as Krasznahorkai's first novel and Tarr's sixth feature, *Sátántangó* represents something notably different in their respective careers—even after we add that the overall artistic evolution of both careers seems to veer increasingly toward allegory, a development culminating in *The Turin Horse* (which Tarr has declared will be his final film). The fact that the Soviet rule of Hungary was still in force when the novel was written but not when the film was made is already a major difference, even though both Tarr and Krasznahorkai have tended to downplay this distinction in the interviews with each that I've encountered.

More generally, the metaphysics of novel and film can't be the same because sentences can pass back and forth between the physical and the metaphysical, but camera movements are perpetually and necessarily mired in the physical. Dan Gunn claims in his review of the novel for the *Times Literary Supplement* (June 1, 2012, p. 19), "What starts as a sentence happening inside one character's head ends inside the stagnation of a puddle or the terror of a cat; the object—a door or a road or a bell—can and does become the actor in its own drama." Perhaps this is a bit hyperbolic, but it does convey the sort of wayward drift that a sentence by Krasznahorkai can take, and clearly a drift of this kind isn't available to a camera and/or microphone in the same fashion. Tarr can only witness or accompany the physicality of an actor/character, and metaphysical or psychological omniscience can figure only in the brief, third-person voiceovers that conclude some of the chapters. (Similar disembodied male voiceovers take over briefly at privileged moments in *The Turin Horse,* signaling once again an acknowledgment of the narrative's literary origins.)

Both *Light in August* and *Sátántangó* qualify as metaphysical and allegorical reveries about the perversion of Christianity and fallen mankind, but the former holds out some form of hope for an earlier model of grace and acceptance, Lena Grove, associated with ancient Greece, while the latter, distributing its pessimistic despair more equitably and universally among its characters, implicitly refuses to categorize any of them as heroes or villains, or even as positive or negative role models. Irimiás may be a shabby con-artist and the villagers deluded fools for trusting him, but there is arguably nothing in the novel or film that suggests they should have given up on the notion of salvation and therefore trusted no one; the speech or sermon delivered by Irimiás over the corpse of Esti may be partially insincere and inadequate in other ways as a form of moral guidance, but it is arguably better than nothing, just as Hightower's well-intentioned impotence and defeat, however abject, might be regarded as morally preferable to the alcoholic doctor in *Sátántangó* who concludes the film by physically shutting out the external world as he boards up his windows.

Whatever his ideological limitations as a white southerner, Faulkner ultimately viewed racism as a metaphysical blight on mankind that turns the racially undefined Joe Christmas into a crucified Christ figure. By contrast, Krasznahorkai and Tarr appear to regard the Hungarian hatred of Gypsies mordantly, as an enduring and even comic-absurdist part of the social landscape (such as when the villagers go to the trouble of dismantling their useless furniture so that the Gypsies can't repossess it before they follow Irimiás to the manor house), but as little more than a glancing detail in their overall abjection (as it appears to be with the father and daughter of *The Turin Horse*), not as any cinching piece of evidence in their fallen state.

It's worth adding that the abjection and miserabilism of *Sátántangó* have become so internalized that its ultimate horror becomes the irrelevance of solipsistic fantasy: the death of Esti ("She brushed the hair from her forehead, put her thumb in her mouth, and closed her eyes. No need to worry. She knew perfectly well her guardian angels were already on the way")[4] or the doctor listening to the "nervous conversation" between his domestic possessions (creaking sideboard, rattling sauce-pan, sliding china plate) in the novel's concluding sentence.[5] The horror of Joe Christmas's death, on the other hand, expands and even ascends to become an imperishable memory surviving in the society that produced it:

> Then his face, body, all, seemed to collapse, to fall in upon itself, and from out the slashed garments about his hips and loins the pent black blood seemed to rush like a released breath. It seemed to rush out of his

pale body like the rush of sparks from a rising rocket; upon that black blast the man seemed to rise soaring into their memories forever and ever. They are not to lose it, in whatever peaceful valleys, beside whatever placid and reassuring streams of old age, in the mirroring faces of whatever children they will contemplate old disasters and newer hopes. It will be there, musing, quiet, steadfast, not fading and not particularly threatful, but of itself alone serene, of itself alone triumphant.[6]

The common thread in both apocalyptic visions is the moral specter of spirituality and acceptance—Christian, post-Christian, or (in the case of Lena Grove), pre-Christian—in the face of nihilistic evil and destruction. Even if it's just a ghost in the (paradoxically) atheistic universe of Krasznahorkai and Tarr, the persistence of that ghost in the very terms of their vision shouldn't be confused with its absence.

Notes

1. Erich Auerbach, *Mimesis: The Representation of Reality in Western Literature*, translated by Willard R. Trask, fiftieth-anniversary edition (Princeton, N.J. and Oxford, U.K.: Princeton University Press, 2003), 11–12.

2. "Anticipate Doom: The Millions Interviews László Krasznahorkai," by Paul Morton," http://www.themillions.com/2012/05/anticipate-doom-the-millions-interviews-laszlo-krasznahorkai.html, posted on May 9, 2012.

3. László Krasznahorkai, *Satantango*, translated by George Szirtes (New York: New Directions, 2012), 27.

4. Ibid., 131.

5. Ibid., 274.

6. William Faulkner, *Faulkner: Novels 1930–1935, As I Lay Dying, Sanctuary, Light in August, Pylon* (New York: Library of America, 1985), 743.

Deep in the Tarr Pit

Recalling the incident in Turin that reportedly occasioned Friedrich Nietzsche's final breakdown into madness—his weeping and embracing a cab horse that was being beaten by its driver for refusing to budge—Béla Tarr's regular screenwriter, novelist László Krasznahorkai, has noted that no one seems to know or ask what happened to the horse. But *The Turin Horse* is only nominally concerned with this riddle. It's more concerned with the horse's driver and his grown daughter, who live in a remote stone hut without electricity, subsisting on an exclusive diet of potatoes and palinka (Hungarian fruit brandy) while a perpetual storm rages outside, then arbitrarily subsides, over a carefully delineated six days. Their abject life remains fixed by a few infernal routines, such as dressing, undressing, drawing water from a well, or looking out the window. (One exterior shot of the daughter doing just that toward the end of the film will haunt me the rest of my life.) What passes for plot gradually becomes even more minimal by the driver's horse first refusing to pull the wagon, then refusing to eat. Eventually father and daughter also become immobilized, confirming one of Tarr's helpful statements—that this is simply a film about the inescapable fact of death. And Tarr is so unconcerned with the usual rules of consistency that he can show us the father and daughter (the latter played by Erika Bók, the little girl in Tarr's *Sátántangó* and Henriette in *The Man from London*) theatrically lit while she refuses to eat, even though the previous scene, ending in total darkness, has shown the lantern repeatedly burning out while it's still full of fuel. So "What is this darkness, Papa?" is a question that goes unanswered. This film is so bound up in what it's doing that it can't be bothered to care about explanations.

The other "major" incidents are no less perfunctory. A neighbor who's run out of palinka stops by for a refill and expounds on the awful state of the world and those who "acquire," "debase," and "destroy" it. Perhaps because this is the film's only extended monologue, some viewers are lured into thinking he must be expounding the filmmakers' "message" rather than merely spouting bullshit (which is what the father suggests). But what Tarr and Krasznahorkai are offering is a vision, not a message. The only other visitors, two women and five men, arrive in a wagon drawn by two robust horses to fetch water from the well, all of them insanely cheerful; the father, who calls them fucking Gypsies and clearly despises them, orders his daughter to chase them away, and after one of them says to her, "Come with us to America," he charges out of the hut with a hatchet, provoking their curses as they ride off. One leaves her a religious book about defilement that she reads aloud from, haltingly, in the next scene. The next day, she discovers the well has run dry, but this is no sort of "message" from the film either, neither retribution nor any sort of causal effect that we can be certain about. Like the neighbor sounding off or the lantern refusing to stay lit or the daughter refusing to eat, it's just another facet of a universe that's blighted by definition—and one that can't be sentimentalized as a blight populated by salt-of-the-earth types, either. Ever since his 1982, seventy-two-minute video production of *Macbeth* in two shots for Hungarian TV (available as an extra in the

Facets edition of *Sátántangó*), Tarr's universe has operated according to some sort of demonic anti-theology that's more a matter of feeling than one of principle; it can't even be counted on to confirm the triumph of evil or pestilence or futility. If this proves to be Tarr's last film, as he now maintains, this may be because it goes beyond any necessity to reach final conclusions about anything but extinction.

I suspect the father partially hates the Gypsies because they're so cheerful. I'm reminded of a hilarious early scene in *Sátántangó*—which has no Gypsies but shows the majority of its major characters peevishly and with great difficulty dismantling the furniture in their collective farm before they abandon it so that the cursed Gypsies won't get their hands on any of it. (In conversation, Tarr confirmed to me that *The Turin Horse,* unlike *Sátántangó,* isn't really Hungarian except for the palinka and "Gypsies"— and by the latter I assume he meant the everyday passionate Hungarian hatred for Gypsies more than the Gypsies themselves. Clearly the father doesn't feel the same way about his gloomy neighbor or even his recalcitrant horse—whom he and his daughter drag along with great effort, in spite of the horse's illness and uselessness, when, after the well goes dry, they attempt to escape. And why do they fail to escape?

The film doesn't say; that's how little it cares about storytelling, apart from conveying the characters and their daily existence. Or unless we redefine storytelling as what the camera does whenever it moves, which happens to be most of the time. That comes close to defining the narrative of *Sátántangó,* thereby implicating us at every turn. But does *The Turin Horse* implicate us morally in the same fashion? Not really, because the turf has become more metaphysical than sociopolitical. Part of this film's mystery is how much it can borrow from the expressive materials of *Sátántangó* (black and white, a droning minimalist Mihály Vig score, horrible weather, rural setting, slow and perpetual camera movements, seeming inactivity, a novelistic narrator summing up what the characters think, feel, and are at the end of various sequences) without expressing the same things or serving the same functions—as if Tarr and Krasznahorkai were contriving to turn a chair into a table, or vice versa. *Sátántangó* used a rain machine and this film uses a wind machine; Tarr is so adept at film illusion that many viewers still believe that he actually killed a cat in *Sátántangó* and that the hut here is some found object, not a constructed set. Like Kiarostami, he resents Hollywood so much that he winds up beating it at its own game, giving us the impression that he's telling a story without actually doing so. *The Turin Horse* may offer an anti-universe according to some anti-theology, but it's one that lives and breathes.

For me the abiding mystery isn't what the film means but how and why we watch it. "Try not to be too sophisticated" was Tarr's suggestion the first time he introduced it at the New Horizons International Film Festival in Wrocław, Poland. A sound piece of advice, but not easy for all cinephiles to follow, especially if the "sophistication" resembles Dan Kois's pseudo-populism masquerading as common sense ("Eating Your Cultural Vegetables") in the *New York Times*. Going beyond the usual middlebrow philistinism, this position suggests that audiences supporting art movies by Akerman, Costa, Kiarostami, Reichardt, Tarkovsky, or Tarr (strange bedfellows, these—back in the '60s they would have been Antonioni, Bergman, Bresson, Dreyer, Godard, or Resnais)—must be masochists wanting to impose their self-inflicted punishments on others.

Factored out of such reckonings are those who regard *Star Wars, Amélie, Slumdog Millionaire, Avatar, Inglourious Basterds,* or even *The Tree of Life* as obligatory cultural vegetables. And meanwhile denying that sensible individuals can find pleasure in Tarr films ultimately means attempting to outlaw the possibility that any might do so. Clearly part of America's eccentric mistrust of art and poetry is bound up with a bizarre association of both with class; the usual pseudo-populist position is to find such activity excusable only when it's interlarded with religion and/or "entertainment" (which in most cases entails colonial conquest, revenge, violence, and/or some form of mush). To fail in this sacred duty apparently means to make films that are lethally boring, so that Rivette's 13-hour *Out 1*, even as a serial, allegedly can't be fun and games like *Twin Peaks*.

Why, then, did I wind up at all three screenings of *The Turin Horse* in Wrocław, three afternoons in a row? Largely because of my fascination with how a film in which practically nothing happens can remain so gripping and powerful, so pleasurable and beautiful. I'm usually reluctant to compare an anti-cinephile like Tarr to any other filmmaker, but even though his diverse technical materials are completely different from those of Erich von Stroheim, there's something about the sheer intensity of both filmmakers as they navigate from one moment to the next that makes the usual rules and logic of film narrative and even the usual practice of following a plot seem almost beside the point—a kind of distraction.

The world of *The Turin Horse* isn't unveiled or imparted or recounted or examined or told; it's simply there, at every instant, as much as possible and more than we can think to cope with, daring us simply to take note of it.

A Personal Report on an Adventure Called film.factory

First of all, what *is* film.factory?

It's usually thought of and referred to as a film school that's been recently set up in Sarajevo, housed at the Sarajevo Film Academy. But Béla Tarr, who created it, isn't happy with this classification. He'd rather call it a workshop or, as its name suggests, a factory that produces films in which he serves as a producer. And he'd rather speak of the sixteen filmmakers he selected late last year from fourteen countries (Austria, the Czech Republic, France, the Faroe Islands, Iceland, Iran, Japan, Mexico, Poland, Portugal, Serbia, Spain, the U.K., and the United States) and hundreds of hours of film-viewing for his three-year-program—all between the ages of twenty-two and thirty-eight—as "colleagues" rather than as students. If he's right, he chose his colleagues well.

But this isn't to say that his aspirations are entirely free of pedagogical designs. When he first spoke to me of his plans a couple of years ago—at the Era New Horizons Film Festival in Wrocław, where he was presenting *The Turin Horse,* already announced as his last film—he said that part of what he had in mind for what he was then calling his "school project" was to explain how everything his students had already been told about filmmaking was a lie. And he asked me to participate by showing them and speaking about American independent films, leaving it entirely up to me how I would define that category and clarifying that this would be an elective "course" or activity, not a requirement.

Early on, I decided to concentrate on an existential, eclectic, and highly personal definition of "independent" that encompassed Stroheim's *Foolish Wives* and *Greed* (the latter had just become commercially available on a Spanish DVD) and Paul Fejos's *Lonesome* as well as Thom Andersen's *Los Angeles Plays Itself,* Charles Burnett's *When it Rains,* Larry Clark's *Passing Through,* Sara Driver's *You Are Not I,* James Benning's *11 X 14,* a few short works by Stan Brakhage and Bruce Connor, Albert Brooks's *Real Life,* Hollis Frampton's *(nostalgia),* Howard Hawks's *Scarface,* Todd Haynes's

Safe, John Huston's *Wise Blood,* Val Lewton's *The Seventh Victim* and *I Walked with a Zombie,* Richard Linklater's *Bernie,* Elaine May's *Mikey and Nicky,* Mark Rappaport's *Exterior Night,* Nicholas Ray's *Bitter Victory,* Mehrnaz Saeed-Vafa's *Jerry and Me,* and Leslie Thornton's *Adynata,* but only *The Struggle* when it came to D. W. Griffith (although I also included a half-hour radio broadcast by Stroheim speaking about Griffith when he died).

Even though I brought along some features by Chaplin, Welles, and Jarmusch, I ultimately opted in most cases for films they wouldn't have otherwise seen or even heard about, and for polemical reasons—to argue against the notion that directorial credits necessarily mattered apart from performances—I devoted my first screening session to Chaplin's *One AM* and most of *Richard Pryor Live in Concert* (for me, one of the greatest performance films in the history of cinema—released in the United States in 1979, although almost completely unknown in continental Europe). My desire to show *Lonesome,* I should add, was spurred not only by the recent release on Criterion of excellent Blu-Ray and DVD editions, but my previous shock at learning that Béla had never seen it. (It was the only screening of mine that he attended, and he was every bit as impressed as I'd hoped he would be; the only previous film by his Hungarian compatriot that he'd previously seen had been *Marie, légend hongroise.*)

The Pryor film was received quite warmly despite the absence of any subtitles (Pryor's body language speaks volumes), but after a screening of Josef von Sternberg's English-language *The Saga of Anatahan* with French subtitles that was met mainly with incomprehension, I opted whenever possible for films with English subtitles. (Among the sixteen, only the oldest and youngest of the members had grown up with English as a first language—respectively, Keja Ho Kramer, the daughter of Robert Kramer, who had previously worked in collaboration with both her father and Steve Dwoskin, and Grant Gulczynski, who hailed from London.) One morning, when I was faced with the prospect of showing Ford's *The Long Voyage Home* with Spanish subtitles, one of the two Serbs offered and then managed to find and synchronize English subtitles in time for a screening after our lunch break.

Regarding the program as a whole, there are no papers or tests or roll-calling—just an expectation that two short films be made by each participant the first year, two more the second year, and hopefully a feature the third. As recently as a year ago, Béla still thought it would be in

Split, Croatia, but late last July he sent out a letter explaining that getting accreditation there to hand out Ph.D.'s was proving impossible, so another location would have to be found; and less than two months later came his email update, with the news that the Sarajevo Film Academy at the local School of Science and Technology would serve as the home base. (Emina Ganić, the Academy's executive director, became the key administrator.) By the time film.factory started in mid-February, Béla's break with his past as both a filmmaker and as a Hungarian had become profound, ending many long-term professional as well as personal relationships and effectively sending him into exile. But he was also clearly and, I think, rightly proud of what he had created: a utopian community that manages to remain intense and relaxed at practically every juncture.

It was established that I would be dividing each day during the second half of May with Mexican filmmaker Carlos Reygadas—Carlos doing "practical" sessions in the afternoons, and my lectures and screenings in the mornings, held for whomever wanted to show up (which also included some M.A. students and other visitors). The original idea was for me to also have public screenings each evening, ideally with some assistance from the U.S. embassy and involving the local community. But shortly before I came, I learned that the embassy hadn't even answered our letter to them, and the further issue of holding public screenings without the proper rights clearances was proving insuperable. All of which is to say that the potential charge of film.factory being an elitist, club-like affair is one that Béla and others are trying to address, even though a satisfactory long-term solution for accomplishing this has yet to be found. (Theoretically, the Sarajevo Film Festival could offer a path, but the fact that it's held in the summer when film.factory is no longer in session rules out that possibility.)

However, instead of simply cutting my syllabus in half when I discovered that public screenings weren't possible, I decided to bring along two or three times as many DVDs as I could possibly show and then thrash out which ones with the students (as I was still calling them at this point), based on their own particular interests and orientations. Before I arrived, I even sent along my preliminary list of possible films to show, along with links to pieces about most of them on my website and the suggestion that they look at my book *Movie Wars* to get some sense of my overall approach. During my two weeks of "official" employment, I also managed to lend out a few other DVDs to match certain individual interests (for example, Martina Kudláček's documentary on Maya Deren, for a filmmaker who was especially interested in her work, apart from my screenings of *Meshes of the Afternoon* and *At Land*, and Jon Jost's *Last Chants for a Slow Dance* for someone else). And during the same period, one of the Spanish filmmakers, Pilar Palomero, introduced me to Luis Garcia Berlanga's corrosive 1963 masterpiece *El verdugo* by making me a subtitled copy.

But things changed again—or at least my perception of them did. Because the entire operations were being planned exclusively, and on a day-by-day basis, by Béla, working only with his thirty-three-year-old assistant and program coordinator, Sunčica Fradelić (a visual artist from Split who had also become my main email contact), I soon discovered that one of the main reasons why film.factory wasn't a school was that it was much closer to a film shoot, something Béla knew and understood a lot better. This meant that everything, my screenings and lectures included, was subject to last-minute revisions owing to weather, equipment, health, sudden inspirations, and other variables. And bearing in mind Orson Welles's definition of a film director as someone who presides over accidents—along with the dawning realization that the same vicissitudes might even apply to film historians, and therefore to what we all know as film history—an important part of my own education over my eighteen days in Sarajevo was simply learning how to roll with all the punches.

Early on, for instance, I discovered that Carlos had already been teaching for a week before I arrived, and would be leaving after only three more days, leaving the remaining afternoons free. (Before he left, I was able to attend his informative afternoon session devoted to showing and discussing his first feature, *Japón*—during which he expressed some irritation about the filmmakers not being as punctual or as assertive as he would have liked.) Thus my own screening and lecture time practically doubled again, especially once it became clear that Tilda Swinton, originally slated to replace Carlos, had to delay her own arrival because of her hectic post-Cannes schedule. But fortunately, after my stint was over, I was able to visit the first two of Tilda's remarkable classes as well as two screening sessions of another lecturer, Manuel Grosso, who hailed from Seville and was focusing on Buñuel. (Among the other visiting lecturers who'd preceded us this year were Jean-Michel Frodon, Thierry Garrel, Ulrich Gregor, Fred Kelemen, and Gus van Sant.)

Among the other fruits of last-minute scheduling were a field trip to Bunker Konjic, about an hour's drive past spectacular mountain scenery from Sarajevo—an underground bomb shelter built by Tito that seemed as large and as crazy as a small country, not to mention a fever dream out of *Dr. Strangelove,* run today by the Bosnian army and currently housing an international art show; a screening of Béla's 450-minute *Sátántangó* one Saturday (the first time Sunčica and nearly all the others saw it), introduced by me and followed the next day by Béla lecturing for four-and-a-half hours about how he filmed it, shot by shot and take by take, using a sort of post-it storyboard as his narrative thread (as with the film itself, there were two intermissions); and an earlier marathon screening arranged by me the previous Saturday, held at an apartment occupied by four of the students, which turned out to be the most memorable session we had. (See below.) Another session of this kind, devoted to the reedit of Welles's *Touch of Evil* that I served as consultant on and, if time and energy permitted, John Gianvito's *The Mad Songs of Fernanda Hussein,* was planned at the request of some of my regulars. But then this had to be postponed when the other Serb filmmaker, who had been filming all week, made a call for crew members and extras (including myself in the latter group), for a lengthy, rowdy shoot inside a local bar inside a basement that was reportedly the only such establishment to survive the war—and which quickly became so filled with cigarette smoke that I only remained for a couple of hours. Then eventually our second viewing session was canceled at Béla's request when he feared that my hefty program of screenings, which eventually totaled twenty-one features and seventeen shorts, might be diverting too much attention and energy away from other parts of the program.

A few words about the *Sátántangó* screening and its aftermath: Béla asked me to give a short introduction, and approved my suggestion that I start by showing a six-minute video in black and white and long takes that Kevin B. Lee made in late 2013—a video that followed me walking in my Chicago neighborhood while discussing the film, aping the film's style in a manner suggested by some of Andre S. Labarthe's TV documentaries. Afterward, I concluded with an argument that I knew both Béla and his cowriter László Krasznahorkai would refute—that the film had something to say about Communist and Stalinist surveillance and bureaucracy. (Admitting that my entire experience of the Communist world consisted of a single afternoon spent in East Berlin, I avowed that, regardless of his and Krasznahorkai's intentions, the film nonetheless reminded me of those few hours, maintaining that sometimes works knew more than their authors did.) The next day, in his lecture and at a meal afterward, Béla respectfully but firmly disagreed, insisting that the film's designs were metaphysical and not political—although his partner, Polish film journalist Małgorzata Sadowska, took my side in the debate.

My own screenings generally consisted of brief introductions by me, watching the films straight through, and discussions immediately afterward. The most popular films were the two Stroheims (especially for the density of the characterizations in *Greed* and the multiple paradoxes involved in Stroheim, an imposter, playing an imposter in *Foolish Wives*), the two Lewtons, *Bitter Victory, Lonesome, Los Angeles Plays Itself, Mikey and Nicky, (nostalgia), Real Life, Safe,* and, most of all, to my delighted surprise, the four films I showed them by Peter Thompson.

This leads me to the one marathon screening we did have. By another accident of chance, I'd received news the night before that Thompson, one of my best friends in Chicago—for me the greatest of all Chicago filmmakers, past or present, even though he continues to be among the least well-known, and someone whom I'd befriended in the late '80s because of how I felt about his work—had died, at age sixty-nine, after eighteen months of terminal illness. (2018: I'm happy to report that a box set including all six of his films and a lengthy interview, meticulously prepared by Peter himself, is currently available from http://www.chicagomediaworks.com/.) I intended to show only his half-hour *Universal Hotel* (1986) on Saturday, but it had such an impact on those present that I wound up screening all three of Thompson's other highly personal films that I'd brought to Sarajevo: *Universal Citizen* (1986) and his *Two Portraits* (1982), the latter about each of his parents. The film about his father, *Anything Else,* stretches out a few seconds of home-movie footage of his father in an airport to almost fifteen minutes of successive stills, accompanied by Peter's own narration.

During his late teens and early twenties, Peter had studied classical guitar with Andrès Segovia and performed at concerts in Europe, and combined with his subsequent academic work in comparative literature, this gives his distinctive voiceovers a literary as well as musical address— "the capacity to suggest infinite reaches with a minimum of photographic 'evidence,' carefully chosen words, and the articulation of his own voice," as I later put it on my own website. And I think what impressed my film.factory colleagues above all in the four films they saw was Peter's narration, which figures in all of them except for the film about his mother, *Shooting Scripts,* despite the absence of any subtitles—both as beautiful, sculpted writing (singled out by Mohammadreza Farzad, who translates contemporary American poetry and fiction into Farsi), and for its inherent musical form of delivery. Also for its feeling, and for what Kaori Oda described to me in a subsequent email as the "strong form" of the rhythm of his images, which made her miss Osaka and "my dear people" there and gave her "a vast space to reflect myself," while responses from several others at the screening, all of which I was able to convey to Peter's widow, were equally strong and personal.

A few years ago, I collaborated with Peter on an article and interview about his work,[1] and here is an "outtake" from our email exchanges that seems especially relevant to what moved my colleagues the most:

> Earlier, Jonathan, you mentioned the films' voice-overs—that they seem to suppress overt emotional expressiveness in order to allow other qualities to surface. You mention "Bresson" in relation to those other qualities. Let me try to amplify what you are pointing to. This style evolved during the voice-over recordings for *Two Portraits*. I was mortified by the first voice-over: it was so over the top, emotionally—an audience would have recoiled. I re-recorded. Again, bad—this time it flew *below* the emotional radar. I realized that I should try to hold the tension between those two emotional states. Five weeks and five recordings later . . . I had a voice-over that seemed to hold that tension. Finally! The difference—besides the positive lessons reaped from the failures—was the memory of a stunningly wonderful concert in 1966: the first visit to France by the Berlin Philharmonic since the outbreak of WWII. Herbert von Karajan conducted Mozart's "Haffner" symphony. Von Karajan stood on the podium, almost immobile, as if anxious not to deflect attention from the music's agonizingly complicated simplicity. He hid his arms and his hands. What *were* visible were his back muscles. They testified to a man on the verge of exploding. The artistic and emotional power generated from his *almost* successfully suppressed emotion seemed to fill Chartres Cathedral. What a balancing act! The tension of that remembered experience became the goal of my subsequent voice-overs.
>
> This goal depends upon honed down scripts and simple writing. . . . I'm an admirer of the *style blanc* practiced by the Polish post-war poets

Czeslaw Milosz, Zbigniew Herbert and Wislawa Szymborska. They write "transparently" with zero extra words and very few adjectives. To shrink downward to that blessed state, I write an embarrassingly large number of drafts because it takes me a while to recognize one word too many.... As you join these three elements together—perceivable rhythm ... the "von Karajan paradox," and the "white style"—a miraculous effect can sometimes occur. I can't judge in advance when, or if, it might happen, but can only recognize with gratitude when it does—suddenly, without warning, everything in the voice-over *accrues* into a quietly overwhelming affect. It's not possible to point to a single word or single utterance that's caused it. *Accrual.* Segovia used to say, "Better to move than to amaze." He moved with small means.

For me, showing Peter's work was the high point of all the sessions I'd initiated, but the comments offered at many of the screenings were often acute; I was particularly struck by Stefan Malesevic's observation about how warmly the characters in *Wise Blood* were portrayed, in spite of all the caustic black humor, which made me realize for the first time how decisively the film differed from Flannery O'Connor's novel, despite the close fidelity to the text. But the two extended lectures of Tilda Swinton I attended more than a week later, about the ethics and practice of dealing with performers, were no less exciting, and interestingly enough, they were no less related to Bresson. Both of her lectures used *Notes on Cinematography* as a major reference point, and even though this might seem eccentric, it turned out to be concrete and practical, especially once Tilda started filming close-ups of everyone in turn, visible on a monitor, while conversing with each of us on the second day. (I was the first guinea pig in this process.) The focus was mostly on how actors/performers, rather than seek to "express themselves," should minimize their expressions to what's needed in a particular shot in order to advance a story, and the public dialogues she had with each of us were demonstrations and elucidations of this process, highlighting the degree to which less—by virtue of being isolated and magnified by the camera—invariably registered as more. Asking each of us to think about something private without verbalizing it was a way of getting us to concentrate and thus empty our faces so that small details started to register. When she asked Pilar—who had previously snapped a photo of Tilda filming me—to pretend she was riding home on a bus, totally exhausted, and so tired that she didn't even have enough energy to close her mouth, the way her open mouth transformed her close-up on the monitor so that it immediately signified "exhaustion" was immediately apparent.

As I said to Tilda afterward, I felt like I had just been through a session with Socrates. This wasn't only because of the interactive nature of her workshop and how responsive she was to what others were saying (at one point during the second half of her lecture, she briefly and pointedly replied to a casual remark I'd made to someone else during a break, which I hadn't even realized she'd overheard), but also because of her solid grounding in so many different kinds of cinema—having begun her career working in the experimental films of Derek Jarman and subsequently traversed everything from the commercial mainstream (Wes Anderson, Michael Apted, the Coen brothers, Cameron Crowe, David Fincher, Spike Jonze) to many kinds of art cinema (Joon-ho Bong, Jim Jarmusch, David Mackenzie, Sally Potter, Lynne Ramsey, Béla Tarr). Such versatility is relatively common in French cinema but virtually nonexistent in the Anglo American world, and her sense of her own identity within that world seems no less acute. (At one point she remarked in passing that she doesn't look like anyone else in films but looks like a lot of other people in paintings.)

In closing, I should note that I didn't start looking at films already made by the "factory workers" until after I returned home,[2] so my experience of film.factory was appreciably different from those of Béla, Carlos, and others more engaged with their actual practice. (The only quality approaching a common trait would be that they mainly have some relation to "art cinema," even though, apart from a preference for black and white among many of them, there are significantly no obvious imitations of Béla Tarr's filmmaking.) For me, it was an adventure having a lot to do with joining and then engaging with a particular community—something I do more often nowadays via the internet, but one in this case that extended my online activity as a writer rather than forge some alternative to it.

Maybe it's some form of teaching after all, despite what Béla says. But as Tilda and her hyper-alertness clarified, it's reciprocal education founded on a Socratic model—conversations and dialogue, not preaching and pronouncements. In the past, I've often felt hamstrung by students firmly convinced that they can learn anything they need to know without reading. So it was no small pleasure to discover back in Chicago that more than two hundred visits from Sarajevo had been paid to my website over the previous month.

Notes

1. "A Handful of World: The Films of Peter Thompson, An Introduction and Interview," *Film Quarterly*, Fall 2009; reprinted in *Cinematic Encounters: Interviews and Dialogues,* University of Illinois Press, 2018.

2. During one of my subsequent film.factory courses—on independent world cinema for MA students in fall 2014—in response to a request from some of the students for a production assignment, I screened Seijun Suzuki's 2001 *Pistol Opera* and assigned them to create five-minute remakes. We screened most of the results nine days later at a party (a couple of the others, unfinished at the time, I have yet to see) and they were really dazzling—and all quite different from one another.

CHAPTER 23

Tsai Ming-liang

The four works of Tsai Ming-liang considered in this section are by no means the only films of his that could warrant detailed discussion. Among my own favorites, I might have also selected *The Hole* (1998) and *What Time is It There?* (2001), both of which I've written about elsewhere—indeed, my exchanges with Australian film critic Adrian Martin about the latter film can be found in the closing pages of *Movie Mutations: The Changing Face of World Cinephilia* (London: BFI Publishing, 2003), a collection that we co-edited—and others might cite *Rebels of the Neon God* (1992), *Vive l'amour* (1994), *The Wayward Cloud* (2005), *I Don't Want to Sleep Alone* (2006), *Face* (2009), or one of his shorts or documentaries—and I'm not even considering the eleven telefilms listed in his Wikipedia entry, none of which I've seen. For an avowed minimalist who keeps recycling many of the same thematic and material elements (including actors, locations, and water), Tsai remains one of the most productive of contemporary Asian filmmakers.

My review of *The River* appeared in the April 14, 2000 issue of the *Chicago Reader*; my consideration of one shot from *Goodbye, Dragon Inn* comes from Chris Fujiwara's excellent 800-page collection *Defining Moments in Movies* (London: Cassell, 2007); and my essay about *Stray Dogs* and *Journey to the West* was written for Cinema Guild's Blu-Ray of those two films, released in mid-January 2015.

City Without Tears (on *The River*)

1. I wouldn't know how to plunge headlong into a single approach toward a film as strange and as shocking as *The River*—Tsai Ming-liang's third feature, playing this week at Facets Multimedia—so a series of alternative perspectives seems desirable. The problem is, even starting off by labeling this movie a masterpiece reminds me how such an assertion in some cases amounts to a gamble more than a certainty, however much one may prefer to pretend otherwise.

What's my alibi for this lack of confidence? First of all, a sense that when one encounters something as downright peculiar as *The River*, the first impulse is not to assert anything at all but to ask, "What the hell is this?" And to pretend to answer such a question, one ultimately has to fall back on one's experience before even attempting an analysis.

In my case, I've experienced *The River* twice, both times in less than ideal circumstances: with German subtitles at the Vienna Film Festival two and a half years ago, and, just before writing this, a copy of an English commercial video, with English subtitles, that a friend was kind enough to make for me when I discovered that there wasn't any other way I could see this film again before reviewing it. Paradoxically, it was the latter experience that was more problematic—if only because the image in all of Tsai's features is immensely more important than the dialogue, which is minimal, and because the size and clarity of the image are both essential to what Tsai is doing. Critic Kent Jones, the friend who made me the dub, aptly wrote about the film's formidable "monumentality" in the French magazine *Trafic* a couple of years ago, and the only reason why I know he's right is my memory of seeing the film in 35mm in Vienna. Seeing it on video less than an hour ago, while it reminds me of all sorts of other details, can only confuse and dilute that first impression.

The fact that I regard *The River* as a probable masterpiece doesn't mean that I consider it fun or pleasant; terrifying and beautiful would be more appropriate adjectives. It's been a subject of dispute ever since it won the Special Jury Prize in Berlin in 1997, and I can't exactly quarrel with those who complain that it's sick and/or boring since these are both possible and perhaps legitimate responses that I don't happen to share. But that it's also the achieved work of a master I have little doubt.

■ ■ ■

2. Tsai—a Taiwanese director born in Malaysia in 1957 who started out in TV dramas (1989–1991), and has made one TV documentary, about AIDS (*My New Friends,* 1995), has made four features to date—*Rebels of the Neon God* (1992), *Vive l'amour* (1994), *The River* (1996), and *The Hole* (1998). All of these features are set in Taipei and deal with loneliness and isolation; the latter, a postmodernist musical of sorts, has also been seen on U.S. cable and elsewhere in a shorter version called *Last Dance*. *The River,* in some ways the most powerful and accomplished of the last three features (I still haven't seen the first), is the one that has been seen the least, probably everywhere, because people don't quite know what to make of it.

* * *

3. The plot—what there is of it—begins with a young woman (Chen Shiang-chyi) who's working on a film crew and runs into an old friend, Hsiao-kang (Lee Kang-sheng), whom she hasn't seen in a couple of years, going in the opposite direction on an escalator in a mall. She invites him to join her, and they ride on his motorbike to the film shoot, where Hong Kong director Ann Hui, playing herself, is trying to get a fake corpse to float convincingly on the polluted Tanshui River. Complaining that the dummy's feet look fake, Hui asks Hsiao-kang during a lunch break if he'd like to play the corpse, and after some hesitation, he agrees. Later his friend takes him to a small hotel to clean up, and they have sex; this is the last we see of her in the film. We also start following the separate daily activities of Hsiao-kang's parents, who live with him, though they're almost never seen together. His mother (Lu Hsiao-ling), an elevator operator, is pursuing a fairly apathetic affair with a man who sells pornographic videos, and his father (Miao Tien), apparently retired, cruises gay saunas in search of anonymous sex. Around the same time that the son starts complaining of a chronic and debilitating pain in his neck, clearly brought on by an infection he got from the river, his father starts noticing a water leak in his bedroom that's gradually becoming more serious; rather than deal with this problem directly, he uses plastic sheeting to form a canopy over his bed and divert the water toward a drain. Meanwhile the father and mother alternately try to find cures for the son's infection, taking him to different doctors who try out various therapies, none of which appears to work. The leak in the father's bedroom begins to flood the

apartment, prompting the mother to climb through a downpour to the empty apartment above to turn off the kitchen faucet. Meanwhile the son is masturbated in one of the dark saunas by an older man, who turns out to be his father. As soon as the father recognizes his son, he slaps him. Father and son sleep in the same bed in a hotel room in a Taipei suburb. In the morning the father, pretending nothing has happened, phones a religious leader, who advises him to return to Taipei with his son and see a doctor, saying they no longer have to visit his temple. The father goes downstairs for breakfast, and Hsiao-kang, before joining him, steps out onto the sunny balcony.

■ ■ ■

4. Stylistically, Tsai favors filming most action in medium shot or long shot, in extended takes, with the camera typically planted in the center of a room—a fairly cool and detached way of dealing with the sadness and isolation of his characters, whether they're alone or not. (No one ever seems to get much enjoyment out of sex or any other kind of social interaction in a Tsai Ming-liang movie.) Most of the settings occupied by these characters are new and relatively anonymous; when the father gets cruised by a young gay hustler in an extraordinarily and beautifully developed long take early in the film, before they proceed to a sauna, it's at a McDonald's.

Ever since I first encountered Tsai's work in *Vive l'amour*, I've tended to regard it as a kind of update on the urban melancholia Michelangelo Antonioni used to specialize in, especially during the '50s and '60s—a reference point that can only take one so far, as it does with another Taiwanese modernist, Edward Yang. One of the main differences may be that Antonioni is a master of alienated moods, but atmosphere tends to be more a given than a creation in Tsai's movies, which conjure up more mysteries in relation to what the characters tend to be inarticulate and confused about—sexuality most of all.

■ ■ ■

5. An obsessive filmmaker, Tsai uses the same lead actor playing virtually the same character in all four of his features to date, and the same actors playing his mother and father in *Rebels of the Neon God* and *The River;* he also uses Chen Chao-jung in central roles in *Rebels of the Neon God* and *Vive l'amour* and in a more minor role (as the gay hustler at

McDonald's) in *The River,* and Yang Kwei-mei as the female leads in *Vive l'amour* and *The Hole* and in a bit part in *The River.* If one adds to this an ongoing obsession with water as a symbol for sexual desire—which crops up no less centrally in *The Hole*—one might say that Tsai has every bit as fixed and narrow a cosmology as Leos Carax. The parallels between the father's sexual desire and the leak in his bedroom, developed concurrently, are as much a part of this system as the fact that water, seen as a life-force, is also the cause of the hero's nearly constant pain—which persists even in the final shot, and is one of the factors that makes the film so unsettling to watch. Furthermore, the urban alienation that seeps into virtually every shot also affects this film's narrative structure, so that at least half an hour passes before it's clear that the son and his two parents are even related, either to him or to each other. (The same principle makes it seem both logical and inevitable when the friend on the film crew whom Hsiao Kang has sex with simply drops out of the film after that.) Furthermore, as Bérénice Reynaud notes in her excellent recent book *Nouvelles Chines, Nouveaux cinémas,* the first time that the son crashes on his motorbike offscreen because of his neck injury and the father, standing nearby, goes to help him, Tsai ambiguously shows the two characters on the street as if they were absolute strangers—making their accidental sexual encounter much later seem a lot more plausible. Tsai's poker-faced distance from his characters may make one think of Buster Keaton or Jacques Tati, as Kent Jones suggests, but it's worth adding that the occasional comic inflections may not always be intentional. In one interview, Tsai mentions that when the father rides behind his son on the motorbike en route to the hospital, holding his head in his hands, this is based on a personal experience Tsai had when Lee hurt his neck during the shooting of *Rebels of the Neon God:* "I thought the image had a lot of pathos," he adds, "but to my surprise everyone seems to find it funny." Squaring Tsai's acute grasp of the contemporary with a particular intentionality may ultimately be beside the point, especially for work that is coded and inflected in so personal a manner. Like a certain form of geometry—or would it be physics, tied to engineering?—the characters and their repressions and longings are so palpably realized that all sorts of improbabilities can intervene without causing a dent. Sex and plumbing, seduction and infection, a spray of steam and a torrent of rain are all factored into the same inexorable flow.

One Shot from *Goodbye, Dragon Inn*

Scene

2003 / *Goodbye, Dragon Inn*—The shot of the empty auditorium near the end.

Taiwan. Director: Ming-liang Tsai. Original title: *Bu san*.

Why it's Key: A minimalist master shows what can be done with an empty movie-theater auditorium.

One singular aspect of Ming-liang Tsai's masterpiece is how well it plays. I've seen it twice with a packed film-festival audience, and both times, during a shot of an empty cinema auditorium, where nothing happens for more than two minutes, you could hear a pin drop. Tsai makes it a climactic epic moment.

Indeed, for all its minimalism, *Goodbye, Dragon Inn* fulfills many agendas. It's a failed heterosexual love story, a gay cruising saga, a Taiwanese *Last Picture Show,* a creepy ghost story, a melancholy tone poem, and a wry comedy. A cavernous Taipei movie palace on its last legs is showing King Hu's 1966 hit *Dragon Inn* to a tiny audience—including a couple of the film's stars, who linger like ghosts after everyone else has left—while a rainstorm rages outside. As the martial-arts classic unfolds on the screen, we follow various elliptical intrigues in the theater, such as the limping cashier pining after the projectionist, whom she never sees. Tsai has a flair for imparting a commanding presence to seemingly empty pockets of space and time.

With the cashier, we peer at the end title on the screen. Then, in a shot lasting well over five minutes, the camera faces the empty auditorium as the lights flicker on and she enters with a broom on the right—recording her slow passage up one aisle, across the middle row, and down the other aisle until she exits on the left. Then we linger for two minutes more, communing with silence and eternity.

Performing Spectators: The Audience as Stray Dogs

Stray Dogs (2013), winner of the Grand Jury Prize at the 70th Venice International Film Festival, is Tsai Ming-liang's tenth theatrical feature. It was described by Tsai at its premiere as his last, and in many ways it's his most challenging. Considered as the apotheosis of his film work to date—which also includes eleven telefilms made between 1989 and 1995, and ten shorts or segments of portmanteau features, culminating in the 2014, fifty-six-minute *Journey to the West*—it constitutes a kind of nervy dare to the viewer, and to prime oneself for it, it might help to look at *Journey to the West* first.

Even though both films flirt with stasis, usually in the midst of extremely long takes, they're also performance pieces that hark back to Tsai's roots in experimental theater and television. And the performers are not only hired actors but also unsuspecting street pedestrians, places, weather conditions, the camera, and, perhaps most crucial of all, viewers watching the activity of all of the above. If Tsai's films typically qualify as questions rather than answers, foremost among the questions is how we perform *as spectators*—a question that we're obliged to pose in relation to all the materials offered. It's hardly coincidental that the longest take in *Stray Dogs*—the penultimate shot, almost fourteen minutes long—is of two characters looking at something offscreen in an abandoned building (a landscape mural that Tsai found during his location scouting, already seen in the film an hour earlier, and viewed once more in the final shot)—a sequence that inevitably forces us to consider our own activity in watching these characters over the same length of time.

In *Journey to the West,* the materials are more clearly those of performance art staged on city streets—Lee Kang-sheng in a monk's red robe inching forward at an almost imperceptibly slow pace, followed at some distance by an equally slow-paced (but more conventionally dressed) Denis Lavant—and the attentiveness or lack of attention paid by innocent bystanders (as well as the viewers of *Journey to the West*) to this spectacle is clearly part of the question being posed.

In *Stray Dogs,* where we have fictional characters—a homeless, alcoholic, and fitfully employed father (again Lee Kang-sheng) with two small children (Lee Yi-cheng and Lee Yi-chieh), and a woman (played by three separate actresses—Yang Kwei-mei in the opening scene, Lu Yi-ching at a supermarket, Chen Shiang-chyi in other scenes) who periodically takes care of the children—but no chronologically continuous or coherent narrative, the questions that we're asked to pose are far more numerous and various. Some of these have to do with our relation to the four characters, and others have to do with our relation to the film as a whole. Their lack of a stable home becomes the equivalent, for us, of our lack of a stable narrative, and this uncertainty persists during certain shots as well as between certain others. In the two most directly performative sequences—when Lee Kang-sheng recites and then sings a patriotic twelfth-century poem by Yue Fei while holding up a real-estate sign at a windy traffic intersection (the only job we ever see him have), and when he discovers on a bed a cabbage that his kids have decorated like a doll's face before attacking, shredding, and devouring it in a paroxysmal frenzy—the shifts in mood and emotional tone are particularly unsettling.

As a rule, continuity editing is maintained in *Stray Dogs*, but only within sequences and not between them. And the status of individual sequences in relation to what we regard as "real" or plausible or consistent with the others is chiefly a matter of how we choose to arrange them all to compose a coherent narrative of our own. When the woman character retrieves the children from their father disembarking in a rowboat in a driving rain, and this sequence is immediately followed by the woman and children presenting the father with a birthday cake in a dry, cozily lit interior, we're obliged to ask not only what happens in between these two scenes—assuming that they unfold in a chronological sequence—but also how much either scene conforms to reality or fantasy in relation to these four characters (and if either scene qualifies as fantasy, whose fantasy it is). Elsewhere, we might ask ourselves, when we see the woman helping one of the children with what appears to be their homework, whether these kids are attending school. (The remainder of the film suggests that they aren't.)

The problem isn't, as one reviewer has suggested, distinguishing between "real" and "stylized," because "realism" is a style in its own right, but how and where we situate ourselves within these conflicting scenes, styles, and modalities. In fact, we wind up shifting our perspectives as often as these characters shift their own living, working, eating, playing, cleaning, evacuating, and sleeping spaces, and the lack of any steady anchor conflates their brooding restlessness with ours.

If anything unites these sequences apart from people, places, weather, and the combined burden and privilege of watching, this is Tsai's melancholy poetics and his mastery of sound and image. Characters cry in this universe, but as the woman remarks at one point, so do buildings, and the rain that falls on both is equally remorseless and relentless. And a key demonstration of Tsai's mastery becomes apparent whenever one has an opportunity to watch one of his masterpieces with others in a crowded auditorium. I'll never forget watching *Goodbye, Dragon Inn* (2003) on two separate occasions at Toronto and Chicago festival screenings, where the attentiveness of a packed audience facing an empty movie house was so hushed that one could hear a pin drop. Whether or not a home viewing of *Stray Dogs* can approximate such an experience is yet another question that this Blu-Ray of the film poses, but I would suggest that watching this film with others is a step in the right direction. Watching it alone might prove vexing at times; sharing its sense of gravity may help to illuminate some of its darkest corners.

CHAPTER 24

Orson Welles

Ever since I started out as a film critic in the early 1970s, when two of my first five contributions to *Film Comment* consisted of my attack on Pauline Kael's "Raising Kane" and my interview with Orson Welles about his *Heart of Darkness* project, Welles has remained a major touchstone for me. My involvement with his work (charted in my 2007 collection *Discovering Orson Welles*) grew when I edited two of his screenplays for a small publisher in Santa Barbara, Santa Teresa Press (*The Big Brass Ring* in 1987 and *The Cradle Will Rock* in 1994) and Welles's coauthored *This is Orson Welles* (with Peter Bogdanovich) for HarperCollins (now available in DaCapo's 1998 edition) and served as a consultant on both the 1998 reedit of *Touch of Evil* and the 2018 completion of *The Other Side of the Wind*. I should add that the four recent essays included here represent only a selection; my 2016 essay about the two versions of Welles's film of *Macbeth,* for instance, written for the Olive Films Blu-Ray, can be found on my website—and, for the record, my favorite of Welles's unfinished late films, explored in the final chapter of *Discovering Orson Welles*, is *Don Quixote*.

The published sources of these essays, in order, are the online *Barnes and Noble Review* (May 18, 2010); the StudioCanal Blu-Ray of *The Trial*, released in Spring 2012; and the Criterion DVD and Blu-Ray of *The Immortal Story*, released in 2016. The final essay was written expressly for this book, although it has also appeared by now in Spanish (*Caimán Cuadernos de Cine*, November 2018), Persian (*Sazandegi*, December 19–20, 2018), and French (*Trafic*, March 2019).

Orson Welles: The Consumerist Version

John Baxter's new foreword to the 1956 novelization of Orson Welles's *Mr. Arkadin,* aptly called "No Pilot Known," correctly discloses on its penultimate page that the novel was actually written in French by one Maurice Bessy, who adapted Welles's original screenplay. This fact is verified by the recent recovery in France of the correspondence between Welles and *Arkadin*'s producer, Louis Dolivet. But none of this has prevented the novel's latest edition, like all the previous ones, from trumpeting the name of Orson Welles as sole author on its cover.

This should come as no surprise. How can a publisher expect to sell the uncredited English translation of a French novelization of an unfinished film, especially if the novel was written by a forgotten film critic? For starters, it has to assume, contrary to Welles, that the film is (or was) finished. This is also why the Criterion box set, released in 2006, insists on calling itself *The Complete Mr. Arkadin,* even though Welles didn't complete any single version of it.

The task of rationalizing Welles's idiosyncratic working methods and fractured film career in consumerist, marketplace terms has invariably led to many obfuscations. Even Baxter's foreword, which starts off quite reasonably, winds up with the usual boilerplate vilifications, claiming without much basis that Welles habitually walked away from films when the budgets ran out, ended his life on charity, and, "For diversion, he dined out—always assuming someone else picked up the check."

Always? That didn't happen when he invited me to lunch in Paris in 1972—and my experience was far from unique. I'd barely published anything at the time, yet a letter sent to him one Saturday at his editing studio, asking him about his first film project, *Heart of Darkness,* yielded a phone call two days later inviting me to an excellent seafood restaurant (the same one seen in *F for Fake,* which he was editing at the time). Our conversation mainly circled around literary subjects. Welles told me that he'd hung out with Nathanael West in Hollywood, that he'd never written a novel of any kind (adding that he'd never even read the *Arkadin* novelization, and that *Une grosse legume,* another "novel" sold under his name and published by Bessy, was actually a film treatment), and, to my disappointment, admitted that he usually preferred John O'Hara as a novelist to William Faulkner. (I'd fantasized him as the ideal adapter of both *Light in August* and Conrad's *Nostromo*—which didn't interest him either, in spite of his reverence for *Heart of Darkness, Lord Jim,* and *Victory,* all of which he'd wanted to adapt as films.)

For me, the closest Welles ever came to writing a novel was probably a screenplay he wrote a decade later, *The Big Brass Ring*. I was particularly gratified when, two years after I managed to get this published in a limited edition in 1987, Gore Vidal gave it a rave review in the *New York Review of Books*. ("He is plainly at the top of his glittering form, which was as deeply literary as it was visual.") But the version of *The Big Brass Ring* most people know—the consumerist version—is the pathetic, nonliterary 1999 film "adaptation" by George Hickenlooper, which shifts parts of Spain to St. Louis (Hickenlooper's hometown) and changes or omits most of the dialogue.

One explanation for why so many filmmakers, actual or potential, continue to use Welles as a mantle (or example) even when they can't approach his essence is that he's seen as a man who once had it all in terms of power and freedom—even though, ironically, many of those same admirers endorse or accept the same studio protocols, such as test marketing and studio revisions, that would have made *Citizen Kane* impossible. Welles stubbornly insisted on keeping his freedom long after he had to relinquish his power, which makes him a troubled role model at best. Some people who continue to envy the power he once had wind up resenting the freedom he continued to exercise, especially when it became the freedom to hold back his work for one reason or another.

This is one reason, among others, why the recent memoir of his eldest daughter, Chris Welles Feder (*In My Father's Shadow: A Daughter Remembers Orson Welles,* from Algonquin Books of Chapel Hill), is such a valuable and bracing corrective. The book's accomplishment isn't really to make Welles more honorable or likable—she leaves little doubt that he was mostly a negligent father—but to dissolve some of the ideological biases and distractions that surround him (such as the dubious notion that his mistress and major collaborator Oja Kodar was "bad" for him and/or his work, which Feder has no truck with), and to make him more life-size.

Even so, the more popular accounts of Welles—Pauline Kael on *Citizen Kane* and David Thomson's *Rosebud*—tend to be both scornful and factually unreliable (as well as scantily researched), perhaps because both seem driven by a sharp sense of what the American public wants to believe. Kael even succeeded in converting *Kane* into a mainstream product after it had lingered uncomfortably in the public imagination as neither fish nor fowl for more than a quarter of a century—an independent feature made with studio resources. By maintaining that in fact it was just a Hollywood newspaper comedy, Kael enabled it to become a treasured classic, even while misrepresenting the substantial role Welles played in writing it in order to celebrate Herman J. Mankiewicz and thereby undermine auteur criticism. The claim of Craig Seligman in *Sontag & Kael* that "who wrote what is something we'll never definitively know" is basically refuted by the research of Robert L. Carringer, but you have to go to academic sources such as James Naremore's "casebook" on the film to discover such details.

In one basic respect, Chris Feder shares with the general public a sense of frustration that the great man didn't furnish what was either wanted or expected of him most of the time; this was his genius as well as his misfortune. In order for an artist (or a father) to be consistent and dependable—that is to say, consumable, offering some sense of security—he has to behave predictably, and this was the last thing Welles was capable of doing most of the time. Producing works that were unforeseeable and therefore somewhat indigestible when they first appeared, which meant that we all often had to spend years catching up with them, he was out of step mainly because he remained ahead of our expectations. He had to pay an enormous price for this, but so did we.

Nightmare as Funhouse Ride: Orson Welles's *The Trial*

"What made it possible for me to make the picture," Orson Welles told Peter Bogdanovich of his most troubling film, "is that I've had recurring nightmares of guilt all my life: I'm in prison and I don't know why—going to be tried and I don't know why. It's very personal for me. A very personal expression, and it's not all true that I'm off in some foreign world that has no application to myself; it's the most autobiographical movie that I've ever made, the *only* one that's really close to me. And just because it doesn't speak in a Middle Western accent doesn't mean a damn thing. It's much closer to my own feelings about everything than any other picture I've ever made."

To anchor these feelings in one part of Welles's life, he was fifteen when his alcoholic father died of heart and kidney failure, and Welles admitted to his friend and biographer Barbara Leaming that he always felt responsible for that death. He'd followed the advice of his surrogate parents, Roger and Hortense Hill, in refusing to see Richard Welles until he sobered up, and "that was the last I ever saw of him. . . . I've always thought I killed him. . . . I don't want to forgive myself. That's why I hate psychoanalysis. I think if you're guilty of something you should live with it."

On the other hand, as Welles fully acknowledged on other occasions, his temperament and background were quite different from Kafka's. The world of Franz Kafka (1883–1924), ruled by male tyrants who make arbitrary decisions, clearly had something to do with his own domineering father in a middle-class Jewish household in turn-of-the-century Prague, whereas Welles, born the year after *The Trial* was written, grew up in much more privileged surroundings in the American Midwest with a strong, disciplinarian mother and a soft, permissive father, a couple who separated by mutual agreement when he was only six—circumstances reflected in various ways in both *Citizen Kane* and *The Magnificent Ambersons*. So even though Welles retained a surprising amount of Kafka's scenes and dialogue in one form or another in his film, it can't be said to qualify as a close adaptation, unlike his versions of either *The Magnificent Ambersons* or *The Immortal Story*. Considering that the novel remains rough and unfinished—even though, unlike the earlier *The Man Who Disappeared* (retitled *Amerika* by Kafka's friend and literary executor Max Brod) and the later *The Castle*, its author had given it a clearly defined conclusion—it offers far more choices to the adapter than any completed narrative would. So it's understandable that Welles would combine two of Kafka's characters—a waitress and prostitute named Elsa whom Josef K. visits every week (although she barely figures in the story's action) and Fraülein Bürstner, a typist who lives in the room next to his—and, casting Jeanne Moreau in this part and calling her Miss Burnster, would produce a character unlike either of Kafka's sketchy figures and arguably somewhat nearer in her bossy temperament to *Touch of Evil*'s Tanya (Marlene Dietrich).

Closer in some ways as an adaptation to Welles's unfinished *Don Quixote* (especially if one considers it in isolation from Jesus Franco's dubious and dull "completion" of that work, which edits in large portions of a hack documentary about Spain while leaving out many of Welles's best scenes), *The Trial* (1962) emerges as a highly personal and slanted reading of a classic that adapts it to Welles's own twisted times—which, all proportions guarded, also makes it comparable to his legendary 1937 stage production of *Julius Caesar* in contemporary Fascist regalia, his even more famously updated 1938 *War of the Worlds* for radio, or his elaborately planned but never filmed first Hollywood feature, *Heart of Darkness*, which years later would inspire Coppola's *Apocalypse Now*. More nightmarish and unsettling in many respects than any of these, *The Trial* has a sense of hallucinatory horror while confronting the corruptions and self-deceptions of the contemporary world that comes even closer to Welles's previous feature and final Hollywood studio production, *Touch of Evil* (1958)—recalled here in both the humiliations undergone by Akim Tamiroff's character and in the near-replication of the earlier film's Hall of Records in a contemporary library of file cabinets (presided over by Paola Mori, Welles's wife). (Conversely, the creepy visit to Titorelli's cramped studio recalls both the slatted bathhouse in *Othello* and Michael Redgrave's antique shop in *Arkadin*.)

Described in Welles's opening narration as a film with "the logic of a dream . . . of a nightmare," it's plainly a film designed to freak us out, and it had precisely that effect on me in my late teens, when it first came out. But, unlike most of Welles's other films, it's an experience to be undergone and felt more than thought about in very much detail. I suspect that Welles arrived at this conclusion himself when he chose to omit his satirical reflections about computers regarded as fortune-tellers—in a scene with Katina Paxinou that survives without sound, and has been subtitled with its scripted dialogue for this release as an extra.

Bogdanovich admitted to Welles that *The Trial* was the only picture of his that he didn't warm to—a judgment he subsequently revised after attending a screening with Welles himself, whose laughter convinced him that the film was much funnier than he had realized. (It's worth recalling, for those who might find this perverse, that Max Brod wrote in his biography of Kafka, "We friends of [Kafka] laughed quite immoderately when he first let us hear the first chapter of *The Trial*. And he himself laughed so much that there were moments when he couldn't read any further.")

Whether or not we laugh much during Welles's version of *The Trial*, it has never found a very secure and comfortable place within his oeuvre, perhaps because it qualifies in some ways as a commissioned work. (When Alexander and Michael Salkind proposed producing a film of his in France, he said he would have preferred directing one of his own stories, but had to select from a list of literary classics believed to have been in the public domain.) It proved to be his only completed film adapted from a literary source not in English, and the difficulty we have in locating its action both geographically as well as historically—and more specifically, in accepting Anthony Perkins as a bureaucrat in an eastern European city with a European uncle and cousin, arrested by cops with American accents, or in adjusting to an updating of the story by almost half a century—has continued to inflect our responses. Such changes inevitably led to others (spoilers ahead): for Kafka's original ending of K. letting himself be stabbed in the heart and dying "like a dog," Welles felt obliged in a post-Holocaust world to have him defy his executioners. And even after retaining most of Kafka's scenes and much of his dialogue, Welles made additions to both in order to incorporate details involving war refugees and computers (though the resemblance of an explosion at the end to a mushroom cloud, by his account, was both accidental and unfortunate).

And yet certain key artifacts of the mid-twentieth century are just as pointedly omitted, such as TV sets. Speaking with an audience of students and film buffs about *The Trial* at the University of Southern California on November 14, 1981—a session filmed but never edited for possible use in a documentary, *Filming The Trial,* conceived as a companion piece to Welles's *Filming Othello* (1979)—Welles said, "In my reading of the book— and my reading is probably more wrong than a lot of people's—I see the monstrous bureaucracy which is the villain of the piece as not only Kafka's clairvoyant view of the future, but his racial and cultural background of being occupied by the Austro-Hungarian Empire.... [So] I wanted a 19th century look for a great deal of what would be, in fact, expressionistic." In short, one might say that Welles wanted to superimpose Kafka's inherited past over his future rather than settle for any ordinary version of his and our present.

Conceptually, Welles also had to alter his own plans to film in elaborately designed studio sets in Zagreb that would gradually disappear over the course of the story, "flying away into the darkness," once budgetary vicissitudes suddenly made this scheme impossible. (The only locations Welles originally planned to use were the huge office where K. works and the streets of Prague and Zagreb at the end where K. is led to his execution.) His main replacement for these sets proved to be various parts of Paris's Gare d'Orsay, which he discovered one night from his room at the Hôtel Meurice—a location that carried, as he described it in a BBC interview, "a kind of Jules Verne modernism."

> The thing that gave it a particular force is that it's not only a very large place to work in, and a very beautiful place to photograph, but that it's full of sorrow—the kind of sorrow that accumulates in a railway station where people wait. . . . And the story is all about people waiting, waiting, waiting for their papers to be filled . . . and it's also a place [of] refugees. People were sent to Nazi prisons from there. Algerians were gathered there.

This was the second time in Welles's career as a European independent that he had to forfeit his carefully planned set designs: in *Othello* (1951), a film that begins with a similar shot (an upside-down close-up of the hero with his eyes closed—later imitated by Coppola to introduce Martin Sheen in *Apocalypse Now*), he also had to devise a makeshift patchwork editing style out of his "found" international locations, creating imaginary places out of diverse details, after his budget for sets (and, in that case, costumes) had evaporated—a methodology carried over to some extent in *Mr. Arkadin* (1955), though arguably far more appropriate here, to match Kafka's own spatial discontinuities. Coincidentally, ninety-odd sheets of Welles's annotated drawings for his production designer on *The Trial,* Jean Mandaroux, were put up for auction at Sotheby's in 2012, while this essay was being written, and the partial glimpses of these drawings found on the Sotheby's website confirm Welles's remark to Bogdanovich that Titorelli's studio and the similarly slatted corridor where the little girls chase K. are the major parts of the production design that remained in the film.

Franz Kafka's second unfinished novel, written about a year before Orson Welles was born and first published eleven years later, in 1925, a year after its author's death, has more than its share of predatory, sexually aggressive women, but not ones who come across as threateningly as those in Welles's adaptation, set almost half a century later. When Leni in the novel, seated in K.'s lap, asks him if he has a sweetheart, he shows her a snapshot of Elsa, but in the film, we're led to assume this must be one of Fraülein Bürstner—even though there's no indication that she and K. have ever gone further than their few casual kisses exchanged during their only long scene together.

Welles himself admitted that "the eroticism is dirty and morbid" in the film, but it doesn't register in quite the same way in the novel—aside from the detail of Josef K. finding obscene books on a table in the empty courtroom (and Welles himself admitted to Bogdanovich that he "got all the dirty eroticism of the rest of the movie out of that one thing.") Speaking at the University of Southern California in 1981, Welles stressed that his film got wonderful reviews in both Europe and the United States when it came out, but Perkins didn't, and that the fault for this was entirely his, attributable not to Perkins's acting but to "my controversial reading of [Josef] K." as a neurotic and ambitious careerist. I personally find Welles's reading quite defensible—the novel is pretty withering about its hero's class snobbery, for instance—but he might have added that casting an American actor in the part, especially one associated in the public mind with *Psycho*'s Norman Bates, probably didn't help matters much. In fact, Welles had wondered more privately to Bogdanovich how much *Psycho* might have been influenced by his own *Touch of Evil*, which planted an undressed Janet Leigh in a remote and otherwise deserted motel with a highly nervous and sexually repressed night clerk—a factor that may have further encouraged him to benefit from Perkins's resulting stardom. But the downside of this was that it yielded a hero who was more repressed, puritanical, and adolescent in his behavior than Kafka's—or than Kafka himself, for that matter. (Despite a popular misconception that Kafka was sexually shy and withdrawn, he frequented brothels with some regularity, as was typical for someone of his class and background in that period.)

The gags about "pornograph" and "ovular" in *The Trial*'s opening scene are Welles's own invention, as are some of the insinuations of sexual impropriety that crop up in later scenes. Moreover, in its overall treatment of sex and predatory women (which enabled Welles to cast some of the sexiest female stars in European cinema at the time—Elsa Martinelli, Jeanne Moreau, and Romy Schneider), *The Trial* can be said to represent a culmination of certain misogynistic traits in Welles's work that were altered by his involvement with Oja Kodar, his muse and mistress for most of the last two decades of his life, whom he met in Zagreb during the shooting. In many subsequent films and film projects—notably *F for Fake, The Other Side of the Wind,* and *The Dreamers*—Kodar's creative involvement as cowriter and actress led to a far more affirmative view of women and their sexuality and an understanding of their viewpoints than can be found in his earlier films. (The second of these, for all of its political "incorrectness," is arguably Welles's only feminist film—as I believe will become clear if it ever sees the light of day—while the third, judging from the filmed excerpts visible in the 1995 documentary *The One-Man Band*, further helps to clarify the extent to which Welles identified with Kodar, exhibitionism and all.)

In the years to come, *The Trial* would clearly (and beneficially) influence various movie touchstones ranging all the way from Jean-Luc Godard's *Alphaville* (1965) to Martin Scorsese's *After Hours* (1985). "*The Trial* begins as farce and ends as tragedy," writes Breon Mitchell, the novel's most recent and probably best English translator, signaling a pattern that also recurs in many of Kafka's best stories. And we can still enjoy most of it today as a perverse kind of roller-coaster or funhouse ride through the sort of mid-twentieth-century modernity that Welles remained forever at odds with, even as he paradoxically continued to shine as one of cinema's greatest modernists.

Divas and Dandies

Aside from William Shakespeare, no writer excited Orson Welles's imagination more than Isak Dinesen, the pen name of Karen Blixen—a Danish baroness who wrote mainly in English—especially when it came to the films he wanted to make. Even though she was born thirty years ahead of him, they shared a capacity for standing outside of their own eras. Both were cosmopolitan twentieth-century aristocrats with nostalgic yearnings for the nineteenth century, who loved to critique the same romanticism in which they enveloped themselves. Both were florid, masterful storytellers, with a developed taste for paradox, irony, and a kind of artifice that unabashedly calls attention to itself. Perhaps even more relevant to this discussion, both were also tireless polishers of their own art, whose apparent simplicity and directness concealed a great deal of subtle craft and nuance. This is especially true when it comes to the architectonics of "The Immortal Story."

Welles once even made a pilgrimage to Denmark to meet Dinesen, but after a sleepless night in Copenhagen, he backed away from the prospect and flew home: "I'd been in love with Isak Dinesen since I'd opened her first book," he later wrote. "Tania was somebody I didn't know. What could a casual visitor presume to offer except his stammered thanks? The visitor would be a bore, and the lover was too humble and too proud for that. I had only to keep silent and our affair would last—on the most intimate terms—for as long as I had eyes to read print." ("Tania" was

Dinesen's nickname to intimates, and one wonders whether Welles might have named Marlene Dietrich's aging, world-weary prostitute after her in *Touch of Evil*.)

Although Dinesen's "The Immortal Story"—included in her final story collection, *Anecdotes of Destiny* (1958), and her personal favorite in that volume—was the only one of her tales that yielded a completed film from Welles, at least half a dozen others attracted his attention as a screen adaptor at one time or another. As early as 1953, he planned to include an adaptation of "The Old Chevalier" (1934) in a sketch film for Alexander Korda called *Paris By Night,* whose other episodes would all be written by himself; and as late as 1985, on the very night that he died, he was planning to shoot part of another sketch film, *Orson Welles Solo,* that would have included his recounting of that same story. His original plan for *The Immortal Story* was to make it part of an anthology of Dinesen stories— either a TV series or a sketch feature—along with "The Heroine" (1942), which he started to shoot with Oja Kodar in Budapest while he was still editing *The Immortal Story* (and then had to abandon a day later when the promised budget evaporated); "The Deluge from Norderney" (1934); and "A Country Tale" (1957). And finally, the most treasured and personal of all his late projects, also starring Kodar, was *The Dreamers,* which he worked on between 1978 and 1985 and based on both the 1934 story of that title and its belated 1957 sequel, "Echoes." (Several excerpts from the half hour or so of Welles's sumptuous test footage for *The Dreamers* are visible in a documentary on Criterion's release of *F for Fake*.)

■ ■ ■

Even for a director expected to do the unexpected, *The Immortal Story* was for many a disconcerting departure for Welles when it premiered theatrically in 1968, in terms of both its seemingly unadorned simplicity and the fact that it was his first released film in color, financed by French television. Although Welles shifted the story's locale from Canton—as Guangzhou, China, was then known—to Macao and compressed or relocated a few of its narrative details, it generally adheres to the original with rigorous fidelity, including its eerie and singsong repetitions of the same embedded story about a sailor and certain spoken phrases, as well as its meditative, almost ceremonial pacing, which suggests at times a hypnotic trance. (There are only a few rapid cuts—such as when a fancy meal is served, and again when several candles are blown out—reminding one that this is the same Welles who had made *Chimes at Midnight* just before, and who would go on to start *The Other Side of the Wind* and make *F for Fake* afterward.)

A wealthy, coldhearted, seventy-year-old merchant named Mr. Clay (Welles) contrives to re-create a legendary and fanciful story he once heard from a sailor, enlisting his accountant, Elishama Levinsky (Roger Coggio), to set the machinery in motion by hiring a local courtesan to play a part. She proves to be the daughter, Virginie (Jeanne Moreau), of a merchant Clay drove to suicide years earlier and whose former house he now occupies; the sailor for the story—a Danish teenager named Paul (Norman Eshley)—is chosen at random and summoned on the street by Levinsky and Clay. The various ways in which Clay's scheme both succeeds and fails over the course of that night constitute the remainder of the tale.

Both the story itself and the tale-within-the-tale are recounted with the sort of elemental purity we associate with myths and fairy tales, and because all four of the characters are solipsistic loners in different ways, and mirrors figure often in the settings, repetitions, echoes, and other rhyme effects involving both words and images recur throughout. This is quintessentially a tale about the lures and perils of storytelling itself—that is, the lures and perils of its processes—and about the power plays among its various participants (tellers, listeners, facilitators, and characters), which helps to account for its personal resonance for both Welles and Dinesen. The fact that Dinesen literally dictated this story, like many of her others, to her longtime secretary (and Danish translator and eventual literary executor) Clara Svendsen must have enhanced her own sense of the interactivity in the yarn-spinning, reflected in Welles's offscreen narration in the opening stretches of the film's English version—and even in his willingness, as in the opening of *The Magnificent Ambersons*, to let gossiping neighbors take up part of the narrating slack, just as Levinsky later completes the telling of the familiar tale that is started by Mr. Clay.

Given the film's apparent sparseness, it's surprising to learn from Jean-Pierre Berthomé and François Thomas's *Orson Welles at Work* that it was shot in both France and Spain, using at least three separate Spanish medieval villages to stand in for Macao. For his cinematographer, after four unsatisfactory days with the old-school studio technician Walter Wottitz, Welles turned to a relative novice, Willy Kurant, who had just recently shot features with Agnès Varda and Jean-Luc Godard, using lighter equipment and a handheld camera, and thus brought a certain New Wave twist to the film's overall classicism. (He would later shoot *The Deep* for Welles.) And even though the shooting lasted only around six weeks, the editing—done at Jean-Pierre Melville's Paris studio—stretched over the better part of a year. This yielded both an English-language version for eventual theatrical release and a shorter French-language version (with Philippe Noiret dubbing Mr. Clay) for French television, and, as Berthomé and Thomas point out, "although only about twelve minutes in the two versions use different takes, they vary in many other ways, like two competing cuts between which it is impossible to choose." Clearly, making the film for TV played a role in Welles's adopting a more minimalist visual and aural palette than was customary for him, as had also happened with his 1958 pilot for American TV, *The Fountain of Youth*. In keeping with this simplicity, and with Dinesen's notion of a blank page as a silence that speaks, a form of Zen-like wisdom, it seems entirely appropriate that *The Immortal Story* should end with both the unheard song of a seashell and a complete whiting out of the image.

Coincidentally, it was thanks to French television—specifically, a program about Erik Satie that Welles saw roughly halfway through his editing—that the filmmaker decided to use several of the composer's sadly reflective solo piano pieces for the film's score, an inspired choice that, as the *New Yorker*'s Alex Ross has pointed out, "soon became clichéd" because of its frequent use by other filmmakers but "was quite new in 1968."

■ ■ ■

According to Dinesen biographer Judith Thurman, this story had a particular personal meaning for its author, having been written after the traumatic dissolution of her intense (albeit chaste) relationship with the Danish poet Thorkild Bjørnvig, for whom she'd served for seven years as muse, literary coach/adviser, and soul mate. Thurman notes, "It was one of the three Dinesen tales concerned with the cosmic meddler, one who, innocent or deluded about his omnipotence, tries to usurp the role of the gods in another person's life, to introduce his own plans for its development and outcome, to graft his own desire onto its fate-in-progress." The first of these tales—which for Thurman "anticipated with an uncanny coincidence of detail" Dinesen's friendship with Bjørnvig—was "The Poet," written in the early 1930s. And the third was "Echoes," her sequel to "The Dreamers," which for Thurman "was the epitaph of that friendship." Hence "The Immortal Story," the centerpiece of this trio, can be read as her complex reflections about her own "cosmic meddling" in the life and destiny of Bjørnvig.

Given Welles's appropriation of both "The Immortal Story" and "Echoes" (not to mention "The Dreamers") into his own oeuvre, it is difficult not to find personal investments of his in this highly allegorical material. "The Dreamers" recounts the story of a famous opera singer named Pellegrina who, after losing her singing voice, resolves to disappear from her life and lead many other, different lives; "Echoes" charts one of those lives, when she tries to mentor a boy in a remote country village who has a beautiful voice and reminds her of her former self, and he winds up denouncing her as a witch.

The fact that Welles shot many of the interiors of *The Immortal Story* in his own villa near Madrid, including much of Clay's house, and all of the material for *The Dreamers* in his own house and backyard in Hollywood, seems to support his personal relation to these stories, even though practical concerns also must have played a part in these decisions. Welles's own long-term relationship with Oja Kodar—whom he also mentored—undoubtedly also played a part, even when it came to *The Immortal Story*. When I first met her in 1986, a few months after Welles's death, she told me that the first work she ever did on one of his films was dubbing Virginie's "lovemaking sighs" during her night with Paul. (In fact, it seems she was alluding to the character's gasp at the moment of orgasm, when she relives the loss of her virginity with an English captain by experiencing an earthquake—an abrupt punctuation to a soundtrack otherwise dominated here by the delicate and intricate orchestration of the chirping of crickets.) And clearly part of what "The Dreamers" meant for Welles related to his identification with Pellegrina (and, by extension, with Kodar) as well as her own best friend and facilitator, a wealthy Dutchman named Marcus Cocoza (whom he played himself), like the character Levinsky, a Jew; and in "Echoes," one suspects, he identified in different ways with both Pellegrina and her young pupil.

So it isn't really a stretch to say that in *The Immortal Story,* Welles identifies with all the major characters—Clay, Elishama, Paul, and Virginie (the last two of whom constitute a clear literary allusion to Jacques-Henri Bernardin de Saint-Pierre's celebrated 1788 novel *Paul et Virginie,* one of the key romances read by Flaubert's Emma Bovary roughly half a century later). Indeed, the fact that both he and Dinesen identify with all four, in equal measures, is central to the primal power of their storytelling.

This cross-identification, then, is something else these two larger-than-life artists shared, a fluidity regarding gender when it came to projecting themselves into others. Dinesen was often called a diva, and Welles was sometimes regarded as a dandy, but clearly it doesn't do justice to either of their respective temperaments or self-images to limit them to such stereotypes. It would be far more accurate to say that both of them were divas *and* dandies, at the same time and at every moment.

The Other Side of the Argument: First Thoughts on Orson Welles's Demonic Fugue

The only time I ever met Orson Welles—in 1972, in response to a letter of mine, to discuss his very first Hollywood project, an updated adaptation of Conrad's *Heart of Darkness* that I was writing about—I also had occasion to ask him about the status of his more recent projects. There was the film called *Hoax* that he was currently editing, which later became *F for Fake* ("not a documentary," he assured me, but "a new kind of film"); two films that he declared were nearly done but he was in no hurry to release, *The Deep* and *Don Quixote*; and a still-unfinished film, *The Other Side of the Wind*, that he wanted to release ahead of the others because it was about movies and "movies are a popular subject now," though he wasn't sure how long this interest would last.

Forty-six years later, a posthumously completed version of the latter, put together by several hands—including Peter Bogdanovich, who also costars as a character much like himself, production manager Frank Marshall, and two later arrivals, editor Bob Murawski and producer Filip Jan Rymsza—is opening in the United States, and as luck would have it, it may be even timelier now than it might have been in the seventies. This isn't because of its ostensible mythic subject, The Death of Hollywood, but because of its other mythic concern, The Death of Macho, which the film proposes as intimately (if covertly) connected with its "popular subject"—indeed, as something akin to a subject that dare not speak its name. All of the film's action unfolds on July 2, pointedly the date of Ernest Hemingway's suicide, and if death of one kind or another remains one of the most common preoccupations of Welles's fourteen released features, the alleged death of Hollywood—combined with the deceptive teaser of a tell-all autobiography about an aging maverick director trying to finance the completion of his final independent feature—is the part of the film's subject designed to get an audience inside the tent. Yet it's the other subject and the other Death that will undoubtedly spark the most debate and controversy. The first Death, mainly fun and games spiced with bantering gossip and the cult of celebrity (featuring such familiar names as Mercedes McCambridge, Cameron Mitchell, Edmond O'Brien, Paul Stewart, and, in bits, everyone from Claude Chabrol, Dennis Hopper, and Curtis Harrington to Henry Jaglom, George Jessel, and Paul Mazursky)—even though it's edited with the rapid, kamikaze shot collisions Welles developed in such globetrotting ventures as *Othello, Mr. Arkadin, The Trial,* and *F for Fake*, pushed here to even more aggressively discontinuous and discombobulated extremes—is clearly the one most cinephiles have been awaiting and expecting, and the one more appealing to mainstream taste. But the second one, pitched in the form of an arty countercultural nightmare about gender reversals (some of which parallel those in Hemingway's posthumously assembled *The Garden of Eden*), sexual humiliation, coitus interruptus, impotence, and castration, without any stars or dialogue, is the one that stings and lingers. The resulting toxic brew may constitute Welles's only feminist film, if only by default, yet the brand of feminism it suggests—predicated in part on the fierce silence of a nameless Native American actress both at the party and in a macho director's unfinished film, glowering in mute and furious judgment at his behavior and world—has too many sinister aspects to be regarded as either affirmative or politically correct. Like the Victorian notions of dirty sex that course through Welles's debatable version of *The Trial*, ravenous nymphets and all, it seethes with demonic unhealthiness.

Why it took almost half a century for *The Other Side of the Wind* to be completed has already been the focus of one book by Josh Karp[1] as well as a documentary feature, Morgan Neville's *They'll Love Me When I'm Dead,* that in some ways confuses as much as it clarifies (by wrongly suggesting, for instance, that the party scenes were mostly improvised rather than scripted, and by being edited in a breezy manner that misrepresents the controlled cacophony of Welles's own style—making it comparable in some ways to the false mimesis of *Chantal Akerman, From Here,* discussed in the first chapter of this book). It's a complicated, dispiriting tale of bad business deals, chicanery, lawsuits, and, finally, impounded footage in

Paris that prevented Welles from editing more than about a third of the two hours of projected running time. When I first met Oja Kodar—the film's lead actress (as the silent Native American) and coauthor—a few months after his death in 1985, which eventually led to both our friendship and her asking me to edit Welles's interview book with Peter Bogdanovich,[2] she told me that the film's correspondence file was as hefty as *War and Peace*. Visiting her at the Villa Welles in Primošten, Croatia early last July, I saw substantial proof of this claim when she finally stacked the file on her kitchen table for me to examine. But apart from assertions by Welles in that pile that confirmed all her shy and mainly reluctant admissions of her creative contributions to the film, which I have been gradually trying to coax out of her for more than three decades, this isn't a tale that I have any appetite for recounting here. What the film says and does is far more interesting.

The Death-of-Hollywood scenario centers on the seventieth birthday party of Jake Hannaford (John Huston), given at his ranch by his old actress chum, Zarah Valeska (Lilli Palmer—a part reportedly offered first to Marlene Dietrich), rendered via super-8 and 16mm footage and still photographs, in both color and black and white, and audiotapes, all allegedly (and sometimes far-fetchedly) recorded by various attendees in a pseudo-documentary style that remained part of Welles's standard arsenal (as in his Shakespearean *Caesar* on stage, *Twelfth Night* on 78 rpm, *The War of the Worlds* on radio, and, in film, the *Citizen Kane* newsreel, the openings of *The Magnificent Ambersons* and *Mr. Arkadin,* and *F for Fake*). Intercut with this material is Hannaford's unfinished film *The Other Side of the Wind,* in color, screened first for a studio honcho (who disdainfully walks out), then at the party, and finally in a nearby drive-in theater after two power outages at the ranch, both of which further evoke impotence and/or interrupted sex. In contrast to the party, full of lively chatter (though almost completely and mysteriously devoid of any couples), this film has no dialogue and basically consists of the flirtations, foreplay, struggles, and sexual encounters between a passive, effeminate, nameless hunk first seen on a motorcycle (Bob Random playing the actor John Dale, mostly and appropriately like a "found" object or one of the many prop dummies representing him that are brought to the party) and an equally nameless Native American radical and dominatrix (Oja Kodar), both of them naked for much of the time—getting it on first in the front seat of a car during a rainstorm (until the driver throws both of them out), then on the bare springs of a mattress-less bed in the open air on a studio backlot.

At the party we learn that the film is unfinished because Dale quit in the midst of shooting. Eventually, in the film being screened, and specifically during the latter sex scene, we discover why: being sexually taunted and humiliated by Hannaford from behind the camera and threatened with a pair of scissors by his costar (until she cuts her bead necklace instead, which is caught in the bedsprings. and her beads spill and scatter like semen), he stomps off the set, with Hannaford instructing his cameraman to film his departure. At the drive-in, we also hear the charge from a journalist (Susan Strasberg playing a cross between Pauline Kael and Barbara Leaming) that super-macho Hannaford has a homoerotic bent—a charge that eventually goads Hannaford into slapping her. (Characteristically, this slap seems calculated to solicit our righteous applause—and not because she's wrong but because she's right.)

Ever since enjoying a mainstream profile in his youth, Welles was reluctant to see himself as an arthouse filmmaker, although this was the status he mainly wound up with. It was only after Kael described *Citizen Kane* as a Hollywood newspaper comedy that his aberrant first feature got ushered belatedly into the mainstream, and the reason Welles gave me in 1972 for holding back his low-budget *Don Quixote* was that he didn't want it to compete with *Man of la Mancha*. So it's unsurprising that he described *Wind* as a movie about movies, his mainstream subject, rather than as an experimental art film about fading sexual confidence and diminished career options.

The fact that it's both becomes an essential part of its fascination: a duet or duel between conflicting self-images. The contrasts between the film's two alternating blocks of material are indeed so striking that they need to be regarded in musical terms, as the separate melodic lines in a fugue: reams of dialogue versus no dialogue at all, old age versus youth, color plus black and white in diverse formats versus just color 35mm, and, perhaps most crucial, lone figures at a noisy party versus a movie couple coupling. Even though the sexual encounters of the latter between a dominatrix and her prey end in coitus interruptus, the two are always continually *engaged* with one another, even in their perpetual conflict, whereas the party guests and hostess are perceived mainly as disengaged and lost, solitary souls seeking some form of social communion. And the musical coupling of these two strands is visceral as well as conceptual:

visual and aural close-ups of Hannaford pouring liquor into a shot glass make voluptuous audiovisual rhymes with the rain splashing against car windows in accompaniment to the movie sex.

Welles's part of the script relates to Hannaford as played by Huston; Kodar's part relates to Hannaford's film in which she implicitly plays Hannaford's sexual surrogate—a predator who, as Kodar has described her conception of the part, resembles a praying mantis. Although this film-within-the-film has often been described as Welles's parody of *Zabriskie Point*—based on his outspoken disdain for Michelangelo Antonioni as an "architect of empty boxes" (though this visual style is notably absent)—Kodar's own acquaintance with Antonioni's work remains minimal, and the artiness and Freudian symbolism of Hannaford's film is chiefly her contribution, even though the anxiety about countercultural androgyny and passivity as a threat to aging macho values clearly belongs to Welles. Kodar directed three sequences—in the car, inside a disco's ladies room, and on a surrealist beach in the final scene, where a giant phallus actually topples in defeat—and a temporary illness prevented Welles from being present at most of the shooting of the second of these scenes, perhaps the creepiest in the film. More generally, Kodar's background as a sculptor—she was the first woman in at least five generations admitted to the sculpture department of Zagreb's Academy of Visual Arts—informs the diverse settings of Hannaford's film, whether they're created or found (as in the MGM backlot, where she and her costar managed to sneak in with Welles and a skeletal crew for about a day and a half of continuous shooting). Most of her sculptures are both abstract and erotic, and the same might be said of the disco nightclub where she cuts the eyes off a doll given to her by her sparring partner—the film's first symbolic castration—in order to wear them defiantly as earrings. (If the disco recalls the funhouse in *The Lady from Shanghai*—and its ladies room evokes the giggling girls peeking through slats into an artist's garret in *The Trial*—this only further suggests that Kodar's multiple collaborations with Welles, however dialectical, could also sometimes attain a genuine osmosis.)

What inspired her to play a Native American radical was an incident during her first visit to Hollywood. As she recounted to me in a public interview held in 2015 in Woodstock, Illinois (the site of Welles's prep school), Welles acquired a car and a driver named Hymie to take her on a solitary tour. On Hollywood Boulevard, "a short, stocky, dark-complexioned man was jaywalking," and an enraged Hymie stopped the car, rolled down a window, and barked out at him, "Move your ass, you red son-of-a-bitch." She got out of the car, not wanting to be driven any further by Hymie, and before she walked back to Beverly Hills, tried to follow the stocky man from a discreet distance, until he gave her a look "and I felt as though I was trespassing."

Kodar knows better than anyone that the public wants a movie by Welles, not a film coauthored by herself, and being mainly a willing outsider to the film world apart from her involvement with Welles, she shares with him the paradoxical temperament of being a reclusive exhibitionist—that is to say, an exhibitionistic artist who treasures her solitude and remoteness. (This remoteness—coupled with living in a Croatian village not far from her birthplace that has limited internet access—has made her an easy scapegoat for some Welles enthusiasts and commentators, mostly male, who feel obliged to fill in various journalistic blanks, so that Josh Karp's assertion that she "allegedly collaborated on the screenplay" of *Wind*[3] is characteristic.) But Welles choosing to complicate his own exhibitionism in *The Other Side of the Wind* by factoring hers into its textures and delivery is a process that he would carry out again, albeit more modestly, in *F for Fake* (as well as in many of the unrealized projects that they collaborated on). Both films combine stories by each of them that involve her brazenly parading her beauty and body (before a fictionalized Pablo Picasso in *F for Fake*) while he no less brazenly parades his verbal wit and eloquence (with John Huston as his fictionalized mouthpiece in *Wind*)—even though she was the one who came up with the titles for both films. As James Naremore has recently pointed out,[4] *Wind* grew out of a story by Welles called *The Sacred Beasts* about a burned-out Hemingway-like aficionado with homoerotic leanings—a tale likely inspired by Welles's first encounter with Hemingway, while recording a voiceover for Joris Ivens's *This Spanish Earth* and being accused by Papa of sounding like a queer—which, according to Welles, led first to fisticuffs and then to an edgy friendship (the sort of ritual commonly enacted by Howard Hawks's heroes). To this story was added Kodar's own tale about an unconsciously homosexual director who sleeps with his leading ladies after they sleep with his leading men, thereby "possessing" his male discoveries at one remove, and is brutally homophobic in the bargain.

How autobiographical *The Other Side of the Wind* actually is will no doubt keep some Welles buffs preoccupied for years to come. Even though Hannaford is plainly modeled on such macho directors as Ford, Hawks,

Walsh, and Huston himself, he's also furnished with such acolytes as Bogdanovich and Joseph McBride (in a smaller role), both known for their associations with Welles and encouraged to parody themselves. Meanwhile, John Dale is assigned a tweedy prep-school mentor named Burroughs (Dan Tobin) who evokes Welles's own beloved Roger Hill in Woodstock, and is shamelessly gay-baited by Hannaford—in one of the film's most nerve-wracking encounters, edited according to their respective stares in a manner calculated to make an audience squirm. (The confrontational power of Welles's editing has, alas, been reduced by the strains of an offscreen piano.)

Yet I find all the elements of an autobiographical fan-dance far less intriguing than the overriding ambiguities of Welles's art regarding the unresolvable mysteries of human personality. He planned to play a gay Kissinger-like figure in *The Big Brass Ring,* but arguably far more relevant is the reporter's assertion in *Citizen Kane* that "I don't think any word can explain a man's life," in contradistinction to "Rosebud" (the mainstream payoff), or the seeming discrepancies between the present and evoked past personae of the title figure of *Mr. Arkadin* or Hank Quinlan in *Touch of Evil.* In keeping with such conundrums, and for better and for worse, *Wind* finally offers us two disparate Jake Hannafords—the charismatic rascal maverick concocted by Welles and Huston and the elusive fag artist in denial devised by Welles and Kodar—who don't really match up. There's a flagrant lack of congruence between the former, American to the core, and the Eurotrashy tang of the latter. The real Hannaford (if there is one), a perpetual enigma, must lie somewhere in between these versions, but precisely where and how he lies (in both senses of the word) is entirely up to us. Indeed, he's so strategically opaque that when he delivers a "witty" racist speech to Kodar's character at his birthday party—even calling her Pocahontas in what must be the timeliest of historical coincidences—he does so in the manner we recognize from Donald Trump's mockery of Elizabeth Warren whereby racism and a conscious parody of racism become indistinguishable and interchangeable.

When I met Welles in 1972, I was disappointed to discover that the man I thought would be the ideal film adapter of *Light in August* (while playing the role of Reverend Hightower) actually preferred John O'Hara, F. Scott Fitzgerald, and Hemingway to William Faulkner. But he also admitted to me that he used to hang out in Hollywood with Nathanael West, and it's surely West's view of Hollywood that informs *The Other Side of the Wind* rather than O'Hara's or Fitzgerald's. One of Hannaford's many stooges and apologists, Billy Boyle, beautifully played by Welles's former director-colleague Norman Foster—a jittery former alcoholic who stays on the wagon by gobbling gumdrops, until the tensions and remonstrations of the evening finally send him back to the bottle (and hardly anyone in his crowd seems to notice, or care)—is a classic loser out of *The Day of the Locust,* a blood brother of Homer Simpson, swimming through the same universe of casual cruelty and thwarted hopes. And the alternate universe provided by Hannaford's stab at a trendy youth movie, even with its glitzy evocations of sex and violence, proves to be even harsher—a blighted view of hippie utopia that could have been hatched in the brain of *Miss Lonelyhearts*' Shrike.

In the interest of full (if belated) transparency, I was one of the two consultants who worked on the completion of *Wind* (Joseph McBride was the other). Even though I have a few, mostly minor differences with Bogdanovich, Marshall, Murawski, and Rymsza, who did most of the work (and with Michel Legrand, who provided the score—lamentably without Welles's supervision, which yielded his excellent contributions to *F for Fake*)—all of whom, along with McBride, are more oriented toward mainstream editing conventions than I am—these differences are secondary to my gratitude that they've finally managed to make available a very radical and challenging work that otherwise would have been lost to history, film history included. So rather than deal with those differences here, I'd like to emphasize that in keeping with Welles's career-long aptitude for defying and confounding most of our expectations about his work, *Wind* can't truthfully be regarded as his "last feature," at least without a great deal of boiling and scraping that entails further obfuscation. Most of it was conceived and shot before *F for Fake* and *Filming Othello* (the latter finally made available on Criterion's recent and superb digital release of *Othello*, which also makes Welles's own two versions of *Othello* fully available for the first time on DVD and Blu-Ray), so trying to assign it the status of Welles's "final" work or statement essentially means trying to give it a marketable form of closure rather than a plausible or meaningful critical definition, a ruse that can only reduce its challenges and provocations. To keep it alive and worrying, as a film addressed to the present moment, I think we need to suspend some of our verdicts until we all become better acquainted with it as a foreign and somewhat scary object. It may even have more to say to us than Welles was aware of. Among other Wellesian specialists, I can think of at least four—three in Europe, a fourth in the United States—who firmly believe that a "completion" of this unfinished work shouldn't have been undertaken in the first place, and even though I disagree with them, I would concede that at least two of them have cogent arguments to support their positions. But now that a film called *The Other Side of the Wind* finally exists as a fait accompli, I would maintain that the primary task we're now faced with isn't so much to determine whether or not it has a right to exist as to question what it is and does. After waiting for it for nearly half a century, a rush to judgment isn't exactly called for.

Notes

1. Josh Karp, *Orson Welles's Last Movie: The Making of* The Other Side of the Wind (New York: St. Martin's Press, 2015).

2. Orson Welles and Peter Bogdanovich, *This is Orson Welles* (New York: HarperCollins, 1992; revised 2nd ed., New York: Da Capo Press, 1998).

3. Karp, *Orson Welles's Last Movie,* 45.

4. "Orson Welles, Citizen of the World," written for the Brazilian/French digital project *Transatlantic Cultures: A Dictionary of Cultural History,* edited by Eduardo Morettin and Caroline Moine. The original English text can be found at jamesnaremore.net.

Index

1+1, 33
1001 Films, 46
11 X 14, 253
24 City, 96, 98–101
36 vues du Pic Saint-Loup /Around a Small Mountain, 225
Les 400 Coups, 52
4 Months, 3 Weeks, and 2 Days, 65
The 5,000 Fingers of Dr. T., 198

Abkarian, Simon, 198
A bout de souffle/Breathless, 56, 139
Abrunhosa, Pedro, 159, 160
Les Abysses, 181
The Abyss/L'Oeuvre en noir, 43, 48
Accatone, 178
Adair, Gilbert, 233
Adynata, 254
Aeschylus, 230, 235, 237, 238
The African Queen, 107
After Hours, 281
L'age d'or, 30
Agee, James, 3, 16
Ahlert, Eve, 136
Aimée, Anouk, 43, 44, 50, 56
Akerman, Chantal, 5, 9–19, 42, 47, 135, 252, 287
À la recherche du temps perdu, 229
L'albero degli zoccoli/The Tree of Wooden Clogs, 171, 174, 176–77
Alexander Nevsky, 197
Algren, Nelson, 83
Allen, Joan, 198
Allen, Woody, 43, 106, 108, 109, 111, 112, 116, 120
All I Need is Love, 125

All the Memory of the World/Toute la mémoire du monde, 212, 214, 218
Almayer's Folly, 11, 19
Alphaville, 55, 218, 281
Álvarez López, Cristina, 237, 238
Amélie, 252
American Film, 202
Amor de Perdição/Doomed Love, 162, 165, 167, 168, 169
L'amour fou, 220, 221, 222, 224, 226, 228, 232, 240
L'amour par terre/Love on the Ground, 221, 225
Andersen, Thom, 34, 70, 76n1, 145–46, 148, 150, 153
Anderson, Arthur, 129
Anderson, Sherwood, 83
Anderson, Wes, 261
Anecdotes of Destiny, 282
Anger, Kenneth, 35
Aniki-Bóbó, 163, 165
L'année dernière à Marienbad/Last Year at Marienbad, 212, 214, 218
Les années 80, 11
Anne of the Indies, 207
Anne Pedersdotter, 59–60
Anouihl, Jean, 219
Anthony, Susan B., 68
Antonio, Emile
Antonioni, Michelangelo, 55–56, 174, 207, 252, 266, 290
Anything Else, 2, 258
Aoki, Tomio "Tokkankozo," 191–92
Apocalypse Now, 277, 279
À Propos de Nice, 164
À Propos de Nice, la suite, 164

Apted, Michael, 261
Archangel, 136, 137, 139
Ardant, Fanny, 43
Arditi, Pierre, 217
Aronovich, Ricardo, 217
Around a Small Mountain/36 vues du Pic Saint-Loup, 225
Arrow Films (DVD label), 96
Artaud, Antonin, 238
Artforum, 32, 220
Artists and Models, 111, 120n3, 226
As Good as It Gets, 21, 22, 24, 25
Ashes of Time, 123
As I Lay Dying, 244, 246, 249n6
"As I Walked Out One Evening" (poem), 123, 125
Astaire, Fred, 128
L'Atalante, 77, 90
At Land, 256
Auden, W. H., 123, 125
Auerbach, Erich, 245–46, 249n1
Aumont, Jean-Pierre, 204
Auster, Paul, 86
Avatar, 252
L'avventura, 174
Ayatani, Chiyoko, 185

B., Scott and Beth, 86
Babel Opéra ou la répétition de Don Juan, 48
Bach, Johann Sebastian, 179
Baecque, Antoine de, 169
La Baie des Anges, 50, 51, 54, 57
Bailey, John, 33
Balderston, John L., 139
Balibar, Jeanne, 33–36, 222
Balliett, Whitney, 227
Balzac, Honoré de, 222, 228, 231, 232, 237
La bande des quatre/Gang of Four, 222, 225
Banditi a Orgosolo, 178
Bankolé, Isaach de, 86, 87, 88, 90, 93
Bardem, Juan Antonio, 65, 168
Barnet, Boris, 39
Barrault, Marie-Christine, 43
Bataille, Georges, 125
The Battle of Algiers, 70
Baxter, John, 273
Bazin, André, 177, 236–37
Beach, Sylvia, 124
Béart, Emmanuelle, 222, 223
Beatty, Warren, 154
Beck, Gustavo, 10
Becker, Jacques, 212
Beckett, Samuel, 87, 166, 244
Becoming Anita Ekberg, 203
Before Midnight, 122
Before Sunrise, 123, 124–25, 126

Before Sunset, 123–27
Behind the Screen, 47, 48
Bel Geddes, Barbara, 149
La Bel Indifférent, 50, 51
The Bellboy, 111, 118, 119
Belle, 43, 45, 47, 48
Belle de jour, 4, 30, 160–61
La belle noiseuse, 221, 222, 225, 226
Belle toujours, 4, 159, 160–61, 163, 165, 167
Bellour, Raymond, 169–70
Benayoun, Robert, 107, 120n3
Benigni, Roberto, 83, 94
Benilde or the Virgin-Mother, 162, 165, 166, 168, 169
Benning, James, 4, 74–75, 253
Benvenuta, 43, 45, 48
Berendt, John, 131
Berger, John, 198
Bergman, Ingmar, 159, 207, 252
Bergstrom, Janet, 12, 19
Berlanga, Luis Garcia, 256
Berlin, Jeannie, 154
Berlin, Louis. 156
Bernie, 122, 130–34, 254
Berthomé, Jean-Pierre, 51, 283, 284
Berto, Juliet, 229
Berto, Michel, 230
Bessa-Luís, Agustina, 166, 167, 169
Bessy, Maurice, 273
The Best Years of Our Lives, 70
Bible, 73, 166, 200, 242, 245–46
The Bicycle Thief, 177
Big, 23
The Big Brass Ring (film), 274
The Big Brass Ring (screenplay), 272, 274, 292
The Big Heat, 34
The Big Money, 243
The Big Mouth, 111
Billiards at Half-Past Nine, 38
The Birdcage, 156
Bird of Paradise, 208
Birkin, Jane, 222
Bitter Victory, 254, 258
Bjørnvig, Thorkild, 284–85
Black, Jack, 132, 133, 134
Blackburn, Robin, 70
Blackwell, Otis, 84, 92
Blair, Betsy, 65
Blake, William, 95
Blanchett, Cate, 83, 92
Blind Husbands, 153
The Blind Owl, 44
Blitzstein, Marc, 128–29
Blixen, Karen, 281. See also Isak Dinesen
Blood/O Sangue, 34, 39
Blue in the Face, 86

296   Index

Blue Jasmine, 109
"Blumfeld, an Elderly Bachelor," 84, 92
Bodard, Mag, 47
Bogarde, Dirk, 217
Bogart, Humphrey, 118
Bogdanovich, Peter, 272, 275, 277, 279, 280, 286, 288, 292, 293, 294n2
La Bohème, 195
Boise, Jean, 229
Bók, Erika, 250
Böll, Heinrich, 38
Bones/Ossos, 34
Bonfanti, Antoine, 47
Bordwell, David, 58, 184, 186
Bouquet, Carole, 30
Boyer, Charles, 218
Boyhood, 122
The Box, 163, 165
Boxoffice, 198
Bradbury, Ray, 83
Brakhage, Stan, 253
Bram Stoker's Dracula, 139
Branco, Camilo Castelo, 167
Branco, Paolo, 162, 167
Braunberger, Pierre, 213
Breaking Away, 23
Breathless/A bout de souffle, 56, 139
Bresson, Robert, 47, 54, 61, 163, 173, 180–82, 210, 212, 240, 252, 259, 260
Broadcast News, 21, 22, 23, 24
Broadway Danny Rose, 109
Brod, Max, 276, 277
Broken Flowers, 88
Brooks, Albert, 24, 25, 26, 253
Brooks, James L., 5, 20–28
"Brother, Can You Spare a Dime?" 114
Brown, John, 68
Bruce, Shelbie, 27
Buñuel and King Solomon's Table, 29
Buñuel, Luis, 4, 5, 22–23, 29–31, 160, 164, 256
Burch, Noël, 184
Burger, Rudolphe, 35
Burn! 70
Burnett, Charles, 77, 253
Buscemi, Steve, 83, 84
Bush, George H. W., 196
Bush, George W., 144
Byrd, Jr., James, 15, 16
By the Law/Dura Lex, 198

Cabrini, Carlo, 175
The Caddy, 111
Caesar/Julius Caesar (stage production), 128, 129, 277, 288
Cahiers du cinéma, 181, 205, 216, 221, 223–26
Caimán Cuadernos de Cine, 211, 272

Calle Mayor/Main Street, 65, 168, 186
Can-Can, 205
The Cannibals, 165
La captive, 11, 17
Caravaggio, 37
Carax, Leos, 90, 267
Careful, 137
Carmen, 53
Caron, Leslie, 223
Carpenter, John, 4
Carrière, Jean-Claude, 30, 31,
Carrière, Mathieu, 45–46
Carringer, Robert L., 275
Carroll, Lewis., 231
Casa de Lava, 34, 39, 40
Cassavetes, John, 4, 154–55
Castelnuovo, Nino, 51
The Castle, 276
Castro, Fidel, 70, 167, 242
Céline et Julie vont en bateau, 220, 221, 223, 224, 228–29, 232
Centro Histórico, 38
Un certo giorno, 176
Cézanne, 74, 213
Chabrol, Claude, 223, 287
Une Chambre en ville, 52, 53, 57
La Chambre Verte, 52
Chandler, Jeff, 208
Chaney, Lon, 145
Chantal Akerman: Four Films, 9
Chantal Akerman, From Here, 10–11, 287
La Chant du Styrène/The Song of Styrène, 212, 213, 214
Chaplin, Charles, 4, 108, 109, 111, 114, 116, 117, 121n7
Chaplin, Geraldine, 222
Clark, Larry, 253
Chávez, César, 73
Chen, Chao-jung, 266
Chen, Jianbin, 99, 100
Chen, Joan, 99, 100
Chen, Shiang-chyi, 265, 269
Cheney, Dick, 87, 88
Cheung, Maggie, 126
Chevalier, Maurice, 117, 205
Chicago, 136
Chicago Reader, 2, 7, 81, 122, 135, 176, 177, 194, 202, 263
Chief Crazy Horse, 68
Un chien andalou, 30
Chimes at Midnight, 283
Christie, Julie, 195, 196, 197
Christopher Columbus, The Enigma, 159, 161
Chronicle of Anna Magdalena Bach, 169
Chronique d'un été, 225
Chu, Tien-wen, 191

Index   297

Clouzot, Henri-Georges, 65, 168, 186
Cinderfella, 107, 111, 116, 118
CineAction, 125
Cineaste, 99, 202
Cinema Guild (DVD label), 96, 263
CinemaScope, 136, 207, 214
Cinema Scope, (magazine) 37, 144, 145, 211
Cinematek, 41, 43, 46, 47
Cinematic Encounters: Interviews and Dialogues, 1, 2–3, 3–4, 202, 262n1
Cintra, Luís Miguel, 159
The Circle Closes, 203, 206
Citizen Kane, 38, 150, 187–88, 274–75, 276, 288, 289, 292
Clan, Wu-Tang, 84, 92
Claudel, Paul, 159, 164
Clementi, Pierre, 138
The Clock, 125
Cloquet, Ghislain, 47, 52, 212
Cocteau, Jean, 51, 54, 72, 219
Coen, Joel and Ethan, 261
Coffee and Cigarettes, 81–87, 92, 93
Coggio, Roger, 283
Coleman, Janet, 155, 156
Coleman, Ornette, 227, 229, 230
Colgate Comedy Hour, 114
Colossal Youth/Juventude em Marcha, 34, 37
Coltrane, John, 35
Come Back, Little Sheba, 108
Commentaires, 214–15
The Complete Mr. Arkadin (DVD box set), 273
Confessions of an Opium Eater, 149
Confidential Report/Mr. Arkadin, 183, 273, 277, 279, 287, 288
Connor, Bruce, 253
Conrad, Joseph, 11, 244, 273–74, 286
Conte, Richard, 207
The Convent, 159, 161, 165
Coogan, Steve, 84, 92
Cook, Adam, 20
Cooper, Gary, 128
Cooper, Lindsay, 195–96
Coppola, Francis, 108, 139, 277
Le Corbeau/The Raven, 65, 168
Costa, Pedro, 32–40, 163, 252
Costello, Lou, 89
Côte, Laurence, 222
Cotten, Joseph, 149
A Couch in New York, 19
A Countess from Hong Kong, 111
"A Country Tale," 282
Cox, Alex, 86
Cracking Up, 115, 119
The Cradle Will Rock (screenplay), 272
Criterion (DVD label), 174, 183, 214, 254, 272, 273, 282, 293

Cronenberg, David, 46
Crowe, Cameron, 261
The Crucible, 63–64
Cry of the City, 207

Daisne, Johan, 43, 44
Dale, Grover, 51
Dali, Salvador, 30
Dalio, Marcel, 203–5, 206
Damnation, 242
Damn Yankees, 116
Dance, Girl, Dance, 197
Daney, Serge, 53, 223
Daniels, Billy, 209
Dante Alighieri, 94, 166
Davis, Harriet Tubman, 68
Davis, Sonny, 131, 132
Day, Doris, 136
Day, Dorothy, 68
Day of Despair, 165, 167
The Day of the Locust, 293
Day of Wrath, 5, 58–66, 186
Days of Being Wild, 123, 126
Dazed and Confused, 123, 134
Dead Man, 81, 82, 91, 95
Deane, Hamilton, 138
The Death of Empedocles, 74
Debbaut, Denise, 42
Debra Paget, For Example, 203, 206–10
Debs, Eugene, 68
The Deep (unfinished film), 284, 286
The Defiant Ones, 192
Defining Moments in Movies, 263
De l'autre côté/From the Other Side, 10, 16–17
Delon, Alain, 88
Delvaux, André, 9, 41–48, 212
Delvaux, Paul, 45
Demetrius and the Gladiators, 207
Demy, Jacques, 5, 47, 49–57, 212
Deneuve, Catherine, 47, 50, 57, 160, 162
Denis, Claire, 212, 223, 245
De Palma, Brian, 148, 150, 238
Depp, Johnny, 95
Descartes, René, 53, 236
Descas, Alex, 85, 86
Il deserto rosso, 174, 181
De Seta, Vittorio, 178
D'est/From the East), 10, 12, 13, 14, 17
Delphy, Julie, 122, 124, 126, 127
"The Deluge from Norderney," 282
Les demoiselles de Rochefort/The Young Girls of Rochefort, 47, 49–54, 57
De Niro, Robert, 116
Deren, Maya, 256
Detto, Loredana, 172
Deux Ans Après, 50

The Devil is a Woman, 30
The Devil, Probably, 240
Devreese, Frédéric, 45
Diary of a Chambermaid, 30
Diaz, Lav, 79
Diderot, Denis, 222
Did You Know Who Fired the Gun? 67
Dieterlen, Arnaud, 35
Dietrich, Marlene, 145, 276, 282, 288
Dinesen, Isak, 281–84, 286
Dionysus in <ap>'69, 238
Discovering Orson Welles, 272
The Discreet Charm of the Bourgeoisie, 29, 30
Disquiet/Inquietude, 162, 165, 166, 167
A Distant Trumpet, 181
The Divine Comedy (film), 159, 165–67
Django Unchained, 102
Doctor Zhivago, 197–98
Dolivet, Louis, 273
Dong, 97
Doniol-Valcroze, Jacques, 229
Don Quixote (unfinished film), 272, 276, 286, 289
Donskoi, Mark, 181
Doomed Love / Amor de Perdição, 162, 165, 167–69
Dorléac, François, 47
Dos Passos, John, 68, 75, 243
Dostoevsky, Fyodor, 166, 246
Douchet, Jean, 191
Douglass, Frederick, 68
Dovzhenko, Alexander, 4, 39, 105, 181
Dowell, Pat, 139
Down by Law, 82, 83
Down There/Là-bas, 10, 11, 12, 16–18
Down with Love, 136–37, 138
Doyle, Chris, 87
Dracula: Pages from a Virgin's Diary, 136, 137, 138–40, 143
Dragon Inn, 268
Drake, Dennis, 136
"The Dreamers" (story), 282, 285
The Dreamers (unfinished film), 280–81, 282, 285
Dreyer, Carl, 6, 7, 58–66, 148, 150, 161, 186, 252
Dreyfuss, Richard, 153
Driver, Adam, 89
Driver, Sara, 253
Drouzy, Maurice, 6, 59, 62, 63
Drum, Jean and Dale M., 62
Dubliners, 83
Duelle, 88, 221, 223–26
Dumas, Alexandre, 237
Duperet, Anny, 218
Duras, Marguerite, 199, 200, 212, 233
Durgnat, Raymond, 7, 30

Dvořák, Antonin Leopold, 161
Dwoskin, Steve, 254
Dyer, Mary, 76
Dziga-Vertov, 39

Eastwood, Clint, 131
"Echoes," 282, 284, 285
L'eclisse, 174
Eco, Umberto, 141
Edison, Thomas, 85
Efron, Zac, 128
Egoyan, Atom, 46
Eisenstein, Sergei, 39, 65, 82, 215
Ekberg, Anita, 203
The Elephant Man, 195
E.L.F. (DVD label), 69
Ellington, Duke, 129
Eminem, 200
English, Rose, 195, 196
Eraserhead, 195
The Errand Boy, 115, 119
Eshley, Norman, 283
Esquire, 174
Essential Cinema, 29, 81, 136
O Estado do Mondo, 34
Europa 2005—27 octobre, 74
Eurydice, 219
Evans, Walker, 16
Evers, Medgar, 68
Everybody Wants Some!! 122, 134
Everything That Rises Must Converge, 84
L'Express, 175
Exterior Night, 203, 254
The Exterminating Angel, 31

Fabian, Françoise, 45, 56, 229
Face, 263
Falk, Peter, 154, 155
The Family Jewels, 111
Family Plot, 150
Fandor Keyframe, 202
La Fanfare a cent ans, 48
Fantômas, 42, 45
Farahani, Golshifteh, 89
Farber, Manny, 1, 3
Far from Afghanistan, 67, 78
Far from Vietnam, 67
Farzad, Mohammadreza, 259
Faulkner, William, 15, 39, 91, 105, 181, 241, 243–49, 273, 292
(F)au(x)tobiographies, 203
Feder, Chris Welles, 274, 275
Fejos, Paul, 253
Fellini, Federico, 47
La femme et le pantin, 30
La femme mariée, 178

Ferreira, Leonardo Luiz, 10
Feuillade, Louis, 212, 237
F for Fake, 273, 280, 282, 283, 286–88, 291, 293
I fidanzati/The Fiances, 174–81
The Fifth Empire: Yesterday as Today, 162, 165, 166
Film Comment, 20, 41–42, 58, 67, 157, 205, 233, 236, 241, 272
Film.Factory, 241, 253–62
Filming Othello, 278, 293
Filming The Trial (unfinished film), 278
Filmkrant, 32
Film Quarterly, 67, 99, 262n1
Film: The Front Line 1983, 4, 202
Fincher, David, 261
"Fine and Mellow," 33
Finney, Albert, 223
First Reformed, 148
Fitzgerald, F. Scott, 292, 293
Flaherty, Robert, 98, 99, 133
Flaming Creatures, 144
Flaubert, Gustave, 285
Foch, Nina, 118
Foolish Wives, 6, 153, 253, 258
Forché, Carolyn, 79
Ford, John, 21, 34, 39, 159, 254, 291
For Example, the Philippines, 77, 78
Fortini/Cani, 74, 240
Foster, Norman, 293
Foundas, Scott, 170
Found Footage (magazine), 135, 202
The Fountainhead, 216
The Fountain of Youth, 284
Fox, David, 142
Fradelić, Sunčica, 256
Frampton, Hollis, 253
Francisca, 162, 165–69
Frankenstein (novel), 90
French, Renee, 85
Frodon, Jean-Michel, 216, 256
From the East, Bordering on Fiction, 11, 13–14
From the East/D'est, 10–14, 17
From the Journals of Jean Seberg, 202, 203, 206
From the Other Side/De l'autre côté), 10, 11, 12, 16–17
Fujiwara, Chris, 5, 110, 113, 115, 120, 263
Fuller, Samuel, 42, 182
Funny Face, 136
Furneaux, Yvonne, 208

Ganić, Emina, 255
Garchik, Jacob, 146
The Garden of Eden, 287
Garrel, Thierry, 256
Gassman, Vittorio, 43
Gazette du cinéma, 224

The General Line, 82
Genesis, 242
Gentleman Prefer Blondes, 1, 117, 208
Gertrud, 58, 59, 181
Ghost Dog: The Way of the Samurai, 81, 82, 85, 90, 91, 92
Gianvito, John, 67–80, 257
Gielgud, John, 217
Ginsberg, Allen, 89
Give a Girl a Break, 221
Les Glaneurs et la Glaneuse, 50
Godard, Jean-Luc, 33, 47, 49, 51, 52, 54, 120n1, 196, 205, 211, 218, 221, 223, 224, 226, 237, 252, 281
Godfather films, 5, 145, 217
Going Home/Xiao Shan, 97
The Gold Diggers, 194–98, 199
Gold Diggers of 1933, 197
Golden Eighties, 11, 19
Goldman, Emma, 68
The Gold Rush, 197
Golestan, Ebrahim, 77
Gone with the Wind, 155, 187
Gonzales, Thia, 71–72
Goodbye Cinema, Hello Cinephilia, 5, 29, 58, 96
Goodbye, Dragon Inn, 268, 271
Goodman, Benny, 129
Goodman, Paul, 68
Good Morning/Ohayo, 55, 183, 188–93
Gorin, Jean-Pierre, 213
Gorman, Cliff, 91
Gracq, Julien, 46, 47
The Graduate, 154
La Grande Illusion, 204
Grant, Cary, 128, 150
Gravity's Rainbow, 227
Greed, 6, 47, 146, 153, 154, 156, 167, 239, 253, 258
Greed (book), 239
The Green Fog, 145–51
Gregor, Ulrich, 256
Gregorio, Eduardo De, 220, 225
Griffith, D. W., 181, 182, 254
Grodin, Charles, 154
Une grosse legume, 273
Grosso, Manuel, 256
Grotowski, Jerzy, 238
Guernica, 213, 214
La Guerre est finie, 212
Gulczynski, Grant, 254
Gunn, Dan, 247
Guys and Dolls, 133
GZA, 84, 86, 92

Haefele, Marc, 220
"Haffner" Symphony, 259–60

Hagakure, or The Way of the Samurai, 90, 91
Hallelujah, I'm a Bum, 53
Hamlet, 90
The Hamlet, 244
Hansbury, Lorraine, 68
Happy Together, 123
Harden, Jacques, 50
Hard Labor on the Douro River, 161
Hardly Working, 111, 115, 117
Harrington, Curtis, 287
Hasumi, Shigehiko, 6, 186–87, 190–91
Hauer, Rutger, 179
Hauptmann, Gerhard, 125
Haut/bas/fragile (*Up, Down, Fragile*), 221, 223
Hawke, Ethan, 122, 124, 126, 127
Hawkins, Coleman, 33
Hawks, Howard, 4, 39, 204, 224, 253, 291
Hay, Alexandra, 56
Haynes, Todd, 253
Heartbreak Kid, The, 6, 153, 154, 155, 156
Heart of Darkness (film project), 272–74, 277, 286
The Heart of The World, 136, 137, 139
Hedayat, Sadegh, 44
Heinrich, André, 214
Hellzapoppin', 197
Hemingway, Ernest, 83, 286, 287, 291
Henderson, Shirley, 201
A Hen in the Wind, 183–88
Herbert, Zbigniew, 260
Les herbes folles/Wild Grass, 212, 214, 218–19
"The Heroine," 282
Herrigel, Eugen, 85
Herrmann, Bernard, 147
Heslin, David, 238
Hickenlooper, George, 274
Hiddleston, Tom, 89
Highlander Folk School, 76
Hill, Roger, 276, 292
Hirano, Kyoko, 184
Hiroshima, mon amour, 199–200, 212, 214
Histoire des treize, 228
Hitchcock, Alfred, 4, 17, 42, 77, 82, 135, 147–51, 212, 218
Hitler, Adolf, 42, 206
Hitler in Hollywood, 42
Hoax, 286. See also *F for Fake*
Hobsbawm, Eric, 137, 158, 170
Hoffman, Dustin, 154
Hofmann, Michael, 179
Hogan, Mike, 83
The Hole, 263, 265, 267
Holiday, Billie, 33
Hollandsworth, Skip, 130–32, 134
Hollywood or Bust, 106, 120n3
Hollywood Reporter, 5, 87, 199

Homer, 141, 245–46
Home Vision Entertainment (DVD label), 152
Hopper, Dennis, 287
Hopper, Edward, 13
Horse Money, 36–40
Hou, Hsiao-hsien, 4, 97, 191
Hou, Lijun, 100
Houseman, John, 129
Howard, Cy, 112
How Do You Know, 21, 22, 24, 26, 27
How to Marry a Millionaire, 136
Hudson, Rock, 136, 146, 149, 151, 202–4, 206
Hughes, John, 233
Hugo, Victor, 237
Hui, Ann, 265
Hunt, Helen, 22, 26
Hunter, Holly, 24
"The Hunting of the Snark," 231
Las hurdes, 30
Hurlevent/Wuthering Heights, 225
Hurt, John, 90, 93
Hurt, William, 24
Huston, John, 254, 288, 290, 291, 292
Hutchinson, Anne, 73, 75

Ida, Akiko, 185
I, Dalio—or The Rules of the Game, 203–5, 206
I Don't Want to Sleep Alone, 263
I'll Do Anything, 20–25, 27–28
The Illustrated Man, 83
I'm Going Home, 162, 165, 167
The Immortals, 166, 168
The Immortal Story (film), 272, 281–86
"The Immortal Story" (story), 281, 282, 285
Impostors, 202
Improvisation, 33
The Indian Tomb, 209
India Song, 240
Inglourious Basterds, 101, 252
An Injury to One, 67
In My Father's Shadow: A Daughter Remembers Orson Welles, 274
In Our Time, 83
In Public, 97
Inquietude/Disquiet, 162, 165, 166, 167
Les Inrockuptibles, 226, 227
In the Company of Men, 65
In the Mood for Love, 123
In Vanda's Room, 37
Ishtar, 152–55, 156, 196
It's Impossible to Learn to Plow by Reading Books, 123
Ivan the Terrible, Part 2, 65
Ivens, Joris, 291
Ivory, James, 161
I Walked with a Zombie, 34, 254

I Want to Go Home, 212
I Was Born, But . . ., 183, 190–92

Jacques Demy ou les racines du rêve, 51
Jaglom, Henry, 116, 287
Japón, 256
Jarman, Derek, 261
Jarmusch, Jim, 4, 5, 6, 81–95, 254, 261
Jaws, 145
Jeanne Dielman, 23 Quai de Commerce, 1080 Bruxelles, 10, 11
Jeanne la Pucelle/Joan the Maid, 222, 225
Jean Renoir, le patron, 222, 225
Jerry and Me, 110, 254
Jerry Lewis, 110, 113, 120n2
Jessel, George, 287
Je t'aime, je t'aime, 212
Jiang, Wu, 104
Jia Zhangke, 96–105, 181
The Job/Il posto, 171–79, 181
John Garfield, 203
"Johnny Guitar," 36
Johnson, Evan, 145
Johnson, Galen, 145
Johnson, Randal, 162–63, 164
jonathanrosenbaum.net, 9, 29, 42, 220
Jones, Kent, 264, 267
Jones, Mother, 68
Jonze, Spike, 261
Joon-ho, Bong, 261
Joudet, Murielle, 23
Jourdan, Louis, 205, 208
Journey to the West, 5, 263, 269
Jousse, Thierry, 191
Joyce, James, 83, 124, 125, 201
Juatco, Teofilo "Boojie," 79, 80
Ju Dou, 65
Jules et Jim, 46, 52
"Just in Time," 126

Kael, Pauline, 5, 54, 205, 217, 272, 274–75, 289
Kafka, Franz, 6, 40, 44, 84, 92, 276–81
Kalfon, Jean-Pierre, 222, 226, 240
Kalmus, Natalie, 233
Kaplow, Robert, 128, 129
Karagheuz, Hermine, 231
Karajan, Herbert von, 259–60
Karp, Josh, 287, 291, 294n1, 294n3
Kauffmann, Stanley, 156
Kaufman, George S., 113
Kavner, Julie, 25
Kazan, Zoe, 128
Keaton, Buster, 109, 267
Keats, John, 245
Kehr, Dave, 23, 177
Kelemen, Fred, 256

Kelly, Gene, 25, 47
Kern, Jerome, 144
Kezich, Tullio, 179
Khoshbakht, Ehsan, 211
Kiarostami, Abbas, 4, 5–6, 251, 252
King, Carole, 23
King, Hu, 103, 268
The King of Comedy, 116
Kinski, Klaus, 125
Kissinger, Henry, 292
Kiss Me, Stupid, 159
Koch, Kenneth, 93
Kodar, Oja, 274, 280–81, 282, 285, 288–92
Kois, Dan, 252
Koran, 200
Korda, Alexander, 282
Kramer, Keja Ho, 254
Kramer, Robert, 72, 192
Kramer, Stanley, 192
Krasznahorkai, László, 241–49, 250, 251, 257–58
Krizan, Kim, 126
Kronos Quartet, 146
Kubrick, Stanley, 108
Kudláček, Martina, 256
Kuleshov, Lev, 151, 204
Kurant, Willy, 283–84
Kurosawa, Akira, 185

Labarthe, André S., 222, 257
Là-bas/Down There, 10, 11, 12, 16–18
LaBute, Neil, 65
The Ladies Man, 107, 117, 118, 119
The Lady from Shanghai, 146, 290
Lady in the Lake, 226
Lafayette, Madame de, 159
Laffont, Colette, 195
Lafont, Bernadette, 229, 240
Lane, Anthony, 136, 145
Lang, Fritz, 4, 34, 207, 209, 221, 222, 224, 233, 236, 237
Langdon, Harry, 109
Lanzmann, Claude, 214
Last Chants for a Slow Dance, 67, 256
Last Dance, 265
Last Flag Flying, 122
The Last Picture Show, 268
Last Year at Marienbad/L'année dernière à Marienbad, 212, 214, 218
Late Spring, 183, 184
Laughton, Charles, 34
Lavant, Denis, 269
Leachman, Cloris, 26
Leaming, Barbara, 275, 289
Léaud, Jean-Pierre, 226, 228, 229, 232, 239, 240

Ledoux, Jacques, 42
Lee, Cinqué, 83, 84, 92
Lee, Joie, 83, 84, 92
Lee, Kang-sheng, 265, 267, 269, 270
Lee, Kevin B., 97, 99, 238, 257
Lee, Spike, 77, 84, 92
The Legend of the Holy Drinker, 176, 178–80, 182n5
Legrand, Michel, 47, 51, 293
Leigh, Janet, 119, 280
Leisen, Mitchell, 209
Leoni, Tea, 24, 26
Lerdorff-Rye, Presben, 60
The Letter, 159, 160, 165, 167
Let Us Now Praise Famous Men, 16
Leung, Tony, 126
Levant, Oscar, 26
Leve, Samuel, 128
Lewis, Jerry, 5, 20, 106–21, 154
Lewton, Val, 37, 39, 108, 254, 258
Life of Riley, 212, 217
Light in August, 243–47, 249n6, 273, 292
Lim, Dennis, 228
The Limits of Control, 5, 81, 87–88, 90, 91, 93
Linklater, Richard, 4, 5, 122–34, 254
Lisbon, 208
Lives of Performers, 198
Living It Up, 107, 120n3
The Living Theatre, 238, 239
Lloyd, Harold, 109
Lockwood, Gary, 56
Loeb, Claire Spark, 73
Logan, Carter, 93
Lola, 50, 51, 52, 54, 56, 57
Lola (online magazine, lolajournal.com), 226
Lonesome, 253, 254, 258
The Long Voyage Home, 254
Lonsdale, Michel, 229, 234, 240
Lopate, Philip, 94
Los Angeles Plays Itself, 145, 253, 258
"Louise," 117
Louÿs, Pierre, 30
The Love Bug, 146
"Love Lifted Me," 132
Love Me Tender, 207
Love Me Tonight, 53
*Love on the Ground/L'amour par te*rre, 221, 225
Lover Come Back, 136
The Lovers, 192
Lu, Yi-ching, 269
Lubitsch, Ernst, 22–23, 212, 218
Lu Hsiao-ling, 265
Lu Luping, 99
Lumière brothers, 98, 99, 133
Lund, John, 112
Luscri, Chris, 238

Lynch, David, 138, 181, 195
Lynn, Diana, 112, 118

Macbeth (Tarr video), 250–51
Macbeth (Welles films), 272
Macdonald, Dwight, 174, 218
Mackenzie, David, 261
MacLaine, Shirley, 26, 111, 133
Madame Bovary, 209, 285
Maddin, Guy, 4, 5, 46, 135–51
Made in USA, 218
Madman (DVD label), 58
The Mad Songs of Fernanda Hussein, 67–68, 69–73, 76, 77, 78, 257
Magic Mirror, 165, 169
Magnani, Anna, 108
The Magnificent Ambersons, 276, 283, 288
Magritte, René, 45
Mahler, Gustav, 87, 138
Mailer, Norman, 217
Main Street/Calle Mayor, 65, 168
Malden, Karl, 147, 149
Malesevic, Stefan, 260
Malick, Terrence, 75
Malle, Louis, 192, 212
Malkovich, John, 161, 162
Malone, Dorothy, 111
Mandaroux, Jean, 279
Mandrake the Magician, 218
The Man from London, 243, 250
Mangolte, Babette, 18, 195
Mankiewicz, Herman J., 275
Manniez, Véronique, 225
Man of la Mancha, 289
Man's Favorite Sport, 181
The Man Who Disappeared/Amerika, 276
The Man Who Had His Hair Cut Short, 41, 43, 44, 48
Margulies, Ivone, 18
Marie et Julien, 223, 225, 226
Marie, légende hongroise, 254
Marignac, Martine, 225
Marker, Chris, 52, 150, 211, 212, 214–15, 216
Marlowe, Christopher, 89, 90
Marnie, 181
Marshall, Frank, 286, 293
Marshall, Penny, 23
The Martian Chronicles, 83
Martin, Adrian, 169, 226, 237–38, 263
Martin, Dean, 107, 111, 112, 113, 115, 117, 118, 159
Martin, Minda, 67
Martinelli, Elsa, 280
Marvin, Lee, 85, 87, 88, 90
The Mary Tyler Moore Show, 23, 24
Masculin féminin, 178
Maslin, Janet, 197

Index 303

Mastroianni, Chiara, 159
Mastroianni, Marcello, 162
May, Elaine, 6, 108, 152–56, 196, 254
May, Mathilda, 56
Mayehoff, Eddie, 117
Mayer, Louis B., 107
Mayer, Sophie, 196
Mazursky, Paul, 287
McBride, Joseph, 292, 293
McCain, John, 71
McCambridge, Mercedes, 287
McCarthy, Joseph, 64
McCarthy, Todd, 88
McConaughey, Matthew, 133
McKay, Christian, 128
McKinney, Mark, 142
McMillan, Ross, 142
McMillan & Wife, 146, 149
McTeague, 6, 47, 239
Mead, Taylor, 86–87
Me and Orson Welles, 127–30
Medeiros, Maria de, 141, 142
Mekas, Jonas, 181
Mélo, 212, 214
Melville, Jean-Pierre, 210, 284
Mengus, Jean-Luc, 203, 208
Mercer, David, 216, 219
Merhar, Stanisla, 11
Merry-Go-Round, 223, 224, 225, 240
The Merry Widow, 153
Meshes of the Afternoon, 256
Metropolis, 221
O Meu Caso, 166
Miao Tien, 265
Michel, Marc, 50
Michiels, Ivo, 43
"Midnight in the Garden of East Texas," 130
Midnight in the Garden of Good and Evil, 131
Mikey and Nicky, 6, 152–56, 254, 258
Mili, Gjon, 33
The Milky Way, 30
Miller, Arthur, 63–64
Milne, Tom, 47, 48, 63, 120n1, 179
Milosz, Czeslaw, 260
Mimesis, 245
Minnelli, Vincente, 125
Miss Lonelyhearts, 246
Mitchell, Cameron, 187
Mitchell, Eric, 86
Mizoguchi, Kenji, 174, 185
Mizukami, Reiko, 185
Model Shop, 50, 52, 54, 55, 56, 57
Modern Times, 243
Molina, Alfred, 84, 92
Molina, Angela, 30
"Momento" (music video), 160
Mon cas/*My Case*, 160, 165, 166, 167, 168

Le Monde, 216, 224
Monk, Thelonious, 162
Mon oncle d'Amérique, 212, 214
Monroe, Marilyn, 56, 117, 208
Montand, Yves, 43, 44, 56
Monteiro, Helder Prista, 166
Montez, Maria, 207
Monthly Film Bulletin, 58, 182n1, 209
Montparnasse 19, 237
Monty, Ib, 59
Moonfleet, 226
Moreau, Jeanne, 50, 276, 280, 283
Moretti, Michèle, 229
Morgan! 216
Mori, Paola, 277
Morin, Edgar, 225
Morrissey, Paul, 4
The Mother of a River, 166
Moullet, Luc, 77, 216, 221
The Moviegoer Who Knew Too Much, 203
Movie Mutations: The Changing Face of World Cinema, 169–70, 263
Movie Wars, 255
Movin, Lisbeth, 60, 66
Moving Image Source, 122, 211
Moving Places, 1, 208
Mozart, Wolfgang Amadeus, 259–26
Mr. Arkadin/Confidential Report (film), 183, 273, 277, 279, 287, 288
Mr. Arkadin (novel), 273
The Munekata Sisters, 186
Mungiu, Cristian, 65
Murawski, Bob, 286, 293
Muriel, 38, 214, 218
Murnau, F. W., 35–36, 140
Murray, Bill, 84, 87, 88, 92
Murrow, Edward R., 119
Music & Literature, 241
The Music Man, 133
My Friend Irma, 106, 111, 112
My Friend Irma Goes West, 111, 112, 113
My New Friends, 265
Le mystère de l'atelier quinze, 214
Mystery Train, 82, 83

Nanook of the North, 98–99, 133
Naremore, James, 99, 275, 291, 294n4
Nasset, Daniel M., 3
Ne Change Rien, 5, 32–36
Négroni, Jean, 215
Neibar, James L., 121nn10–11
Neiiendam, Sigrid, 61
Neill, Sam, 201
The Neon Wilderness, 83
Ne touches pas la hache/*The Duchess of Langeais*, 225
Neville, Morgan, 287

A New Leaf, 153, 154, 155
News from Home, 12
The Newton Boys, 123, 131, 134, 156
The New Yorker, 54, 145
The New York Review of Books, 274
The New York Times, 71, 197, 199, 228, 252
Niagara, 208
Nice—À Propos de Jean Vigo, 164
Nichols, Mike, 154, 156
Nicholson, Jack, 22, 24, 25, 27
Nietzsche, Friedrich, 166, 249
Night and Day, 19
Night and Fog, 212, 213, 214
Night of the Demon, 34
The Night of the Hunter, 34
Night on Earth, 82
Nilsson, Josefine Bernardine, 59
No Country for Old Men, 109
No Home Movie, 9, 12
Noiret, Philippe, 284
Nolte, Nick, 20
No, or the Vainglory of Command, 165, 166, 170
Noroît, 220, 223–27, 240
Norris, Frank, 6
North by Northwest, 150
(nostalgia), 253, 258
Nostromo, 244, 273
Notes on Cinematography, 260
Not on the Lips, 212, 214
Not Reconciled, 38
La notte, 174
Novak, Kim, 147, 150, 151
Nugent, Marjorie, 130–32, 133
The Nun/La réligieuse, 222, 224
The Nutty Professor, 107, 111, 113, 115, 118

O'Brien, Edmond, 287
O'Connor, Flannery, 83–84, 156, 260
O'Connor, Sinéad, 23
October, 82
Oda, Kaori, 258
The Odyssey, 245
L'Oeuvre en noir/The Abyss, 43, 48
Ogier, Bulle, 46, 88, 160, 222, 229, 232, 240
O'Hara, John, 273, 292, 293
Ohayo/Good Morning, 55, 183, 188–93
Okuda, Ted, 121nn10–11
"The Old Chevalier," 282
Old Testament, 245
Oliveira, Manoel de, 4, 5, 157–70
Ollier, Claude, 218
Olmi, Ermanno, 4, 171–82
One A.M., 254
One-Man Band, 281, 282
One More Time, 111
One Night, a Train/Un soir, un train, 41, 43, 44, 47

Only Lovers Left Alive, 89, 91, 92
On the Waterfront, 107
Ordet, 58, 59, 148, 169
Orlando, 197
Orphée, 219
Orson Welles at Work, 283
Othello (film), 277, 278, 279, 287, 293
The Other Side of the Wind, 272, 280, 283, 286–94
Our Stars, 203
Out 1, 77, 220, 221, 223–26, 227–40, 252
Out 1: Spectre, 224, 228–36, 239, 240
Out of the Past, 210
Ozu, Yasujiro, 5, 6, 49, 54–55, 183–93, 233

Padgett, Ron, 94
Paes, João, 166, 168
Paget, Debra, 203, 206–10
Paine, Thomas, 68
Pakula, Alan J., 23
Palmer, Lilli, 288
Palmo, Holly Gent and Vincent, 128
Palomero, Pilar, 256, 260
Panseri, Sandro, 172, 173
Papas, Irene, 162
Papatakis, Nico, 181
Parade, 33
Paradise Now, 239
Paramour, 35
Les Parapluies de Cherbourg, 50–55
Paris Belongs To Us/Paris nous appartient, 220, 221, 224, 228
Paris by Night (film project), 282
Parker, Charlie, 33, 35
Parker, Junior, 84, 92
Parks, Rosa, 75–76
Parolini, Marilù, 225
Parronaud, Vincent, 65
Parsi, Jacques, 159, 163
Party, 165
Pasolini, Pier Paolo, 177, 238
Passing Through, 253
The Past and the Present, 164
Paterson, 81, 88–95
Patrício, António, 166
The Patsy, 115
Paul et Virginie, 285
Paul Gaughin, 213, 214
Pavese, Cesare, 77
Paxinou, Katina, 277
Peau d'Âne, 50, 53, 54
Pedersdotter, Anne, 60, 63
Pederssøn, Absalon, 60
Peña, Richard, 170
Penn, Arthur, 108
A People's History of the United States, 73, 77n6
Peranson, Mark, 37, 38, 138

Index   305

The Performance Group, 238
Perkins, Anthony, 278, 280
Permanent Vacation, 92
Perrin, Jacques, 57
Persepolis, 65–66
Persona, 197
Peters, Jean, 207
Le Petit Soldat, 52
The Phantom of Liberty, 30
Phénix, 225
Piaf, Edith, 56
Picasso, Pablo, 291
Piccoli, Michel, 57, 160, 162
Pickpocket/Xiao Wu, 97, 99
Pierrot le fou, 120
Pillow Talk, 136
Pirandello, Luigi, 222
Pistol Opera, 192, 262n2
Pitts, Zasu, 154
Placing Movies, 1, 58, 167
Les Plages d'Agnès, 50
Platform, 96, 97, 99, 101
Plath, Sylvia, 9, 13
Platoon, 154
Pocahontas, 292
Poe, Amos, 86
Poe, Edgar Allen, 109
"The Poet," 284
Point Blank, 87, 88, 90
Poitier, Sidney, 149
Polanski, Roman, 213
Le Pont du Nord, 224
Pop, Iggy, 86, 89
Porto of My Childhood, 165, 166
Positif, 107
Il posto/The Job, 171–79, 181
Potemkin, 82
Potter, Sally, 5, 194–201, 261
Pound, Ezra, 246
Pour finir encore et autres foirades/Fizzles, 166
Powell, Michael, 140
The Power of Emotions, 198
Presley, Elvis, 84, 92, 107, 108, 109, 200
Price, Vincent, 149
Primary Colors, 156
Prince, 23
The Princess of Clèves, 159
Princess of the Nile, 207
Private Fears in Public Places, 212
Privett, Ray, 70
Profit Motive and the Whispering Wind, 67–68, 69, 70, 73–76, 77, 79
Promenade, 164
Prometheus Bound, 230, 238, 239
Proust, Marcel, 11, 229
Providence, 5, 211, 212, 214, 216–17, 219

Pryor, Richard, 254
Psycho, 82, 280
Puccini, Giacomo, 195
La Putain respectueuse, 15
Pynchon, Thomas, 84, 156, 227, 246

Queen Christina, 197
Queen Kelly, 155
Queneau, Raymond, 214
Quinn, Anthony, 108

Rabal, Francisco, 31
Radziwilowicz, Jerzy, 223
Raft, George, 119
The Rainmaker, 108
Raise the Red Lantern, 65
Ramsey, Lynne, 261
Rand, Ayn, 215
Randall, Tony, 136
Random, Bob, 288
Ranvaud, Don, 179, 182n1
Rappaport, Mark, 4, 5, 136, 202–10
Rashomon, 90
The Raven/Le Corbeau, 65, 168
Ray, Nicholas, 4, 34, 36, 39, 182, 254
Rayns, Tony, 48, 104, 209
Real Life, 253, 258
Rear Window, 17, 150
Rebels of the Neon God, 263, 265, 266, 267
Rechtshaffen, Michael, 87
Redgrave, Michael, 277
"Red Hollywood" (essay), 70, 76n1
The Red Shoes, 1976
Reed, Peyton, 136
Régio, José, 166, 169
La règle du jeu, 204
Reichardt, Kelly, 252
El-Rei Sebastião, 166
Reisz, Karel, 216
La réligieuse/The Nun, 222, 224
Rembrandt, 66
Rendez-vous à Bray/Appointment in Bray, 42, 43, 45, 46–47, 48
Les Rendez-vous d'Anna, 19
Resnais, Alain, 4, 5, 45, 47, 51, 52, 178, 199, 200, 211–19, 226, 252
Reville, Alma, 42
Rexroth, Kenneth, 6
Rey, Fernando, 30, 31
Reygadas, Carlos, 255, 256, 261
Reynaud, Bérénice, 267
Rice, Bill, 86–87
Rice, Elmer, 163
Rich, Ruby, 195
Richard, Nathalie, 222
Richard Pryor Live in Concert, 254

Richardson, Joely, 24
Richie, Donald, 184, 187, 188
Riding, Laura, 136, 141
Riding in Cars with Boys, 23
Rigano, Joe, 85
Riis, Jacob, 40
Rite of Spring (film), 163, 165
The River, 263, 264–67
The River's Edge, 209
Rivette, Jacques, 4, 21, 52, 77, 88, 178, 220–40, 252
Rivette: Texts and Interviews, 220, 226
Robeson, Paul, 68
Rock Hudson's Home Movies, 136, 202, 203, 206
Rodriguez, E. J., 83, 85
Rohmer, Eric, 125, 223, 231
"Le Roi Cophétua" (story), 46
The Rolling Stones, 33
Roose, Thorkild, 60
The Rose Tattoo, 108
Ross, Alex, 284
Rossellini, Isabella, 141
Rossellini, Roberto, 224
Roth, Joseph, 178, 179
Rouch, Jean, 47, 72, 225, 237
Rouge (online magazine, rouge.com.au), 233
Rousseau, Henri, 181
Rousseau, Jean-Jacques, 127
Routine Pleasures, 213
RR, 74, 75
Rudd, Paul, 26, 27
Ruiz, Raúl, 31, 158, 164
Runyon, Damon, 112
Rymsza, Filip Jan, 286, 293
Ryu, Chishu, 186, 189
RZA, 84, 86, 92

The Sacred Beasts (film project), 291. See also *The Other Side of the Wind*
The Saddest Music in the World, 135, 141–45
Sadowska, Małgorzata, 258
Saeed-Vafa, Mehrnaz, 110, 254
Safe, 254, 258
The Saga of Anatahan, 218, 254
Sailor Beware, 107
Saint, Eva Marie, 150
Saint-Pierre, Jacques-Henri Bernadin de, 285
Salazar, António de Oliveira, 161, 163
Salinger, J. D., 156
Salkind, Alexander and Michael, 277
Same Old Song, 212
Samuels, Charles Thomas, 173, 175, 176, 182nn2–4, 182n8
Sandrelli, Stefania, 162
Sartre, Jean-Paul, 15
Sátántangó (film), 168, 241–49, 250, 251, 257

Sátántangó (novel), 241–49
Satie, Erik, 284
The Satin Slipper, 159, 164
Sato, Tadao, 187, 187
Satrapi, Marjane, 65
Saturday Night Fever, 115
Saturday Night Live, 83
Saulnier, Jacques, 217
Saura, Carlos, 29
Scarface, 253
Scènes de la vie parallèle, 223
The Scenic Route, 209, 210
Schechner, Richard, 238
Schiffmann, Suzanne, 228
Schmidlin, Rick, 32
Schneider, Romy, 280
Schrader, Paul, 148, 150
School Days, 48
The School of Rock, 123
Scorsese, Martin, 108, 115, 137, 281
Scott, Dustin, 72
Screen, 196
The Searchers, 41
Seberg, Jean, 202, 203, 204, 206
Sécret defense, 222, 225
The Secret Life of Moving Shadows, 203
Segovia, Andrès, 258, 260
Seligman, Craig, 275
Send Me No Flowers, 136
Sergeant Rutledge, 34
Seven Against Thebes, 230, 238
The Seventh Victim, 221, 226, 254
Shakespeare, William, 118, 128, 161, 198, 281
Shapiro, David, 93
Sheen, Martin, 279
Shepherd, Cybill, 154
She Wore a Yellow Ribbon, 34
Shoah, 213–14
Shooting Scripts, 2, 259
Shuck, John, 151
Sicilia! 34
Sight and Sound, 58, 150, 220, 241
Signoret, Simone, 56, 204
The Silence of the Lambs, 109
Silva, Henry, 85, 91
Silveira, Leonor, 159, 162
Silver, Joel, 26
The Silver Screen: Color Me Lavender, 203
Simon, Neil, 154
Simon & Garfunkel, 154
Simonds, Carioline, 206
Simone, Nina, 126
The Simpsons, 23
Sinatra, Frank, 111, 219
Singin' in the Rain, 107
"Sing, Sing, Sing," 129

Index   307

Slacker, 123
Slow Learner, 84
Slumdog Millionaire, 252
The Smiling Madame Beudet, 197
Smith, Jack, 144
Smoking/No Smoking, 212
Snow, Michael, 168
Socrates, 261
Un soir, un train/One Night, a Train, 41, 43, 44, 47
Sojcher, Frédéric, 42
Soledad (painting), 45
"The Song is You," 144
"Song of Myself," 158
Sontag, Susan, 5, 6, 217
Soon-Mi, Yoo, 67
Sorel, Jean, 160
The Souls of Black Folk, 90
The Sound and the Fury, 244, 246
The Sound of Jazz, 33
Sousa, John Phillip, 209
South/Sud, 10, 11, 12, 14
Spanglish, 21, 22, 23, 24, 26, 27
Le Spectateur qui en savait trop, 203
Spielberg, Steven, 137, 153
Spione, 209
Sqürl, 93
Stardust Memories, 43
Stars and Stripes Forever, 209
Star Trek IV, 146
Star Wars, 145, 252
The State of Things, 198
Les Statues meurent aussi/Statues Also Die, 52, 211, 212–16
Stavisky . . ., 212, 218
Stephens, Uriah Smith, 76
Sternberg, Josef von, 30, 140, 144, 218, 254
Stevens, Brad, 229
Stewart, James, 149, 150
Stewart, Paul, 287
Still Life, 96, 97, 99, 102, 103
Stoker, Bram, 138, 139
Stone, I. F., 73
Stoneback, Shane, 93
The Stooge, 117
The Story of Marie and Julien, 225, 227
The Story of the Last Chrysanthemums, 174
Stranger Than Paradise, 82, 85
Strasberg, Susan, 289
Straub-Huillet (Jean-Marie Straub & Danièle Huillet), 13, 34, 38, 39, 74, 163, 213, 233
Stravinsky, Igor, 179
Stray Dogs, 5, 263, 268–71
Street Scene, 163
Strode, Woody, 34

Stroheim, Erich von, 4, 6, 47, 108, 140, 152–57, 239, 252–54, 258
Strong, Benjamin, 76
The Struggle, 254
StudioCanal, 30, 272
SubUrbia, 123
Sud/South, 10, 11, 12, 14
Sugimura, Haruko, 189
Summer and Smoke, 108
Sunrise, 36
Sunset Boulevard, 210
Suzuki, Seijun, 192, 262n2
"Suzy," 166
Svendsen, Clara, 283
Svierjier, Anna, 61
Sweet Exorcism, 38
Swinton, Tilda, 88, 89, 93, 256, 260–61
Szirtes, George, 242, 249n3
Szymborska, Wislawa, 260

Taft, William Howard, 79
Take the Money and Run, 109
Tales from the Gimli Hospital, 137
A Talking Picture, 160, 162, 165
Tamiroff, Akim, 277
Tanaka, Kinuyo, 184
Tape, 123, 124
Tarafal, 34
Tarantino, Quentin, 101–2
Tarkovsky, Andrei, 75, 77n5, 252
Tarr, Béla, 4, 5, 241–62
Tashlin, Frank, 49, 54, 55, 110–11, 120, 214
Tati, Jacques, 33, 42, 109, 180–81, 182, 189, 267
Taxi, 23
Taxi Driver, 103, 147
Tchalgadjieff, Stéphane, 225, 234, 235, 240
Téchiné, André, 224
Il tempo si è fermato, 176
The Ten Commandments, 146, 207
The Tender Trap, 136
Terms of Endearment, 21, 22, 23–24, 26
Tesla, Nikola, 84, 85
Thalberg, Irving G., 153, 154
Tharp, Twyla, 23
That Obscure Object of Desire, 29–30, 31
That's My Boy, 109, 112, 118
They Caught the Ferry, 58
They Had it Coming, 67
This is Orson Welles, 272, 294n2
This Spanish Earth, 291
Thomas, François, 217, 283, 284
Thomas Gordeyev, 181
Thompson, Peter, v, 2–3, 77, 194, 258–60, 262n1
Thomson, David, 5, 21–23, 129, 274
Thoreau, Henry David, 68, 75, 246

Thornton, Leslie, 254
Three on a Couch, 115, 119
Thriller, 195
Thurman, Judith, 284–85
Ticket of No Return/Bildnis Einer Trinkerin, 179
Tiede, Bernie, 130–32, 133
The Tiger of Bengal, 209
Tih-Minh, 220, 237
Tito, Josip Broz, 257
Tobin, Dan, 292
To Have and Have Not, 204
Tokyo Story, 49, 54
Toles, George, 135, 141, 144
Tomorrow We Move, 19
Too Early, Too Late, 13, 74
Touch of Evil, 32, 145, 168, 257, 272, 276, 277, 280, 282, 292
A Touch of Sin/Tian Zhuding, 5, 96, 101–5
A Touch of Zen, 103
Tourneur, Jacques, 4, 34, 37, 39, 140, 254
Toute la mémoire du monde/All the Memory of the World, 212, 214, 218
To Woody Allen, From Europe with Love, 43
Trafic (magazine), 23, 81, 202, 241, 264
Trains du soir (painting), 45
Travolta, John, 115
The Tree of Life, 252
The Tree of Wooden Clogs/L'albero degli zoccoli, 171, 174, 176–77
Trepa, Ricardo, 159, 160, 162
The Trial (film), 195, 197, 272, 275–81, 287, 290
The Trial (novel), 276, 277, 281
von Trier, Lars, 77
Trilling, Lionel, 127
Tristana, 30
Trois places pour le 26, 51, 53, 55, 56, 57
Truffaut, François, 51, 52, 171, 178, 221, 223
Trump, Donald, 28, 91, 292
Trump, Melania, 292
Tsai Ming-liang, 263–71
The Turin Horse, 241, 242, 247, 248, 249–53
Twelfth Night, 288
Twilight of the Ice Nymphs, 137
Twin Peaks, 252
Two Portraits, 2, 258, 259–60
Tybjerg, Casper, 63
Tyner, McCoy, 33, 35
Tyszkiewicz, Beata, 47

Ubu Roi, 197
Ulysees, 124, 125, 201
The Uncertainty Principle, 165
Universal Citizen, 2, 258
Universal Hotel, 2, 258
Unknown Pleasures, 97, 99

U.S.A., 75
Useless, 97

Valley of Abraham, 165, 167
Les Vampires, 237
Vampyr, 58
Van Gogh, 213, 214
Van Hool, Roger, 46
The Vanity Tables of Douglas Sirk, 203
Van Sant, Gus, 256
Vapor Trail (Clark), 77, 78, 79
Varda, Agnès, 49–50, 283
Varela, Vitalina, 38–39
Variety (magazine), 5, 88, 199
Va savoir, 222, 225
Vatnsdal, Caelum, 140
Vega, Paz, 27
Vella, Vinny, 85
The Velvet Light Trap, 220
E venne un uomo, 176
Ventura, 34, 36–39
El verdugo, 256
Verne, Jules, 279
Vertigo, 17, 135, 147–48, 149, 150–51, 164
Vidal, Gore, 108, 274
Video Watchdog, 229
Vierny, Sacha
Vig, Mihály, 251
Vigo, Jean, 77, 90, 140, 164
Viridiana, 29
Visconti, Luchino, 53
Visit or Memories and Confessions, 157, 164
Visit to a Small Planet, 108, 118
A Visit to the Louvre, 213
Viva Zapata! 70
Vive l'amour, 263, 265, 266, 267
Vivre sa vie, 178
Vogel, Amos, 220
La Voix humaine, 51
Vous n'avez encore rien vu/You Ain't Seen Nothin' Yet, 217, 218–19
Voyage to the Beginning of the World, 162, 165

Waits, Tom, 86
Wajda, Andrzej, 47
Wake (Subic), 77–80
Waking Life, 123
Walden, 246
Walking Down Broadway, 155
Wallis, Hal, 107–8, 112
Walsh, Raoul, 181, 292
Wang, Baoqiang, 104
Wang, Wayne, 86
Warhol, Andy, 86, 200
The War of the Worlds (radio show), 277, 288

Warren, Elizabeth, 292
Warshow, Robert, 64
Wavelength, 168
Way Down East, 197
The Wayward Cloud, 263
Wedding March, The, 6, 155
Weekend at Bernie's, 147
Welles, Orson, 4, 5, 6, 41, 77, 116, 117, 127–30, 157, 183, 195, 254, 256, 257, 272–94
Welles, Richard, 275–76
West, Nathanael, 273, 292–93
What Nobody Saw, 77
What Time is it There? 263
When it Rains, 253
Where Lies Your Hidden Smile? 34
Which Way to the Front? 110, 115
White, Jack and Meg, 84, 85, 92
Whitaker, Forest, 90
Whitman, George, 124
Whitman, Walt, 158
Wiers-Jenssen, Hans, 59–60
Wikipedia, 5, 15, 51–52, 204, 263
Wild Grass/Les herbes folles, 212, 214, 218–19
Wilkerson, Travis, 67
Williams, Tennessee, 108
Williams, William Carlos, 90, 94
Will Success Spoil Rock Hunter? 136
Wilson, Marie, 112
Wilson, Owen, 27
The Wind in the Willows, 90
Winesburg, Ohio, 83
Wise Blood, 254, 260
With Dieric Bouts, 43, 48
Witherspoon, Reese, 27
Wolcott, James, 5, 217
Woman in a Twilight Garden, 43, 48
A Woman of Paris, 111
Wong, Kar-wai, 4, 123
Wood, Robin, 125
The Wooster Group, 238
Word and Utopia, 165, 167

Workers, Peasants, 74
The World, 96, 97, 99–103
Wottitz, Walter, 283
Wright, Steven, 83
Wright, Whittni, 20, 24
The Wrong Man, 150
Wynn, Ed, 116

X, Malcolm, 68
Xiao Shan/Going Home, 97

Yakir, Dan, 45
Yang, Edward, 4, 266
Yang, Kwei-mei, 266–67, 269
Yeats, William Butler, 54
Yes, 194, 197, 198–201
You Ain't Seen Nothin' Yet/Vous n'avez encore rien vu, 217, 218–19
You Are Not I, 253
Young, Lester, 33, 35
The Young Girls of Rochefort/Les demoiselles de Rochefort, 47, 49–54, 57
The Young One, 29
You're Never Too Young, 107, 118, 120n3
YouTube, 44, 160, 208–9
Yu, Fei, 270
Yu Tang Chun, 103

Zabriskie Point, 56, 290
Zellweger, Renee, 136
Zen in the Art of Archery, 85
Zéro de conduite, 77
Zhai Yongming, 99
Zhang Wei-qiang, 138
Zhang Yimou, 65
Zhou Enlai, 100
Zimmerman, Paul D., 115
Zinn, Howard, 73, 75, 76, 77n6
Zucca, Pierre, 235
Zugsmith, Albert, 149